# Yugoslavia Unraveled

## Advance Praise for *Yugoslavia Unraveled*

"*Yugoslavia Unraveled* makes a solid contribution to our understanding of the Balkan tragedies of the 1990s. The book shows clearly how the Western powers undermined Yugoslavia's sovereignty and thereby helped cause the ensuing bloodshed and chaos. The policies pursued by those powers will have implications far beyond the Balkans for decades to come. Thomas has written a powerful account that should be must reading for policymakers and interested laymen alike." **—Ted Galen Carpenter**, Cato Institute

"In *Yugoslavia Unraveled*, Raju Thomas and other authors explore the tragedies of self-determination gone amok, of 'morality as a product of power' on the part of interventionist countries, of the destructive role that 'advocacy scholarship' and the new 'government-media-academia complex' played in tearing Yugoslavia apart during the 1990s. In short, a valuable work." **—David Binder**, *New York Times*

"*Yugoslavia Unraveled* should be required reading for the enthusiasts of humanitarian U.S. interventionism and for the policymakers who have prematurely declared the Balkan tragedy a 'success story.' The contributors to this compendium offer solid evidence that highlights the inherent dangers of using ethnic stereotyping as a substitute for the rule of law. **—Nikolaos A. Stavrou**, Editor of *Mediterranean Quarterly*

# Yugoslavia Unraveled

## Sovereignty, Self-Determination, Intervention

Edited by
Raju G. C. Thomas

LEXINGTON BOOKS
*Lanham • Boulder • New York • Oxford*

LEXINGTON BOOKS

Published in the United States of America
by Lexington Books
A Member of the Rowman & Littlefield Publishing Group
4720 Boston Way, Lanham, Maryland 20706

PO Box 317
Oxford
OX2 9RU, UK



British Library Cataloguing in Publication Information Available

**Library of Congress Cataloging-in-Publication Data**

Yugoslavia unraveled : sovereignty, self-determination, intervention / edited by Raju G.C. Thomas
cm.
Includes bibliographical references and index.
ISBN 0-7391-0517-5 (cloth : alk. paper)
1. Yugoslavia—Politics and government—1980–1992. 2. Yugoslavia—Politics and government—1992– 3. Nationalism—Yugoslavia. 4. Yugoslavia—Ethnic relations. 5. Intervention (International law) 6. Yugoslavia Wars, 1991–1995. I. Thomas, Raju G. C.
R1302 .Y845 2003
47.703—dc21 2002014324

Printed in the United States of America

∞™ The paper used in this publication meets the minimum requirements of American National Standard for Information Sciences—Permanence of Paper for Printed Library Materials, ANSI/NISO Z39.48-1992.

# Contents

# Prologue

## Making War, Peace, and History

*Raju G. C. Thomas*

From creation in 1918 to destruction in 1991, primarily outside Great Powers made war, peace, and history for Yugoslavia. The concept was that of President Woodrow Wilson at the end of World War I, with mainly Slovenians and Croatians pushing for the new state to avoid the punitive peace treaties about to be imposed by the victors on the vanquished at Versailles. Subsequently, twice in the last sixty years of the twentieth century, Germany intervened in Yugoslavia—militarily in 1941 and diplomatically in 1991—and twice it led to war, death, and destruction among the southern Slavs. In the end, U.S. political and military intervention in the 1990s changed the course of events and history irretrievably. During the 1991–1999 conflict, images of Serbian "aggression" and "genocide" flooded the Western and especially American media, accompanied by official policy making that reacted accordingly. The Yugoslav crisis of the 1990s was reduced to a simple story of good versus evil. No doubt, many Serbs had committed horrible atrocities in the wars among the peoples of the former Yugoslavia. But the projection of the images of the war and the explanations provided were selective and prejudicial against one side, whereas all sides were to blame in varying degrees for the tragedy—not unlike the culpability of all sides during World War I, where only Germans were blamed and punished.

Indeed, we would have to go back to the hysteria toward Germans and German Americans that prevailed in the United States during World War I to understand the nature of the treatment of "the Serbs" during the Yugoslav crisis of the 1990s. John Gurda, an urban historian of Milwaukee, recorded what happened:

> America was officially neutral when the shooting started in 1914. As residents of the most German city in the nation, Milwaukeeans felt free to express their support for the Kaiser's cause. . . . A dizzying about-face occurred as soon as America entered the war in 1917. As if to overcompensate for its earlier shows of sympathy, Milwaukee became a stronghold of anti-German feeling that devolved into simple hysteria. Self-appointed patriots went looking for traitors and professed to find them everywhere—in classrooms, on the stage, even in the pulpit. The superpatriots' ultimate goal was to rid the community of every last vestige of Germanism. In Milwaukee, that was a challenge equivalent to erasing a leopard's spots, but it didn't prevent a full-scale effort.[1]

Gurda continued:

> *The Milwaukee Journal* gave voice to the sentiments of the superpatriots. F. Perry Olds, who had joined the paper just a year before, began to work a full-time disloyalty beat in 1916. Olds spent his days translating stories from Milwaukee's German-language press and publishing excerpts that he considered especially treasonous. The excerpts would fall easily under First Amendment rights today, but Olds' exposes were enough to win the *Journal* a Pulitzer Prize in 1919.

Under a similar but more subdued and carefully crafted media-generated hysteria against Serbs and Serbianism in 1992, Roy Guttman of *Newsday* and John Burns of the *New York Times* won Pulitzer Prizes for their sensationalized one-sided exposés of the war in Bosnia.[2] Parallels were drawn with "the holocaust," thereby trivializing this unprecedented tragedy in the history of mankind. The concept of genocide was reinvented to encompass "ethnic cleansing." If this is so, then the greatest genocide against a single ethnic group was that against the Germans at the end of World War II, when some fifteen million Germans were ethnically cleansed from Poland, Czechoslovakia, and other parts of Eastern Europe and the Soviet Union with the tacit blessings of President Harry Truman and Prime Minister Winston Churchill.

## THE WAR PSYCHOSIS

The behavior of the ethnic groups of the former Yugoslavia and that of the governments and mass media of the Western powers was troubling. There was a compulsion toward violent behavior by the Yugoslav ethnic groups and a preference for military solutions by the Western powers. Perhaps this phenomena may call more for psychological and sociological analysis rather than political and security. Psychological theories of war usually point out certain standard prevailing characteristics among hostile groups and their supporters:[3]

1. At the core of interethnic antagonism is a diabolical enemy image mirrored by the other side.[4] The enemy is seen as devoid of moral values. They can do nothing right. Empathy is nonexistent all around.
2. Correspondingly, there is a strong moral self-image where our nation is believed to be without fault. We can do no wrong. The moral high ground is on our side.
3. This is accompanied by selective attention or inattention to historical and current facts. Only those facts and events that support preconceived beliefs are accepted. Those that do not are rejected. The possibility that all sides may have grievances and that all sides may be guilty is not worthy of consideration.
4. A sense of military overconfidence builds up in the mind of the self-righteous nation. In preparation for war, "the enemy" is demonized and dehumanized. Killing becomes palatable, denying principles of fairness to the enemy becomes understandable, and violating international law becomes acceptable. We are, after all, the "good guys" and may be excused or forgiven for whatever we do because our actions are always for the greater good of humanity.
5. War and the slaughter of "the enemy" then becomes justified. Killing innocents by the thousands is merely "collateral damage." Every life we lose is precious and unacceptable. We feel the pain of our fallen soldiers and their "loved ones." On the other hand, the enemy is not loved, nor does it have "loved ones" who suffer pain and anguish.
6. Eventually, the "enemy" is demolished in a happy outcome. Good prevails over evil.

Now it is understandable that such beliefs may exist among the warring Serbs, Croats, Muslims, and Albanians. What may not be easily understood was the frequent demands for violent retribution that were widespread in the U.S. Congress and the media (and, to a lesser extent, their counterparts in Europe) during the Yugoslav interethnic conflicts. Many in the United States and elsewhere were outraged by the war and genocide during the Yugoslav conflict, blamed mainly on "the Serbs." But was there not also a certain expectation and satisfaction in provoking and viewing the bloodshed?

This unusual human behavior of desiring war while denouncing its evil was explored by J. Glenn Gray in his 1959 book, *The Enduring Appeals of*

*Battle*.[5] Gray pointed out that, while we proclaim our abhorrence to the horrors of war, there is still an underlying allure and satisfaction in the occurrence and conduct of them.

First, war is a "spectacle" to behold which excites and thrills us, especially if this can be done without risk to our own lives. "Anyone who has watched people crowding around the scene of an accident on the highway realizes that the lust of the eye is real." During the Yugoslav tragedy, there was a steady stream of war-hating voyeurs into Sarajevo. They included Pulitizer prize–seeking journalists, publicity-seeking politicians, hopeful best-selling authors, and feminists craving rape victims to augment their sense of outrage. They were lodged at the Holiday Inn in Sarajevo to witness the horrors of war "with their own eyes," as the cliché goes. All returned unharmed, as they knew they would. Bosnia became the most celebrated cause as no other cause in the world, although far greater tragedies were taking place in Abhkazia, Ngorny-Karabakh, Chechnya, Jaffna, Kigali, Srinagar, and Kandahar, places many of these war voyeurs probably had not even heard of, or would not care or dare to visit if they had.

Second, wars generate a sense of community and "comradeship." Gray noted that "the cause that calls comradeship into being may be the defense of one's country, the propagation of the one true religious faith, or a passionate political ideology; it may be the maintenance of honor, or the recovery of a Helen of Troy." During the Cold War, the cause was containing communism. During the Yugoslav wars, the cause was advancing humanitarianism, no less a political ideology than other past "isms" since the concept and its parameters are the subject of serious dispute and the raison d'etre for wars extolled especially by the new age, Western, liberal establishment.

Third, according to Gray, "there is a delight in destruction" in the human psyche. "*Happiness* is doubtless the wrong word for the satisfaction that men experience when they are possessed by the lust to destroy and kill their kind. Most men would never admit that they enjoy killing, and there are a great many who do not." Actually "happiness" may be the right word to describe this phenomena. Extremely bloody and destructive war movies are always popular as it allows for a vicarious satisfaction in the savagery portrayed on the screen, the next best thing to being involved in the real thing. Indeed, much of the American media and attentive public was enthralled at the "spectacle" of the U.S. bombing of Serbia in 1999 (or that of Iraq in 1992 and Afghanistan in 2001). The first major "humanitarian war" in history evoked a sense of patriotism and moral superiority. Western governments, the media, and the public were swift to condemn Serbian "ethnic cleansing," "genocide," and "rape." Yet when this was shown not to be factual on the scale alleged, as in the case of Kosovo (the flight of Albanian refugees was the result of NATO bombing), there was disappointment and even a sense of being cheated out of genocide instead of relief and satisfaction.

## THE MORALITY OF THE POWERFUL

In the post Yugoslav conflict era, a plethora of books and articles have been written by journalists, policymakers, and public activists determined to record their one-sided version of events for posterity. The main characteristic of nearly all of these writings is a self-righteous moral undertone. For example, Richard Holbrooke in his book *To End a War* depicts how the United States ended a brutal war of aggression, genocide, and rape by Serbs.[6] Through American diplomatic skills and military power, good eventually triumphed over evil. To a considerable extent, such self-righteous and one-sided perspectives and policies may be attributed to the end of the Cold War and the collapse of countervailing power. This was not only the triumph of the West (capitalism and democracy) over the East (socialism and totalitarianism), but it also heralded the triumph of a new moral liberalism which emphasized global humanitarianism over the old, cynical, state-centered realism. The concept of state sovereignty embodied in the 1649 Treaty of Westphalia was declared obsolete in the new U.S.-dominated world order, except when the self-interest or survival of the United States and its allies and friends were at stake.

A statement that the U.S. sets different standards for itself compared to what it inflicts on others, and that the United Nations cannot judge U.S. and NATO actions, is reflected in a speech delivered by the then leader of the U.S. Senate Foreign Relations Committee, Senator Jesse Helms, to the UN Security Council on January 20, 2000.[7] According to Helms, the American people would not tolerate "the majority of the UN members routinely voting against America in the General Assembly," nor " the reports of the raucous cheering of the UN delegates in Rome, when U.S. efforts to amend the International Criminal Court treaty to protect American soldiers were defeated." Nor would they tolerate the investigation of a UN Special Rapporteur who, despite all the human rights abuses taking place in dictatorships throughout the world, "decided his most pressing task was to investigate human rights violations in the United States—and found our human rights record wanting."

On the possibility of war crimes investigations being conducted against NATO in its war against Yugoslavia, Helms stated: "Most recently, we learn that the chief prosecutor of the Yugoslav War Crimes Tribunal has compiled a report on possible NATO war crimes during the Kosovo campaign. At first, the prosecutor declared that it is fully within the scope of her authority to indict NATO pilots and commanders. When news of her report leaked, she backpedaled. She realized, I am sure, that any attempt to indict NATO commanders would be the death knell for the International Criminal Court." Helms explained why the United States should be exempt from international law and justice: "No UN institution—not the Security Council, not the Yugoslav tribunal, not a future ICC—is competent to judge the foreign policy and national security decisions of the United States. American courts routinely refuse cases where they are asked to sit in judgment of our government's national security decisions, stating that they are not competent to judge such decisions. If we do not submit our national security decisions to the judgment of a Court of the United States, why would Americans submit them to the judgment of an International Criminal Court, a continent away, comprised of mostly foreign judges elected by an international body made up of the membership of the UN General Assembly?"

Helms continued: "Americans distrust concepts like the International Criminal Court, and claims by the UN to be 'the sole source of legitimacy' for the use of force, because Americans have a profound distrust of accumulated power. Our founding fathers created a government founded on a system of checks and balances, and dispersal of power." Thus, Senator Helms believes that whatever military action the United States conducts abroad is legally and morally right because the United States is infallible.

Proclaiming to carry the moral high ground, the United States was determined to fulfill its new "Manifest Destiny" worldwide. As Richard Holbrooke concluded in his book (italics are his): "*There will be other Bosnias in our lives*—areas where early outside involvement can be decisive, and American leadership will be required. The world's richest nation, one that presumes to great moral authority, cannot simply make worthy appeals to conscience and call on others to carry the burden. The world will look to Washington for more than rhetoric the next time we face a challenge to peace."[8] Other American leaders have referred to the United States as the "indispensable nation" and the beacon of light in a world where much darkness prevailed. Such outlooks reflect the Machiavellian dictum that morality is the product of power.

However, if American military interventions in Vietnam, Panama, Nicaragua, and Yugoslavia are the yardsticks, Holbrooke's threat to do more good to the rest of the world should be taken seriously. Just as democratic rights and individual liberties cannot be guaranteed without a system of checks and balances within a state, the territorial integrity of states and freedom and justice cannot be guaranteed among states without a system of countervailing power in the international system. If there are no physical or economic costs to the dominant and unrivaled military power, what will stop it from resorting to force instead of peaceful negotiations to resolve issues? As

Secretary of State Madeleine Albright told General Colin Powell, then Chairman of the Joint Chiefs of Staff who refused to bomb the Serbs, "What is the point of this superb military that you are always talking about if we cannot use it?"[9] Invariably, moral invocations by unrivaled and dominant leaders, states, or corporations conceal self-serving goals or, at best, debatable moral outcomes.

## MAKING AND UNMAKING HISTORY

Napoleon reportedly once said that "history is nothing more than a mutually agreed upon set of lies." If I may add, the lies and selective half-truths of history are written usually from the perspective of the powerful and the victorious. Through repetition and frequent citations, one-sided interpretations become formalized as historical truth. In reality, the truth may be subjective or inconclusive. No single interpretation of history should be accepted as final. Instead various versions must be accommodated. Access to all information is never always available, and every historian and political scientist must select and interpret subjectively. Especially during the wars of Yugoslavia's disintegration, most American politicians, journalists, scholars, and other observers supported or condemned one side with a passion.

Thus, a comparison of the history of the region that became Yugoslavia written by British, French, and American scholars in the decades before 1991 and by the new breed of instant experts and scholars during the crisis of the 1990s will reveal the stark difference in perceptions and interpretations. News reporting and scholarship before 1991 consisted mainly of dispassionate research and analysis and, in the 1990s, mainly passionate one-sided expositions. The images and roles of ethnic groups during the two world wars and of centuries earlier have been entirely recast. The past has now been rewritten to fit the prejudice of the present.

Much of the writings during the conflict in the former Yugoslavia may be described as advocacy scholarship of varying degrees. However, many of the views represented in this book were widespread during the Yugoslav crisis of the 1990s decade but were given little or no exposure in the mainstream print and audiovisual media. Frequently, their ethnic backgrounds, political affiliations, or family linkages were the justification for shutting out their views. The same rules did not apply to the other side, which conformed to the standard version. There was nothing "revisionist" or "denialist" about such interpretations as they started to find outlets in the mainstream publications. They were always there but marginalized or shut out during the crisis. Perhaps this is because, if they were allowed to be heard at the time, the edifice of the standard story line of "good versus evil" may have crumbled. There are some parallels here with the Vietnam experience in America.

In his article "How Could Vietnam Happen? An Autopsy," James C. Thompson Jr., a member of President Lyndon Johnson's White House staff, defined several factors that led to America's Vietnam disaster.[10] These included the following: (a) "the abuse and distortion of history"; (b) "the legacy of the 1950s," especially McCarthyism, which had driven out many experts who disagreed with official policies; (c) "a general perception of China-on-the march" that was declared to be a general threat to the security of Asia; (d) a widespread conviction in the "domino theory," which argued that, if Vietnam fell to communism, all of Asia and the world would fall eventually; (e) "the domestication of dissenters," whereby dissenters were compromised by being made to feel at home while their views were marginalized; (f) "the effective trap," where dissenters remained silent for the time being in order to prove effective at an opportune time later; (g) "a preoccupation with Vietnam public relations as opposed to Vietnam policy-making"; (h) "rhetorical escalation oversell," whereby the war advocates sold themselves their Vietnam policy by repeatedly exaggerating the critical importance of Vietnam to U.S. security; (i) that the war "posed a fundamental test of America's national will"; and (g) "a steady give-in to pressures for a military solution."

Thompson's Vietnam analogies and analysis has some fit with American Yugoslav crisis decision making. First, Croatian and Muslim versions of Yugoslav events and history were quickly accepted unchallenged and carved into the minds of American decision makers and the media to the total exclusion of the Serbian version. Second, Milosevic and Karadzic's "Greater Serbia" project was declared a threat to the stability of Europe. If Slobodan Milosevic and other Serb leaders were not stopped, other similar leaders would gain inspiration and go on a destructive rampage in other parts of the world. The lessons of appeasement at "Munich" that led to World War II must not go unheeded. Third, (and I am speculating here) dissent, if any, within the policy-making bureaucracies on this standard viewpoint probably was compromised through minor accommodations. Other leaders, bureaucratic decision makers, academics, and journalists who disagreed with Washington's Yugoslav policy held back their views in the hope of fighting the policy another day when conditions became more favorable.

Fourth, as in the prolonged Vietnam crisis, Yugoslav policy was driven by a poll-driven and public relations–minded President Clinton, who was more interested in how his decisions played at home and was also mindful of the fact that there were over one billion Muslims and a similar size Catholic population overseas. On the other hand, there were only 10 million Orthodox Christian Serbs backed mainly by Orthodox Christian Russia and Greece. The first could be ignored because it was then an economic basket case dependent on the West for survival, and the second was a marginal player within NATO and the European Union. Fifth, as in the global communist threat read into the Vietnam civil war, Serbian efforts to carve a "Greater Serbia" out of the territories of a disintegrating Yugoslavia so as to keep all Serbs within a single state was assessed to be the greatest evil since Hitler's efforts to unite German-inhabited territories of Austria, Czechoslovakia, and Poland. This was the greatest evil because we said it was so, whether this claim made any comparable or proportionate sense or not. Finally, all of this was viewed as a test of America's moral, political, and military credibility. Serbia, like Vietnam, had erred badly in attempting to challenge, defeat, and humiliate a superpower and was made to pay the price.

Unlike Vietnam, American military involvement in the Yugoslav crisis was not at any time likely to degenerate into a Vietnam-like quagmire, mainly because of the U.S. ability to conduct wars from the air without much risk to American soldiers. A quick military solution became the most desirable option. It should be recalled that, in spite of the large sacrifice of American lives in distant Vietnam, most Americans supported the war initially because it was perceived to be in defense of democracy and capitalism against a monolithic, communist totalitariat directed from the Kremlin. It was only after the Tet Offensive of 1968, when hundreds of Americans suddenly lost their lives, that the validity of the traditional interpretation of the underlying cause of the Vietnam War began to be questioned. The struggle in Vietnam was reinterpreted thereafter as a war of nationalism against foreign forces—Japanese, French, and finally American—amidst a civil war between the state's communists and noncommunists. However, it had little to do with the advance of international communism aided by, and directed from, the Kremlin.

Given that no American lives were at risk during the Yugoslav wars, no serious examination was made of American policy except briefly, during NATO's bombing of the remnant Yugoslavia when a flurry of alternative views were allowed to be heard. This included one by ex-President and Nobel Peace Prize–winner Jimmy Carter, who observed:

> The approach the United States has taken recently has been to devise a solution that best suits its own purposes, recruit at least tacit support in whichever forum it can best influence, provide the dominant military force, present an ultimatum to recalcitrant parties and then take punitive action against the entire nation to force compliance. . . . Instead of focusing on Serbian military forces, [U.S.] missiles and bombs are now concentrating on the destruction of bridges, railways, roads, electric power, and fuel and fresh water supplies. Serbian citizens report that they are living like cavemen, and their torment increases daily.[11]

## TO BOMB OR NOT TO BOMB

It was commonplace to use the word "international community" during the Yugoslav crisis as some concrete organization that was always in consensus when interpreting the monumental upheavals that occurred in the former Yugoslavia. However, much of the rest of the world, including Russia, China, India, Vietnam, Mexico, Argentina, and much of Latin America, disagreed with those standard interpretations, especially those that prevailed in the United States. There was dissent in Britain (except the official line of the Tony Blair government) and even more so in Europe, where it increased in magnitude as one moved to the Orthodox Christian countries. The bombing of Serbia brought out widespread worldwide condemnation in Asia and Latin America and even in the Arab Middle East with the notable exception of Jordan. Washington Post correspondent Anthony Faiola observed:[12]

> Here in Argentina, one of Washington's closest Latin American allies, a poll last week showed that 64 percent of the public opposed the NATO air campaign against Yugoslavia. More respondents had a negative opinion of NATO than of Yugoslav President Slobodan Milosevic. In Latin America, Asia, Africa, the Middle East and other regions with little direct interest in the conflict, opposition is surfacing in statements by elected officials, newspaper editorials, opinion polls, public protests, Internet banter and street graffiti. Increasingly, there is little subtlety in NATO-bashing.

In Russia, China, and India, condemnations of NATO were severe and widespread both within and outside their governments.[13] While the intense reactions against NATO in Russia and China were reported in the American media, the sweeping denunciations by India went unreported and, therefore, in the Western public's mind, never happened. Among the more radical Arab Muslim states of Iraq, Syria, Libya, and Algeria "the suffering of the Kosovars was completely neglected as the common experience of perceived U.S. aggression, double standards and imperial hegemonism was constantly evoked."[14] The Clinton administration's spokesman, David Leavy, attributed this phenomena to the fact that "President (Slobodan) Milosevic has an extensive propaganda machine. We've worked very hard to try to counteract that propaganda machine."[15] Likewise, in Britain, where there was much criticism of NATO's bombing, Prime Minister Tony Blair's spokesman, Alastair Campbell, accused British journalists of being duped by the Serb "lie machine" and of being too lazy to cover the Kosovo conflict properly.[16] Given eight years of international sanctions on Serbia and Serbs, and the bankruptcy caused by war and economic sanctions, this massive and well-financed worldwide "Serb lie machine" of President Milosevic—as alleged by the

Clinton and Blair governments—could not have existed. On the contrary, in much of the world, the well-financed and highly sophisticated Western media was the only source of information.

Overall, however, nearly all states have "bandwagoned" with the United States and the West in the new unipolar military and economic world of the post–Cold War era, even more so after Al Qaeda's massive terrorist attack on the United States on September 11, 2001. Rightly, the new global "war" against international terrorism led by the United States is a common cause. However, the policies to be adopted, including the utility of conventional force against a shadowy threat composed of elusive individuals and groups, should remain open to debate. But what is surprising is that, long before September 11, much of the Western media and academia had also bandwagoned with their governments in support of its foreign policies.

Even a star-studded Hollywood movie entitled *Wag the Dog,* released the year prior to the U.S. bombing of Serbia in 1999, was an insufficient hint to the American media and intelligentsia that the Clinton administration, led by Secretary of State Madeleine Albright, had engineered a pretext for war to cover up the President's escalating sex scandals at home. In the movie script, White House aides contrived images of a major atrocity against Albanian civilians by Serb forces—all staged exclusively in a Hollywood studio—in order to distract public attention from a sex scandal involving the film's fictitious U.S. president. Real life then imitated fiction when an alleged Milosevic-directed massacre of Albanians at Racak in January 1999 turned up just in time. A month later, a State Department–devised ultimatum was delivered to Serbia at Rambouillet—an ultimatum that was designed to be rejected. The bombing of Yugoslavia ensued.

However, Hollywood has since chosen to endorse the official government interpretation of good versus evil. *The Scott O'Grady Story* and *Behind Enemy Lines* glorify the story of a U.S. Air Force pilot whose fighter plane was shot down in Serbian territory but managed to get back without being captured. The assumption here is that Serbs were the enemies of Americans during the Yugoslav wars, and had Scott O'Grady been caught, he would have been killed. O'Grady's expectation of the worst was belied later when three American soldiers captured by Serb forces during the 1999 Kosovo war, were treated humanly and released unharmed.

Regarding the use of force in the new U.S.-dominant world, American debates were reduced to whether the United States should bomb now or bomb later; whether to send in ground forces or to rely on aerial bombardment and unmanned cruise missiles; whether to go it alone or muster a coalition of forces to give military actions the appearance of international legitimacy. Whereas on domestic policy issues the U.S. media and academia remain as alert and vigorous as ever, demonstrating the robust and vibrant nature of the American democracy, the same cannot be said now of foreign policy issues. A new "government-media-academia complex" appears to have replaced the old "government-military-industrial complex." Freedom of thought and expression had given way to a new government-controlled and directed intellectual patriotism.[17] This condition is commonplace in most countries of the world, including some democracies, but it is surprising that such a political culture surfaced in the United States during the Yugoslav wars.

Echoing my sentiment of the earlier U.S. bombing of Yugoslavia in 1999, one American citizen living outside London questioned the dearth of criticism of American military actions in Afghanistan in 2001–2002. She wrote:

> Can I say something now? Because no one's been able to do so. . . . People with differing opinions on military action have been accused of being unpatriotic, of not loving America anymore. . . . But I'm an American too, even if I live overseas. I have my passport; I pay taxes; my kids are American, love the U.S. and plan to live there when they are finished with school. I fly a huge American flag outside my house every 4th of July whether my English neighbors like it or not. . . . Questioning information, forming opinions, arguing, discussing—it's all part of democracy. We don't want a nation of Stepford Citzens.[18]

*Yugoslavia Unraveled* provides some alternative and diverse interpretations of the crisis. Not all the views and analysis found in this book may be acceptable to all readers. And unlike other books on this subject, where its authors believe they are providing definitive and objective assessments, this book does not claim to be the final verdict. The title of the book reflects both the dismantling and disintegration of the former Yugoslavia and the varied subjective expositions presented here as to why this happened. Whether the reader agrees with these views or not, the contributions to this volume must be viewed as serious attempts to expound alternative versions of the historical events that unfolded in the former Yugoslavia.

The genesis of this book goes back to papers that were presented at the American Political Science Association (APSA) conventions in San Francisco (1996), Boston (1998), and in Washington (2000) and at the Association for the Study of Nationalities (ASN) convention in New York (2001.) Papers presented or oral presentations made at the ASN were those of Milica Bookman, Gordon Bardos, Summantra Bose, Maya Chadda, Prem Shankar Jha, Robert Hayden, and Raju Thomas (parts of chapter 2). Papers presented at the APSA were those of Kelly Greenhill, Alan Kuperman, and Raju Thomas (parts of chapter 1). Later, chapters were invited from Edward Herman, Peter Liotta, Michael Mandelbaum, Michael Mandel, and Satish Nambiar on the media's role, religion and war, comparative nationalisms, international law and war crimes, and peace-keeping operations. Subsequently, these papers were revised and updated, some reconfigured entirely, to form the basis of this edited book. The chapters represent the views of the individual contributors and not those of the collective group or their affiliates.

## NOTES

1. See John Gurda, "Recalling Another Time When War Divided City," *Milwaukee Journal Sentinel*, January 5, 2002. www.jsonline.com/news/editorials/jan02/10229.asp

2. Roy Guttman won a Pulitizer Prize for his book *A Witness to Genocide*, New York: Macmillan Publishing Company, 1993. John Burns won the prize for his reporting from Bosnia. The claim made by Guttman in the book's title is impossible when the commanders of the United Nations Protection Force (UNPROFOR) and the 28,000 men under them witnessed no such thing. I demonstrate later that Burns's death toll of 200,000 during the first ten months of the war in Bosnia is conjecture.

3. For a variety of psychological theories of war, see James E. Dougherty and Robert L. Pfaltzgraff, *Contending Theories of International Relations*, New York: Addison Wesley Longman, 2001, pp. 231–263.

4. To justify the use of force, an enemy needs to be identified and designated. Sometimes, this may done to rationalize the utilization of large-standing military establishments.

5. See J. Glenn Gray, "The Appeals of Battle," in John F. Reichart and Steven R. Sturm, eds., *American Defense Policy*, Baltimore: Johns Hopkins University Press, 1982, pp. 839–851. The chapter in the above edited volume is extracted from his book, *The Warriors* (originally titled *The Enduring Appeals of Battle*), New York: Harcourt Brace and World, 1959, pp. 25–58

6. Richard Holbrooke, *To End a War*, New York: Random House, 1998.

7. Text of Senator Helms before the UN Security Council, January 20, 2000 (Senate Foreign Relations Committee chair makes blunt appraisal) (4550). It was the first time in the history of the United Nations that a representative of the U.S. Congress had ever addressed the UN Security Council. www.usis.it/wireless/wfa00120/A0012011.htm

8. Holbrooke, *To End a War,* p. 369.

9. Cited by Lord David Owen in his *Balkan Odyssey*, San Diego: Harcourt Brace, 1995, p. 135.

10. James C. Thompson Jr., "How Could Vietnam Happen? An Autopsy," in Steven L. Spiegel, ed., *At Issue:Politics in the World Arena,* New York: St. Martin's Press, 1972, pp. 377–387. (This article was first published in the *Atlantic Monthly*, April 1968.)

11. Jimmy Carter, "Have We Forgotten the Path to Peace?" *New York Times*, May 27, 1999.

12. See Anthony Faiola, "Air Campaign Ignites Anti-U.S. Sentiment," *Washington Post Foreign Service*, May 18, 1999. Faiola quotes Indian Prime Minister Atal Bihari Vajpayee in a fiery speech as follows: "NATO is blindly bombing Yugoslavia. There

is a dance of destruction going on there. Thousands of people rendered homeless. And the United Nations is a mute witness to all this. Is NATO's work to prevent war or to fuel one?"

13. For analyses of media reactions to NATO's bombing, see Ed Hermann and Philip Hammond, *Degraded Capability: The Media and the Kosovo Crisis*, London: Pluto Press, 2000.

14. Roland Dannreuther, "Perceptions in the Middle East," in Mary Buckley and Sally N. Cummings, eds., *Kosovo: Reflections of War and Its Aftermath*, London: Continuum Press, 2001, p. 210.

15. "Govt Unit To Control Flow of US News," by Anne Gearan, Associated Press, August 8, 1999.

16. "Serb Lies Duped Media, Claims No 10," by Michael Evans and Carol Midgley, *Times* (London), July 10, 1999.

17. See Edward S. Herman and Noam Chomsky, *Manufacturing Consent: The Political Economy of the Mass Media*, New York: Pantheon Books, 1988.

18. Elizabeth Thomas (no relation or acquaintance of the author), "Speaking Out About Citizens' Silence: Curtailing Criticism of the President is Not the Way to be a Patriot," *Chicago Tribune*, May 28, 2002. The reference is to the movie *The Stepford Wives*, where husbands in a New England town turned their wives into robots ready to serve and obey them at all times with a smile on their faces.

# I

# NATIONS, STATES, AND NATIONALISM

# 1

# Sovereignty, Self-Determination, and Secession: Principles and Practice

*Raju G. C. Thomas*

## HOW YUGOSLAVIA UNRAVELED: AN INTERPRETATION

### The Death of a Sovereign Independent State

The coming apart of Yugoslavia between 1991 and 1992 has been referred to variously as the "fall," the "disintegration," the "collapse," and the "tragedy" of Yugoslavia.[1] In reality, Yugoslavia was "dismembered" through a selective and prejudicial international recognition policy of its internal "republics." Unlike the Soviet Union, a legacy of the Czarist empire, which fell apart broadly because of Gorbachev's liberalizing policies and specifically from the failed military coup of 1991, Yugoslavia's creation and destruction was fundamentally different. It was a state created voluntarily in 1918 by its various nationalities and destroyed in 1991–1992 by the West's ad hoc recognition policy.

Donald Horowitz, a leading American specialist on nationalism and ethnic conflict, noted appropriately that the secessions of Slovenia, Croatia, Macedonia, Montenegro, Bosnia, and Serbia followed the violent patterns of state dissolution elsewhere. He pointed out that states with no history of independence, such as Bosnia, were swiftly recognized without considering the consequences. "*Led by Germany, European and American recognition of the former Yugoslav republics was accomplished in disregard of international law doctrine forbidding recognition of secessionist units whose establishment is being resisted forcibly by a central government.*[2]"

My thesis rejects the current widespread argument that Yugoslavia fell apart mainly because of domestic struggles and militant Milosevic-led Serbian nationalism, although this was a significant contributing factor. All along, the Tudjman-led and diaspora-supported Croatian nationalism was as bad as Serbian domestic nationalism. However, neither Serbian nor Croatian nationalism was sufficient to destroy Yugoslavia. Such domestic, competing nationalism was not unique to Yugoslavia. The dissolution of Yugoslavia had much to do with the political intrusions of the Western powers, especially Germany and the United States, in support of their favored ethnic groups and to advance their own policy agendas.[3] More specifically, the key individual actors responsible for the mess were German Foreign Minister Hans Dietrich-Genscher and the last American ambassador to Yugoslavia before it fell, Warren Zimmermann.

Referring to the dismemberment of Yugoslavia through international recognition policy, a foreign service officer of the Indian Ministry of External Affairs assessed the problem succinctly: "If we [India] were a small country like Yugoslavia, they [the Western powers] would probably have done it to us also."[4] Unilateral declarations of independence by Muslim Kashmir, Sikh Khalistan, or Hindu Assam and swift international recognition would have caused India to unravel, leading to large-scale massacres, ethnic cleansing, and nightmarish refugee flows. In 1994 when I posed the question of what India would do if the West went ahead and recognized an independent Kashmir and a Sikh "Khalistan" (as they did with Slovenia and Croatia) against India's objections, an Indian security analyst in New Delhi told me, "We would have 100 nuclear bombs ready by tomorrow morning." India went nuclear in 1998 and rationalized this decision, *post hoc*, following the bombing of Yugoslavia in 1999. An Indian nuclear weapons capability was declared to be essential for deterring potential Western interventions in India's internal wars of secession.

Countries such as Russia, with secessionist problems in Chechnya, China in Tibet, India in Kashmir, and Indonesia in East Timor, are big countries. While Indonesia failed to stop the secession of East Timor through Western diplomatic intervention, Russia, China, and India, all nuclear weapons states, will not tolerate such intervention and the destruction of their territorial integrity. Apart from peaceful or violent decolonization movements for independence, and except for the peaceful dissolution of Czechoslavakia and the violent but successful movements for independence by Bangladesh in 1971 and Eritrea in 1993, virtually all secessionist movements have been prevented through massive force by central government forces or have simply dissipated over time. They include Biafra from Nigeria; Katanga from Zaire; the Kurdish areas from Turkey and Iraq; South Yemen from North Yemen (a union which had only been forged in 1990); Punjab, Assam, Nagaland, and Mizoram from India; Baluchistan and Sind from Pakistan; Tamil Ealam from Sri Lanka; Shans and Kachins from Burma; and the Moros from the Philippines. Even Abraham Lincoln chose civil war to prevent the Confederate South from seceding from the United States. In all of the above cases, the right of self-determination and secession was rejected, and the territorial integrity of the state was almost always asserted.

Given these precedents, why did the United States and Germany so recklessly push for the secessions of Croatia, Slovenia, Bosnia, and Macedonia from Yugoslavia? Were issues of right and wrong, justice or injustice greater in the former Yugoslavia than in other parts of the world? If the 1975 Helsinki Accords Final Act guaranteeing the territorial integrity of European state frontiers could be discarded in the case of Yugoslavia, why are the new international frontiers of the former internal "republics" of Yugoslavia being preserved at all costs? It is important to record here that there were no killings or even human rights violations taking place in any of the "republics" of Yugoslavia when Germany, the Vatican, and Austria began to encourage the secessions of the Catholic Yugoslav republics—Slovenia and Croatia—or in Bosnia when the United States promoted the secession of that province. That there was a domestic constitutional crisis in Yugoslavia in 1990–1991—a perennial Yugoslav situation—cannot be denied. However, it was promises of support for secession followed by formal recognition that led to the tragedy of Yugoslavia.

German and American actions that led to the dissolution of Yugoslavia may not have been deliberate, although a historic German and a newly formed American prejudice toward the Serbs may have had something vaguely to do with it. Wolfgang Schloer is right when he points out that the recognition of Slovenia and Croatia was not motivated by renewed ambitions arising from a newly independent Germany: "Indeed, these initiatives were not in the German national interest. In the context of overall German foreign policy and in the light of the German attitude to the continuing conflict in Yugoslavia, this policy has to be understood as a unique combination of situational factors, personal idiosyncracies, inexperience, and misperceived domestic pressures."[5]

Schloer rejects Serbian allegations that Germany wanted to separate Croatia and Slovenia from Yugoslavia as part of some grand geostrategic plan to gain a foothold on the Adriatic or to guarantee access to their vactionland in Dalmatia. First, Germany felt remorse for not having supported the allied powers adequately in the 1991 Gulf War to dislodge Iraq from Kuwait and believed it needed to take the leadership in the Yugoslav crisis. Second, Germany believed that the recognition of Croatia and Slovenia would stop the Yugoslav Army from continuing with its destructive war operations in Croatia. Germany simply had not anticipated the tragedy that unfolded. The voice of Croatian guest workers numbering some five hundred thousand of the seven hundred thousand Yugoslavs in Germany also produced a significant one-sided perspective and impact on German policy. However, it should be noted that the Yugoslav Army's military operations in Croatia to carve out large sections of the seceding territory began only after the unilateral declaration of independence by Croatia in June 1991, which they did under German, Austrian, and Vatican encouragement.

Beverly Crawford provides a variation of Schloer's "domestic" explanation, indicating that it was a narrow section of the German elite that had pushed for recognition generated mainly by leadership rivalries and domestic party politics that eventually produced a "bandwagoning" effect in support of self-determination and recognition of Croatia and Slovenia. "It was formed neither by external forces—that is, by Germany's new geopolitical interests in a changing international environment—nor by the internal pressure of public opinion, interest groups, or the media. Rather, elites preferred to recognize these two states because a recognition policy was most consistent with Germany's entrenched foreign policy norms and the incentives structured by party politics. . . . The unilateral action was caused by a spiral of mistrust that emerged in international negotiations in the face of German domestic pressure for a policy of diplomatic recognition."[6] Whether or not Germany's actions were derived from longer historical ties in the region, broader geostrategic interests, or from more immediate domestic politics, its policy was to put pressure on the European Union to recognize Slovenia and Croatia while threatening to move ahead on its own.

French President Francois Mitterand and British Prime Minister John Major, backed by British Foreign Secretary Douglas Hurd, had strongly opposed German pressure to recognize Slovenia and Croatia. They succeeded in preventing Hans Dietrich Genscher from having his way until December 1991 when, at the EU foreign ministers' meeting at Maastricht, they were pressured again by Genscher. Retired American diplomat Walter Roberts described the meeting this way: "The vote in this gathering was 8 to 4 against recognition, but the German foreign minister insisted that he would not leave the table until the EC foreign ministers would unamimously support him. It was 10 P.M. By 4 A.M., he had his way. Would it not have been wiser if the British and the French foreign ministers had declared that *they* would not leave the table until Germany and its three allies agreed with the majority not to accord recognition?"[7]

If Germany was largely to blame for promoting the secession of Slovenia and Croatia in 1991, the United States was mainly to blame for promoting the secession of Bosnia in March 1992. Under the Bush administration, the initial U.S. position was to maintain the territorial integrity of Yugoslavia, warning Slovenia and Croatia against secession. In testimony before the U.S. House of Representatives International Relations Committee in 1995, former Secretary of State James Baker stated:

> What I said was that if there were unilateral declarations of independence followed by the use of force that foreclosed possibilities for peaceful breakup, peaceful negotiations, as required again by the Helsinki Accord, that it would kickoff the damndest civil war they had ever seen. And that's exactly what happened. And the fact of the matter is that it was Slovenia and Croatia who unilaterally declared independence in the face of these kinds of warnings. They used force to seize their border posts, and that, indeed, triggered the civil conflict that we suggested was going to happen.[8]

By the spring of 1992, following the eight months of war in Croatia, this American position was reversed. In the United States, the Croatian diaspora had established a quick lock on the U.S. government and media with their version of Yugoslav history and politics. The United States now took the lead in taking the rest of Yugoslavia apart in opposition to European preferences. In February 1992 at a meeting in Lisbon, a proposal was put together by the Portuguese Foreign Minister and Secretary General of the European Union, Jose Cutileiro, and the British EC representative to the former Yugoslavia, Lord Carrington, that provided for a Canton system for Bosnia based on the Swiss model. This plan, often referred to as the "Cutiliero Plan" or the "Lisbon Plan," allotted to the Serbs 44 percent of dis-contiguous Bosnian territory in their cantons. Bosnia was to be a loose, independent confederation with only one international personality. This plan was accepted by Alija Izetbegovic for the Muslims, Radovan Karadzic for the Serbs, and Mate Boban for the Croats. In December 1995, Cutileiro recounted what had happened:

> After several rounds of talks our "principles for future constitutional arrangements for Bosnia and Hercegovina" were agreed by the three parties (Muslim, Serb and Croat) in Sarajevo on March 18th as the basis for future negotiations. These continued, maps and all, until the summer, when the Muslims reneged on the agreement. Had they not done so, the Bosnian question might have been settled earlier, with less loss of (mainly Muslim) life and land. To be fair, President Izetbegovic and his aides were encouraged to scupper the deal and fight for a unitary Bosnian state by well-meaning outsiders who thought they knew better.[9]

These "well-meaning outsiders who thought they knew better" were members of the U.S. State Department and, in particular, the Ambassador to Yugoslavia, Warren Zimmermann. Zimmermann appeared in Sarajevo on March 28, ten days after all sides had accepted the Lisbon Plan, and discussed the plan with Izetbegovic. Thereafter, Izetbegovic backed out of the plan. Laura Silber and Allan Little claim that this episode has been misrepresented: "Zimmermann, a staunch advocate of human rights, was under instructions to support any agreement reached by the three sides. He said that he had advised

Izetbegovic that if the Bosnian President had made a commitment he should uphold it."[10] This explanation is dubious. John Mearsheimer and Stephen Van Evera observed: "Tragically, the Lisbon plan failed when Bosnian leader Alija Izetbegovic changed his mind and scuttled it. Although Warren Zimmermann, the American representative at the talks, now denies it, most reliable reports suggest that Izetbegovic acted with U.S. approval."[11] David Binder quotes Warren Zimmermann as saying: "Our view was that we might be able to head off a Serbian power grab by internationalizing the problem. Our hope was the Serbs would hold off if it was clear Bosnia had the recognition of Western countries."[12] Referring to Izetbegovic's meeting with Zimmermann following his return from Lisbon, Binder quotes Zimmermann as saying: "He said he didn't like it. I told him, if he didn't like it, why sign it?" Izetbegovic publicly renounced the agreement after having talked to Zimmermann. Needless to say, Zimmermann has absolved himself completely from all blame. In his book *Origins of a Catastrophe: Yugoslavia and its Destroyers*, Zimmermann claimed:

> The prime agent of Yugoslavia's destruction was Slobodan Milosevic, president of Serbia. Milosevic claimed to defend Yugoslavia even as he spun plans to turn it into a Serb-dominated dictatorship. His initial objective was to establish Serbian rule over the whole country. When Slovenia and Croatia blocked this aim by deciding to secede . . . [Milosevic] would bring all of Yugoslavia's Serbs, who lived in five of its six republics, under the authority of Serbia, that is, of himself. . . . Franjo Tudjman, elected president of Croatia in 1990, also played a leading role in the destruction of Yugoslavia. A fanatic Croatian nationalist, Tudjman hated Yugoslavia and its multiethnic values. He wanted a Croatian state for Croatians, and he was unwilling to guarantee equal rights to the 12 percent of Croatia's citizens who were Serbs.[13]

Such competing nationalisms between Serbs and Croats were not sufficient to destroy Yugoslavia, a problem that occurs in other multiethnic states.[14] The proverbial "foreign hand" made the decisive difference between the integrity of Yugoslavia and its destruction. Just as in the case of Croatia, when war began with referendums to secede and unilateral declarations of independence supported by Germany, war in Bosnia followed a Serb boycotted referendum and a Muslim-Croat declaration of independence supported by the United States against the wishes of the Bosnian Serbs.

One of the basic problems of the Yugoslav crisis between 1991 and 1995 was that, while the Serbs were looking backward and remembering the enormous destruction of Serbian lives during World War I and World War II, the Americans were looking forward and worrying about the post–Cold War territorial and nationalities problems in the former Soviet Union and Eastern Europe. From the American standpoint, allowing the Serbs to achieve their Greater Serbia out of the former Yugoslavia would have meant that Russians would also have the right to carve out a Greater Russia out of the former Soviet Union. A concession to the Serbs would have justified Russian nationalist demands that more than twenty-five million Russians stranded in the newly independent former Soviet Republics be retained within the Russian Federation through drastic territorial revisions of all the republics that seceded.

## THE REALITIES OF POWER IN THE POST–COLD WAR ERA

The territorial outcome in the former Yugoslavia demonstrates one of the basic dictums of international politics theory, namely that the lack of *countervailing power* in the world will not guarantee the sovereignty and independence of states, especially states that are small. Small states become vulnerable if the dominant powers in a unipolar world, acting in concert, seek to destroy their territorial integrity. The collapse of the Soviet Union left the United States and its newly united German partner with unrestraind power to dictate the new order in the Balkans. They have declared their actions to be morally justified.

If Serbian military power was about to determine the territorial boundaries of the new states out of a disintegrated Yugoslavia unfairly and through violent means, German and American politial and military power changed those equations in favor of their proteges, especially the Croats. The new territorial order imposed in the former Yugoslavia through American military intervention, both covert (Iranian arms) and overt (bombing of the Serbs), is not morally superior by any means to that which the Serbs were about to impose in the region to their advantage. The Serbs sought what they could have had for the asking at the end of World War I, a Greater Serbia. This was the historic mission of the Serbs in the nineteenth century and was no different from the uniting of Italians and Germans into the consolidated states of Greater Italy and Greater Germany in the 1860s and 1870s. If Croats and Slovenes had not agreed to join the South Slav Union, these states, in 1918, would have been very small while the "victorious Serbs would undoubtedly have succeeded in enlarging the territory of prewar Serbia to include sections of Croatia and Bosnia where many hundreds of thousands of Serbs had lived under Austro-Hungarian rule."[15] Instead, the quest for a Greater Serbia out of the territories of the former Yugoslavia—*not out of the bordering territories of independent states such as Hungary, Romania, Bulgaria, or Albania, which would be a case of irredentism and aggression*—was declared to be unacceptable by the United States.

Meanwhile, by 1995, Croatia and Croat Bosnia had become ethnically pure regions. A unified de facto Greater Croatia, consisting of the Republic of Croatia and the Croatian Republic of Herceg-Bosnia, was in operation since 1992 with no outcry from the international community. As of mid-2002, the Muslim-Croat Federation in Bosnia remains, as before, a fiction of the American imagination, although the United States and the German governments continue to force this federation into becoming a reality in order to demonstrate their belated commitment to the territorial integrity of multiethnic states.[16] This Muslim-Croat union was first a marriage of convenience agreed to by the Bosnian Croats and then, from 1994, an American compelled shotgun marriage. Bosnian Croats have shown no desire to be part of this Muslim-Croat federation, and, indeed, they voted with the Muslims in March 1992 to take Bosnia out of Yugoslavia for the sole purpose of joining their areas with Croatia into a "Greater Croatia." If Croatia had the right to secede from Yugoslavia, then it made sense for Bosnian Croats to want to become part of a united Croatia. In 1995, John Mearsheimer and Stephen Van Evera pointed out the following reality at the time:

> The Bosnian Croats can destroy the Federation at will. Their political organization, the Republic of Herzog-Bosna, already boasts all the trappings of a state. It has its own 50,000 man army. It delivers the mail, runs the schools, and collects taxes. . . . It is already closely linked to its mother state: Bosnian Croats carry Croatian passports, use Croatian currency, and Croatian license plates, route their telephone calls through Croatia, and vote in Croatian elections, as they did in Croatia's October 29, 1995, parliamentary elections.[17]

Indeed, while accusations of "Serbian aggression" were being directed at Serbia and the Bosnian Serbs, Peter Reid, a Boston columnist, noted in 1993 that "there is no dispute that 40,000 Croatian troops, including the HOS troops [a neo-Nazi Croatian militia] riding tanks, are in Bosnia."[18] A "Greater Croatia" was prevented on paper by the Dayton Accords of 1995, which created an autonomous Muslim-Croat federation out of 51 percent of the land and a boomerang-shaped Republika Srpska of the remaining 49 percent but divided by the Brcko corridor at the corner of the reverse, upside-down, L-shaped territory. Both parts remained within the independent state of Bosnia-Herzegovina held together by NATO powers. The Serb-inhabited areas of Krajina and Slavonia were taken over by Croatia following military assaults by Croatian forces in 1995, resulting in the expulsion and flight of nearly all Serbs from Croatia. The denial of the historic goal of a Greater Serbia for the Serbs in 1991–1992 and the de facto creation of an ethnically pure Greater Croatia for the Croats by 1995 were not coincidences or accidents. It was the natural outcome of Great Power politics and a preponderance of power at the end of the Cold War.

The argument that Serbia was attempting to secede from Yugoslavia while carving out the boundaries of a "Greater Serbia" from the internal "republics" of Croatia and Bosnia is quite misleading. The claim here is based on the pronouncements of Serbian intellectuals, led by Dobrica Cosic, in the late 1980s. Laura Silber and Allan Little stated that the Memorandum of the Serbian Academy of Sciences and Arts, "an unfinished draft," declared that Serbs were the victims of economic and political discrimination by their Croat and Slovene countrymen although Serbs had made the greatest military contribution and suffered the most casualties over the last century.[19]

According to Vesna Pesic, these Serb elites felt that the concept of Yugoslavia was a Serbian delusion not shared by Croats and others. They argued that there was a conspiracy to keep Serbs poor, weak, and exploited by the richer Croats and Slovenes. Serbs were exposed to hatred and Serbophobia among other ethnic groups.[20] Pesic quotes some Serbian nationalists as follows:

> After genocide [1941–1945] . . . after the 1974 constitution . . . it is difficult to understand why Serbs today do not reasonably and obstinately aspire to a state without national problems, national hatreds, and Serbophobia. Serbs must learn to live without others within their own national state. This was an issue of freedom and the right to exist for the Serbian ethnos as the whole of its spiritual, cultural, and historical identity, irrespective of the present-day republican boundaries and the Yugoslav Constitution. If this freedom and right are not respected, then the historical goal of the Serbian people—unification of all Serbs in one state—is not realized.

Pesic quoted Dobrica Cosic as saying that "the enemies of Serbs made Serbs Serbs." Another nationalist is quoted as saying: "The Serbian issue was started and opened by others. They straightened us out by blows, made us sober by offenses, woke us up through injustices, brought light and united us by coalitions. They hate us because of Yugoslavia, and now it seems they do not leave her, but us."

Silber and Little claimed that "a member of the Academy, Cosic, went so far as to explain, rather unconvincingly, that the Memorandum was not 'nationalist' but 'anti-Tito and pro-Yugoslav.' In the 1970s, disgruntled intellectuals rallied around him. Cosic held clandestine monthly meetings on the need for democratic reform in Yugoslavia."[21] A draft by Serbian intellectuals in the late 1970s narrating Serbian grievances can hardly be considered sufficient excuse for Great Powers to move in and take Yugoslavia apart more than a decade later. These Serbian grievances would appear to be well founded, as later events showed. Dissident Slovenes, Croats, Bosnian Muslims, and Macedonians chose to leave Yugoslavia. The Serbs were demonized and dehumanized by the Western media and their united Serbian state destroyed through the actions of a German-led Europe and the United States.

There was a significant difference between the concept of Greater Croatia and Greater Serbia. In the decades before 1918, it was the Croatian intelligentsia that favored a broader South Slav state, and it was the Serbian intelligentsia and leaders that sought a Greater Serbia for Serbs alone.[22] After the creation of the South Slav state in 1918, the Croatian national question was always secessionist, which required taking with it all of the territories of Dalmatia, Krajina, Slavonia, and the western part of Bosnia-Herzegovina, territories they would never have had if the South Slav union had not been accepted by the Serbs in 1918. On the other hand, the Serbian national question after 1918 was not necessarily secessionist but involved carving out the boundaries of a Greater Serbian Republic within Yugoslavia to redress their traditional grievance that the perpetuation of these internal boundaries of the republics was not acceptable, whether historic or not. The Serbian goal was secessionist to the extent that, if the international frontiers of Yugoslavia were not to survive, then they would fight to obtain what they could have had in 1918, namely, a Greater Serbia encompassing the Serb territories of post-1945 Titoist Croatia in Krajina, parts of Dalmatia and Slavonia, and all of Bosnia-Herzegovina (which historically had a Serb pluralist majority before the extensive destruction of Serbian lives in two world wars), Montenegro, and Macedonia (which before 1918 used to be South Serbia).

The intensity of Croatian nationalist demands after 1945 reached its height between 1967 and 1972. In 1967, demands were made that Croatian language alone be used in the Croatian republic. Barbara Jelavich wrote: "The Serbs immediately countered with the request that the 700,000 of their people living in Croatia receive reciprocal rights."[23] In 1971, Croatian nationalists declared that Croatia was "the sovereign national state of the Croatian nation" possessing "sovereignty based on the right to self-determination, including the right to secession." They reiterated that Croatian would be the only language that could be used in the republic. While Tito suppressed Croatian nationalism during this time, he then conceded much of the Croatian demands in the formulation of the 1974 Yugoslav Constitution to the detriment of Serbian interests.[24] Croatia was strengthened; Serbia was weakened.

In retrospect, the earlier erasure of the autonomy of Kosovo and Vojvodina by Milosevic, which Tito had imposed unilaterally on Serbia, would appear fortuitious. If it were not for Milosevic's actions, Kosovo and Vojvodina would also have been separated from Yugoslavia through American and German dictates on the basis that internal provinces of a sovereign state have the right to become international states based on the principle of self-determination. Indeed, in the early phase of the conflict, the United States encouraged the secession of Montenegro so as to complete the secession of all republics as in the case of the Soviet Union. Milosevic and the Serbian nationalists attempted to secede from Yugoslavia with a Greater Serbia through force from mid-1991 onward only when they realized that, under German pressure, Slovenia and Croatia would eventually be recognized within their prevailing internal boundaries.

In the complex domestic situation of Yugoslavia there were legitimate complaints on all sides. The primary Serbian complaint was that Marshal Josip Broz Tito, a half Croat and half Slovene, ran Yugoslavia on the principle that "A Weak Serbia Makes for a Strong Yugoslavia."[25] Thus, he created autonomous provinces of Vojvodina and Kosovo but not autonomous provinces of Dalmatia, Slavonia, or Krajina. In the former Yugoslavia, Serbs constituted only 38 percent of Yugoslavia's entire population and even today represent only 70 percent in the "rump" Yugoslavia. Together with Macedonia, what is left of Yugoslavia constitutes one of only two multiethnic states that emerged out of the former Yugoslavia. This is in stark contrast to an ethnically pure Greater Croatia established with willing or inadvertent German and American assistance. The Croatian claim that Serbs of Krajina and Slavonia followed their nationalist leaders into Bosnia and Serbia "voluntarily" fails to explain the Serbs' historical fears for resisting German-sponsored Croatian independent rule, not to mention the sudden terror of the American-supported military assaults on Western Slavonia and Krajina.[26]

Cedric Thornberry, deputy head of UNPROFOR (United Nations Protection Forces) in the former Yugoslavia from 1992 to 1994, noted: "But one of the most puzzling features of the Yugoslav tragedy has been the comparative lack of significance the world has attached to events in the Krajina region when the Croatian army recaptured it last year. . . . Today, through the 'ethnic cleansing' that has occurred, Croatia has become the most 'ethnically pure' state in the whole of the former Yugoslavia."[27] Referring to the earlier Croatian incursion into Medak, which set the standard in Krajina, Thornberry observed:

> The Croatian Army assault was well-planned. The advancing soldiers killed or destroyed everyone and everything in their path—the few Serb defenders, the mostly aged inhabitants, and all their livestock. Using dynamite and engineering precision, the invaders leveled every single building. Three days after the Croatian army's withdrawal under international pressure, I could find only one chicken alive during a full day's survey of the 100-square-mile area. . . . Our Canadian military experts concluded that the goals of the incursion had been to carry out a program of 100 percent scorched earth and slaughter, and that it had been systematically planned, and that such planning could only have been endorsed at the highest level of the Croatian Army—at the least. The most disturbing feature of this event was the cold-bloodedness with which it had evidently been implemented.

Similarly, Andre Liebich noted: "Croatia has solved its minority problem by overrunning the Serb autonomous areas whose refusal to accept a diminished constitutional role in an independent Croatia triggered war in 1991."[28] Rarely is it mentioned now that Croatia's unilateral declaration of independence in June 1991 was accompanied by the restoration of the old Nazi-Ustashe symbols of World War II, the denial of citizenship rights to Serbs, the dismissal of Serbs from their jobs, and the expulsion of some 30,000 to 50,000 of them from Zagreb, and that Serb residents who remain sign loyalty oaths to obtain Croatian citizenship.[29] That led to the expulsion of some 80,000 to 100,000 Croats from the Serbian majority areas of Krajina almost immediately. And, eventually, nearly all Serbs, numbering some 200,000, were driven out of Krajina and Slavonia by Croatian forces by 1995. The difference in the culpability between Serbs and Croats was that less mass murder and ethnic cleansing needed to be done by Croatians to achieve their ethnically pure Greater Croatia than by Serbs to achieve their ethnically pure Greater Serbia. Moreover, Tudjman was assisted by the United States in achieving his goal by 1995, while Milosevic was prevented. However, the Croatian and Serbian objectives were the same. These were not unusual expectations on a continent composed mainly of nation-states.

Under the more moderate post-Tudjman regime of President Stipe Mesic, Croatia has offered to take back Serbs who fled. But even if many return and others remain, there is the unusual problem of Serbian identity being lost through their conversion to Catholicism. The essential difference between a Serb and a Croat is Orthodox Christianity and Catholicism, with race and language remaining the same. Facing continued demonization and discrimination in Croatia, large numbers of younger Serbs have converted to Catholicism in order to become Croats and have changed their more obvious Serbian names to more Croatian ones.[30] Children of Serbs are refusing to be Serbs and insist on being Croats. The parallel to this situation would be Jews who convert to Christianity, losing their ethnic Jewish identity, except that the switch from Orthodoxy to Catholicism within Christianity is more facile. With younger Serbs likely to convert, the Serbian minority problem in Croatia will dissipate shortly as elderly Serbs who cling to their identity pass away.

Arguments were made by those supporting the Croatian point of view that Serbs and Croats are different, one European and the other Asiatic, and therefore cannot live together. To be Catholic and Croat was to be more Western and enlightened; to be Orthodox and Serbian was to be more Eastern and "Byzantine," implying backwardness.[31] This "Huntingtonian" civilizational mindset was central in the demand for the separation of Croats from Serbs, although Christianity is an Asian religion that emerged from

Judaism in the Middle East. Indeed, all the great living religions of the world are Asian. The mentality of higher and lower cultures is puzzling, since knowledge of European history, politics, and culture is accessible to anybody who wishes to learn. In the age of satellite and cyber communications and the Americanization of the world, such claims are meaningless. Yugoslavia was declared to be an artificial state—though Bosnia was not—where the right of self-determination had to be granted to its distinct "nationalities." Secessions became inevitable in order to allow the more European, and presumably more civilized, parts to become democratic and eventually part of the European Union. That Western liberals pushed this narrow-minded agenda made it even more surprising. Michael Libal, who was the Southeast European Director of the German Foreign Ministry during the Yugoslav crisis, writes:

> by showing a ruthless disdain for human rights in general and minority rights in Kosovo, Serbian nationalism posed an insuperable obstacle to the chances for a democratic and European future of Yugoslavia as a whole and by implication of the smaller republics and nations. Serbian national communism made it inevitable for these smaller entities to separate. . . . The alleged allurements by pro-Slovene and pro-Croat forces in Central and Western Europe played an insignificant role besides the expectations based on memory of what a restored Serbian hegemony would mean for the other Yugoslav nations.[32]

Where in Slovenia, Croatia, Bosnia, or Macedonia did the Serbs show "a ruthless disdain for human rights in general" before 1990? I was unable to find any report that would fit this extreme generalization during this time. How does this allegation compare with Turkish policies in its Kurdish areas, Russia in Chechnya, China in Tibet, India in Kashmir, or Indonesia in East Timor? What exactly were "the expectations based on memory of what a restored Serbian hegemony would mean for the other Yugoslav nations"? During World War II, some five hundred thousand to seven hundred thousand Serbs were slaughtered by the Nazi-backed Croatian Ustashe. The terrible memory belonged mainly to the Serbs. Between 1945 and 1980, Yugoslavia was ruled with an iron fist by Marshall Tito, a non-Serb communist dictator. Most command positions in the civilian, military, and foreign service bureaucracies were held by Slovenes and Croats. Indeed, this is what Slobodan Milosevic was complaining about bitterly.

Earlier, between 1918 and 1940, how many Croats, Slovenes, Bosnian Muslims, and Macedonians died because of Serbian repression under a Serbian monarchy? According to my inquiries, nobody seems to know, perhaps a few dozen in two decades. The two significant killings were the assassination of Stjepan Radic, leader of the Croatian peasant party in 1929, and then the assassination of the Serbian King Alexander in Paris in 1934. Again, between 1980 and 1990, how many of these national minorities died from Serbian repression ("a ruthless disdain for human rights in general" as Libal puts it)? According to my inquiries, none other than the average crime statistics. That there was intense Serb-Croat rivalry is not in dispute. Kosovo was a special case for the Serbs, not unlike the Israelis' emotional attachment to Jerusalem, and not unlike Israeli repression in the West Bank and Gaza, where Jewish "settlers" felt threatened but where they had less right to be "settled" compared to the Serbs in Kosovo.

## SOVEREIGNTY VERSUS SELF-DETERMINATION

### The Problem and Its Implications

The underlying cause of the tragedy of Yugoslavia was the ad hoc rejection of the principle of the territorial integrity and sovereignty of states. In September 2000, at the United Nations summit in New York, President Bill Clinton of the United States, Prime Minister Tony Blair of Britain, and Prime Minister Jacques Chretien of Canada, supported by the UN Secretary-General, Kofi Anan, endorsed the idea of humanitarian interventions within sovereign states.[33] They proposed the setting up of a permanent UN peacekeeping force to undertake such actions. Anan declared that states cannot hide behind the principle of sovereignty when indulging in "evil" within its borders. Anan and Western leaders are, of course, referring to events in Bosnia, Kosovo, East Timor, Rwanda, and Sierra Leone. By contrast, during the summit, China, Russia, and India invoked the principle of state sovereignty and noninterference in the internal affairs of states—the basis of the UN Charter, although the original terms of the Charter had already eroded with the passage of the 1948 Genocide Convention, the 1948 Universal Declaration on Human Rights, and other multilateral agreements on individual and minority rights.

Undoubtedly, the enforcement of human rights worldwide is a noble and worthy goal. Who could object to humanitarian intervention by the international community to stop genocide and ethnic cleansing by state authorities within its national borders? However, there is a problem that is usually overlooked. Often the threat and willingness to intervene politically and militarily by the "international community" (which in reality means the United States and not the United Nations) in the internal affairs of sovereign states actually provokes and causes further bloodshed and human rights violations that may not otherwise have occurred. Further, where the territorial integrity of the state is violated and territorial secessions are encouraged, it leads to more demands by other ethnic or ideological groups for the same right of secession leading to more violence, more death and destruction, and greater human rights violations. Disgruntled minorities and ethnic groups then have a vested interest in provoking the state authorities into massive human rights violations in order to invite "humanitarian interventions" by the "international community." Where such problems were restricted and localized at one time, it now becomes more massive and widespread.

Indeed, the encouragement of the right of self-determination, an unwillingness to respect the sovereignty of the state, and the willingness to indulge in humanitarian interventions would create the conditions where such an active international policy posture would become necessary. A standing or threatened policy of humanitarian intervention by the United States and the West then becomes the cause of human rights nightmares. Although NATO and their supporters now claim routinely that it attacked Serbia in violation of the UN Charter in order to return the one million Albanians driven out of Kosovo, it was NATO's illegal assault that caused the flight. During the year prior to NATO's bombing of Kosovo, which commenced on March 24, 1999, some 2,000 Albanians and Serbs had died, some 300,000 Albanians had been internally displaced, and another 70,000 may have moved out of Kosovo to Albania and safer areas abroad because of the overreaction of Serbian security forces against the Kosovo Liberation Army. It is not an unusual phenomenon for the insurgents and terrorists to be unknown and hidden within the civilian population, for example, Chechnya, Kurdistan, and Kashmir. Allegations have been made that the expulsions of all Albanians had been planned by Milosevic before NATO's assault and the assault provided the needed excuse to do so. However, as Kelly Greenhill points out in her chapter in this book, there is no evidence that such a "Horseshoe Plan" existed.[34]

Following NATO's war over Kosovo, efforts were made to sever Kosovo from Serbia and to encourage the secession of Montenegro from the remnant Yugoslavia. Such actions do not lead to less human rights violations but more, often with the onetime victims conducting such violations against their former oppressors. Thus, a U.S.-led NATO, with a pliant United Nations in tow, has set itself up for an active role in world affairs, now that there is no challenge from the defunct Soviet-led Warsaw Pact countries or, indeed, little challenge from anywhere to anything that the West may choose to do in the name of a self-defined and selective morality.

Such a policy posture could undermine the unity and stability of multiethnic states thus contradicting the other noble Western goal of promoting interethnic tolerance and coexistence within a state of different linguistic, religious, and cultural groups. Human rights violations could then reach epidemic proportions and could keep the proposed UN peacekeeping force busy indefinitely and increase the need for even more peacekeepers. Consequently, two large bureaucracies, the UN and NATO, by creating new roles for themselves, have become self-serving and self-perpetuating. Besides, the lofty declarations and proposals made at the UN summit in September 2000 by Clinton, Blair, Chretien, and Anan may be applied only to small and weak states, not to states such as Russia, China, and India.

Ironically, with the fall of Milosevic in September 2000, the West reversed itself on the question of the territorial integrity of the remnant Yugoslavia. No further moves were made to sever Montenegro and Kosovo from Yugoslavia. Indeed, UN Security Resolution 1244, which brought the war to an end in June 1999, upheld the territorial integrity of the remnant Yugoslavia that included Kosovo and the confining of NATO forces only to Kosovo and not throughout Yugoslavia. These were the main reasons for Serbia's refusal to accept the U.S. dictate at Rambouillet in February 1999. An implication of NATO's war over Kosovo appears to be that the United States and its Western allies have the right to abandon the principle of the territorial integrity of states if there are human rights violations taking place.

## SECESSIONIST MOVEMENTS AND STATE SOVEREIGNTY

Some disturbing international precedents were set in the Yugoslav case that could lead to more chaos and injustice rather than political stability in the rest of the world, especially India. Traditionally, the unwritten rules of the "old world order" were as follows:

1. When the right of self-determination is invoked by secessionist ethnic groups, the state almost always invokes the principles of the territorial integrity and sovereignty of the state and the inviolability of its borders. This invariably leads to civil war. A "Unilateral Declaration of Independence" (UDI) against the objections of the federal authorities and the wishes of the majority population who are engaged in resisting the secessionists is considered a violation of international law.[35] In 1965, for instance, Britain refused to recognize the UDI by Prime Minister Ian Smith's White minority government in Rhodesia declaring the act as illegal under international law. Supporting the British position, the United Nations then proceeded to impose economic sanctions on Rhodesia as punishment for its illegal UDI.
2. The notion of state sovereignty in the past meant that other states did not have the right to interfere in its internal matters. While multilateral economic and arms control treaties signed voluntarily for the mutual bene-

fits they provide have increasingly placed limitations on state sovereignty, such self-limitations do not extend to the right of external interference in the internal struggle between the state and the secessionists.

3. The state's "standard operating procedure" in dealing with secessionist demands and accompanying insurgency or terrorism is the attempt to crush it through counterinsurgency and counterterrorist means. The level of violence by the state then invariably exceeds that of the separatists. Human rights violations are committed by both sides. States usually justify such an overwhelming military response with its human rights violations on the grounds that it produces less tragedy and suffering in the long run by deterring other separatist movements and by preventing the collapse of the state into anarchy. This is hardly a satisfactory condition, but the policy of humanitarian interventions may be less desirable.
4. Apart from the long-standing states of Europe and a few others elsewhere, such as Japan, Thailand, Persia, and Ethiopia, most states came about haphazardly with the end of empires: the end of the Spanish and Portuguese empires in the Americas in the eighteenth and nineteenth centuries; the Austro-Hungarian and Ottoman empires in Europe and the Middle East at the end of World War I; and the end of all European empires in Asia and Africa over a period of decades after World War II. There is no serious rationale for the existence of large states, such as the United States or China, and small states, such as Trinidad or Tuvalu. Tuvalu, with a population of 11,000, and East Timor, with a population of 8,000 were the two most recent states to be admitted to the UN in 2000 and 2002. The formation of new states from an existing state through successful separatist violence aided by outside powers or through mutual agreement between the state and the secessionists have been rare, for example, Bangladesh from Pakistan, Eritrea from Ethiopia, and the several states out of the former Soviet Union and Yugoslavia. However, the reference to the right of self-determination in the United Nations Charter applies only to decolonization, although state formation as the result of decolonization may carry no logic or consistency. Most states are accidents of history.
5. When a state attempts to crush secessionist movements through military force, the term "aggression" as defined by the United Nations Charter does not apply. This is civil war, not war among states. A state has the legal right to preserve its territorial integrity by force with a moral obligation to minimize human rights violations. While the state may be accused of "crimes against humanity" under conditions of civil war, this does not give outside powers the right to dismantle the state through a policy of new state recognitions, as in the case of the former Yugoslavia.

6. According to the Guidelines of the Montevideo Convention of 1933, new states are to be recognized on the empirical evidence that they possess clearly demarcated territorial boundaries, a stable population, and a government in control.[36] Political preference and moral considerations are less relevant. These conditions were not met in 1992 when Bosnia-Herzegovina was recognized as an independent state. The boundaries of Bosnia were being contested by Serbia and Croatia at the time. Its population was unstable amidst ethnic cleansings and refugee flows. Between 1992 and 1995, the Muslim government in Sarajevo under Alia Izetbegovic did not have control over the Serbian and Croatian occupied territories, which constituted the bulk of the land and the population. Although sometimes a requirement for recognizing new states includes the expectation that the "state's government be established consistent with the principle of self-determination," this principle, according to Hurst Hannum, "seems to be applicable only in the context of decolonization, such as the refusal of the world community to concede statehood to Southern Rhodesia from the time of Ian Smith's unilateral declaration of independence in 1965 to the establishment of majority rule in 1980."[37]
7. If parts of an existing state manage to secede, the rights of the old state are retained by the remnant state if this part still remains the equal or greater part than the single or each of the several parts that seceded from the old state. There are precedents establishing this rule: India became the successor state when Pakistan, with the minority population, seceded in 1947; Pakistan became the successor state when Bangladesh, with the majority population, seceded in 1972; and Russia was declared the successor state when the rest of the Soviet Republics, with a combined population slightly greater than Russia, seceded in 1991.
8. When the old state ceases to exist, either through secession or disintegration, the former internal boundaries of the state, whether they are called provinces, "states," or "republics," cannot automatically become the boundaries of the new state. For example, when Ireland seceded from Britain in 1992, Northern Ireland was separated from Ireland. When Pakistan seceded from India in 1947, the provinces of Bengal and Punjab were divided.
9. Secession may be considered immoral when it leads to the denial of past benefits to the rest of the country; when it compels other units also to secede, leading to state disintegration; and where such actions lead to war, chaos, and human tragedy.

The above principles and practices were discarded in cavalier fashion by the "international community" in the case of the former Yugoslavia, setting precedents elsewhere in the world that will generate more violence and instability.[38] In retrospect, it is difficult to believe that the sudden media-generated hysterical hate and mass prejudice against the Serbs that swept the West in the 1990s could have led to such a transformation of the rules of the international system. UDIs and new state recognition in the former Yugoslavia, or the intention to recognize new states as in the case of Slovenia and Croatia, caused the subsequent wars.

However, these new rules do not apply to the West. In August 1998, the Canadian Supreme Court, while acknowledging that Canada is not indivisible, declared that Quebec could not secede through a simple majority vote among its residents.[39] The terms of secession would have to be negotiated with the rest of Canada as an amendment to the Canadian constitution. The nine Canadian justices indicated that, while such a secession would be theoretically feasible, it would be difficult, painful, and costly, suggesting that it was not likely to be accepted in practice. More importantly, the Canadian Supreme Court (that included three judges from Quebec) declared that, under international law, there is no right of unilateral secession except territories that are judged to be colonies and specially oppressed peoples. Quebec fulfills neither category. The court warned that unilateral secession by French Canadians would likely be rejected as illegitimate by the "international community," presumably the same international community, including Canada, that rushed to recognize the unilateral declarations of secession by Slovenia and Croatia.

Another anomaly exists in the West's policy of recognition. This was the "unseating" of the remnant Yugoslavia at the United Nations on the grounds that it was not the successor state of the former Yugoslavia. This decision was made despite the fact that the Kingdom of Serbs, Croats, and Slovenes, created in 1918 and renamed Yugoslavia in 1929, was the successor state to the Kingdom of Serbia, which was recognized as a sovereign independent state at the 1878 Congress of Berlin. Yehuda S. Blum pointed out that this decision appeared to have nothing to do with international law or with precedent but with international revulsion over the tragic events in Yugoslavia.[40] According to Blum, the Permanent Representative of the United States to the United Nations, Edward Perkins, declared to the General Assembly that "the Belgrade authorities" carried the "overwhelming responsibilities for the terrible events that have occurred" on the territory of the former Yugoslav federation. Perkins added that changes in Yugoslavia had "fundamentally altered the previous structures" and therefore Serbia and Montenegro would have to reapply for membership "and be held to the same standards as all other applicants. Specifically, they must prove to the Members of the United Nations that the *so-called* Federal Republic of Yugoslavia is a peace-loving state."[41]

Blum points out a "glaring inconsistency" in the U.S. position. While the United States rejected the "so-called Federal Republic of Yugoslavia," consisting of Serbia and Montenegro, as the successor state to the former Yugoslavia, the delegates from this so-called state continued to occupy the seat of the former Yugoslavia at the United Nations. Yugoslavia was one of the founding members of the League of Nations and the United Nations. The demand that states be "peace-loving" is found in Article 4 (1) of the Charter. However, the breakup of Yugoslavia was similar to the breakup of British India in 1947 amidst violence, war, and massive refugee flows. According to Blum, despite Pakistan's claim that both India and Pakistan were new states, the UN Secretariat declared:

> From the viewpoint of international law, the situation is one in which a part of an existing State breaks off and becomes a new state. On this analysis, there is no change in the international status of India; it continues as a State with all the treaty rights and obligations, and consequently, with all the rights and membership in the United Nations. The territory that breaks off, Pakistan, will be a new state; it will not have the treaty rights and obligations of the old State, and it will not, of course, have membership in the United Nations.[42]

According to Blum, "by any objective yardstick—whether factual or legal—it is difficult to deny the 'Belgrade authorities' the right to occupy the seat of Yugoslavia at the United Nations, however reprehensible their policies may seem to some—or even the overwhelming majority—of the Organization's members."[43] The claim that the Federal Republic of Yugoslavia was the successor state to the old Yugoslavia was rejected by the UN Security Council in May 1992 (Resolution 757). In September of that year, the United Nations General Assembly, endorsed the Council's resolution by a vote of 127 to 6, with 26 abstentions and 20 absences. Even after this vote, "the allegedly non-existent Yugoslavia" continued to occupy the same seat in the General Assembly, while its modified red, white, and blue flag, without the star of the communist federation in the middle, continued to fly outside at the UN building. Blum concluded: "The procedure resorted to in the instant case clearly plays havoc with the criteria laid down in the wake of the partitioning of India in 1947 and consistently applied ever since—criteria that by and large have served the United Nations and the international community well over the past decades."[44]

As regards Serbia's claim to Kosovo, it was no different than most other cases, such as Russia's to Chechnya, Spain's to the Basques areas, India's to Kashmir, China's to Tibet, Israel's to the lands it occupies, or even that of the United States to Texas, New Mexico, and California, which were wrested from Mexico by force in the nineteenth century. Kosovo was annexed by Serbia in 1912 during its quest to consolidate historic Serb territories and unite the Serbian people into a single state. The goal of uniting Serbs, Croats, and Albanians would be no different from the uniting of Italian territories in the 1860s into a "Greater Italy," under the leadership of Giuseppe Garibaldi and Conte Camillo di Cavour, and the uniting of German territories into a "Greater Germany," under the leadership of Chancellor Otto von Bismarck. Moreover, Serbia could have had its "Greater Serbia" for the asking at the end of World War I for having fought and sacrificed enormously on the side of the victorious Entente Powers.

Efforts to carve out a "Greater Serbia," following the unilateral declarations of independence and the subsequent recognition of Croatia and Bosnia, involved keeping within the remnant Yugoslavia as much of the old territories of Yugoslavia where Serbs lived. This was not the same thing as Nazi Germany's attempts to annex the German inhabited territories of the Sudetenland in Czechoslovakia or Silesia in Poland. Serbia did not seek to annex by force the territories of Austria, Hungary, Romania, Bulgaria, or Albania. Indeed, if the rules applied to the former Yugoslavia were applied elsewhere in the world, few of the existing state boundaries would survive, especially those in Africa and the Americas. It would open up a pandora's box of UDIs leading to civil wars, refugee flows, and global chaos. For example, amidst political turmoil in Indonesia following the overthrow of President Suharto, the dislodging of East Timor from Indonesia by the "international community" through diplomatic pressure has encouraged further violent demands for secession among other ethnic groups in Aceh, Ambon, Irian Jaya, and the Moluccan Islands.

## THE BOUNDARIES QUESTION FOLLOWING STATE SECESSION

When new states are forged through secession from an existing state, one significant principle established in two earlier cases was that the former internal boundaries of the state cannot automatically become the external boundaries of new states.[45] Thus, when Catholic-majority Ireland seceded from Britain in 1921, the Protestant-majority areas of Northern Ireland were dislodged from Ireland and retained by Britain, despite the protests of Ireland and the Catholics of Northern Ireland. When Pakistan seceded from India in 1947, Punjab and Bengal were divided between India and Pakistan, despite protests by Pakistan that the majority in these two British provinces were Muslim.

In both the breakup of Yugoslavia and the Soviet Union in 1991, no such territorial and boundary changes of their former internal "republics" were allowed by the international community. The post-Soviet boundaries of Russia were particularly puzzling because the boundaries of Russia had fluctuated over the centuries. One post-disintegration analysis of the Soviet Union stated: "Because Russia became an empire before the Russians consolidated as a nation, the psychological limits of the state and of the Russian identity have always been problematic. Russia has always been a pre-modern empire with a center and a periphery."[46] Another analyst pointed out: "The Russian state has never existed within its current borders."[47] The origins of the Russian state are found in Kiev, the capital of Ukraine, around the ninth century. The distinctions among the Orthodox Christian peoples of Russia, Ukraine, and Beylorussia (now Belarus) are relatively minor. Certainly, the differences are much less than various ethnic groups, such as Chechins and Tatars, seeking secession from post-Soviet Russia.

In the case of the former Soviet Union, the rationale for the emergence of independent states based on its pre-1991 internal boundaries was that there existed no more than fifteen "republics" within the former Soviet Union, whether or not these fifteen republics alone made sense. Russian-majority Crimea is a part of independent Ukraine after 1991 because Khrushchev decided to transfer Crimea to the Ukrainian republic in 1954. The reason that Armenian-majority Ngorno-Karabakh became part of independent Azerbaijan instead of Armenia is that Stalin decided to transfer it from Armenia to Azerbaijan in 1921.[48] As long as the Soviet Union remained one state, these internal boundary questions among its "republics," on whether there ought to be more than fifteen "republics" for the USSR's more than one hundred nationalities were not burning issues. But they become matters of "life and death" when the state disintegrates and when historic memories of conflict or persecution exist among the new minorities.

Similar problems prevailed in the former Yugoslavia with even greater complications. On the territorial question, Susan Woodward points out the conflicting views about boundaries that existed in Yugoslavia at the time of its dissolution. These viewpoints included the following: boundaries were to be based on *historical claims*; on the *democratic principle* that allows ethnic groups to carve out states where they are in a majority; on the *territorial integrity* principle that declares the inviolability of international frontiers (the 1975 Helsinki Accords Final Act); on *the realist principle* that accepts changes to borders through a fait accompli; and on the *feudal principle* (as invoked by Karadzic in Bosnia) based on land ownership and occupation.[49] Disagreements about such territorial rights and claims among Yugoslavia's constituent nations and republics were unresolved prior to the state's breakup. The argument is often made that, when Marshall Tito drew the internal boundaries of Yugoslavia toward the end of World War II, he was merely adhering to historic boundaries. Therefore, Tito's internal boundaries should be maintained, and Serbian claims denying such rigid and unchangeable boundaries are distortions intended to justify their "aggression."

In a severe critique of Susan Woodward's book *Balkan Tragedy*, Michael Libal, former Director of the German Foreign Ministry in charge with dealing with the problems of the former Yugoslavia, made the following observation:

> Because the frontiers of Slovenia, Croatia, and Bosnia-Hercegovina were on the whole historical frontiers, the choice was easier to make. Nothing, therefore, is further from the mark than Woodward's claim that "new" states were being created out of Yugoslav territory. No "new" states had to be created. Just as there is a state of Bavaria in the Federal Republic of Germany, and as there was a state of Slovakia in the Czechoslovak republic and a state of Georgia in the former USSR, there existed states in the former Yugoslavia. . . . And in this context, contrary to what Woodward pretends, the Serbs were granted exactly the same, albeit rather limited, right of self-determination, as all other Yugoslav nations. They were allowed to claim international recognition for their republic (Serbia) and respect for its territorial integrity, which meant denying the right to secession to the Albanians in Kosovo and the Muslims in the Sanjak.[50]

This statement is not only wrong from the standpoint of international law and politics among sovereign states, but it is highly dangerous. Except for the Kingdom of Serbia before 1918, Slovenia, Croatia, Bosnia-Herzegovina, and Macedonia were never states under international law over the last five hundred years, at least, and never possessed an international legal personality to act independently. Libal's claim that the internal "republics" of the former Yugoslavia were "virtual reality states" (my term) under international law is patently absurd. Their status under international law was no different from that of Kosovo or Sanjak within the Serbian republic of Yugoslavia, or that of Dalmatia, Krajina, and Slavonia within the Croatian republic of Yugoslavia. Internal boundaries have no sanctity under international law and may be changed. In many cases, internal boundaries may have no political or legal justification within the state and may be the subject of intense domestic controversy, as in the case of Serbian complaints prior to 1991.

While Croatian-American historians and their supporters may claim that Tito followed historical boundaries of provinces that existed within the Austro-Hungarian and Ottoman empires, Yugoslav specialists such as David Martin claim that Yugoslavia's internal borders were essentially the "recent inventions of a Communist dictator [Tito] and have no historical validity."[51] Similarly, the British author Nora Beloff noted: "The internal borders, which we treat as permanent features of Yugoslavia, were in reality drawn up secretly by Tito's men in 1943 and were designed as administrative boundaries, within a centrally planned Stalinist state."[52]

There are few states in the world today whose "historic" boundaries have been constant. Many had no past boundaries of any kind at all until they emerged as independent states following decolonization. No ethnic logic prevails in the boundaries of African states, except the colonial legacy. This was the argument made by the Catholic Ibos of Biafra who had declared independence from Nigeria and were crushed by Muslim federal forces in a brutal civil war between 1967 and 1970. At the time of British India's independence, there existed several large British Indian provinces proper and over 580 autonomous Indian princely states ruled by maharajahs and nawabs. After independence, the new Indian government changed all those internal boundaries such that virtually none of the old historic boundaries remained.

The important question is whether, when provinces secede from a sovereign state, internal boundaries should automatically become external boundaries. From the standpoint of equity and justice, this should not be allowed to happen. No government of India of any political party or persuasion would tolerate Michael Libal's argument that internal provinces, whether they are called states or republics, have the right to become independent states within those borders. Indeed, as far as India is concerned, they have no right to become independent states whatever their borders. And by implication, unilateral declarations of independence are considered acts of war, which India will prevent by all possible means. This resolve is no different elsewhere in the world, including the United States, as evident in the civil war that it fought in the nineteenth century. Yugoslavia was prevented from exercising this right of preserving its territorial integrity by the Western powers.

Libal is wrong even about the territorial status of some of the "virtual reality" republics of the Soviet Union. The boundaries of Tajikstan and Uzbekistan were drawn by Stalin to keep Tajiks and Uzbeks weak. Much of historical Tajikstan that included Tashkent and Samarkand was deliberately given to Uzbekistan, and the Uzbek population was divided between the two republics. Nations and international boundaries of these two states did not coincide after they became independent, something which did not matter when both Tajikstan and Uzbekistan were part of the Soviet Union. And exactly how historic is "historic" for internal provinces to claim that they are "virtual reality" independent states waiting to break free and be recognized instantly, as in the case of Slovenia and Croatia?

Second, internal boundaries, whether historic or not, cannot justify the perpetuation of those internal borders when provinces secede. Territories must be renegotiated. There are some real dangers in accepting the territorial principles applied in allowing various internal republics of the Soviet Union and Yugoslavia to secede without changes to their boundaries. The central governments of states, dominated by an ethnic majority, will be motivated to set up highly centralized political systems in the future based purely on administrative district boundaries, thus preventing autonomous self-government for provinces. That would aggravate ethnic dissatisfaction, secessionist pressures, and internal conflict. Alternatively, there could be an escalation in conflict between ethnic majorities and minorities for the creation of more internal "states" or "republics" along ethnic lines in case the multiethnic state disintegrates in the future.

## THE POPULATION-TO-LAND PROPORTIONALITY QUESTION

Assuming that the principle of the territorial integrity of existing states is to be abandoned and that such new state boundaries must be renegotiated, then the question arises whether territory should be parceled out according to population proportions. In Bosnia, the international community was outraged that the Serbs seized 70 percent of the territory when they constitute only 33 percent of the population. This land-to-people proportionality principle hardly made any more sense than allowing internal republics to secede with their prevailing boundaries. The more appropriate criteria for territorial renegotiation would be to examine the location, quality of land occupied or to be received by the various sides, and claims of historical residence, which may have been usurped by others in more recent times.

Land allotted at the time of secession must encompass as much of the population of the seceding ethnic group or, conversely, retain as much of the population of newly created ethnic groups that do not wish to be part of the new state. Territorial carve-ups must also ensure territorial contiguity for single-resident ethnic groups, something that the Vance-Owen Plan of 1993 failed to fulfill. Likewise, vast acres of agricultural or barren land cannot be equated with small territories of resource-rich or industrialized land. Sarajevo alone is worth much more than all of the 49 percent of the land allotted to the Serbs, which is mainly mountainous and lacks industries or power plants. According to Peter Brock, Serbs were wary of the Vance-Owen Plan because they would have received only $6.1 billion of the total $31.5 billion identified assets in Bosnia; none of the known deposits of bauxite, lead, zinc, salt, or iron; none of the ten hydroelectric power plants, which would all fall under Bosnian Croat jurisdiction; 160 of the 960 kilometers of railroad lines; and 200 kilometers of the improved roadways.[53] Finally, some attention must be paid to historical residential claims, although it may be difficult to reverse migrations and settlements once they have occurred. Besides, historical residential claims are also subject to considerable manipulation by all sides. Here, Serbs faced the loss of 24 percent of the land that they had held for generations.

One Serbian claim is that they constituted the overall pluralistic majority in Bosnia-Herzegovina before 1940, as demonstrated in the 1910 Austrian census. The 1910 Austrian census showed the following distribution:[54]

| *Religion* | *Population* | *% Population* | *% Servile Tenure* |
|---|---|---|---|
| Orthodox | 825,418 | 43.5 | 74.0 |
| Muslims | 612,137 | 32.4 | 4.6 |
| Catholics | 434,061 | 22.8 | 21.4 |
| Uniates | 8,136 | 0.4 | —— |
| Jews | 11,868 | 0.6 | —— |
| Protestants | 6,342 | 0.3 | —— |
| Total | 1,897,972 | 100.0 | 100.0 |

The percentage distribution of Serbs, Croats and Muslims had clearly undergone substantial transformation by the 1990s. Serbs are now 33 percent of the population, Muslims 45 percent, and Croats 20 percent. Serbs argue that this change was not due entirely to higher birthrates among Muslims, but because of the enormous loss of Serbian lives during World War I and II.

What is even more significant is that Serbs, as mainly farmers and peasants, owned or occupied 74 percent of the land in 1910. They claimed that, before the outbreak of hostilities in Bosnia in 1992, they owned or occupied 65 percent of the land, although this land had several pockets of more valuable industrialized cities where the Muslims were a majority. This distribution of poorer Serbs in the country and richer Muslims in the city caused the human explosion in Bosnia. Territorial demarcation according to ethnicity became impossible except through violent "ethnic cleansing." Carving out a Greater Serbia to encompass the Serbian diaspora of Bosnia and Croatia within the old Yugoslavia could have been done no other way except by "punching corridors" through Muslim majority areas and laying seige to Muslim majority cities.[55] At the heart of this tragedy was the U.S. decision to push for the recognition of an independent Bosnia against the wishes of the Bosnian Serbs. The United States failed to take into account historical grievances and the territorial distribution of Serbs, Muslims, and Croats in Bosnia in advocating recognition.

There have been similar situations in other parts of the world. The effort to create a territorially contiguous and viable Jewish majority state of Israel out of Palestine through war resulted in the flight of almost a million Palestinians. No formula of proportionality between population and land was applied in determining the distribution of land between the proposed states of Israel and Palestine in 1948. Likewise, the potential problem underlying Sikh demands in Indian Punjab for an independent Sikh state of Khalistan was that Sikhs are the overwhelming majority in the countryside while Hindus are the majority in nearly all the cities scattered throughout Indian Punjab. If Hindu Punjabis were to refuse to be part of a Sikh state, a Bosnia-like situation might have developed in an independent Khalistan.

The dilemma of territorial carve-ups when a state disintegrates also raises the question of resource and investment distribution in the newly forged states. Especially in centrally planned Communist and socialist states, the central government usually places industries and other economic projects to favor certain groups or regions as a reward for supporting the party and its policies, or places them based on the ethnicity or ethnic preference of the dictator. This may lead to uneven economic growth and prosperity in the various regions. In the case of Yugoslavia, the distribution of investments was uneven, with Slovenia and Croatia receiving greater and more technically sophisticated investments compared to Serbia, Montenegro, and Macedonia. In these circumstances, secessions without some form of economic redistribution or compensation would then appear to be grossly unfair. Underlying the South Slav conflict is an economic struggle between rich and poor: richer Croats and Bosnian Muslims against poorer Serbs, and richer Serbs against poorer Albanians in Kosovo.

Irrespective of whether internal boundaries are historical, there are precedents that, when a region or province inhabited by a particular "nation" secedes, boundaries may be renegotiated. As noted earlier, precedents were set when Northern Ireland was separated from Ireland when Ireland seceded in 1921 and when Punjab and Bengal were divided when Pakistan seceded from India in 1947. Indeed, if Yugoslavia's international boundaries could be taken apart through unilateral declarations of independence followed by immediate Western recognition, then why not also regions within the former internal boundaries of Yugoslavia which now constitute the international frontiers of new states? If the territorial integrity of states is no longer to be upheld, then all states must be subject to potential dismantling, both old and new, especially if ethnic groups are able to establish de facto states by whatever means. Republika Srpska and the Croatian Republic of Herzog-Bosna in Bosnia and the Serb Republic of Krajina in Croatia had all successfully broken free and declared their independence.

One of the basic Western inconsistencies on Yugoslavia was that the West, led by Germany and the United States, discarded the principles laid down in the 1975 Helsinki Agreement Final Act, which guaranteed the boundaries of the existing states of Europe. According to this agreement: "The participating states will respect the territorial integrity of each of the participating states. Accordingly, they will refrain from any action . . . against the territorial integrity, political independence, or the unity of any participating state."[56] The former Yugoslavia was party to this agreement, not the new states (which subsequently invoked the Helsinki territorial principles to preserve their boundaries) that were carved out from the old state.

## DEMOCRACY AND THE SELF-DETERMINATION PRINCIPLE

In dealing with the various conflicting demands and rights of self-determination and territorial integrity in the former Yugoslavia, the international community embarked on a confused and contradictory set of goals and policies. Hurst Hannum writes: "Perhaps no contemporary norm of international law has been so vigorously promoted or widely accepted as the right of all peoples to self-determination. Yet the meaning and content of that right remain as vague and imprecise as when they were enunciated by President Woodrow Wilson and others at Versailles."[57] Is there a universally accepted international norm that "nations" have the right to "secede" from an existing sovereign state under the principle of national self-determination? There is none.

Allen Buchanan warned against confusing democratic rights with secessionist rights based on the principle of self-determination.[58] He pointed out the need to view the two concepts and their objectives together to understand its distinctions and to avoid the likely adverse consequences of confusing the two concepts. While there is "widespread, unambivalent endorsement of the goal of democratization," there are serious doubts about destroying the state itself through secessions in advancing this goal of democratization. "There is good reason to be apprehensive. Attempts at secession, and the efforts of states to resist them, have frequently led to severe economic dislocations and massive violations of human rights. Ethnic minorities have won their independence only to subject their own minorities to the same persecutions they themselves formerly suffered."[59] Buchanan further points out the misleading parallels between democratization and secession. "Both democratization and secession, it may seem, are exercises of the right of self-determination. If democracy is popular sovereignty—participation in government by the people—then secession may be seen as the effort of various peoples to govern themselves, to be politically self-determining, in the most literal sense, by forming their own independent, fully sovereign states." Buchanan provides two reasons for rejecting self-determination and secession as an extension of democracy. First, secessionist struggles have generated massive human rights violations on all sides and economic destruction and deprivations. Second, "as Abraham Lincoln argued, secession can pose a lethal threat to democracy: If a discontented minority can exit the polity whenever it is outvoted by the majority on an issue it deems of great importance, then the majority does not rule. In addition, if secession is considered as a real option, then a minority group may use the threat of 'exit' as a form of 'voice' that serves as an effective veto on majority rule."[60]

It is at least debatable whether "nations" have the right to "secede" from a sovereign state under the principle of national self-determination. In the more liberal interpretation of freedom, subject ethnic groups within a state are considered to have the right to hold referendums to determine whether they wish to remain part of the state or secede from it. This right of national self-determination is, however, mentioned only obliquely and in passing reference in Article 1 (2) of the United Nations Charter, which reads: "To develop friendly relations among nations based on respect for the principle of equal rights and self-determination of peoples, and to take other appropriate measures to strengthen universal peace." Articles 73 to 91 essentially deal with "Non-Self-Governing Territories" and the "Trusteeship System" but have nothing to do with granting self-determination to peoples within existing sovereign independent states. The 1970 "Declaration on Friendly Relations" elaborated on the Charter and went beyond to declare that the principle did not only apply to colonial territories, but also to "all peoples," giving them "the right freely to determine without external interference, their political status."[61] The principle was emphasized in Article 1 of the "International Covenant on Civil and Political Rights" passed in 1976 and ratified by 113 by the end of 1991. However, the rights of minorities to self-determination, according to the Covenant, did not include the right to secede. It implied the right of peoples in all states "to free, fair and open participation in the democratic process of governance freely chosen by each state."[62] A 1990 meeting of the Conference on Security and Cooperation in Europe (CSCE) in Copenhagen went far in affirming democratic rights and human rights of peoples but did not go so far as to endorse the right to secede.

In his book *Secession*, Allen Buchanan provides various moral arguments for and against secession.[63] Secession may be morally justified: (a) to protect liberty; (b) to escape severe economic exploitation; (c) to preserve one's culture, which is in danger of being wiped out; (d) as an instrument of self-defense against state-organized violence against the ethnic group; (e) to rectify an unjustified or illegal past annexation; and (f) because there is inherent merit in the right of ethnic groups to exercise self-determination. Conversely, secession may be opposed on moral grounds: (a) to protect the legitimate expectations of the rest of the people, which may be jeopardized by the secession of one group; (b) in self-defense if secession makes the remnant state economically nonviable; (c) to protect the principle of majority rule, which may be jeopardized if those who do not agree are allowed to secede; (d) where there has been no serious political or civil violation of the minority group; (e) to prevent anarchy through the domino effect whereby the entire state may unravel; (f) to prevent the seceding territory wrongfully bolting with the heavy central government investments in the region; and (g) where the "Haves" simply wish to separate themselves from the "Have-Nots" for no other reason than because they are rich and the rest are poor.

Buchanan has made arguments for and against secession on all of the above criteria. However, even if the morality of such principles are self-evident in theory, application in particular cases can become extremely messy. Some of the criteria above may be applied with favorable and nonviolent outcomes in some regions but not in others, even if the grievances and moral arguments are the same. The problem in the case of the former Yugoslavia was that the moral justification for secession was questionable, even by the above criteria, compared to other parts of the world where secessions have been denied. Some logical explanation must be provided as to why the principle of the right to secede was applied selectively to Slovenia, Croatia, and Bosnia but not (for example) to Tibet, Kashmir, Chechnya, and Kurdistan. Ultimately, power and ability prevailed in the former Yugoslavia. States that have seceded successfully are those that (a) acquired the independent power to do so (Ireland); (b) were assisted by external powers to break free (Bangladesh, the Turkish Republic of Northern Cyprus, and East Timor); (c) were voluntarily allowed to go by the Union (Singapore and Slovakia); or (d) because the federal authorities became too weak to resist secession (the ex-Soviet republics and Eritrea). The initial support to the secessionists in Slovenia and Croatia by a German-led West, backed later by the U.S., made the difference in allowing these two Yugoslav republics to secede. Morality and justice were irrelevant in determining the outcome.

## LESSONS AND PROSPECTS

From the standpoint of equity and fairness, two related questions may be asked. If the principle of national self-determination with the meaning of "the right to secede from a state" could be granted to Slovenians, Croatians, Bosnian Muslims, and Macedonians, then why could not the same principle be granted to the Serbs of the newly recognized states of Croatia and Bosnia? And, if the Serbs demand this right, then why should not the Albanians of Kosovo demand the same right? If national self-determination extending to the right to secede is the new overriding norm of world politics today, then it must be granted also to new minorities created by state secessions. Or, some logical explanation must be provided as to why the principle of the right to secede was applied selectively to Slovenia, Croatia, and Bosnia but not to other ethnic groups demanding secession elsewhere in the world. Domestic political disputes, minority ethnic grievances, and armed secessionist struggles have been far more intense and prolonged elsewhere than in the former Yugoslavia.

From a global-comparative perspective, it is difficult to justify Slovenia and Croatia being allowed to "jump the queue" ahead of other self-proclaimed nations demanding the right to secession and international recognition. As regards the claim of Serbian domination, it is not unusual for dominant ethnic groups to insist on more centralized political arrangements that they control. Such complaints have been made in the past against the English in Britain by the Irish, Scots, and Welsh; against the English-speaking settlers in Canada by the French-speaking settlers in Quebec province; against the WASPs (White Anglo-Saxon Protestants) in the United States by African Americans and Hispanics; against the Punjabis in Pakistan by Bengalis, Sindhis, and Baluchis; against the Hindi-speaking Hindus of India by other linguistic and religious minorities; and against the Russians in the former Soviet Union and the new Russia by other linguistic and religious minorities. Majority versus minority nationalist politics have taken place in all of these countries.

The former Yugoslavia was treated differently from the standard practice and experience. First, Germany, Austria, and the Vatican pushed the European Union to recognize the independence of Slovenia and Croatia, their favored Catholic regions of Yugoslavia. Next, the United States pushed the rest of the world to recognize the independence of Bosnia-Herzegovina before it became a functioning state with a government in control. The criteria of recognition here was selective and arbitrary. And finally, all the internal "republics" of the former Yugoslavia were then granted the right to secede, which led to the recognition of the remaining province, Macedonia. Other would-be independent secessionist nations elsewhere in the world did not receive such powerful and influential patronage.

Consider the following inconsistency: The rationale for taking Yugoslavia apart in 1991 and 1992 was that Serbs, Croats, and Muslims, and Serbs and Albanians, could not live together. Having declared this, the West now expects the same ethnic groups to live together in Bosnia and Kosovo, whether they like it or not. Writing in March 2001, Wolfgang Petritsch argued that perpetuating a multiethnic Bosnia consisting of Serbs, Croats, and Muslims was the right policy because monoethnic states do not exist anywhere in Europe except perhaps Iceland.[64] Germany, Austria, and the Vatican should have thought of this during the period 1990 to 1991 when they pushed for the secession and then rushed to recognize

Slovenia and Croatia out of Yugoslavia because these were Catholic and more prosperous provinces. And the United States should have recognized that Croatians joined Muslims in a February 1992 referendum on secession, only for the purpose of joining up with a monoethnic Croatia in a Greater Croatia. If these governments felt that Serbs, Croats, and Muslims—all of the same race and speaking the same language—could not continue to live together in the former Yugoslavia when there was no violence among them (until they were given hopes of secession and recognition), then why do they now insist that the same ethnic groups live together in Bosnia after years of violence and bloodshed?

The fundamental problem was not what the Serbs did but what the Western powers did: namely, the violation of Yugoslavia's territorial sovereignty, the rush to advance the principle of self-determination, and the reckless use of massive force in violation of the UN Charter on humanitarian grounds. Recognition, or the promise of recognition, led to the unraveling of Yugoslavia and to widespread bloodshed and ethnic cleansing. There was no violence before the declarations of independence by Slovenia, Croatia, and Bosnia in defiance of the Serbs and Serbian-dominated federal authorities in Belgrade. The promise of external support for independence encouraged the Albanians of Kosovo to provoke the Serbian security forces into committing human rights violations in order to invite NATO military intervention.

The Yugoslav crisis reflects one of the growing problems of the post–Cold War era. Various ethnic groups who see themselves as a nation seek statehood for a variety of reasons that range from: (a) a sense of exploitation in the larger multiethnic state; (b) the belief that greater prosperity may be obtained by breaking away from the existing state; (c) the belief that national aspirations cannot be fulfilled without statehood; and (d) the need to follow other ethnic secessions in a disintegrating state. However, the application of the self-determination principle has been highly selective. Slovenes, Croats, Muslims, and Albanians have all been conceded the right of self-determination, but the Serbs of Croatia, Bosnia, and Kosovo have been denied this right.

In choosing between the principle of the right of self-determination and the principle of the territorial integrity of sovereign states, the "international community" has now established the following self-contradicting and dangerous precedent and principles in the Yugoslav case: (1) The internal boundaries of a sovereign state will automatically become international frontiers without change if that sovereign state is taken apart through new state recognition policy; and (2) These newly recognized international frontiers of the newly created sovereign states that have been recognized will be preserved and enforced at any price, thus contradicting the earlier decision to take the international frontiers of the preexisting sovereign state apart based on the right of self-determination and secession.

## NOTES

1. This part has been adapted from the first sections of my article "Self-Determination and International Recognition Policy: An Alternative Interpretation of Why Yugoslavia Disintegrated," *World Affairs*, vol. 160, no.1, June 22, 1997, 17–33.

2. Donald L. Horowitz, "Self-Determination: Politics, Philosophy and Law." MacArthur Foundation Program in Transnational Security, Working Paper Series, 1995, p. 11. Center for International Studies, Massachusetts Institute of Technology, and the Center for International Affairs, Harvard University. Italics mine.

3. For a rather strong indictment of German and American responsibility for the Yugoslav mess, see T. W. Bill Carr, "German and US Involvement in the Balkans: A Careful Coincidence of National Policies?" Monograph issued by *Defense and Foreign Affairs*, London, 1994.

4. The implication of this statement was that if India was small, Khalistan, Kashmir, Assam, Nagaland, and other Indian "states" would have all been recognized as independent. This official made the comment off the record and does not wish to be identified.

5. Wolfgang F. Schloer, "Germany and the Breakup of Yugoslavia," in Raju G. C. Thomas and H. Richard Friman, eds. *The South Slav Conflict*, New York: Garland Publishing, 1996, p. 315. T. W. Bill Carr, the Associate Publisher of *Defense and Foreign Affairs* (London), claims that Franjo Tudjman visited in Germany in 1988 where he met Chancelor Helmut Kohl and other senior government officers. Here the first seeds of Slovenian and Croatian secessions were laid. See T. W. Bill Carr, "German and U.S. Involvement in the Balkans: A Careful of Coincidence of National Policies?" Paper presented at the Yugoslavia Past and Present symposium, Chicago, August 31–September 1, 1995.

6. Beverly Crawford, "Explaining Defection From International Cooperation: Germany's Unilateral Recognition of Croatia," *World Politics*, vol. 48, no. 4, July 1996, pp. 484–485.

7. See Walter R. Roberts, "The Tragedy in Yugoslavia Could Have Been Averted," in Thomas and Friman, *The South Slav Conflict*, p. 370.

8. Hearing of the House International Relations Committee chaired by Representative Benjamin A. Gilman, Thursday, January 12, 1995. Cited in footnote by Rodoljub Etinski, "Has the SFR Yugoslavia Ceased to Exist as a Subject of Inernational Law?" in *International Law and the Changed Yugoslavia*, Institute of International Politics and Economics, Belgrade, 1995.

9. Letters to the Editor, *The Economist*, December 9, 1995. See also David Owen, *Balkan Odyssey*, Orlando, FL: Harcourt Brace, 1995, p. 62.

10. See Laura Silber and Allan Little, *Yugoslavia: Death of a Nation*, New York: TV Books, 1996, pp. 219–220.

11. John J. Mearsheimer and Stephen Van Evera, "When Peace Means War," *The New Republic*, December 18, 1995, p. 16.

12. David Binder, "U.S. Policymakers on Bosnia Admit Errors in Opposing Partition in 1992," *New York Times*, August 29, 1993.

13. See Warren Zimmermann, *Origins of a Catastrophe: Yugoslavia and Its Destroyers*, New York: Times Books, 1996, pp. Viii–ix.

14. See Raju G. C. Thomas, "Competing Nationalisms: Secessionist Movements and the State," *Harvard International Review*, vol. 18, no. 3, Summer 1996, pp. 12–17.

15. Walter R. Roberts, "The Tragedy in Yugoslavia Could Have Been Averted," in Thomas and Friman, *South Slav Conflict*, p. 364.

16. See David Rieff, "In Bosnia, A Prelude to Partition," *New York Times*, August 14, 1996.

17. John Mearsheimer and Stephen Van Evera, "When Peace Means War," *The New Republic*, December 18, 1995, p. 17.

18. Peter Reid, "World Must Be Wary of Fascist Croat Forces," May 23, 1993. See also Kenneth Roberts, "Unreconstructed Nazism on Display," *The Spectator* (London), March 19, 1994.

19. Silber and Little, *Yugoslavia*, pp. 31–32.

20. Vesna Pesic, *Serbian Nationalism and the Origins of the Yugoslav Crisis*, Washington, DC: United States Institute of Peace Monograph, 1996, p. 18.

21. Silber and Little, *Yugoslavia*, p. 32.

22. See Leonard J. Cohen, *Broken Bonds: Yugoslavia's Disintegration and Balkan Politics in General*, Boulder, CO: Westview Press, 1995, 1–44.

23. See Barbara Jelavich, *History of the Balkans: Twentieth Century*, Cambridge: Cambridge University Press, 1983, pp. 396–397.

24. For a short discussion of this period, see Fred Singleton, *A Short History of the Yugoslav Peoples*, Cambridge: Cambridge University Press, 1985, pp. 255–270.

25. See John Zamatica, *The Yugoslav Conflict*, Adelphi Paper, no. 242, London: International Institute for Strategic Studies, 1992.

26. In a letter to an American newspaper, the Croatian ambassador in Washington, Miomir Zuzul, declared: "When this region [Krajina] was liberated, many Serb residents chose to follow the remnants of the Serb nationalist forces to Serbia and Bosnia and Herzegovina." The ambassador stated that this was not ethnic cleansing, an interpretation endorsed by the OSCE. *New York Times*, July 27, 1996.

27. Cedric Thornberry, "Saving the War Crimes Tribunal," *Foreign Policy*, no. 104, fall 1996, p. 79.

28. Andre Liebich, "Getting Better, Getting Worse: Minorities in East Central Europe," *Diessent*, Summer 1996, p. 88.

29. These approximate figures are from my many readings.

30. I obtained this information from some Serbs living in Zagreb who did not wish to reveal their identities.

31. A Russian Orthodox priest and professor of theology narrated this story to me of the experience of a delegation from the World Council of Churches to Yugoslavia in the late 1980s. After spending some time in Belgrade, they flew to Zagreb and were greeted with the words: "Welcome to Europe from Asia." I have heard from Croatians that "Europe begins at the Drina River," indicating again that Serbs are lesser Asiatics. Peter Reid, a Boston columnist, noted after a visit to Croatia in 1993: "Croats see themselves as protectors of the European frontier, and they see Serbs as inferior Asiatics to be pushed out or pushed down." Peter Reid, "World Must be Wary of Fascist Forces," *Times Union* (Albany, New York), May 23, 1993. Article first published in the *Miami Herald.*

32. Michael Libal, "The Balkan Dilemma: An Interpretation of the Crisis," *Harvard International Review*, vol. 18, no. 2, Spring 1996, p. 67.

33. The UN summit and the comments of leaders were reported widely in the press at this time.

34. Kelly Greenhill's chapter in this book is a revised version of her paper "People Pressure: The Coercive Use of Refugees in the Kosovo Conflict," presented at the American Political Science Association Convention, Thursday, September 1, 2000 Marriot Wardman Park Hotel, Washington, DC.

35. See Donald L. Horowitz, "Self-Determination: Politics, Philosophy and Law." MacArthur Foundation Program in Transnational Security, Working Paper Series, 1995, p. 11. Center for International Studies, Massachusetts Institute of Technology, and the Center for International Affairs, Harvard University.

36. See Hurst Hannum, *Autonomy, Sovereignty and Self-Determination: The Accommodation of Conflicting Rights*, Philadelphia: University of Pennsylvania Press, 1990, p. 16.

37. Hannum, *Autonomy,* p. 16.

38. See William E. Ratliff, "Madeleine's War and the Costs of Intervention: The Kosovo Precedent," *Harvard International Review*, (Special issue on Sovereignty), vol. 22, no. 4, Winter 2001, pp. 70–76.

39. See Anthony DePalma, "Canadian Court Rules Quebec Cannot Secede on Its Own," *New York Times*, August 21, 1998.

40. See Yehuda Z. Blum, "UN Membership of the 'New' Yugoslavia: Continuity or Break?" Belgrade: Institute of International Politics and Economics, 1995, pp. 11–18.

41. Blum, "UN Membership," p. 11. Italics mine.

42. Blum, "UN Membership," p. 13.

43. Blum, "UN Membership," p. 17.

44. Blum, "UN Membership," p. 17.

45. For a study on this issue, see Frederick Barth, ed., *Ethnic Groups and Boundaries*, Boston: Little Brown, 1976.

46. Paul Goble, "Russian Break-Up," *NEFTE Compass*, vol. 2, no. 2, January 15, 1993, p. 11. Cited in Jessica Eve Stern, "Moscow Meltdown: Can Russia Survive?" *International Security*, vol. 18, no. 4, Spring 1994, p. 42.

47. Stern, "Moscow Meltdown," p. 42. See also Jack Snyder, "Nationalism and the Crisis of the Post-Soviet State," *Survival: The IISS Quarterly*, vol. 35, no. 1, Spring 1993, pp. 5–26. For a study of the South Asian case involving similar issues, see Raju G. C. Thomas, "Secessionist Movements in South Asia," *Survival: The IISS Quarterly*, Summer 1994, vol. 36, no. 2, pp. 92–114, and my "Competing Nationalisms: Secessionist Movements and the State," *Harvard International Review*, vol. 38, no. 3, Summer 1996, pp. 12–15, 76.

48. For a discussion of Crimean and Nagorno-Karabakh issues, see articles by Roman Popadiuk, "Crimea and Ukraine's Future," and Stephen H. Astourian, "The Nagorno-Karabakh Conflict: Dimensions, Lessons and Prospects," *Mediterranean Quarterly*, vol. 5, no. 4, Fall 1994, pp. 30–39, and pp. 85–109.

49. Susan Woodward, *Balkan Tragedy: Chaos and Dissolution After the Cold War*, Washington, DC: Brookings Institution, 1995, p. 212.

50. Michael Libal, "The Balkan Dilemma," *Harvard International Review*, vol. 18, no. 2, Spring 1996, p. 87. See my article in the following issue where I proposed in the case of South Asia that, while the states in this region may seek to move toward confederal arrangements, they should recognize for the sake of avoiding tragedy that "the existing international borders, whether good or bad, legal or illegal, are inviolable; and that none of the states in the region will aid and abet each other's separatist movements." Raju G. C. Thomas, "Competing Nationalisms: Secessionist Movements and the State," *Harvard International Review*, vol. 18, no. 3, Summer 1996, p. 76.

51. See David Martin, "Croatia's Borders: Over the Edge," *New York Times*, November 22, 1991.

52. Nora Beloff, "Hope and History in Yugoslavia," *The Overseas Guardian Weekly*, December 1, 1991.

53. Peter Brock, "Dateline Yugoslavia: The Partisan Press," *Foreign Policy*, Winter 1993/1994, pp. 168–169.

54. From Stephen Cissold, H. C. Darby, R. W. Seton-Watson, Phyllis Auty, and R. G. D. Laffan, *A Short History of Yugoslavia: From Early Times to 1966*, Cambridge: Cambridge University Press, 1966, p. 71. These figures in the book were obtained from L.von Sudland, *Die Jugoslaviche Frage*, Vienna, 1918, p. 211.

55. See Stephen Van Evera, "Hypothesis on Nationalism," *International Security*, vol. 18, no. 4, Summer 1994, p. 20.

56. Clause IV of the Declaration of Principles Guiding Relations Between Participating States.

57. Hannum, *Autonomy*, p. 27.

58. For a detailed study of the moral arguments for and against secession, see Allen Buchanan, *Secession: The Morality of Political Divorce from Fort Sumter to Lithuania and Quebec*, Boulder, CO: Westview Press, 1991, pp. 27–125.

59. Allen Buchanan, "Democratization, Seccession and the Rule of International Law." MacArthur Foundation Program in Transnational Security, Working Paper Series, 1995, pp. 2–3. Center for International Studies, Massachusetts Institute of Technology, and the Center for International Affairs, Harvard University.

60. Buchanan, "Democratization," p. 4.

61. Cited in Thomas M. Franck, "The Emerging Right to Democratic Governance," *American Journal of International Law*, vol. 86, no. 4, 1992, p. 58.

62. Thomas Franck, "Emerging Right," p. 59.

63. The moral arguments for and against secession are taken from Buchanan, *Secession,* pp. 27–125.

64. Wolfgang Petritsch, "Don't Abandon the Balkans," *New York Times*, Op-Ed, March 25, 2001.

# 2

## The Future of Nationalism

*Michael Mandelbaum*

The great question at the heart of nineteenth-century European politics was who should govern—the princes or the people? The question was settled by World War I, which swept away the Continent's dynastic monarchs and their empires, only to give rise to another: just how are the people to govern—through elected representatives whose powers are limited, or through self-appointed political elites exercising total control over those they rule? In the wake of World War II and the Cold War, totalitarianism in Europe has been vanquished, leaving, however, yet a third question, one that underlies the large-scale violence that has followed the collapse of communism and the end of the East-West rivalry on the Continent: Who, for the purposes of self-government, *are* the people?

This is a matter of maps. Government requires a state. A state must have borders. A method for determining them is therefore needed.

The issue is not a new one. The nineteenth century knew it as the national question. It stemmed, then as now, from the quest of self-identified nations for their own states. To the question "who are the people?" the answer then seemed obvious: a few great nations—the German, the Italian, the Hungarian, and the Polish—imprisoned in autocratic multinational empires. Once the empires were destroyed, they would take their places in the company of the British, the French, and the Russians as the peoples entitled to govern themselves in sovereign states. In the twentieth century, however, Europe discovered that the matter was not so simple. The empires were indeed destroyed, but in their wake came not few but many claims to sovereignty, claims that were both overlapping and conflicting. How were they to be adjudicated?

First Europe and then the world embraced two rules for deciding the location of borders. One is the principle of national self-determination, the rule that every self-identified nation should have its own sovereign state. The other is the principle that existing sovereign borders are sacrosanct and should not be altered. The two are not always compatible. Often they are in conflict. The conflict between them was submerged during the Cold War but has resurfaced in its wake. That conflict lay at the heart of the wars in the former Yugoslav republics of Croatia, Bosnia, and Kosovo and the fighting between Armenians and Azeris, Georgians and Abkhaz, and Russians and Chechens on the territory of the former Soviet Union. In each case, one side went to war to change borders in order to make them conform more closely to the principle of national self-determination, while the other fought to retain existing borders.

The twentieth-century history of the conflict between the two principles for determining borders is one of alternation and compromise, accompanied by surprisingly little debate about their respective merits. The lesson of that history for the twenty-first century is that, although Europe—and the world—would be better able to manage and prevent conflict if one or the other principle were firmly established as the unchallenged international norm, this is not possible. Both are rooted in history and logic; neither can be entirely eliminated. The prospects for resolving twenty-first century national conflicts—both in Europe and the rest of the world—depend on finding compromises between the two. The late twentieth-century history of the national question, including the war in Kosovo, shows how difficult this is.

## CHANGING NORMS

The twentieth century saw three great bursts of state creation, occasioned by the demise of three sets of empires: the dynastic ones of Central and Eastern Europe after World War I, the overseas empires of Western Europe after World War II, and the communist empires in Europe after the Cold War. In the wake of each upheaval there was a change in the international norm governing the determination of borders.

Until the twentieth century, borders were set by Europe's dynastic rulers on the basis of military might. Blood and iron determined where one ruler's domain ended and another's began. The empires governed by the Habsburgs, the Hohenzollerns, the Romanovs, and the Ottoman Turks were as large as their rulers' power could make them. When they fought each other, the winners gained territory at the expense of the losers. Indeed, the quest for expanded territory was an important reason for going to war in the first place.

This norm changed at the end of World War I, in the first of the major twentieth-century shifts. The Paris Peace Conference that convened in 1919 proclaimed that the allocation of sovereignty would be based on justice, defined as the fulfillment of national aspirations. Borders were to be drawn so as to put people of the same nationality in a single sovereign political unit. But this requirement was not entirely fulfilled, nor could it have been. In some areas national populations—Hungarians and Romanians, for example, in what had been Hungary and would become Romania—were intermingled.

The post–World War I settlement had important elements of continuity with the imperial past. The Great Powers retained the prerogative of deciding where borders were to be drawn, and they ignored the precept of national self-determination when this suited their purposes. The Bolsheviks were able to incorporate many different national groups into their new Soviet state because they had won the power to do so on the battlefield. The Germans were scattered among several different states because defeat had deprived them of the power to prevent it. The Great Power prerogative was still in force after World War II, although the changes of boundaries were more modest. Stalin moved the borders of the Soviet Union westward, into what had been Poland, and simultaneously moved the Polish border westward as well, placing lands that had been ethnically German for centuries within the Polish state.

So it was not World War II but rather the second period of twentieth-century state creation—the one triggered by the end of the West European empires in Asia, Africa, and the Caribbean in the three decades after World War II—that raised the concept of the inviolability of existing borders to an international norm. This second stage of imperial dissolution multiplied the number of sovereign states. When the United Nations was founded in *1945*, it had *50* members. By 1999 its membership had grown to over *190*.

The European-imposed borders in Asia and Africa were deemed immutable precisely *because* there were so many of them that were so arbitrarily drawn. They included so many different groups that had not previously been part of the same political unit (and also divided several that had) that, without the norm of inviolability, all would have been subjected to challenge; and once challenged, there would have been no widely shared concept, no legitimate principal, no viable formula on the basis of which they could be redrawn peacefully. The alternative to the preservation of all existing borders, no matter how capriciously or even mischievously established, seems to be widespread chaos, violence, and bloodshed. There was also another motive. What is called the international community is, among other things, a trade association of governments. Each has an interest in preserving its own prerogatives and so is disposed to protect the prerogatives of the others. To put it differently, the international community may be seen as a cartel, the members of which seek to ration, so as to preserve the value of, their common product: sovereignty.

This norm of inviolability was bolstered by the Cold War. The United States and the Soviet Union worried that trying to change existing borders had the potential for creating conflicts into which they could be drawn, with conceivably disastrous consequences. For that reason, and because they competed for the allegiance of third countries around the world, both Washington and Moscow supplied arms and money that weak Third World governments of dubious legitimacy used to retain power over their recognized territories.

The rule of inviolability was on vivid display in West Africa at the outset of the 1970s. The Ibos of eastern Nigeria, resentful of the domination of the country by the Muslim Hausas of the north and the Yoruba of the west, tried to secede. The federal government of Nigeria crushed the secession in a bloody civil war. Only a few countries, and none outside Africa, supported the Ibo cause.

Just as the national principle of the post–World War I period was not faithfully applied in the postcolonial era, the postcolonial commitment to the inviolability of borders was not sustained when communist rule in Europe collapsed. When that happened, the inviolability norm gave way to a third precept for allocating sovereignty and defining borders, a rule that might be called "orderly promotion." For the communist multinational states, the Soviet Union and Yugoslavia collapsed, in part, because, unlike the multinational states of the Third World during the Cold War, the West would not, and the East could not, support them. Upon their collapse, the world recognized as sovereign the next-largest subordinate administrative units of both countries: the six constituent republics of the former Yugoslavia and the fifteen constituent republics of the former Soviet Union.

This new method of creating sovereign states was neither formally proclaimed nor systematically debated. It was a compromise between the difficulty, and, from many points of view, the undesirability, of keeping communist multinational states intact, on the one hand, and, on the other, the need for as consistent a principal of sovereignty as possible so as to minimize the disruption and violence that a revision of borders would surely provoke.

This kept the maps of post-communist Europe relatively orderly. The thick black lines marking off the Soviet Union and Yugoslavia disappeared; the dotted lines that had denoted their constituent republics were thickened in recognition of their newly bestowed sovereignty. But if the maps were preserved, the politics were transformed. Peoples who had been part of political majorities became minorities and vice versa, leading, in some places, to violence on a large scale. Thus, neither national self-determination nor the sanctity of existing sovereign borders had been fully embraced or definitively dismissed. Nor was it feasible for either principle entirely to displace the other.

## THE IMPOSSIBILITY OF CONSISTENCY

In the twentieth century, nationalism as a principle for allocating sovereignty has received unfavorable reviews from both scholars and diplomats—and for good reason. It is, in the first place, impossible to apply consistently because it is impossible to define clearly. There is no single definition of a nation that can serve as the basis for determining where state borders should be drawn. Language is a rough, but not a foolproof, standard. Serbs and Croats can conduct disputes with each other from their separate states using the same language; united India, by contrast, contains seventeen different major languages. Religion is often, but not always, germane. Protestants and Catholics are both loyal Germans; but a common Islamic faith did not keep Bengalis from seceding from Pakistan.

The most nearly viable definition of a nation turns out to be a tautology: nations are groups that believe they are nations and mobilize themselves to secure their own state. But even that definition can give an erroneous impression of how some contemporary states have become sovereign, especially in the post-communist period. The successor states of the Soviet Union in Central Asia, for example, were not created by national movements that wrested power from the Soviet authorities. There was no Uzbek or Kyrgyz national movement, or even much nationalist sentiment worthy of the name, in either place. When the Soviet Union collapsed, the two were, for a variety of reasons, union republics and so had sovereignty thrust upon them by the principle of orderly promotion.

Even if it were coherent, national self-determination would still, its critics have said, be objectionable in principle, because it stresses a set of similarities within groups as the basis for political organization. It thus automatically places equal, and perverse, emphasis on what divides these groups from others. Nationalism is at once narrow, exclusive, and potentially chauvinistic.

And even if it were not incoherent in theory and objectionable in principle, national self-determination would be—indeed has proved to be—unmanageable in practice. Lines of political division that are acceptable to all cannot be drawn on the basis of this principle. During the Paris Peace Conference, Woodrow Wilson's secretary of state, Robert Lansing, wrote of self-determination in his diary: "The phrase is loaded with dynamite. It will raise hopes, which can never be realized. It will, I fear, cost thousands of lives."[1] So it has. For while it is impossible to draw borders so that every state contains the members of one and only one nation, the principle does permit any self-described nation to claim the right to its own sovereign state.

The boundaries of state and nation can be made to conform by changing not the borders but rather the people living within them. Group identities can be, and have been, altered. Assimilation is a common feature of social life, but it is not a universal one and not one to which all-national minorities are attracted. On the contrary, some such minorities—the Hungarians in Romanian Transylvania are one example—actively seek to retain the identities they and their forebears have borne, the languages they have spoken and the homes they have inhabited for centuries.

Alternatively, people can and do move. More or less voluntary—or at least not murderously coerced—migrations have often followed the shift of borders, the creation of new states, and the political division of previously united nations. After World War I, Germans moved to Germany from territories that had long been German but that the postwar settlement had made part of Poland. Similarly, Hungarians left what became diaspora communities for the new, shrunken Hungarian nation-state. In the post-Soviet period, Russian nationals have left Central Asia for Russia. But the twentieth century has also seen all too many instances of forced population transfer, a process that lately has come to be known, courtesy of the horrors of the former Yugoslavia, as "ethnic cleansing." The international community may not always be able to prevent this practice, but it can hardly accept it as a legitimate tool of statecraft.

Yet self-determination cannot be discarded. National self-consciousness is a powerful fact of contemporary international life. The cement of national solidarity may, as scholars argue, be composed of dubious materials—myths about the past, illusions concerning the future, resentments in the present—but it is no less powerful for that. And national homogeneity has its uses.

A vivid illustration of its potentially soothing effect is to be found in Poland, the largest country in Central Europe. Poland's population is among the most uniform in all of Europe, with virtually all citizens speaking the same language and professing the same faith. National, ethnic, and religious conflict is almost entirely absent, in contrast to the Polish experience in the interwar period when one out of every three people living in the country was not a Polish-speaking, Catholic, ethnic Pole.

The method by which Poland became homogeneous—the Nazi murder of its Jews and the eviction of its Germans—can scarcely be commended, and the correlation between national homogeneity and political stability may be spurious. But even if it is not desirable, the principle of national self-determination is unavoidable. As the basis for apportioning sovereignty, it is firmly embedded in international theory and practice. As such, it is self-reinforcing. Every group with a claim to being a nation now believes that that claim brings with it the right to a state. Like the Microsoft operating system for personal computers, once nationalism was established as the world standard, every group seeking the benefits of statehood acquired an interest in professing allegiance to and conformity with it.

Because national self-determination is so well established, it is not possible to enshrine the inviolability of borders as the unchallenged international norm for assigning statehood. A determined national group dissatisfied with the borders within which it lives will press to change them, sometimes resorting to violence on a large scale. This, after all, was the basis for the war in Kosovo in which NATO intervened in March 1999. Such a group will claim that the borders to which it objects are arbitrary and unfair, and such claims almost always contain at least a measure of truth. This is the case even with the borders set by the post–Cold War attempt at a compromise between national self-determination and the inviolability of existing borders—sovereignty was simply conferred on the next-largest unit of the collapsed communist multinational states of Yugoslavia and the Soviet Union.

That attempt turned out to be historically perverse. It meant that everything Lenin, Stalin, and Tito did was discredited and discarded *except* the borders they enforced, which were deemed sacrosanct. It meant that Russian-speaking communities in Ukraine and Kazakhstan, although previously part of a Russian-dominated state and although contiguous to post-Soviet Russia, could not choose to belong to it. It meant that Bosnia had to be a sovereign state within its Yugoslav borders, despite the fact that the majority of the people living within those borders were violently opposed to this, while Kosovo could *not* be sovereign, despite the fact that the vast majority of its inhabitants desired independence and were increasingly willing to fight for it.

Still, while it cannot always be implemented, neither can the commitment to maintaining existing borders be wholly abandoned in favor of the promise of a sovereign state for every nation. For there are simply too many potential nations. By one estimate, in 1995 there were 184 independent countries, 600 living language groups, and 5,000 distinct ethnic groups.[2] While efforts to enforce the principle of inviolability have led to turbulence and bloodshed, abandoning that principle altogether would likely produce at least as much turbulence, and perhaps more.

The conflicts between dynastic and popular rule, and between democratic and totalitarian governance, were each settled decisively in favor of one of the two competing principles. The conflict between the twentieth century's two principles for allocating sovereignty—national self-determination and the inviolability of existing borders—will not be. Neither principle can entirely supplant the other; both will persist into the twenty-first century. Thus, many sovereign states will contain more than one nation, and in some of these states, one or more of the nations they contain will be dissatisfied with the way its borders are drawn.

The uneasy coexistence of different nations, or ethnic or tribal groups, within a single state is also a feature of political life outside Europe, even where what is in dispute is not the location of borders but rather the question of which group will control the state: in Rwanda and the Congo in Africa, for example, and in Afghanistan and Iraq in West Asia.

If, in the twentieth century, international tranquility depended on peaceful coexistence between and among sovereign states, the governments of which rested on different principles of legitimacy, it would require peaceful coexistence among nations *within* the same state that embrace different principles for determining sovereignty. In some places—Bosnia and Kosovo, for example—this may not be possible. Over the long term, separation—a division rather than a sharing of sovereignty—may be necessary. But elsewhere, the practical problem that the twenty-first century version of the national question raises is how to make this coexistence more peaceful than it has been in the twentieth.

## CONSOCIATIONAL DEMOCRACIES

A leading candidate for easing conflicts of all kinds is economic growth. Prosperity is widely regarded as a powerful, all-purpose solvent of every political stain and blight, a miracle drug for social and economic ills. It certainly has some healing properties. Prosperous countries are, all other things being equal, more harmonious than those that are poverty-stricken. When the economic climate turns harsh, minorities, whether or not they have actually contributed to the economic distress, become targets of anger, discrimination, and persecution on the part of the majority, something that ethnic Chinese learned when the Asian fiscal crisis struck Indonesia in 1997 and 1998, and that Jews in Europe have had painful, indeed tragic, occasion to know for centuries. From the standpoint of communal harmony, economic activity is beneficial in and of itself because it requires, and therefore fosters, cooperation, including cooperation across national and ethnic divisions.

But while prosperity may erode those divisions, it cannot eradicate the grievances, not all of them economic in character, that cause conflict where different nations inhabit the same state. Moreover, economic growth cannot be produced on demand.

In the post–Cold War period, the political equivalent of prosperity is democracy: something universally desirable if not quite universally desired, a source of all blessings, a necessary part of the public agenda of virtually every sovereign state, new or old. The attitudes and institutions necessary for managing the conflicts within sovereign states are common in the public life of Western democracies but almost nowhere else: tolerance, wide opportunities for effective political participation, and social space for the expression of cultural differences. But Western democracies are *liberal* democracies, which combine the rule of the majority with constitutional and cultural protections for minorities. Liberal or constitutional democracy is a system both for determining how governments are chosen and for limiting what they can and cannot do with the power vested in them. The first feature empowers the majority; the second protects minorities.

It is perfectly possible to have the first without the second, and democracies that are illiberal can aggravate rather than reduce national tensions when they lack well-established political institutions and practices. In such states, political competition is intense, and nationalism becomes the most promising material out of which to fashion a political appeal. Contenders for power find it advantageous to evoke—or provoke—fears among the majority that their patrimony is being diminished or subverted or is otherwise at risk from the minority.[3]

Even the successful establishment of liberal, constitutional democracy may not ensure harmony where nations coexist within a single state. The constitutions of the major Western democracies protect the political rights of individuals. What national minorities demand, however, is constitutional protection for groups. In lieu of the partition of territory, they seek the partition of sovereignty. Here the appropriate models are the smaller states of Western Europe—Belgium, the Netherlands, and Austria—whose constitutional arrangements aim at just such an outcome.

The elaborate form of power sharing that is practiced in each country has several defining features: close collaboration among the elites of the different groups, often in a single governing "grand coalition" in the national parliament; veto power for each group in areas of importance to it; proportional representation in the parliament and in government employment; and a high degree of autonomy for each group in its own internal affairs.

Such institutions and practices have taken root in a particular kind of political soil, which is not, alas, widely distributed. The "consociational democracies" are small and wealthy.[4] Within their borders, values such as tolerance, compromise, and nonviolence are well established. They are situated in the sunny liberal uplands of the international system. Outside Western Europe, this approach to sovereignty has a poor track record: it collapsed after a period of success in Lebanon and was rejected when proposed in Cyprus. The Yugoslavia that failed to survive the Cold War had several of the relevant features. The establishment of consociational democracy is like an organ transplant: a delicate, difficult operation that is likely to succeed only when the recipient is, in other ways, in robust health.

Nor is the record of success appreciably better when outside powers are charged with protecting the political prerogatives and cultural preferences of national minorities. At the Paris Peace Conference after World War I, minority treaties were drawn up and applied to the new states of Eastern Europe that harbored substantial national minorities. These obliged the signatory governments to accord the minorities the right of collective organization and to respect their distinctive religions and cultures. Violations of the treaties could be appealed to the League of Nations, which, in theory, was the agent of enforcement. But the League did not enforce the treaties. Britain and France would have had to take responsibility for enforcement, but neither was willing to do so.

The more recent constitution for Bosnia mandated by the Dayton Conference of 1995 resembles consociational arrangements. It provides for a very weak central Bosnian government and reserves major powers to two designated constituent units—the Serb republic and the Muslim-Croat grouping. While NATO troops have been deployed to Bosnia, they have policed a cease-fire rather than enforced the controversial provisions of Dayton, such as apprehending suspected war criminals and ensuring the safe return of refugees to their original homes; nor has NATO enforced the prerogatives, such as they are, of the central Bosnian government.

Governments such as those of Britain and France in the interwar period and of the members of NATO after the Cold War were and are generally unprepared either to spend political capital or to suffer casualties on behalf of the accords to which they are party. There is, to be sure, a major difference between the two historical periods: in the first, enforcement was avoided because it was too dangerous. Fearing German revanchism, the West European powers were more interested in maintaining solidarity with the Central European governments against Germany than in protecting national minorities against the depredations of these same governments. In the second, the Western powers have balked at enforcing Dayton's provisions because they face no danger in southeastern Europe and so cannot justify to their publics paying any serious price to police the region.

NATO's 1999 war in Yugoslavia might seem to be an exception, but it is an exception that proves the rule. Outside powers did intervene in the war between the government in Belgrade and the ethnic Albanian Kosovo Liberation Army. But the Atlantic Alliance adopted military tactics—bombardment from high altitudes—that ensured that there would be few Western casualties. Having driven the Serbs from Kosovo using these tactics and having occupied the province itself, NATO is left in a position to enforce the political settlement it favors, which is autonomy. This is very much in the spirit of the post–World War I treaties and consociational democracy, a compromise between complete control of Kosovo from Belgrade and complete independence for Kosovo. But the Albanian Kosovars seek full independence, laying the basis for a conflict between the forces that occupy Kosovo and the people who live there. In the event of such a conflict, it is doubtful that NATO would be any more willing to pay a price in blood to defeat the Albanians than it had been to defeat the Serbs. Nor is it at all likely that NATO will repeat its Kosovo experience in other similarly troubled places.

This reluctance is, in one sense, good news. The clashes of the principles of legitimacy that dominated the nineteenth- and twentieth-century international politics of Europe led to three great international conflicts. The competition between principles with which Europe and the world will have to cope in the twenty-first century—between national self-determination and the integrity of existing borders—leads to local bloodletting, which, Kosovo notwithstanding, the rest of the world can largely afford to, and therefore will, ignore. That, in turn, means that the prospects for resolving these local, isolated conflicts will depend not on outside powers but on the parties themselves; and those prospects, while not uniformly bright, are by no means hopeless.

## FATIGUE—AND DIMINISHED STAKES

The precedents that give rise to optimism for the resolution of the various incarnations of the national question in the twenty-first century are to be found where outside powers have *not* seriously intervened. In Northern Ireland, Catholics and Protestants are moving slowly and painfully toward mutually acceptable forms of power sharing; in the Middle East, Israelis and Palestinians are moving, at a comparable pace and with even more attendant violence, toward a formula for a division of sovereignty with which each community can live. The American government has played a highly visible but substantively marginal role in each "peace process." The impetus for reaching a settlement comes in both cases from the parties themselves, as it did with the arrangements between the government of Russia and the Muslim province of Tatarstan, with the establishment of a regional parliament for Scotland, and with the treaty signed by the governments of Hungary and Romania protecting the cultural rights of ethnic Hungarians in Romania.

The lesson of these varying (and not necessarily eternal) arrangements for accommodating the collective demands of national minorities is that what is most needed to settle such conflicts is not ingenuity of constitutional design: there are, after all, many ways to build a structure in which two or more families can live comfortably but separately under the same roof. The necessary and all too rare ingredient for a solution to the contemporary version of the national question is the political will to settle.

National conflicts are settled by those who are party to them when they are "ripe" for resolution. Perhaps the most common source of ripeness is fatigue.[5] Parties to a conflict will be ready to compromise when they are exhausted from waging it, as in the cases of Northern Ireland and the Middle East.

The debilitating expenditure of blood and treasure will not be the only incentive for settling national conflicts in the twenty-first century. Prudence, rationality, and the observation of what can happen in the absence of a settlement are not unknown and have evidently played a role in post-communist relations between Russians and Tatars and between Hungarians and Romanians.

Yet another trend in twenty-first-century international politics, however, may turn out to be the most effective solvent of national conflicts: the obsolescence of sovereignty itself.

The national question has been so contentious because the stakes have seemed so high: control of the machinery of the modern state, a supremely important twentieth-century institution that is the product of the two forces that first shaped Europe and then the world—the French Revolution and the Industrial Revolution. These forces conferred upon the political societies of Europe two tasks for which a powerful instrument was necessary: modern war and economic management. The French Revolution led to mass armies to wage wars; the Industrial Revolution produced ever more complicated, expensive, and deadly weapons with which those armies could be equipped. Only a powerful state could recruit, train, and support the soldiers and develop and purchase the weaponry.

Modern war was born in the nineteenth century. In the twentieth, sovereign states assumed another responsibility for which a powerful state was needed: economic management. In communist countries, the state's economic responsibility was total. The economic role of the central government elsewhere was more modest but still considerable: appropriating an increasing share of the society's output through taxation; providing, with the taxes it collected, an expanding array of services and public works; and using fiscal and monetary tools to cushion the shocks and abbreviate the downturns to which market economies are prone.

While neither great task has by any means disappeared, in the wake of the Cold War, both are in decline. Also in decline, therefore, is the institution responsible for them, the state itself. Major war, the kind fought by men with weapons that only the powerful modern state can provide, is going out of fashion. While not impossible, it is less likely than at any time in the past two centuries.[6] The communist economic system is discredited; with the exception of North Korea, no sovereign state now seeks to control all facets of economic life. In other countries, where the balance between government control and the impersonal rules of the market in the governance of economic activity has periodically shifted, it has swung, in the wake of the Cold War, sharply in favor of the market.

The retreat from government control of economic activity is most noticeable where the national question began: in Europe. There, in the second half of the nineteenth century, what had previously been regarded as agglomerations of politically inert peasants rather than true nations began demanding their own sovereign states, producing a raft of conflicting claims that could not all be fulfilled. Emblematic of this trend were the Czechs, who, as the twentieth century began, were unwilling to conduct their political business under German rule or their private transactions in the German language.

As the century ends, the Czech people, living in their own state, have no higher aspiration than for their interest rates to be set in Germany. Of course, if the Czech Republic succeeds in joining the European Union, its interest rate would be set by a European, not a German, Central Bank in Frankfurt. But that is just the point. Even mighty Germany, in economic terms Europe's most powerful state, has given up what was once a cardinal feature of sovereignty, the control of its own monetary policy.

The eclipse of the nation-state has been regularly foretold; now, as in the past, the state is not on the verge of withering away. But its once overweening and still formidable powers are plainly, if slowly and unevenly, declining. It is possible that its powers may someday diminish to the point at which the borders of sovereign states will have no more significance than those of American postal zones and that the bitter twentieth-century conflicts over borders will seem as distant and puzzling as the theological disputes that provoked battles and persecutions in medieval Europe do to us today. On that day, the national question will have vanished; no one fights about the location of postal zones. But to the unhappy regions of the planet where, on the eve of the twenty-first century, the national question is still a virulent, poisonous one, that happy day will be a long time in coming.

## NOTES

This chapter was previously published in *The National Interest* 57, Fall 1999, 17–26.

1. Quoted in Daniel Patrick Moynihan, *Pandaemonium: Ethnicity in International Politics*, New York: Oxford University Press, 1993, p. 83.

2. Will Kymlicka, ed., introduction to *The Rights of Minority Cultures*, New York: Oxford University Press, 1995, 5.

3. On the two types of democracy, see Fareed Zakaria, "The Rise of Illiberal Democracy," *Foreign Affairs,* November/December 1997. On the combustible potential of fledgling democracy, see Edward Mansfield and Jack Snyder, "Democratization and the Danger of War," *International Security,* Summer 1995.

4. The term is from Arendt Lijphart, *Democracy in Plural Societies: A Comparative Exploration*, New Haven, CT: Yale University Press, 1977.

5. The concept originates with I. William Zartman, *Ripe for Resolution*, New York: Oxford University Press, 1985. See also Zartman, "Ripeness Revisited," in *The Resolution of Conflict*, Washington, DC: National Academy of Science, 1999.

6. See my "Is Major War Obsolete?" *Survival* 38, no. 3, Fall 1998.

# 3

## Transnational Causes of Genocide, or How the West Exacerbates Ethnic Conflict

*Alan J. Kuperman*

Since the end of the Cold War, a series of extremely violent intrastate communal conflicts—involving ethnic cleansing and/or genocide—has captured the attention of Western publics, media, policymakers, and scholars. Academic and popular literature has burgeoned with prescriptions for reducing such violence, including preventive diplomacy to avert its outbreak, humanitarian intervention to mitigate its consequences, and conflict management to resolve it and prevent its recurrence. A common assumption in this literature is that insufficient Western attention and involvement have contributed to the outbreak, intensity, and persistence of such violence. In normative terms, the sin of the West is characterized as one of omission, rather than commission. Accordingly, the usual prescription is for more active diplomacy and intervention to prevent such deadly conflicts.[1]

This chapter proposes a contrary theory: that the substantial level of attention already paid to nascent conflicts by the international community is actually a causal variable in exacerbating their violence. The first section of the chapter lays out this theory, contrasts it with several alternative explanations of such violence, and formulates predictions that should obtain if the theory is correct and the alternatives wrong. The second section conducts a preliminary test of the theory by tracing four post–Cold War cases of massive communal violence, in which the main victims were Iraq's Kurds in 1991, Bosnia's Muslims in 1992, Rwanda's Tutsi in 1994, and Kosovo's Albanians in 1999. The final section draws conclusions, discusses potential policy prescriptions, and offers suggestions for further research.

## THE THEORY

Although the words "genocide" and "ethnic cleansing" are commonly associated with an irrational, emotional outburst of hate, it has been demonstrated conclusively that such violence in most cases is a rational response by one group to the threat posed by another.[2] As Helen Fein writes, genocide "is usually a rational act. . . . Since 1945, most genocides have been state responses to rebellions or challenges by ethnic groups excluded from power—that is, challenges to the structure of domination."[3] During the period 1945 to 1988, she identifies thirteen cases of genocide in Africa, Asia, and the Middle East.[4] Of these, seven are classified as "retributive" (that is, in response to a rebellion) and two as "preventive" (that is, in anticipation of such a revolt).[5] Thus, nine of thirteen, or 69 percent, of the identified genocides were a rational response by a state's dominant group to a challenge by a subordinate group.[6]

A theoretical framework can be constructed to account for this evidence by observing that the traditional relationship between a dominant and a subordinate societal group fits Thomas Schelling's model of a successful coercive relationship.[7] As Schelling aptly observes in the context of limited war, successful coercion is not total victory for one side, as might appear superficially, but rather a bargain to which each side willingly consents. The stronger side refrains from destroying its opponent and thereby saves resources, while the weaker side makes concessions and thereby avoids destruction. Adapting this to the domestic context of communal competition, we can see a similar two-sided bargain: the dominant group refrains from inflicting overt violence on the subordinate group—which it clearly has the means to inflict—so long as the subordinate group accepts inferior status, rights, and rewards. This relationship may be "peaceful" for decades or centuries, either because it is ingrained culturally or because both groups perceive that they enjoy higher utility by eschewing overt violence.

However, when and if the subordinate group chooses to break its side of the bargain—by pursuing equal rights, political autonomy, secession, and/or the revolutionary overthrow of the existing regime—the dominant group is likewise freed to break its side of the bargain. Indeed, the dominant group may perceive a self-interest in inflicting massive violence, including genocide and ethnic cleansing, against the subordinate group, either to reestablish the original coercive relationship or to eliminate the group permanently as a potential threat to its interests.

In light of this theoretical framework, we are presented with a conundrum heretofore under-explored in the literature: why would a group sufficiently vulnerable to face the punishment of genocide provoke that very outcome by launching an ill-fated challenge against the dominant group?

Insight again is offered by the literature on interstate wars. According to Geoffrey Blainey, such wars generally are caused by "optimistic miscalculation." If both sides had perfect information, the weaker would concede to the demands of the stronger prior to the outbreak of war, thereby obtaining the same eventual outcome but avoiding the human and financial costs of fighting.[8] A leading cause of such miscalculation, he says, is the false expectation of obtaining assistance from allies.

In the domestic context, analogously, genocides and ethnic cleansing may occur when a vulnerable subordinate group rises up because it miscalculates optimistically that it will receive assistance from an outside source. When such assistance does not materialize, the group is crushed. This chapter proposes that, in the post–Cold War era, a main source of such optimistic miscalculation has been the expectation by subordinate groups that the "international community" will intervene to protect them on humanitarian grounds if their challenge to authority provokes retaliatory violence.

This false expectation arises from two main factors. First, in the wake of the Cold War, Western politicians increasingly have engaged in public condemnation of, and threats against, leaders of foreign states for oppression of subordinate groups within their own borders.[9] Second, the West in some cases has followed up such rhetoric by launching humanitarian military interventions on behalf of the victimized groups—notably in Somalia, Bosnia, and Kosovo—after media coverage of suffering civilians prompted calls for action. Although such interventions have not been launched quickly enough to prevent massive violence, they ultimately have aided the subordinate groups.

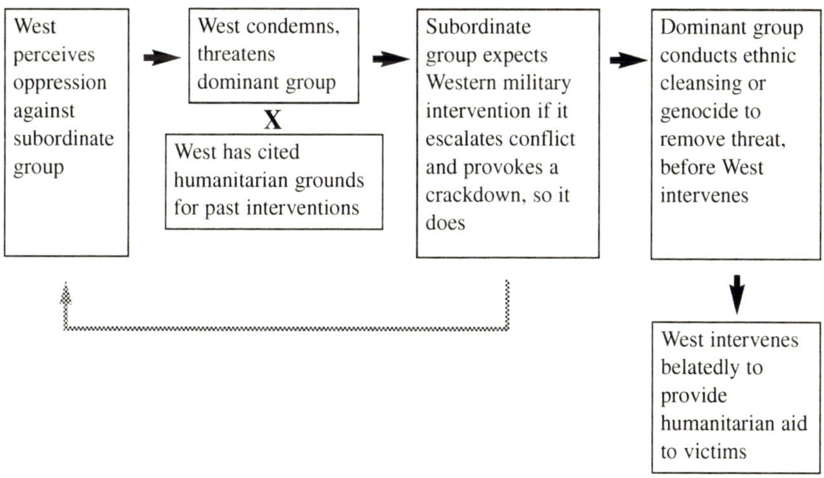


**Figure 3.1. How the West Inadvertently Causes Genocide and Ethnic Cleansing**

This new Western policy exacerbates conflict in two ways. First, where violence already is nascent, Western criticism and threats increase the subordinate group's expectation of receiving military assistance and thereby encourage it to escalate the fighting. Second, where violence has not yet broken out, weak subordinate groups have a perverse incentive to initiate violent challenges against much stronger opponents in order to provoke a violent crackdown against their own people, in hopes of compelling sympathetic media attention, Western threats, and ultimately military intervention.[10]

## Alternative Theories

Many other theories have been offered for massive intercommunal violence. One category of theories assumes that communal groups do not behave as unitary rational actors. Thus, if the subordinate group rises up, it is because persistent discrimination has led to frustration and then aggression, without prior calculation of expected outcome.[11] If the dominant group initiates violence, it is due to irrational hatreds within the dominant group[12] or escalatory outbidding among its non-unitary elite in a competitive political environment.[13] Such irrational dominant-group aggression also may spur the subordinate group to launch an uprising preventively, on grounds that it expects to be annihilated anyway and therefore has nothing to lose.

A second category of theories, based on the security dilemma, assumes the two sides are unitary rational actors who would both prefer to avoid conflict and alleviate the discriminatory situation. They are prevented from achieving this positive-sum outcome only by overarching anarchy, which compels them to take precautionary measures that inadvertently threaten the other. This leads to an escalatory spiral and preemptive or preventive conflict.[14]

A third category of theories is similar to that proposed above in assuming that subordinate groups rationally choose to launch violent uprisings against stronger opponents, but this category finds different causes for such ill-fated challenges. These putative causes include: a false belief that the dominant group would never inflict massive retaliation against its own countrymen; a high tolerance for such retaliation as the price of victory; an expectation of outside support from non-Western strategic allies (as opposed to Western humanitarian interveners); or simple risk-proneness.

## Predictions

If the proposed theory is correct, and the alternatives wrong, we should expect to observe several predictions:

1. Prior to the genocide and/or ethnic cleansing, leading politicians in the West condemned and threatened the dominant group for its perceived oppression of the subordinate group.
2. Subordinate-group leaders believed the West would aid them if they provoked a crackdown, and this motivated them to escalate the conflict.
3. Subordinate-group leaders did not believe they could prevail in armed conflict against the dominant group without Western military intervention.
4. Subordinate-group leaders knew in advance that the dominant group was willing to resort to massive violence in response to a challenge to its dominance.
5. The dominant group had not resorted to genocide or ethnic cleansing in the past—and did not threaten to—in the absence of a provocative challenge to its authority.
6. The West did not intervene on a timely basis to prevent the ethnic cleansing or genocide, although it subsequently may have provided aid to reverse some of the damage.
7. The challenge to the state's authority was not triggered by an escalatory spiral of insecurity.
8. Subordinate-group leaders acted on the basis of rational calculation (though possibly with imperfect information) rather than impulse or risk-prone behavior.

## THE CASES

### Iraq

Iraq's minority Kurds, who live mainly in the North, and its majority Shiite Muslim Arabs, who live mainly in the South, have long been disgruntled due to discrimination at the hands of Iraq's minority Sunni Muslim Arab elite, who dominate the ruling Ba'ath party in Baghdad. Several times over the past few decades, Baghdad has launched deadly attacks against the Kurds and/or Shiites, in response to their demands for autonomy and/or independence. However, at other times when the groups have accepted Baghdad's authority and the domination of its Sunni elite, they have been spared violence and have even received rewards. This case study focuses on Baghdad's relationship with the Kurds,[15] although the case of the Shiites is similar.

One period of peaceful coexistence between Baghdad and the Kurds was the two years prior to the 1991 Gulf War. It followed a particularly vicious crackdown against the Kurds—the 1988 Anfal campaign in which Saddam employed chemical weapons against civilians, notably at Halabja. Also in

1988, the end of Iraq's eight-year war with Iran meant the Kurds lost support from Tehran, while Saddam was able to focus more energy on crushing domestic dissent. When the Kurds realized their hope of victory was dashed, they chose to accept Baghdad's rule, and in return, Saddam stopped attacking them. For two years, there was no major conflict between Baghdad and the Kurds.

Things changed near the end of the Gulf War. In mid-February 1991, during the war's air campaign, President George Bush declared "the Iraqi people should take matters into their own hands to force Saddam Hussein the dictator to step aside."[16] When the ground war ended two weeks later, with Saddam's troops in retreat and hundreds of thousands of American troops poised in and around Southern Iraq, Bush repeated the call.[17] This same message was repeated in millions of pamphlets dropped by U.S. military psychological-operations (psyops) units inside Iraq. The U.S. Central Intelligence Agency also sponsored a radio station, "Voice of Free Iraq," that repeated such calls and told the Iraqi opposition "that the whole world was behind them."[18] When the Gulf War ended, the Kurds and Shiites did indeed rise up, and Saddam predictably responded by ordering his army to crush the uprisings.[19] Kurdish leaders then appealed to President Bush for help on grounds that "you personally called upon the Iraqi people to rise up against Saddam Hussein's brutal dictatorship."[20]

However, Bush had long ruled out the possibility of deploying U.S. ground troops deep inside Iraq and now declined to deploy even the limited option of air power to shoot down Iraqi helicopter gunships that were punishing the rebels. Saddam's forces, which enjoyed overwhelming superiority, crushed the uprisings and within a month cleansed an estimated half- to one million Kurds in Iraq's northern reaches and neighboring states. United States officials later revealed that their rhetoric had been intended only to encourage a coup from within the Sunni elite of the Iraqi Army.[21] The rebel uprising took U.S. officials by surprise because the Administration had cut off all communications with the rebels several years earlier in deference to Turkey. When Washington realized the rebellion was being led by communal groups in the North and South, it feared rebel victory would lead to de facto partition of Iraq and a power vacuum in which neighboring revolutionary Iran could expand its regional influence, so it chose to let the uprisings be crushed.[22] Only after the rebellions were suppressed did the United States provide humanitarian aid by airlifting supplies to the displaced, establishing a safe zone, and imposing a no-fly zone in Northern Iraq to enable many Kurds to return home.

## Bosnia

Intermittent interethnic violence has been a fact of life in the Balkans for centuries. Still, Bosnia's history includes long stretches without violence, including its tenure as a republic within Yugoslavia from 1945 to 1992. In the 1980s, several factors—including the death of Marshal Tito, the global decline in the legitimacy of communism, and local economic troubles—contributed to an internal crisis in Yugoslavia. By most traditional measures, Serbia had been the dominant republic: Serbs dominated the federal army; the federal capital was also Serbia's capital—Belgrade; Serbs were the most numerous ethnic group in Yugoslavia and had large populations in several republics outside Serbia; and though Slovenia and Croatia were richer on a per capita basis, the Yugoslav tax system redirected some of this wealth toward Serbia and the other poorer republics. Accordingly, as communism withered in the late 1980s, Serbia sought to ensure perpetuation of the federal Yugoslav state and its own preeminence therein. Several other republics, led by Slovenia and Croatia, chafed at this Serb domination and pursued independence. Serbian President Slobodan Milosevic responded by warning that he would not consent to such secession until border changes were negotiated so that Serb-populated areas of the seceding republics were ceded back to Yugoslavia.

In mid-1991, however, Slovenia and Croatia seceded unilaterally. Serbia responded by launching a half-hearted attack on Slovenia, which contained virtually no Serbs, but a vicious attack on Croatia, which had a Serb population of 12 percent. The fight was lopsided because Belgrade could employ the federal army, while Croatia had to rely on poorly equipped and trained militia and former army troops. Within a few weeks, Yugoslav forces had captured one-third of Croatian territory, ethnically cleansed tens of thousands from their homes, and left thousands dead. In early 1992, Croatia's independence was recognized by the international community, a cease-fire was negotiated, and UN peacekeepers were deployed to the occupied areas, effectively locking in Serb territorial gains temporarily.

Bosnia's Muslim President Alija Izetbegovic was more cautious. He had long been wary of confronting Serbia with unilateral secession,[23] and this fear was reinforced by events in Croatia. He knew that Serbia was even more covetous of Bosnia, because Serbs represented nearly one third of the republic's population and lived on about half the territory, and because Bosnia provided a land bridge from Serbia to Serb-controlled areas of Croatia. Moreover, Bosnia was less able to defend itself from Serbia because its military forces were weaker than Croatia's, and the Yugoslav army had moved additional troops into Bosnia from Slovenia and Croatia. Accordingly, Izetbegovic initially took a more accommodating approach. Rather than pursuing full independence, he called for relaxing Belgrade's central control and transforming Yugoslavia into a looser confederation. When Belgrade rejected this proposal, he did not immediately pursue unilateral secession.

In late 1991, however, the international community became more involved in Yugoslavia. Spurred by German pressure, the European Commission's Badinter panel recommended recognizing the independence of Yugoslavia's republics if they met certain requirements. Many observers believed that such recognition carried with it a commitment to defend a republic's sovereignty, as guaranteed under the UN Charter. Indeed, less than a year earlier, a UN military coalition had successfully defended the sovereignty of Kuwait against external aggression, which President Bush said symbolized a "new world order."

The Badinter panel said Bosnia needed to approve a referendum on independence to qualify for EC recognition, so the republic's Muslim leaders quickly held one at the end of February 1992, which was approved with the overwhelming support of Muslim and Croat voters. However, the Serb portion of the population boycotted the vote, and their leaders warned that if Bosnia seceded from Yugoslavia, the Serb areas would secede from Bosnia, virtually assuring war to determine final borders.[24] To avert this impending disaster, the European Community appointed Portuguese mediator Jose Cutileiro to negotiate a power-sharing compromise prior to independence, under which Bosnia's three ethnic groups would be given substantial autonomy and veto power over any central Bosnian decisions affecting them. In late February 1992, all three Bosnian groups signed the accord, which some observers criticized as de facto partition but which offered the only realistic hope of avoiding civil war in Bosnia.[25]

Before the plan could be implemented, however, U.S. Ambassador Warren Zimmermann met with Izetbegovic. Zimmermann asked the Bosnian President why he had signed an agreement for de facto partition, and Izetbegovic explained that he had been pressured to do so by the EC mediators. Zimmermann replied that Izetbegovic should not agree to something he didn't believe in and reassured the Bosnian President he could get a better deal, upon which Izetbegovic renounced his consent. Cutileiro scrambled and managed to persuade all three parties to sign a revised version in mid-March, but by the end of the month, Izetbegovic had again reneged, after receiving U.S. assurances that he could win recognition without signing on to the plan.[26] A week later, despite the absence of any agreement between the three Bosnian parties, the United States and EC recognized Bosnia's independence. Almost immediately, Bosnian Serb forces and the Yugoslav army attacked, as they had promised to do if confronted with unilateral secession.[27] The UN responded by withdrawing virtually all of its forces from Bosnia, where they were headquartered for the peacekeeping mission in neighboring Croatia. Within a few months, by August 1992, Serb forces held two-thirds of Bosnia, had killed tens of thousands of Muslims, and had ethnically cleansed hundreds of thousands more from the territory under their control.[28] Only then did UN peacekeepers return to assure delivery of humanitarian aid.

## Rwanda

Rwanda's minority Tutsi had ruled and dominated Rwanda during its precolonial and colonial periods, when they constituted about 17 percent of the population. During the transition to independence starting in 1959, however, control switched to the majority Hutu, who comprised virtually all the rest of the population. Over the next few years, exiled Tutsi leaders repeatedly sought to return to power by launching attacks from Uganda and Burundi. Rwanda's Hutu leaders repulsed those attacks and perpetrated reprisals against domestic Tutsi suspected of supporting the invaders, spurring the flight of about half the Tutsi population as refugees to neighboring states. By the late 1960s, the Tutsi rebels had accepted the futility of their struggle and halted their invasions. In Rwanda, meanwhile, a 1973 coup brought to power Juvenal Habyarimana, a Hutu from the northwest region. The new regime disproportionately favored Hutu from the president's region at the expense of Tutsi and other Hutu, but—in the absence of any Tutsi uprising or invasion—it perpetrated no significant communal violence for seventeen years.[29]

In the 1980s, however, two dynamics in Uganda revived the aspirations of Rwandan Tutsi refugees to return home. First, and more important, many Tutsi refugees served in the Ugandan rebel army of Yoweri Museveni, which captured power in Kampala in 1986, thereby providing a blueprint for the exiles' return to power in Rwanda. Second, Tutsi continued to be viewed as outsiders in Uganda even after their ally Museveni took power. Persistently insecure in their adopted country and emboldened by their newfound military skills, Ugandan Tutsi led the formation in 1987 of the "Rwandan Patriotic Front" (RPF). Rwandan President Habyarimana suspected that an invasion might be imminent, so in 1990 he invited Uganda's Tutsi refugees to return home peacefully. Instead, in October 1990, the RPF invaded Rwanda.

In a virtual repeat of the 1960s experience, Rwanda's Hutu leaders repulsed the initial invasion and launched reprisals against domestic Tutsi. This time, however, the Tutsi-led RPF successfully regrouped and gained control of a small swath of territory in the north of Rwanda, from which it launched further offensives from 1991 to 1993. The rebels also forged political alliances with disgruntled Hutu inside Rwanda. Habyarimana was forced to call on French military reinforcements to defeat the initial invasion, and several times subsequently.[30] His regime also responded by escalating its rhetorical and violent attacks against domestic Tutsi, in the hope of unifying domestic Hutu support for the government by sowing fear of a common Tutsi enemy.

The RPF was acutely aware that its attacks were triggering undesired consequences—including reprisals against domestic Tutsi, increased French military intervention, and international criticism. Accordingly, the rebels instead tried to negotiate their way into power—reserving the military option as a last resort.

Starting in about 1992, the international community became heavily involved in the Rwandan power struggle, mainly on behalf of the RPF and the domestic opposition. From 1992–1994, Western officials used the leverage of foreign economic and military aid to force President Habyarimana to sign and begin to implement the Arusha Accords, which effectively required that the president hand over power to the rebels and his domestic political opponents.[31] To the president's clients and cronies, such a deal was unacceptable, because they would lose their privileges and face potentially deadly reprisals from the new leaders.[32]

Confronted by this looming threat, extremist Hutu concocted a full-fledged plot of political assassination and genocide, which included death lists, nationwide youth militias, and hate media to foment and guide the killing. Because both sides now felt threatened, the international community pledged at Arusha to deploy a multinational force to Rwanda to "guarantee overall security of the country" during the transition.[33] However, as the accords began to be implemented in late 1993—starting with the replacement of French troops in the capital by UN peacekeepers and a battalion of rebels—the Hutu extremists feared the worst. On April 6, 1994, Habyarimana's plane mysteriously was shot down, and the extremists immediately implemented their plan to kill all Tutsi and moderate Hutu. The UN force in Kigali lacked the troops, equipment, or mandate to stop the killing, and the international community, rather than beef up the peacekeeping mission, chose instead to withdraw it almost entirely. Genocide ended only after the rebels defeated the extremist Hutu government three months later, in July 1994, by which time three-fourths of Rwanda's Tutsi had been killed. UN-authorized troops did not return to Rwanda until late June, when the killing of Tutsi was virtually over.

## Kosovo

Kosovo, a province of Serbia, has been the scene of a power struggle between Serbs and Albanians for centuries, and whichever ethnic group has held power has oppressed the other. Early in the twentieth century, each group represented about half of the province's population, but Albanians have since come to predominate. After World War II, Tito was generous to the ethnic Albanian portion of Kosovo's population, motivated in part by his desire to woo Albania to join Yugoslavia. In the 1960s, he removed an oppressive administrator and steadily increased local control, which tended to favor the more numerous Albanians, culminating in a constitutional grant of substantial autonomy in 1974. Over time, the province's demographics tilted sharply toward Albanians due to differential fertility rates, immigration from Albania, and ethnic outmigration of Serbs that was motivated by economics and perceived hostility from Albanians. By the late 1980s, Serbs represented only about 10 percent of Kosovo's population, and this small remaining population was subject to harassment by extremist Albanians who sought an ethnically pure province, secession from Yugoslavia, and ultimate unification with Albania.[34]

As Yugoslavia's central communist authority waned in the 1980s, Slobodan Milosevic came to prominence in Serbia largely on the nationalist issue of protecting Kosovo's Serbs. Starting in 1989, he successfully pushed through reforms that revoked Kosovo's autonomy, required use of the Serbo-Croatian language in its government institutions, and removed Albanians from government jobs—the only good ones in a centralized economy—by dismissing them or requiring loyalty oaths that they refused to swear. In addition, a new Serb police force began to harass Albanians and commit human rights violations as it hunted separatists.

For nearly ten years, however, there were no attempts at ethnic cleansing or genocide against the ethnic Albanians because Kosovo—unlike Croatia and Bosnia—did not attempt to secede forcefully from Yugoslavia, even though Belgrade's oppression was heaviest there. Two factors explain this absence of violent secession. First, the Badinter guidelines did not offer to recognize the province's independence, so the Albanians had no expectation of outside assistance against powerful Yugoslav forces. Second, Kosovo was led by the charismatic pacifist Ibrahim Rugova, who sought to avoid carnage by pursuing independence gradually through civil disobedience. Boycotting Yugoslav elections, taxes, schools, and health care, Kosovo's Albanians, by 1991, had established their own parallel institutions. Though they lacked a police force and remained second-class citizens in the province, by the mid-1990s, they had reestablished a degree of de facto autonomy. Rugova was confident that demographics—the dwindling number of Serbs in the province—would lead eventually to independence. Rejecting calls for an immediate uprising, he explained in 1992 that "the Serbs only wait for a pretext to attack the Albanian population and wipe it out. We believe it is better to do nothing and stay alive than to be massacred."[35]

Things changed in late 1997 when a fringe group of secessionist Albanians, calling themselves the Kosovo Liberation Army (KLA), escalated their more violent tactics.[36] After the rebels shot several Serb policeman, Belgrade responded by intensifying its counterinsurgency activities, including the massacre of an extended family associated with the rebels in March 1998. This crackdown backfired by galvanizing support for the rebels among both Kosovo's Albanians and international observers. U.S. Secretary of State

Madeleine Albright immediately declared: "We are not going to stand by and watch the Serbian authorities do in Kosovo what they can no longer get away with doing in Bosnia."[37] In June 1998, NATO staged practice bombing raids in neighboring Albania and Macedonia, attempting to deter Milosevic from further brutalities. It is possible, though not documented, that this saber-rattling deterred Milosevic from immediately employing a strategy of mass expulsion. However, the undeniable effect of the West's threats against Belgrade was to embolden the rebels to escalate their offensive, which predictably triggered an even bigger crackdown by Serb forces. Although NATO declared repeatedly that it would not serve as "the KLA's air force," Kosovo's Albanians believed such military intervention was inevitable if fighting escalated.[38]

The onset of winter and an interim agreement to insert international human rights monitors into Kosovo temporarily curtailed fighting and permitted most Albanians displaced by the fighting to return home temporarily. However, by early 1999, fighting had renewed, which spurred the West to convene an international conference in Rambouillet, France, to resolve the conflict. American officials drafted an agreement that largely favored the Albanians—demanding a referendum on independence after three years and free passage for NATO troops throughout all of Yugoslavia—and presented it to Belgrade as an ultimatum, threatening to bomb if Milosevic were responsible for "cratering" the negotiations.[39] The rebels eventually signed the agreement but Belgrade refused. Living up to its threat, NATO started bombing in late March 1999, expecting to compel Milosevic's quick acceptance. Instead, Belgrade launched a massive campaign of ethnic cleansing in Kosovo, expelling nearly half of the Albanian population, internally displacing most of the rest, and killing thousands of rebels and Albanian civilians.[40]

After eleven weeks of NATO bombing that inflicted billions of dollars of economic damage and killed hundreds of civilians, Milosevic agreed to a somewhat less demanding peace deal.[41] Albanians who had survived were able to return home, where many took revenge on Serb civilians, compelling them to flee the province. The result today is that Kosovo, except for a few small enclaves mainly in the north, is a virtually pure ethnic Albanian province—the longtime goal of the province's Albanian extremists.

## ASSESSING THE THEORY'S PREDICTIONS

### 1. Western politicians condemned/threatened the dominant group for its oppression prior to the genocide/ethnic cleansing.

In Iraq, the West had not explicitly warned Saddam Hussein about his treatment of internal communal groups immediately prior to his crackdown but had imposed sanctions and fought a two-month war against him for "naked aggression" against the Kuwaiti people. In Bosnia, the West repeatedly had warned Serbian President Slobodan Milosevic that it would "oppose the use of force or intimidation to resolve political differences" or to keep Yugoslavia together.[42] In Rwanda, the West had applied economic sanctions against the government for failing to share power and criticized it for human rights abuses during the two years prior to the genocide. In Kosovo, the West condemned Milosevic starting in the late 1980s, and as early as 1992, the United States issued its so-called Christmas warning: "In the event of conflict in Kosovo caused by Serbian action, the U.S. will be prepared to employ military force against Serbians in Kosovo and in Serbia proper." Starting in March 1998, Washington reiterated this threat regularly for a year, culminating in Albright's ultimatum at Rambouillet, which immediately preceded NATO's bombing and Serbia's response of launching an ethnic cleansing campaign.[43] This prediction is clearly fulfilled in Bosnia, Rwanda, and Kosovo and somewhat fulfilled in Iraq.

### 2. Subordinate-group leaders believed the West would aid them if they provoked a crackdown, and this motivated them to escalate the conflict.

In Iraq, Kurd leaders expected such aid due to Bush's statements, the psyops leaflets and CIA radio broadcasts. As a U.S. colonel who directed psyops concedes, "I think you could say we contributed to" the uprising.[44] The Kurds also were motivated by Saddam's perceived weakness after defeat in the Gulf War, but historically they had not risen up without outside assistance and encouragement. In Bosnia, the Muslim leadership explicitly avoided unilateral secession on grounds it would be too provocative to Serbia, until the EC offered recognition and urged it to hold an independence referendum. Even after the referendum, Izetbegovic signed on to the Cutileiro plan agreeing to Bosnia's de facto partition until the U.S. ambassador told him he could do better and that the United States would recognize Bosnia's independence in any case.[45] After war broke out, Muslim forces repeatedly launched attacks against better-armed Serb forces, expecting this would lead to retaliatory killing that would attract international support, according to several UN commanders.[46] In Rwanda, the rebels had no expectation of Western military aid when they launched their invasion, but during the Arusha peace negotiations, Western diplomatic support emboldened them to make demands that threatened Rwanda's ruling elite. Had the West not sided with the rebels but instead continued to support the Hutu government, the rebels might have reduced their demands, thereby mitigating the threat to the Hutu elite and avoiding a genocidal backlash.[47] In Kosovo, the KLA believed from the start that its only hope of victory was to draw the international community into the fight on its behalf by militarizing the conflict.[48] As a KLA negotiator later conceded, "The more civilians were killed, the chances of international intervention became bigger, and the KLA of course realized that."[49] This prediction is clearly fulfilled in Iraq, Bosnia, and Kosovo and somewhat fulfilled in Rwanda.

**3. Subordinate-group leaders did not believe they could prevail in armed conflict against the dominant group without humanitarian military intervention.**

In Iraq, the Kurds knew they could not prevail against Saddam's army under ordinary conditions but may have perceived Saddam's control as weakened by defeat in the Gulf War. In Bosnia, in early 1992, Muslim government leaders had just witnessed Belgrade's crushing of Croatia, which was stronger than Bosnia and had fewer Serbs than Bosnia. They did not believe victory was possible without foreign assistance, which is why they initially urged the West not to grant recognition to any of the republics until a negotiated solution was found. In Rwanda, the rebels doubted they could triumph militarily so long as France reinforced the Hutu government with troops and equipment. Thus, the main "intervention" they sought was a halt in French military assistance to compel the government to surrender power. In Kosovo, the Albanians knew they could not prevail without Western intervention.[50] This prediction is clearly fulfilled in Bosnia and Kosovo and somewhat fulfilled in Iraq and Rwanda.

**4. Subordinate-group leaders knew in advance that the dominant group was willing to resort to massive violence in response to a challenge.**

In Iraq, the Kurds had suffered chemical weapons attacks from Saddam in response to their previous challenge and had been warned by a top Baghdad official in January 1991—just five weeks prior to the uprising—that "if you have forgotten Halabja, I would like to remind you that we are ready to repeat the operation."[51] Bosnians were aware of the horrible atrocities suffered in neighboring Croatia after its unilateral secession and had been warned by Bosnian Serb leader Radovan Karadzic in March 1992—just three weeks prior to Bosnia's secession—that such a step without agreement of the Serbs would lead to "a civil war between ethnic groups and religions with hundreds of thousands dead and hundreds of towns destroyed."[52] Rwanda's Tutsi had been subject to massacres and ethnic cleansing in the 1960s in response to previous rebel invasions, so RPF officials expected their invasion to trigger approximately ten thousand retributive killings of Tutsi. In the months prior to the genocide, as warning signs proliferated, they began to fear a much higher level of retributive killing, but this did not induce them to reduce their demands.[53] Kosovo's Albanians had witnessed Serb atrocities in Croatia and Bosnia and had no illusions about Serb tactics in response to armed secession. This prediction is clearly fulfilled in all four cases.

**5. The dominant group had not resorted to genocide or ethnic cleansing, and did not threaten to, in the absence of a provocative challenge to its authority.**

In Iraq, Saddam had not threatened or attacked the Kurds for two years prior to their uprising in 1991. In Bosnia, Serbs did not launch large-scale violence until the republic unilaterally seceded in 1992. In Rwanda, the Hutu government had not committed massacres against Tutsi for seventeen years until expatriate Tutsi refugees invaded from Uganda in 1990. In Kosovo, Serb forces did not kill or displace large numbers of Albanians until the KLA escalated its attacks in 1997 and did not turn to full-blown ethnic cleansing until NATO began bombing in 1999. This prediction is clearly fulfilled in all four cases.

**6. The West did not intervene on a timely basis to prevent the ethnic cleansing or genocide, although it subsequently may have provided aid to reverse some of the damage.**

In Iraq, the rebellion had been crushed and more than a half-million Kurds had been cleansed before the United States intervened to provide humanitarian aid. In Bosnia, Serbs had cleansed two-thirds of the republic before the UN deployed troops to provide humanitarian assistance. In Rwanda, approximately three-fourths of the Tutsi population had been killed and the rebels had already captured most of the country before a UN-authorized intervention was launched. In Kosovo, almost half the Albanian population was ethnically cleansed from the province, and most of the rest displaced internally, before NATO's air campaign compelled a withdrawal of Serb forces. This prediction is clearly fulfilled in all four cases.

**7. The challenge to the state's authority was not triggered by an escalatory spiral of insecurity.**

Some "defensive realists" argue that all desire for power is merely a reaction to insecurity, so that all conflict stems from the security dilemma. However, for the concept of the security dilemma to have theoretic utility, it should not be applied to conflicts that stem originally from a lust for power rather than any acute fear. In Iraq, the Kurds launched their uprising during a period when they were relatively secure, rather than out of any acute insecurity. In Bosnia, there was no acute insecurity until the Muslims and Croats began agitating for the republic's independence in the face of Serb opposition. Thus, the security dilemma was a consequence, not a cause, of the secession. In Rwanda, the Tutsi invasion was triggered mainly by the rebels' desire to retake power in Rwanda, not by any acute Tutsi insecurity either in Rwanda or Uganda. Had the Tutsi in Uganda merely sought to reduce the insecurity inherent in their refugee status, they could have accepted President Habyarimana's invitation to return to Rwanda in 1990, prior to the invasion. Moreover, in Rwanda, it is unclear whether either side ever was motivated more by fear than by lust for power, or whether, in the absence of insecurity, either would have preferred compromise over confrontation—both of which are requirements for the security dilemma to be at work. Kosovo fits the same pattern as the other cases, because the KLA escalated its attacks at a time of relative security and increasing de facto autonomy for Albanians. Thus, in all four cases examined, the outbreak of violence stemmed not from acute insecurity but rather from a lust for power.

### 8. Subordinate-group leaders acted on the basis of rational calculation (though possibly with imperfect information) rather than impulse or risk-prone behavior.

In Iraq, the Kurds rose up only after being urged to do so by the United States, which had hundreds of thousands of troops deployed in the theater, and after Saddam was weakened by defeat in war.[54] In Bosnia, Muslim leaders eschewed secession until they were urged to hold an independence referendum, promised recognition, and told to reject compromise by Western powers that had intervened to ensure Kuwait's sovereignty a year earlier. In Rwanda, expatriate Tutsi had planned for several years to return to Rwanda by force and did so at the moment they calculated their chances were optimal. Their decision making during the civil war likewise was calculated by an executive committee subject to input from RPF members around the world.[55] In Kosovo, the KLA chose violence because it believed this was the only way to attract the international intervention necessary to end Serb domination in the province. In each case, the subordinate group chose to launch its challenge because it rationally calculated that it would succeed at acceptable cost based on its information at the time, which later turned out to be imperfect. This prediction is clearly fulfilled in all four cases.

To summarize, there is strong evidence for the theory in each of the cases, but it is confirmed definitively only by the Bosnia and Kosovo cases. In Iraq, the remaining counterfactual question is whether the Kurds would have risen

**Table 3.1. Summary of Findings**

| Predictions | Iraq | Bosnia | Rwanda | Kosovo |
|---|---|---|---|---|
| 1 West Had Threatened, Condemned Dominant Group for Oppression | ✓ | ✔ | ✔ | ✔ |
| 2 Subordinate Group Expected Western Military Aid If It Escalated Conflict | ✔ | ✔ | ✓ | ✔ |
| 3 Subordinate Group Expected Failure without Such Western Intervention | ✓ | ✔ | ✓ | ✔ |
| 4 Subordinate Group Aware Government Willing to Retaliate Extremely Violently | ✔ | ✔ | ✔ | ✔ |
| 5 Dominant Group Eschewed Extreme Violence until Authority Challenged | ✔ | ✔ | ✔ | ✔ |
| 6 West Did Not Intervene Successfully until Violence Virtually Complete | ✔ | ✔ | ✔ | ✔ |
| 7 Challenge to State Not Triggered by Escalatory Spiral of Insecurity | ✔ | ✔ | ✔ | ✔ |
| 8 Subordinate Group Leaders Acted on Rational Calculation | ✔ | ✔ | ✔ | ✔ |

KEY ✔ = Clearly Fulfilled
✓ = Some Evidence

up even without U.S. urging in the wake of Saddam's defeat in the Gulf War.[56] In Rwanda, the question is whether the rebels would have pressed maximal demands even without Western backing so that they still would have threatened the Hutu extremists sufficiently to trigger a genocidal backlash.

## CONCLUSIONS

In at least two recent cases of massive communal violence—and perhaps all four under examination—the causal chain of the proposed theory is in evidence. The West, attempting to deter violence with criticism and threats, inadvertently encouraged a vulnerable group to escalate its challenge against a more powerful group by raising its expectation of forthcoming military aid. Because such assistance did not materialize in a timely manner, the subordinate group fell victim to ethnic cleansing or genocide when the dominant group attempted to remove the threat and/or restore the status quo ante.

Several lessons can be drawn. First, and most obviously, it is potentially dangerous for the West to criticize and threaten a foreign government for alleged abuses against a subordinate group if the West has no intention of intervening militarily in a timely manner. However, it is conceivable that such empty threats sometimes do deter abuses by foreign governments. Thus, further research is necessary before definitive conclusions can be drawn about the wisdom of such diplomatic bluffing.

Second, each instance of Western humanitarian military intervention appears to raise expectations of future such interventions. The UN-authorized interventions to defend Kuwait's sovereignty in 1990–1991 and to keep peace in Croatia in early 1992 raised Bosnia's Muslims' hopes of similar aid if they sparked war by seceding unilaterally. Similarly, NATO's 1995 intervention against Serb forces in Bosnia raised the KLA's hopes that it could benefit from such intervention by provoking civil war in Kosovo in 1998.[57] Any cost-benefit assessment of humanitarian military intervention must take note of such negative spillover effects.

Third, all the cases under examination demonstrate a remarkable phenomenon in which Western rhetoric apparently is believed by subordinate groups but largely discounted by dominant groups. The subordinate group is sufficiently encouraged to rise up, but the dominant group is not sufficiently deterred to eschew massive retaliation. In each case, the dominant group's assessment proved more accurate in the short run, as it was able to inflict massive violence before the West intervened successfully. Eventually, however, belated Western intervention did assist the subordinate groups to varying degrees. In Iraq, most Kurds were able to return home. In Bosnia, ethnic cleansing was partially reversed after three years by Western military aid, training, and air strikes, although the dead could not be brought back to life and hundreds of thousands have been unable to return to their homes. In Rwanda, an arms embargo against the genocidal government helped the rebels to defeat the government in just three months, but not before three-quarters of Rwanda's Tutsi were killed. In Kosovo, military intervention largely reversed ethnic cleansing and compelled the departure of Serb forces within about four months, but not until thousands of Albanians had been killed and hundreds of thousands traumatized by forced displacement. In the long run, the subordinate groups' expectation of intervention was fulfilled, but only after they paid a higher price than expected (except Kosovo, where the ultimate price may have been within initial expectations). Moreover, in all the cases but Rwanda, the subordinate group had to settle for an outcome short of its goal of full independence for its entire territory.

In most of the cases, it is doubtful that the subordinate-group leaders would have chosen to launch their challenges in the same way had they known Western intervention would be so belated and circumscribed as to significantly raise their costs and prevent attainment of their desired outcome. This appears to be the case at least for the leaders of the Iraqi Kurds, Bosnian Muslims, and Rwandan Tutsi. (By contrast, Kosovo's Albanian rebel leaders might have, from the start, viewed the prospect of approximately five thousand Albanian civilian deaths as an acceptable cost for restoration of the province's autonomy and long-term defense by NATO.) This raises the question of why learning appears to be uneven—in that subordinate groups apparently learn to expect intervention, but fail to learn that it will be belated and inadequate.

## Prescriptions

In light of the above theory and cases, three potential policy prescriptions can be considered.

*1. The West should avoid encouraging false hopes of intervention in cases where it will not actually intervene on a timely basis.*

While this prescription can be inferred from the theory, it has several problems. First, Western democratic governments cannot know in advance where they will intervene because the decision is subject to many political factors not under their control, including the nature and degree of press coverage. Second, "the West" is not a unitary actor likely to speak with a single voice. In 1991, most Western countries opposed recognition of unilateral declarations of independence by Yugoslavia's republics, but Germany and Italy favored recognizing Slovenia and Croatia, which was sufficient to encourage those republics to secede. Even individual Western democracies do not speak with a single voice. In 1995, the U.S. executive branch opposed formally lifting the UN arms embargo on the former Yugoslavia that hindered the military efforts of Bosnia's Muslims, but the U.S. Congress repeatedly threatened to do so, which sent a mixed signal about forthcoming assistance. Third, although there is little evidence, it is possible that raising false expectations of intervention may in some cases actually deter violence by dominant groups. Thus, this prescription is largely impracticable and potentially counterproductive. Still, policymakers should keep in mind the important, but rarely noted, lesson that well-intentioned rhetoric can backfire. In places where the West has no desire or intention to intervene effectively on a timely basis if a subordinate group provokes violence, Western diplomats should employ considerable effort to convey that message to the subordinate group.

*2. The West should avoid all interference in the domestic affairs of sovereign states.*

This was the traditional Westphalian rule intended to promote international order at the expense of universal conceptions of morality, but it has begun to be displaced by a norm that universal human rights take precedence over state sovereignty. The theory and cases above suggest that returning to the Westphalian norm would promote not only international order but domestic tranquility in states with ethnic communal-based power structures by removing false hopes of timely Western intervention. If the West had maintained such an explicit non-intervention policy during the 1990s, it is unlikely that the Iraqi Kurds, Bosnian Muslims, or Kosovo Albanians would have dared to launch military challenges against much stronger government forces, which led to retaliatory atrocities. In Rwanda, if the West had maintained support for the state in the early 1990s, the Hutu regime probably could have fended off the Tutsi rebels without feeling compelled to resort to genocide against Tutsi civilians. Ironically, the evolving norm of intervention to safeguard human rights has thus inadvertently fostered some massive atrocities. However, it is unrealistic that the West will return to a policy of Westphalian restraint. Moreover, such an overly broad policy would prevent the protection of innocents even in cases of unprovoked genocide such as the Nazi Holocaust. Finally, it is possible that Western human rights conditionality has promoted political liberalization and stability in some cases, especially where it has been applied prior to the outbreak of violence. Thus, this prescription in its purest form is neither practical nor necessarily advisable.

*3. The West should intervene with significant force on a timely basis in all cases of ethnic cleansing or genocide.*

This prescription has been advocated for years by human rights groups and was endorsed by President Clinton in the aftermath of intervention in Kosovo, leading some to dub it the "Clinton Doctrine."[58] In theory, such a policy would prevent atrocities initially by physical interdiction and subsequently by deterrence, when such intervention came to be expected. In practice, however, the concept has several problems. First, as demonstrated by the cases above, military intervention often will arrive too late or be too feeble to prevent atrocities. In Iraq, Bosnia, and Kosovo, hundreds of thousands were ethnically cleansed in a matter of weeks. In Rwanda, hundreds of thousands were killed in the first three weeks. Deploying a properly equipped intervention force to a remote conflict requires weeks or months, especially if it must be airlifted, which means such forces cannot get there in time to prevent violence in many cases.[59] Second, such conflicts are too common for the West to launch intervention in every case. For instance, some respected commentators have written that intervention should be considered in any civil conflict where the killing exceeds five times the U.S. murder rate.[60] However, during the 1990s alone, that standard would have included seventeen conflicts—Albania, Algeria, Angola, Azerbaijan (Nagorno-Karabakh), Bosnia, Cambodia, Congo Republic, Croatia, Ethiopia, Kosovo, Liberia, Rwanda, Sierra Leone, Somalia, Sudan, Tajikistan, and Zaire—an impossibly large agenda. Third, by the logic of the theory proposed in this chapter, such a doctrine inadvertently would encourage further armed uprisings by subordinate groups and thereby more retaliatory atrocities. Because intervention often will arrive after much of the damage is already done, the West's primary objective should be to prevent the initial outbreak of such violence. Unfortunately, this goal could be undermined by a standing rule of humanitarian intervention.

To summarize, none of the above prescriptions can or will be fully implemented by Western democracies. Politics in such societies makes it impossible for a government either to (1) know perfectly in advance where it will have sufficient public support to launch intervention, (2) remain silent about well-publicized foreign oppression, or (3) dedicate massive resources for repeated overseas interventions. Instead, Western states will continue to intervene on an ad hoc basis in cases where the costs and risks of doing so are outweighed by the national interest or by political pressures from allies, news media, domestic co-ethnics of foreign subordinate groups, and domestic political opponents.

Nevertheless, the declaratory policy of the West could have important consequences. The cases above indicate that Western threats of intervention appear able to encourage uprisings by subordinate groups but unable to deter violent retaliation by dominant groups. If that is actually the case, a declaratory policy of routine intervention would increase the number of uprisings and thus the amount of retaliatory ethnic cleansing and genocide in the world. A middle-ground policy of declaring in advance which cases are worthy of intervention would also tend to foster some uprisings and retaliatory violence. By contrast, a declared policy of nonintervention could discourage uprisings by weak subordinate groups and thereby—counterintuitively—reduce ethnic cleansing and genocide.

This does not mean the West must eschew all humanitarian military intervention. However, a declaratory policy of routine intervention such as the Clinton Doctrine is likely to be counterproductive, inadvertently spurring the very violence it is intended to stop. Even without such an explicit doctrine, the problem of moral hazard is unavoidable. Each time the West intervenes militarily on behalf of a subordinate group, it increases expectations of future such interventions, regardless of any declared policy, and thereby encourages further uprisings. To mitigate this problem, when the West does intervene, it should emphasize the unique aspects of the case that compelled action and declare that no precedent is being set.

Such a declaratory policy of restraint would be subject to several criticisms.[61] First, some would argue it could perpetuate oppression by dissuading subordinate groups from trying to overthrow discriminatory regimes. However, such uprisings rarely end oppression and often trigger retaliatory atrocities.

Even where Western assistance can enable a subordinate group to triumph, such as Kosovo, oppression may not be eliminated but merely reversed—which is no better from a moral or human rights perspective. By contrast, if violent uprisings can be avoided, history suggests that discrimination may ease over time as states become richer, especially if they adopt Western liberal values and institutions, as appears to be the general trend according to scholars such as Francis Fukuyama.[62] If so, a better policy to help oppressed groups would begin with efforts to keep them alive on their home territory by discouraging armed uprisings. In addition, economic and other incentives could be offered to dominant groups to encourage them to reduce discrimination and oppression sooner than might occur naturally.[63]

A second potential criticism is that a declared nonintervention policy would increase genocide and ethnic cleansing by eliminating a threat that deters some dominant-group leaders from launching such violence. However, the cases above and Fein's earlier studies indicate that dominant-group leaders generally do not launch such attacks in the absence of a direct threat to their authority. Moreover, once their authority is sufficiently challenged, dominant-group leaders apparently are not deterred from violent retaliation by the threat of intervention. A few exceptional cases exist, such as Nazi Germany, in which dominant-group leaders launched genocidal violence against a subordinate group without any apparent provocation. Such psychotic behavior would not be stopped by the proposed declaratory nonintervention policy. However, neither would it be deterred by a policy such as the Clinton Doctrine. Irrational mass killing is a rarity not explained by the proposed theory and should be treated differently. If the West intervenes in such cases, as many urge, Western officials should make clear they are doing so because the violence was unprovoked and was not, as is more typical, the by-product of a power struggle.

## FURTHER RESEARCH

The cases above were not selected scientifically and were intended only to demonstrate that the causal pathway of the proposed theory has operated in a variety of settings. Further process tracing should be carried out on the four cases to determine with higher confidence if the theory's causal mechanism was at work. In addition, further research is necessary to determine the robustness of the theory and under what conditions it operates. One useful research design would introduce variation on the dependent (or intervening) variable of armed uprising. Cases would be selected in which the West criticized dominant groups for their oppression, but only in some of which the subordinate group launched an uprising, to determine the other condition variables for such uprisings and to explore if Western condemnation ever induces dominant-group moderation that averts uprisings. Another research design could select cases where subordinate groups rose up, but in some of which the dominant group failed to launch massive retaliation, to determine if Western threats or other factors had any deterrent effect. A third research design could focus on cases of uprisings that triggered retaliation, but in which there was no threat or expectation of Western intervention, to explore other putative causal variables. Finally, a key finding of this study—that Western criticism and threats encourage subordinate groups to rise up but do not deter dominant groups from retaliating violently—requires further investigation. Additional process tracing should be employed to determine whether these two audiences really have systematically divergent perceptions of the credibility of such threats—and, if so, why—or whether they merely respond differently because of other factors, including domestic politics, risk proneness, tolerance for casualties, or differing time horizons.

## NOTES

An earlier version of this chapter was presented at the Annual Meeting of the American Political Science Association, Atlanta, GA, September 2, 1999. Preparation was assisted by financial support from the Institute for the Study of World Politics, the Brookings Institution, the Federation of American Scientists, the Harvard-MIT MacArthur Transnational Security program, the MIT Department of Political Science, the U.S. Institute of Peace, Harvard's Belfer Center for Science and International Affairs, and the University of Southern California's Center for International Studies.

1. See, for example, Carnegie Commission on Preventing Deadly Conflict, *Preventing Deadly Conflict: Final Report* (Washington, DC: Carnegie Corp. of New York, 1998).

2. The common misperception is probably the consequence of several factors: association of the word "genocide" with the Holocaust, which was an atypical case of genocide in that the violence was not a rational response to a threat; the cognitive tendency to think of a group that commits mass murder as the "cause" of that killing, which has been exacerbated by some media and historical accounts; and conflation by Western observers of "immoral" with "irrational" behavior.

3. Helen Fein, "Patrons, Prevention and Punishment of Genocide: Observations on Bosnia and Rwanda," in Helen Fein, ed., *The Prevention of Genocide: Rwanda and Yugoslavia Reconsidered* (New York: Institute for the Study of Genocide, 1994), p. 6.

4. Helen Fein, "Accounting for Genocide after 1945: Theories and Some Findings," *International Journal on Group Rights*, No. 1 (1993), pp. 79–106. She also identifies during this period one genocide each in Europe, Central America, and Latin America, which she excludes from her study because "one aim of the study was to later make comparisons between perpetrators of genocide and non-perpetrators by

region." Fein's preferred definition of genocide is "sustained purposeful action by a perpetrator [usually the state] to physically destroy a collectivity." She distinguishes it from "genocidal massacres" or "pogroms," which are briefer or more episodic, and from "mass political killings," a term she does not define clearly but which appears to refer to killings of civilians during civil wars.

5. Fein identifies the retributive cases as China/Tibet 1956–1960, Burundi 1972–1973, Indonesia/East Timor 1975, Uganda 1979–1986, USSR/Afghanistan 1980–1989, Ethiopia 1983–1984, and Iraq/Kurds 1987–1988; the preventive cases as Rwanda 1962–1963 and Pakistan/Bengalis 1971–1972; and the other cases as Indonesia/Communists/Chinese 1965–1966, Uganda 1971–1979, Kampuchea 1975–1979, and Iran/Bahai 1979–1988.

6. Stating that genocide is a "rational" choice in such situations does not preclude the availability of other non-genocidal options or make any claim to the morality of such a choice.

7. Thomas C. Schelling, *Arms and Influence* (New Haven, CT: Yale University Press, 1966).

8. Geoffrey Blainey, *The Causes of War, Third Edition* (New York: The Free Press, 1988). More generally, the German sociologist Georg Simmel argued a century ago that imperfect information was the root of most conflict: "The most effective prerequisite for preventing struggle [is] the exact knowledge of the comparative strength of the two parties." Quoted in Lewis A. Coser, *The Functions of Social Conflict* (Glencoe, IL: Free Press, 1956), p. 133.

9. Although this phenomenon has increased after the Cold War, it is not entirely a novelty of the current era. During the Cold War, the West similarly encouraged a failed uprising in Hungary in 1956.

10. This strategy of attempting to provoke Western intervention is not completely new. Among the nineteenth-century Balkans, it was known as the "fight option," according to Wallace Sagendorph ("Deconstructing Kosovo," unpublished manuscript). "During the Ottoman occupation, Serbs and other insurgent groups knew they could never defeat the Ottoman armies in open warfare . . . [but could] put up enough of a fight to arouse the sympathies of Europe's Great Powers, who, hopefully would then intercede on their behalf. This worked for the Serbs in their drive for independence, which culminated successfully in 1878." More than a century later, in 1991, Croatia used the same tactic to wrest independence from Yugoslavia, according to Yugoslavia's former ambassador to the European Community Mihailo Crnobrnja, *The Yugoslav Drama* (Montreal: McGill-Queen's University Press, 1994), p. 167: "The Croatian leadership was also fully aware that . . . they could not hope to achieve a clear victory on the ground. . . . So the best bet was to provoke the JNA [Yugoslav Army] into the type of action that would lead to international condemnation, thus securing sympathy and support for the Croatian cause."

11. This theory was formalized by John A. Dollard et al., *Frustration and Aggression* (New Haven, CT: Yale University Press, 1939). Initial tests were conducted by Ivo K. Feierabend and Rosalind L. Feierabend, "Aggressive Behaviors Within Polities, 1948–1962: A Cross-National Study," *Journal of Conflict Resolution*, Vol. 10 (September 1966), pp. 249–71.

12. The notion of irrational hatreds is a folk theory, often drawing on analogies to Nazi Germany and lent credence by the political rhetoric of Western leaders in their efforts to build support for intervention. Thus, in recent years, both Saddam Hussein and Slobodan Milosevic have been compared by Western officials to Hitler.

13. Escalatory outbidding is noted by, among others, Donald Horowitz, "Making Moderation Pay: The Comparative Politics of Ethnic Conflict Management," in Joseph V. Montville, *Conflict and Peacemaking in Multiethnic Societies* (New York: Lexington Books, 1991). He analyzes several cases that involved "significant intraethnic party competition, which has exacerbated interethnic tensions . . . as moderates were outbid by extremists." This is a timeless concept, as Thucydides also reported extremists who "carried the revolutionary spirit further and further . . . [by arguing that] prudent delay was the excuse of a coward; moderation was the disguise of unmanly weakness." Quoted in Crane Brinton, *The Anatomy of Revolution* (Englewood Cliffs, NJ: Prentice-Hall, 1938), excerpted in James Chowning Davies, *When Men Revolt and Why* (New York: The Free Press, 1971), p. 322.

14. The security dilemma is analyzed formally by Robert Jervis, "Cooperation Under the Security Dilemma," *World Politics*, Vol. 30, No. 2 (January 1978), who defines the situation as one in which both sides "are satisfied with the status quo" but cannot attain "goals that they recognize as being in their common interest." Barry R. Posen, "The Security Dilemma and Ethnic Conflict," *Survival*, Vol. 35, No. 1 (Spring 1993), attempts to use the term more broadly to explain the outbreak of conflict in situations where at least one side clearly is not satisfied with the status quo.

15. For a description of this recurrent pattern among the Kurds, including crackdowns by Saddam Hussein in 1975 and 1988, followed immediately by periods of peaceful relations, see Kamran Karadaghi, "The Two Gulf Wars: The Kurds on the World Stage, 1979–1992," in Gerard Chaliand, ed., *A People Without a Country: The Kurds and Kurdistan* (New York: Olive Branch Press, 1993).

16. Tony Horwitz, "Forgotten Rebels: After Heeding Calls to Turn on Saddam, Shiites Feel Betrayed —U.S. Played an Active Role in Encouraging a Revolt Despite Lack of Strategy—A Successful 'Psyop' Effort," *Wall Street Journal*, Dec. 31, 1991, p. 1, citing a February 15, 1991, statement by Bush.

17. President George Bush, press conference, March 1, 1991: "The Iraqi people should put Saddam aside."

18. Horwitz, "Forgotten Rebels."

19. The allied campaign was halted on February 28, 1991; the Shiite uprising began on March 1; the Kurd uprising began on March 5. Faleh Abd al-Jabbar, "Why the Uprisings Failed," *Middle East Report*, Vol. 22, No. 3 (May/June 1992), p. 8.

20. Michael M. Gunter, *The Kurds in Iraq* (New York: St. Martin's Press, 1992), p. 53.

21. Shiite Muslims represent 80 percent of the ranks of the Iraqi army but only 20 percent of its officer corps. Top positions are dominated by close allies of Saddam Hussein, many from his Tikriti clan. Abd al-Jabbar, "Why the Uprisings Failed," pp. 5–6.

22. Gunter, *The Kurds*, p. 56, cites several other reasons for the Administration's refusal to intervene: the danger of becoming enmeshed in a protracted Iraqi civil war;

Turkish opposition to an Iraqi Kurd mini-state, which could be a model and a rear base for Turkey's own Kurdish rebels; and the danger of such a mini-state becoming a disgruntled zone of stateless refugees like Israel's Gaza strip. This was not the first time—nor the last, as a subsequent 1996 CIA fiasco demonstrated—that the United States would give false hope to Iraq's Kurds only to abandon them to Saddam's mercy. See Jim Hoagland, "How CIA's Secret War on Saddam Collapsed," *Washington Post*, June 26, 1997.

23. John Newhouse, "The Diplomatic Round: Dodging the Problem," *New Yorker*, August 24, 1992, reports that "Bosnia's leaders pleaded with Western capitals to withhold recognition of Slovenia and Croatia, fearing that if it was granted Serbs and Croats would instantly fall upon Bosnia" and divide it between them. Izetbegovic believed Bosnia's prospects would be improved if a comprehensive settlement were negotiated for all the republics, so he opposed recognition for any of the republics as late as a November 1991 trip to Bonn.

24. Crnobrnja, *The Yugoslav Drama*, p. 176.

25. An initial version of Cutileiro's plan was adopted by the three sides in Lisbon on February 23, 1992, but soon was rejected by the Muslims. A revised version was adopted in Sarajevo on March 18. The plan included a de facto ethnic veto in that important decisions required a four-fifths majority of the Bosnian Chamber of Constituent Units. The revised version was rejected by the Muslims on March 25 and by the Croats on March 24. Saadia Touval, "Tangled Peacemaking: Mediation in the Yugoslav Wars, 1990–1995," draft manuscript, April 1999, p. 7–9, claims the Croats backed away from the revised version because the Muslims did, although this does not jibe with the timing of their final decisions. James Gow, *Triumph of the Lack of Will* (New York: Columbia University Press, 1997), p. 81–87, says the Bosnian Croats pulled out because the plan would have left most Croats living in areas controlled by the other two sides. Gow harshly criticizes the Cutileiro plan as tantamount to the appeasement of Hitler at the Munich conference, where Nazi Germany was given part of Czechoslovakia. "The EC and its ambassadors were urging Izetbegovic in what was essentially an exercise in appeasement." Gow says the plan's reliance on "the principle of ethnically determined territorial units" was a "cardinal mistake," because it encouraged ethnic cleansing. The reality, however, is that large-scale ethnic cleansing occurred only after the plan was rejected by the Muslims.

26. David Binder, "U.S. Policymakers on Bosnia Admit Errors in Opposing Partition in 1992," *New York Times*, August 29, 1993, first reported Zimmermann's account of his conversation with Izetbegovic: "He said he didn't like it. . . . I told him, if he didn't like it, why sign it?" Binder also quoted Zimmermann conceding, in retrospect, that "the Lisbon agreement wasn't bad at all." This article prompted Zimmermann, "Bosnian About-Face," *New York Times*, September 30, 1993, to deny ever encouraging Izetbegovic's reneging and to claim instead that he actually "encouraged him to stick by his commitment." However, Binder quotes an unnamed U.S. State Department official confirming explicitly that the Bush Administration "policy was to encourage Izetbegovic to break with the partition plan. . . . We let it be known we would support his government in the United Nations if they got into trouble." The department's desk officer at the time, Richard Johnson, also confirms that Secretary of

State James Baker "told the Europeans to stop pushing ethnic cantonization of Bosnia . . . [and] to move forward on recognition." Zimmermann later conceded that U.S. policy was based on the hope that "internationalizing the problem . . . would deter Milosevic. Unfortunately it didn't. We were wrong on this." See "Interview with Noah Adams," *National Public Radio*, March 18, 1994. Jose Cutileiro also confirms that "President Izetbegovic and his aides were encouraged to scupper that deal and to fight for a unitary Bosnian state by well-meaning outsiders who thought they knew better." As a result, "the Muslims reneged on the agreement. Had they not done so, the Bosnian question might have been settled earlier, with less loss of (mainly Muslim) life and land." See "Letters," *Economist*, December 9, 1995. Zimmermann claims that the Serbs would have attacked even had the West not recognized Bosnia, but he offers no explanation for why they did not launch a major attack until recognition. See also Gow, *Triumph*, p. 88. See also, Warren Zimmermann, *Origins of a Catastrophe* (New York, Times Books, 1996), pp. 188–92. Izetbegovic is more honest, acknowledging in retrospect that "we could not have escaped this [violent fate] when we decided for independence. We could have possibly avoided it if we remained in Yugoslavia." Quoted in Lenard J. Cohen, *Broken Bonds: Yugoslavia's Disintegration and Balkan Politics in Transition*, 2d ed. (Boulder, CO: Westview Press, 1995), p. 244.

27. In retrospect, the head of the panel, Robert Badinter, concedes that recognition of Bosnia "was a mistake and it was immediately understood." Quoted in Robert M. Hayden, "Reply," *Slavic Review*, Vol. 55, No. 4 (Winter 1996), p. 768.

28. Prior to the war, because Serbs lived in rural areas, they had predominated in about 55 percent of Bosnian territory even though they represented only about one-third of the population. Crnobrnja, *The Yugoslav Drama*, p. 176.

29. Dixon Kamukama, *Rwanda Conflict: Its Roots and Regional Implications* (Kampala, Uganda: Fountain Publishers, 1993).

30. Belgium and Zaire also sent troops to Rwanda in 1990 in response to the initial RPF invasion. However, the Zairian troops were asked to leave within weeks because they were accused of pillaging. The Belgian troops merely guarded the airport for a short period of time. Unlike the French, neither Zaire nor Belgium again deployed troops to Rwanda during its civil war until Belgian peacekeepers arrived to help implement the Arusha peace accords in late 1993.

31. Alan J. Kuperman, "The Other Lesson of Rwanda: Mediators Sometimes Do More Damage Than Good," *SAIS Review*, Vol. 16, No. 1 (Winter/Spring 1996).

32. This perspective is explained by Jean-Bosco Barayagwiza, *Rwanda: Le Sang Hutu Est-Il Rouge?* (Yaounde, Cameroon, 1995).

33. Cited in *Rwanda: Lettre ouverte aux parlementaires, Le texte du rapport du groupe "Rwanda" du Senat* (Brussels: Editions Luc Pire, 1997), p. 85.

34. Marvine Howe, "Exodus of Serbians Stirs Province in Yugoslavia," *New York Times*, July 12, 1982. David Binder, "In Yugoslavia, Rising Ethnic Strife Brings Fears of Worse Civil Conflict," *New York Times*, November 1, 1987.

35. Tim Judah, "Inside the KLA," *New York Review of Books*, June 10, 1999.

36. Chris Hedges traces the KLA's first attack to May 1993, but the rebels did not emerge as a significant threat until 1997. Four possible causes for this escalation have

been identified. First, during Albania's 1997 civil war, armories in that country were looted, liberating tens of thousands of small arms for the Kosovo rebels. Second, the 1995 Dayton accords, which resolved the Bosnian civil war, were silent on Kosovo, leading Kosovo's secessionists to grow increasingly frustrated with Rugova's pleas for patience. Third, peace in Bosnia also made available thousands of Albanian fighters, who had gone to Bosnia to fight alongside that republic's Muslims, to fight in Kosovo. Fourth, the NATO air campaign against Bosnian Serb forces in summer 1995 suggested that if the situation in Kosovo were militarized, the West would side against the Serbs. See Stacy Sullivan, "From Brooklyn to Kosovo," *New York Times Magazine*, November 22, 1998, pp. 50–56. Chris Hedges, "Kosovo's Next Masters?" *Foreign Affairs*, Vol. 78, No. 3 (May/June 1999), pp. 24–42. KLA officials reveal that the first and fourth causes were decisive. The sudden availability of arms enabled them to implement a strategy that was premised on attracting the international intervention necessary to defeat the Serbs. KLA officials, interviews with author, Pristina, Kosovo, August 2000.

37. R. Jeffrey Smith, "Yugoslavia Will 'Pay a Price,' Albright Warns," *Washington Post*, March 8, 1998.

38. By March 1998, this phenomenon was noted by Richard Huckaby, director of the U.S. Information Agency office in Kosovo: "One of our main struggles is to convince them that we really don't support independence. . . . They just don't get it." R. Jeffrey Smith, "U.S. Envoy Warns Serbs, Kosovo Rebels; U.S. Urges Restraint on Both Sides of Strife," *Washington Post*, March 11, 1998, p. 21. By July 1998, a Western diplomat noted that successful Western efforts to compel Serb restraint had backfired: "Instead of calming things down and letting us figure out how to get everyone to the negotiation table, what we've done is give the Albanian fighters a feeling of euphoria. . . . This makes them bolder, and it also makes other Albanians want to join them." Mike O'Connor, "Rebels Claim First Capture of a City in Kosovo," *New York Times*, July 20, 1998, p. 3. In January 1999, another press report noted that "the guerrillas held onto the idealistic hope that America would inevitably support them because their struggle for independence was right and good." An American official confirmed: "They think we support their goals." See Michael Ignatieff, "The Dream of Albanians," *New Yorker*, January 11, 1999. See also Gary T. Dempsey, "Washington's Kosovo Policy," CATO Institute, Washington, DC, October 8, 1998.

39. Charles Trueheart, "Kosovo Accord Proves Elusive," *Washington Post*, February 22, 1998. For a critique of this strategy, see Alan J. Kuperman, "Rambouillet Requiem: Why the Talks Failed," *Wall Street Journal*, March 4, 1999.

40. Eight hundred and fifty thousand Albanians were made refugees out of a population of less than two million, according to Tim Judah, *Kosovo: War and Revenge* (New Haven, CT: Yale University Press, 2000), p. 241. As for deaths, by 2001, approximately four thousand bodies had been found, and a Hague prosecutor said the confirmed count might go as high as five thousand as mass grave sites were uncovered in Kosovo and elsewhere in Serbia. See Joanne Mariner, "Kosovo's Unquiet Dead," *CNN Findlaw Forum*, June 20, 2001, www.cnn.com/2001/LAW/06/columns/fl.mariner.kosovo.06.20/ [downloaded November 11, 2001]; Gregory Piatt, "Kosovo Death Toll Climbs as KFOR Finds More Graves," *Stars and Stripes*, August 27, 2000.

41. The deal Milosevic signed was less demanding than Rambouillet in that it reaffirmed Yugoslavia's sovereignty over the province, contained no requirement for an independence referendum, confined NATO troops to Kosovo, and provided for UN authorization of the occupation. The agreement was stricter than Rambouillet in demanding that all Serb forces initially depart the province—which was necessary to facilitate the return of Albanian refugees who had been driven from the province during the bombing—and in permitting fewer Serb forces to remain in the long run. On this question, see a published interchange between the author and the Assistant Secretary of State. Alan J. Kuperman, "Botched Diplomacy Led to War," *Wall Street Journal*, June 17, 1999; James P. Rubin, "Milosevic Sabotaged U.S. Diplomacy," *Wall Street Journal*, July 6, 1999; Alan J. Kuperman, "Albright Painted Milosevic into a Corner," *Wall Street Journal*, July 14, 1999.

42. James A. Baker, III, *The Politics of Diplomacy* (New York: G. P. Putnam's Sons, 1995), pp. 479–82. The former Secretary of State reports this was the message he took to all of Yugoslavia's leaders in June 1991, four days prior to Slovenia and Croatia seceding. Baker says this message was intended to deter the republic leaders from seceding, as well as to deter Milosevic from using force to hold Yugoslavia together. He also warned Yugoslav President Markovic "about any use of force to preserve the federation" and told him, "if you force us to choose between unity and democracy, we will always choose democracy." The leaders of the disgruntled republics understood this and aimed to set up such a choice.

43. Judah, *Kosovo: War and Revenge*, pp. 73–74, 150.

44. Horwitz, "Forgotten Rebels."

45. Crnobrnja, *The Yugoslav Drama*, p. 177, asserts: "The Muslims, led by Alija Izetbegovic . . . decided to use all means to have the international community put pressure on the Serbs and the JNA and, if need be, to fight them."

46. The first UN deputy commander, Canadian General Lewis MacKenzie, became angry at Muslim leaders after the outbreak of war because they repeatedly broke cease-fires "in the hope of provoking a US intervention," according to Gow, *Triumph*, p. 96. A subsequent UN commander, British General Sir Michael Rose, *Fighting for Peace: Bosnia 1994* (London: Harvill Press, 1998), p. 141, reports that Muslim forces continued this strategy through 1994 based on the logic that "if the Bosnian Army attacked and lost, the resulting images of war and suffering guaranteed support in the West for the 'victim State.'" Crnobrnja, *The Yugoslav Drama*, p. 180, concurs that Bosnia's "Muslims and Croats engaged the JNA even when they were outgunned and out-numbered, in the hope of involving the international community on their side."

47. Kuperman, "The Other Lesson."

48. Senior KLA officials, interviews with author, Pristina, Kosovo, August 2000. Also see Diane Johnstone, "Hawks and Eagles: 'Greater NATO' Flies to the Aid of 'Greater Albania,'" *Covert Action Quarterly*, No. 67 (Spring/Summer 1999), who reports that in 1998 the Kosovo Albanians' "intransigence was largely the result of their certitude that they ultimately commanded full United States and NATO support."

49. Dugi Gorani, quoted in Allan Little, "Moral Combat: NATO at War," *BBC2 Television*, March 12, 2000.

50. Rugova stated clearly in 1992: "we would have no chance of successfully resisting the army." Cited in Judah, "Inside the KLA." This judgment had not changed by mid-1998, when a senior advisor to Rugova stated: "NATO is the only force that can bring democracy and independence to Kosovo . . . [but that] depends on how we look on CNN." Cited in Gary Dempsey, "Another Blunder in Kosovo Policy?" *Washington Times*, July 9, 1998. The KLA rebels also repeatedly urged NATO intervention to avert their defeat.

51. Gunter, *The Kurds*, pp. 49–50, quoting Izzat Ibrahim, deputy chairman of the ruling Revolutionary Command Council of the Ba'ath party, as cited in *International Herald Tribune*, January 25, 1991.

52. Binder, "U.S. Policymakers on Bosnia."

53. RPF officials, interviews with author, Kigali, April 1999. Rather than reducing their demands, the RPF tried unsuccessfully to arm and train Rwandan Tutsi to defend themselves before the killing began.

54. Abd al-Jabbar, "Why the Uprisings Failed," pp. 8–11, claims the uprisings were a spontaneous reaction by defeated Iraqi soldiers returning from the Kuwaiti theater, and that opposition leaders claimed credit only after the uprisings initially appeared to succeed. (After the uprisings were crushed, the opposition leaders disavowed responsibility and claimed they had been spontaneous.) However, Gunter, *The Kurds*, p. 50, notes that Kurdish leaders had imported extra rebels prior to the uprisings, which suggests they were planned in advance.

55. RPF officials, interviews with author, Kigali, April 1999.

56. Interestingly, Kurd leader Jalal Talabani stated in November 1990 that his forces would not rise up without strong assurances of Western support. "We have been deceived many times by foreigners. We are determined not to make the same mistakes again." Gunter, *The Kurds*, p. 49.

57. As a Kosovo Albanian was quoted in June 1998: "We hope that NATO will intervene, like it did in Bosnia, to save us." Chris Hedges, "Both Sides in the Kosovo Conflict Seem Determined to Ignore Reality," *New York Times*, June 22, 1998, p. 1.

58. Michael Kelly, "A Perfectly Clintonian Doctrine," *Washington Post*, June 30, 1999. This doctrine was elucidated by the President in Macedonia on June 22, 1999: "Whether you live in Africa or Central Europe or any other place, if somebody comes after innocent civilians and tries to kill them en masse because of their race, their ethnic background or their religion and it is within our power to stop it, we will stop it." See also, Jim Hoagland, "Kosovos to Come," *Washington Post*, June 27, 1999.

59. See Alan J. Kuperman, *The Limits of Humanitarian Intervention: Genocide in Rwanda* (Washington, DC: Brookings Institution Press, 2001).

60. Michael O'Hanlon and Stephen Solarz, "Deciding When to Go," *Washington Post*, Outlook section, February 7, 1999, p. B–1. The authors claim that only eight conflicts exceeded this threshold from 1992–1999. However, during the 1990s, at least the seventeen cases that I identify in the text arguably surpassed this threshold, based on death estimates from the Stockholm International Peace Research Institute (SIPRI) and other organizations. Even O'Hanlon and Solarz do not advocate automatic intervention when this threshold is surpassed, saying that other considerations should include whether intervention would work and whether it would risk provoking war with

another major power. Solarz is a former subcommittee chairman on the House Foreign Affairs Committee. They have made this argument in greater detail elsewhere, including Stephen J. Solarz and Michael O'Hanlon, "Humanitarian Intervention: When is Force Justified?" *Washington Quarterly*, Vol. 20, No. 4 (1997), pp. 3–14.

61. See several opinion pieces by this author and the responses they aroused. Alan J. Kuperman, "False Hope Abroad: Promises to Intervene Often Bring Bloodshed," *Washington Post*, June 14, 1998, "Kosovo Option: Conditional Surrender," *Washington Post*, September 25, 1998, and "Support of Rebels Was a Mistake," *Los Angeles Times*, April 11, 1999.

62. Francis Fukuyama, "The End of History," *National Interest*, No. 17 (Summer 1989).

63. Steven R. Ratner, "Quietly Preventing Conflict," *Christian Science Monitor*, August 18, 1999, argues that such positive incentives have helped avert ethnic conflict in the former Soviet Union and Eastern Europe.

# 4

## Religion and War: Fault Lines in the Balkan Enigma

*P. H. Liotta*

> Listen, then, to what you do not know. The three rivers of the ancient world of the dead—the Acheron, the Phlegethon, and the Cocytus—today belong to the underworlds of Islam, Judaism, and Christianity; their flow divides the three hells—Gehenna, Hades, and the icy hell of the Mohammedans—beneath the one-time Khazar lands. And there, at the junction of these three borders, are confronted the three worlds of the dead: Satan's fiery state, with the nine circles of the Christian Hades, with Lucifer's throne . . . the Moslem underworld . . . kingdom of icy torment; and Geburah's territory to the left of the Temple, where the Hebrew gods of evil, greed, and hunger sit in Gehenna. . . . In the Jewish hell, in the state of Belial, the angel of darkness and sin, it is not Jews who burn, as you think. Those like yourself, all Arabs or Christians, burn there. Similarly, there are no Christians in the Christian hell—those who reach the fires are Mohammedans or of David's faith, whereas in Iblis' Moslem torture chamber they are all Christians and Jews, not a single Turk or Arab.[1]

In 1995 a series of videotapes were submitted as evidence to the International Tribunal on War Crimes in the Former Yugoslavia, The Hague, which included interviews and "battle" footage from a number of Serbian paramilitary organizations operating in the ethnically Serb-dominated Krajina region of Croatia or in support of Bosnian Serbs in Bosnia-Herzegovina. Most notorious among these paramilitary groups were "The Tigers" of Zeljko Raznatovic—more popularly known as Arkan—whose militia began the "ethnic cleansing" of the Bijeljina region of eastern Bosnia in 1992.

Although the tribunal did not "unseal" its indictment against Arkan until 1999, some noteworthy symbolism appeared in the video footage submitted four years earlier. The expected symbols of Serbian unity (which came to be a marker of death in Bosnia), of course, appear in the opening credits: the four Cyrillic S's, the abbreviation for the Serbian slogan "Only Unity Saves the Serbs." Literally, this Serbian expression means that only harmony will liberate the Serbs, an especially crucial distinction. One could argue that the mistranslation of this saying, which emphasized ethnic unity over interethnic harmony, actually destroyed the Serbs. Of at least equal significance, however, was that the opening sequences of these videos, inflamed with Serbian nationalism, took place not on a battlefield but in a Serbian Orthodox church.

The video opens with a voiceover in the reverent intonations of a Serbian renaissance hymn during a ritual ceremony in which an Orthodox priest blesses Arkan's Tigers. In effect, this image potently symbolizes Serbs as holy warriors, embraces Serbian resistance to centuries of Ottoman occupation, and emphasizes how Serbs had turned on their fellow South ("Yugo") Slavs in permanently destroying the Yugoslav ideal and the Yugoslav nation-state.

Against this intimate linking of Serbian violence performed in the name of orthodoxy stands an equally powerful series of Catholic images. A decade ago, while studying Serbo-Croatian under a Fulbright fellowship at the East European Language Institute in Pittsburgh, I learned of a Croatian Catholic church named St. Mary's that held a unique series of frescoes and murals. Receiving the pastor's permission to visit, I discovered an edifice that more closely resembled an Orthodox basilica than a more traditional "Western" church.

On the far wall of the church there is a massive mosaic of Mary, Queen of Peace, cradling the Christ child—work of both skillful precision and serene grace. But in the entranceway and along the outer walls that line the pews there exists a series of images no less powerful and far more disturbing: one mural depicts scenes from the Austro-Hungarian front of World War I. Amidst the trenches of mass slaughter and gas warfare, Christ hangs crucified; beneath, dressed in a World War I uniform and resembling nothing so much as a U.S. doughboy of the period, a Serb infantryman (as ersatz Roman legionnaire of the New Testament) taunts Christ on the cross, probing his wounds with the tip of a bayonet affixed to a rifle. In the far distance, Serb soldiers swarm down from the hills, and, in the foreground, inexplicably, the Virgin Mary, wearing a gas mask, is framed in an extraordinary Pietà: she holds the crucified Christ in her arms, as an unseen Serb stands looming behind with a raised axe ready to execute her.

Against the clear Balkan enmity between Serb and Croatian, an apparent East-West tension marked by religious difference, there exists a third religious element. In 1970, in the Yugoslav Republic of Bosnia-Herzegovina, Alija Izetbegovic, a devout Muslim, was imprisoned by the Communist regime for his Islamic activism and, partly, for his book *The Islamic Declaration: A*

*Programme for the Islamisation of Muslims and the Muslim Peoples*, which argued for "the incompatibility of Islam with non-Islamic systems. There can neither be peace nor coexistence between the Islamic religion and non-Islamic social and political institutions."[2] Izetbegovic advocated that an Islamic movement within a state should consolidate power and create a purely Islamic republic when the opportunity becomes present; almost a decade later, he expressed praise for Ayatollah Khomeini during the overthrow of the Shah by revolution and in the creation of the Islamic Republic of Iran.

Izetbegovic argued that education, media, government authority—in effect, an Islamicized version of the Yugoslav Communist model of "Social Management"—should be in the hands of people whose Islamic moral and intellectual authority is indisputable.[3] Following the February 29, 1992, referendum (which Bosnian Serbs boycotted), Izetbegovic, as leader of the Muslim Party of Democratic Action (SDA), became the first president of the independent and internationally recognized nation of Bosnia-Herzegovina a year later; in 1996, he received a majority of votes and became the first to preside over a three-man presidency of the joint Bošniak-Croat Federation and the Republika Srpska within the parastate today known as Bosnia.

Throughout 1998, Bosnia received training and military supplies from the United States. President Clinton equally expressed concern about Bosnia's "stability," stating obliquely that "things we knew from the beginning would be difficult have been difficult."[4] Although Izetbegovic promoted a multiethnic state in public declarations, any variety of sources confirm that positions of authority within the Bosnian administration and armed forces became largely Muslim, as indeed similar positions within the nominally "Yugoslav" army (*Vojska Jugoslovenska*) became almost exclusively Serb. Notably, Izetbegovic never publicly repudiated his *Islamic Declaration.*

Yugoslavia, as a nation of roughly twenty-three million in its final days (including eight and a half million Serbs), directly affected the course of European and world history in the twentieth century with its agonizing process of self-destruction. The elements that comprise the "Balkan Enigma" cannot divorce the significance of religion from the culture in which it lives, just as culture cannot be divorced from politics. As one seasoned observer has correctly noted, "Without an understanding of the culture and religion one can never understand the politics."[5] Religion was a social component of the forces that helped dismember the Yugoslav "Experiment" (as it was known in the Cold War years with an odd fondness). In retrospect, it seems *one* of various ecological factors considered in this study (rather than an exclusive cause) that helps explain the disintegration of Yugoslavia.

Religious difference, nevertheless, was a contributing influence in recent Balkan conflict. Deep cultural rifts, marred by history and violence and never reconciled on terms with which all sides could find peace, seem to mark the perfect illustration of the "dynamics" that create, in Huntington's terms, "fault line wars"—wars that are the inevitable consequence when cultures, if not civilizations, collide.[6] Indeed, Misha Glenny has argued that the wars of the last days of Yugoslavia "increasingly assimilated the characteristics of religious struggle, defined by three great European faiths—Roman Catholicism, Eastern Orthodoxy and Islam, the confessional detritus of the empires whose frontiers collided in Bosnia."[7] On the surface, of course, such an analysis seems reasonable, just as Huntington's "Clash of Civilizations" paradigm—which claims that in the post–Cold War era the "fundamental source of conflict . . . will be cultural"—seems largely true in application, even as its implications appear inherently racist. Such an assertion of religious and cultural "holy war" fails, nonetheless, by numerous exceptions to the paradigm. As such, the arguments against Huntington have often been used to justify circumstances when conflict either does *not* occur or to provide examples when cultures within civilizations have been able to solve differences other than through violent means to reconcilable ends.

Huntington, unsurprisingly, received an immense amount of criticism. According to the editors of *Foreign Affairs*, in which "The Clash of Civilizations?" originally appeared in 1993, the journal received more letters in response to the essay than had occurred in the previous three decades. In 1996, the Council on Foreign Relations published *The Clash of Civilizations: The Debate*, which contained the criticisms and counterarguments of a number of scholars. The scholar Kishore Mahbubani, whose essay titled "The West and the Rest" sparked the first post–Cold War "civilizational" debate, is included in this collection of largely negative positions regarding Huntington's thesis.[8]

Perhaps the most outspoken of Huntington's critics is Edward Said. Said, whose academic discipline is comparative literature, is most widely known as the author of *Orientalism*, the title of which defines an embedded and condescending "Western" attitude that, Said argues, has been consistent both in racist media and in foreign policy.[9] Regarding the civilization paradigm, Said quickly dismisses Huntington as "a crisis manager, rather than student of culture or reconciler" who boils down cultural complexity to a formulaic response that "foreign policy elites and Pentagon planners will understand easily."[10]

The weakness of Said's argument, however, lies in how the criticism of Huntington tends to focus almost exclusively on a pivot of "Western" versus "Islamic" (and in Said's response, largely Arabic) difference and tends to ignore the broad canvassing of issues and ideas that Huntington presented in his 1996 book, *The Clash of Civilizations and the Remaking of World Order*. Further, Said's criticisms appear to be targeted not so much against Huntington as against the work of fellow Middle and Near Eastern scholar Bernard

Lewis. Lewis, who first proposed the term "clash of civilizations" in his essay in the *Atlantic Monthly* titled "The Roots of Muslim Rage," nonetheless, treats Islam with respect and not condescension.[11] To his argument's overall detriment, Said tends to delve into both ad hominem insult *and* substantive critique.[12]

The strength of Said's critique justifies how the battle is not between civilizations, but inside them. Yet what happened in former Yugoslavia confirms Said's assertion: a pertinent example of both intrastate as well as intracivilizational conflict rather than interstate conflict (the more historically recognizable contest of war between states). Yugoslavia, as the most pertinent and violent example of a state's disintegration in the wake of the Cold War, died a gradual, methodical, and ineluctable death. As various ecological factors (in particular, shrinking economic power) influenced the decline of the state, religion, as particular cultural component, played an increasingly dynamic part in setting the stage for conflict.

Yugoslavia represented an extraordinary tapestry of national differences among nationalities. Among the South Slavs themselves, those who trace their origins to the mythic "Wandering of the Peoples" in the Dark Ages and who came to settle in the region, there emerged cultural differences so acute that it seems, in retrospect, only acts of violence against each other could be the natural result. Nowhere is that difference more culturally marked than in religion. Religion provided an occasion, but was not the cause, for the death of Yugoslavia. A brief examination of religious elements within the former Yugoslavia that still exist today would prove helpful to correct analysis, one that considers economic potential, politics, history, social identity, and religion as inextricably linked.

## CATHOLICISM

> I know of Saint George's church. We shall break the door of the Holy Church. We shall burn fire in it, So that God will send us luck.
>
> —Croation Epic of the Uskoks of Senj, sixteenth century

The epigraph above illustrates how too much attention to religious difference alone in the Balkans fails to distinguish the often misunderstood "practicality of the usually practical South Slavs."[13] In this particular example, a war party of Uskoks, faced with freezing to death from exposure to a winter storm or breaking into a Catholic church and essentially defiling it, choose the practical solution. Their faith in their Church, associated with a national spirit, and their own sense of reverence, even as they sin, do not prevent them from taking action. Yet in more recent times, the manipulation of Catholicism and its identity with, variously, a Yugoslav identity or Croatian nationalism has been the rule of practice.

In 1991, in the last days of the Yugoslav republics, sociological studies suggest there were approximately 3 million *practicing* Catholics, 1.5 million *practicing* Muslims, and 1.2 million *practicing* Serbian Orthodox (in contrast to various religious officials in the country who claimed 7.3 million Catholics, 3.8 million Muslims, and 10 million Orthodox).[14] Marshal Tito recognized these figures as representing significant forces within Yugoslavia; under his regime and in the decade following his death, various experiments were made to manipulate religion as a cultural component of revolutionary identity, as part of a central national identity, or a target of control within the various stages of federalist experiment. Finally, in the last years of the Socialist Federal Republics of Yugoslavia, and within the confederalist idea that spelled doom for the nation itself, the state itself was undone partially by religious identities that aligned with nationalist claims—Catholicism within Slovenia and Croatia; Orthodoxy within Serbia, Montenegro, and throughout Macedonia; Islam within Bosnia-Herzegovina, Western Macedonia, and the Kosovo province of Serbia.

Various attempts by the Yugoslav Communist governments to build a coherent socialist structure recognized that seemingly irreconcilable cultural differences could not be erased simply by the stroke of a revolutionary pen—or sword, for that matter. In a similar vein of manipulation, one fueled by nationalism, newly elected Croatian president Franjo Tudjman in 1990 quickly identified the Catholic Church as both a force that had resisted Communist oppression and had nurtured Croatian national consciousness.[15]

The cultural tensions that marked Catholicism in the former Yugoslavia can best be identified generally by two figures and one event: Bishop Juri Josaj Strossmayer (1815–1905), who predated the ideal type of Yugoslavia by promoting the cultural unity of the South Slavs—the Slovenes, Serbs, Croats, Montenegrins, and "Bulgarians" (all of whom Strossmayer referred to as "Illyrians"); the controversial Cardinal Alojzije Stepinac (1898–1960), symbol of Croatian nationalism and spirited defiance; and finally, the significance of the Vatican II Council (1962–1965), in which the "Catholic Church rejects nothing of what is true and holy in [other religions] . . . and urges her sons to enter with prudence and charity into discussion and collaboration with members of other religions."

It would seem that the Vatican would have held Bishop Strossmayer in highest regard for his progressive social programs, his charitable acts, and his refusal to take any hand in the movement to persecute the Orthodox Church, which set the Croat against the Serb.[16] In reality, it was Cardinal Stepinac who came to be seen as a guardian of the "Church of the poor" of Vatican II.[17] Pope John Paul II, whose own cultural heritage springs from Poland in the years before World War II (where he was known prior to his ordination as a priest as Karol Wojtyla) and in the Cold War itself, was all too aware of the oppressions in Central and Eastern Europe that characterized the twentieth century's last half. As such, Cardinal Stepinac, for Pope John Paul, came to symbolize the essential responsibility of the religious leader to resist Communist oppression.

Further, Stepinac was imprisoned by the Tito regime for his refusal to break ties with Rome after World War II. If he had "modified" his position on breaking from Rome and advocated the creation of "a Croatian Church, separate from Rome," in the words of once prominent Tito establishment politician (and eventual imprisoned dissident himself) Milovan Djilas, he would have been "raised to the clouds!"[18] Stepinac refused such compromise and became a political martyr. His noble act, nonetheless, tends to obscure his own involvement with, and at least partial support in World War II for, the quisling Croatian regime of *Ustashe* (literally, "Insurrectionists") leader Ante Pavelic. Pavelic was a devout Catholic and a demon at the same time. Some might best remember him for his alleged regular "tribute" made to Nazi leaders in St. Mark's Square during the years of occupation: a basketful of human eyes taken from Croatian *Ustashe* death camps.

Stepinac, as both symbol and individual, represented (and represents) for Serbs and other former Yugoslavs Nazi collaboration flagged under a Croatian mantle of support for the brutal *Ustashe* Fascist regime, which claimed the lives of hundreds of thousands of Serbs, Jews, Croatians, and Gypsies at the Jasenovac concentration camp in World War II. For Croatians and other former Yugoslavs, Stepinac is a hero, the symbol of resistance both to Nazi oppression and *Ustashe* brutality. He is no less controversial a figure today, regarded—depending on your cultural point of view—as either a "beloved saint" or "a murderer." In what may be an apocryphal description, a former representative of the Belgrade Communist regime claimed that, in World War II, priests under Stepinac's direction "officiated at mass conversions of Orthodox Serbs minutes before their execution by Croatian *Ustashe*, just so they could go to heaven."[19]

Thus, Stepinac's ghost serves as a fundamental symbol of the cultural tensions that drove Serbia and Croatia into conflict, what would appear now to have been an inevitable struggle in which, as Robert Kaplan frames it, "the battle between Communism and capitalism [was] merely one dimension of a struggle that pits Catholicism against Orthodoxy, Rome against Constantinople, the legacy of the Habsburg Austria-Hungary against that of Ottoman Turkey—in other words, West against East, the ultimate cultural conflict."[20]

As a consequence of that same cultural tension, Pope John Paul II emphasized Stepinac's eventual noble resistance to an oppressive regime and overlooked the human frailties that confront anyone who lives and has influence during times of immense historical significance. This oversight also forced the Vatican, for some, to become immersed at the very heart "of a Croatian nationalism that saw itself as culturally superior to Serbs—the very nationalist tradition that had inspired Stepinac's original desire to see the Serbs converted to Catholicism."[21] For some then, the Vatican's "complicity" was an active dynamic in the clash between cultures: "the Vatican became a partisan in the conflict [declaring] Croatia 'a rampart of [Western] Christianity.'"[22] In practice, the Vatican diplomatically recognized Slovenia and Croatia before the European Union, thus hardening the perception that religious identity was a crucial marker for cultural distinction.[23]

One could argue, of course, that the Pope acted exclusively in the interest of his religious flock rather than simply to defend Croatian or Slovenian nationalism. At the same time, he was not singularly guilty of defending Croatia and accusing Serbia. The "West" itself tended to often betray its own cultural myopia, most often in condemning Serbian human rights violations and ignoring similar Croatian violations. As one example, the revamped Croatian army's attack on the Serbs of Krajina in 1995, Serbs who had lived in the region for centuries, received an essentially silent response from the "West."[24]

By taking such a defense, however, the Pope helped place an imprimatur on the *perception* that many Croats themselves believed: Croatia "as the gallant frontier guardians of the West against Orthodoxy and Islam" (Huntington 1996, 273). For some—most especially Orthodox Serbs, Jews, and Gypsies—then, the Pope's refusal to set foot in Yugoslavia until he could pray at the tomb of Stepinac in Zagreb Cathedral displayed a myopic stance of anti-Communism while ignoring the Church's "wider historical role and attitudes in this part of the world."[25]

The Pope did not come to Yugoslavia until 1994—by then a place that no longer existed—and seemed to be reacting more to Tito and Communism (which had made Stepinac a symbolic martyr in the struggle between Communism and religion in the post–World War II Yugoslav state) and less to post–Cold War realities. To secure permission for his visit, it had taken two decades of Vatican efforts. Yet when he did arrive on 10 September 1994, the Pope appeared to have been well aware of the symbolism of his presence and the dangers of too close an affiliation with Croatian nationalism. Speaking the next day in fluent Croatian before a crowd of one million people in Zagreb, the Pope warned of "the risk of idolizing a nation, a race, [or] a party and justifying in their name hatred, discrimination, and violence."

Thus, his visit represented in one sense the triumph of faith in the Cold War's aftermath in a region torn by nationalism and self-inflicted violence; in the Pope's own words, he sent "a kiss of peace" to the Serbian Orthodox leadership and urged Croatian Catholics to become "apostles of a new concord between peoples."[26] Yet the Pope's Zagreb pronouncements produced shock waves when he openly praised the late Croatian Cardinal Stepinac.

Two destinations on his itinerary thus soon became lost opportunities: Pope John Paul's planned "pilgrimage for peace" to former Yugoslavia included both a visit to war-torn Sarajevo and reconciliation with Serbian Patriarch Pavle. The patriarch, nonetheless, refused the Pope's offer of peace, terming his visit "inopportune"; Bosnian Serbs soon after refused to guarantee the Pope's security and even made "vague threats, implying that they were prepared to blame the Muslims for any mishaps."[27] Although both Bosnian president Izetbegovic and Croatian president Tudjman enthusiastically supported the Pope's visit, the United Nations succeeded in dissuading a papal visit to Sarajevo on the grounds that security guarantees were impossible, and bowing to the inevitable, Pope John Paul canceled his Bosnian "pilgrimage."

Pope John Paul, whose papacy has marked the "coming of the world church," would not visit Sarajevo until April 1997, and then at the invitation of the three-member joint Bosnian presidency—a Croatian, a Muslim, and a Serb—and under more secure circumstances, though still in a landscape lacking clear resolution. By then, his visit had lost the interest of media and he became less a target and more a self-proclaimed "messenger of peace."

Thus, the tensions and the symbolism that existed in Yugoslavia, and Catholicism's place within the current of those tensions, still exist today. Cardinal Stepinac may well represent the most appropriate symbol of Balkan fault lines, fault lines that have existed for centuries, and will exist for centuries to come, among the South Slavs. The true genius of unity and advocate for religious tolerance and spiritual unity long before the Vatican II Council—Bishop Strossmayer—is largely forgotten. The tensions created between Tito's Yugoslavia and the Vatican's concern for the care of its Catholic flock seem to have ensured his erasure from history. Strossmayer's monument, sculpted by the famed Ivan Mestrovic, stands in a small park behind the Art Pavilion in Zagreb; by contrast, within the walls of Zagreb's cathedral stands another Mestrovic monument, the tomb of Alojzije Stepinac.

On the back wall of the cathedral, however, there stands an equally impressive memorial, one that many have chosen to ignore or simply have not been able to recognize: the Ten Commandments, written in stone nearly twenty meters high, and in the Glagolithic alphabet of Saints Cyril and Methodios, a reminder that the same language (Old Church Slavonic) and the same alphabet were once the same liturgical language for both Roman Catholic and Orthodox churches in the Balkans.

## ISLAM

> Land of Albania! let me bend mine eyes
> On thee, thou rugged nurse of savage men!
> The cross descends, thy minarets arise,
> And the pale crescent sparkles in the glen.
> —Lord Byron, "Childe Harold's Pilgrimage"[28]

Byron, who came to champion the cause of Greek independence and died in 1824 after serving only three months as commander in chief of the perpetually squabbling Greek forces who sought to throw off their Ottoman rulers, seems an appropriate figure for the West's romantic notion of Islam as mysterious, barbaric, and "foreign" culture—even within the Balkans. Byron (whose heart is buried outside the small, coastal village of Messolónghi) represented a figurehead in how, in struggling for Greek independence, the "West" came to champion both freedom and cultural values in casting off the dark forces of the "East."

Odd as these romantic notions may seem today, they still help illustrate how Europe views its own boundaries and its own cultural identities.[29] In 1993, a senior member of the Greek military told this researcher bluntly: "The only reason you Americans are involved in Bosnia is because of Saudi Arabia."[30] Indeed, Huntington's "cultural" paradigm reveals a *perception* of Islam, and Islam in the Balkans, that is troubling: "Europeans . . . expressed concern that the establishment of a Muslim state in the former Yugoslavia would create a base for the spread of Muslim immigrants and Islamic fundamentalism, reinforcing what [French President] Jacques Chirac referred to as '*les odeurs d'Islam*' in Europe."[31]

Huntington, in presenting the core tenets of his cultural paradigm, tends to dwell on "Western" perceptions and then present such perceptions as fundamental truths. Nowhere are such gross misperceptions so consistently applied than with regard to Islam in the Balkan conflict. Further, it proved to be the United States, not Europe, that acted more out of principle than in "the vital interest" of preserving the North Atlantic Alliance (NATO) as a viable entity, to aid Bosnians—that is, largely Bosnian Muslims—who portrayed themselves, and often were, the victims of massacres and Serbian aggression.[32] Thus, a paradoxical development *may have occurred*: the United States acted on "the [European] source—the *unique source*" (in the words of Arthur M.

Schlesinger Jr.) of the ideas of "individual liberty, political democracy, the rule of law, human rights, and cultural freedom."[33]

Beyond such myopic European perspective, the thoughts of two observers who lived with the culture of Islam within their borders prove useful in addressing the place of Islam as a cultural fault. The first thought comes from a Greek, Theodoros Couloumbis, director of the Hellenic Foundation for Defense and Foreign Policy and a member of the American University faculty: "Our real problems will never be solved if we continue to frame our relationships in a Byzantine versus Ottoman struggle, rather than a relationship between the modern Greek state and the modern Turkish one."[34] The place of Islam will hold a central cultural reference point within the center of any evolving relationship; as such, the "ideal" of evolving state-to-state relationships must recognize and base relationships on the recognition of difference as much as similarity. By contrast, Huntington argues that Greece and Turkey will see their "ties to their NATO [and European] states [as] likely to attenuate."[35]

The second observation is by former Russian prime minister Yevgeny Primakov (and former key figure within the Russian intelligence apparatus): "In regards to *fundamental* [emphasis added] Islam, one must not confuse it with Islamic extremism. Extremism is those forms through which are exposed this or that social group or this or that movement, which attempts to export and impose the Islamic form of life, the Islamic model, sometimes with the use of armed force."[36]

For the Balkan example, the non-Muslim perception persistently remains that Islamic "fundamentalism" and "extremism" are synonymous. Radovan Karadzic, ersatz leader of the Republika Srpska, spoke with passionate belief "about having a mission to eradicate the last traces of the Ottoman Turkish empire in Europe."[37]

Within U.S. domestic policy circles, the issue came to the forefront in 1995 when ambassador to Croatia Peter Galbraith and then national security adviser Anthony Lake provided a means (by simply stating the United States had "no position" on the issue) for Iran to ship arms to Bosnia via a Croatian transport conduit. Iran, a target at the time (along with Iraq) under the U.S. National Security Strategy of a "policy of dual containment," was regularly associated with being an "extremist" state by American, though not necessarily West European, standards.

By implication, then, Bosnia-Herzegovina, aided and abetted by Iran, was on its way—through arms supplies, military "advisers" from Iran, Afghanistan mujahedeen, liberal funding from Saudi Arabia, moral support from Turkey—to establishing a fundamentalist Islamic regime (with extremist elements). Huntington has suggested that Bosnia employed a strategy that "convincingly portray[ed] itself as the victim of genocide" while receiving "significant assistance from civilizational kin," those Muslim brethren with whom Bosnia shared cultural religious ties.[38]

Yet the strength of Huntington's argument becomes rapidly blurry with the insertion of the intentionally explosive adjective "*extremist*" in describing how the government of Alija Izetbegovic attempted to establish a *fundamentalist* Muslim government. Further, Huntington ignores how a fundamentalist Islamic regime, while not a theocracy per se, is one in which the religious and political cultural links are, in the ideal type, synonymous. This is not true of "Western" states, where the role of the church is separate and distinct from the role of secular government. Yet Huntington suggests that Izetbegovic may not have fully secured his policy/religious goals in the wake of the Dayton Peace Accords and wanted more in the post-Dayton Bosnia: "The victory of *the extremists* [emphasis mine] is not necessarily permanent."[39]

Igor Sevostianov, former deputy director for the Ministry of Foreign Affairs in Russia, takes a significantly contrasting view: "One must not reduce the diverse ranges of expression of the Islamic factor down to extremism, [or] limit the strategies of approaching the Moslem world to the opposition of extremism. . . . [In] Russia, more than anywhere else, there [exists] the synthesis of various civilizations, uniting in one community the East and the West. The role of 'defender of the West against the Islamic East' for us is organically impossible."[40]

Even within the nodes of extremism, there are degrees of difference. It may come as some surprise for many to learn that, within the Islamic Republic of Iran, "the imams [literally, 'Islamic teachers'] have derided the ruling *Taliban* [literally, 'religious student'] of Afghanistan's militia regime [for its] rigid belief."[41]

Thus, the difference of extremes in Islam may simply lump together, in the Western *weltanschauung* of Islam as a cultural component of religion, particularly one regarded as non-Western, into a category exempt from the process of inculturation within Western civilization(s). Such perception, as Huntington rightly notes, disregards the truth that Westernization is not a process of universal appeal. Consider the examples of language, religion, and Western values:

> In 1958, roughly 9.8 percent of human beings spoke English; in 1992, 7.6 percent did. A language foreign to 92 percent of the world's population is not a world language. . . . [Regarding religion] at some point in the next decade or so the number of Muslims [the fastest growing religion in the United States] will exceed the number of Christians. . . . The West—and especially the United States, which has always been a missionary nation—believes that the non-Western peoples should commit themselves to the Western values of democracy, free markets, limited government, separation of church and state, human rights, individualism, and the rule of law, and should embody these values in their insti-

> tutions. . . . What is universalism to the West is imperialism to the rest. . . . Imperialism is the necessary, logical consequence of universalism, yet few proponents of universalism support the militarization and brutal coercion that would be necessary to achieve their goal. Furthermore . . . the West no longer has . . . the dynamism to impose its will on other societies. Westerners will come to appreciate the connection between universalism and imperialism and to see the virtues of a pluralistic world.[42]

Huntington advocates the alignment of similarities into blocs that are linked by cultural identities (often in which religion is a crucial cultural component). Under such a rubric, neither globalism nor isolationism, multilateralism nor unilateralism will best serve American interests in working with its "European" partners. Cultural diversity within Europe, such as Izetbegovic's desire to create a fundamentalist Islamic state within Bosnia, creates problems; in extremis, such diversity shocks conflict out of latent dormancy. Such cultural alignment equally rejects the notion that Bosnia, within the Balkans, is even *part* of Europe—an approach Europe itself has done its best to practice over centuries of neglect, often with disastrous results.

With regard to Islam itself within the culture of Europe, we may record with horror Dame Rebecca West's assertion that "[the Slavs] knew that Christianity was better for man than Islam, because it denounced the prime human fault, cruelty, which the military mind of Mohammed had not even identified."[43] Such broad generalization, of course, finds numerous exceptions in the practice and fallibility of both ancient and modern Christian cultures. It also points to the essential paradox that retired Foreign Service Officer Michael Menard pointed to, with some emotion, in *Foreign Policy*: "The U.S. Department of State [has] been unable to accept the fact that neither the Serbs nor the Croats can possibly feel safe in a state with a 44 percent Muslim plurality that by the end of this century is likely to become an absolute majority. . . . The strong evidence of fundamentalism among the Muslim leadership in Bosnia-Herzegovina has been largely withheld from the American public. As a result, Izetbegovic has been made to appear a martyr instead of someone who belongs in a courtroom dock with the rest of the war criminals."[44]

The latent or suppressed fear of Islam as the cultural core of the nation-state—within Bosnia, within Europe—represents a threat, as it were, to the existing order. "Albanian Muslims and Bosnian Muslims are in this together," two "Yugoslav" journalists told Professor Sabrina Ramet in a Belgrade café in 1989. "They want to see a Khomeini in charge here. . . . They will continue to advance until they have taken . . . all the great cities of Europe."[45] Such fears masked the positive cultural aspects that Islam brought to the Balkans, which include a rich literary and religious heritage, among other developments, unique to the region.[46]

Islamic communities, keenly aware of their perceptions held against them by other cultures within Yugoslavia, remained far more silent than either the Serbian Orthodox Church or the Roman Catholic Church within the former Yugoslavia. In some way, perhaps, the more vocal and obvious advocacy of Islam—both in Bosnia and Albania—is the process of more liberal religious policy within states that maintain a fragile political structure. The process of linking religious culture within political structure, or at least the attempt to establish the process, ought to be viewed as a natural force within Islam, much as (within the "West") economic, political, and social pluralism are prime movers.[47] Further, with all the debate over extremism and fundamentalism, little attention has been paid to the particular identity in the Balkans that Islamic practice within cultural context has taken on. Women in particular have assumed an integral role with the religious communities that would seem unthinkable in other regions. As early as 1986, female imams were educated and delivering sermons within mosques, despite the objections of some (fundamentalist) male Muslims.[48] Indeed, the Islamic Central Board in Skopje (then part of the Yugoslav Republic of Macedonia) viewed the issue of women within mosques as one of simple "equality."

Although Huntington might find such cultural identities jarring, he might assert that, with the outbreak of war, Islam within former Yugoslavia "identified . . . with its broader cultural community and defined itself in religious terms."[49] Thus, according to Huntington, Bosnian Muslims, perhaps the strongest supporters of multiculturalism prior to war's outbreak (if only because they suffered the greatest abuse under Tito's oppression), became ardent Islamic "hard-liners" in the face of cultural conflict. It remains unclear if, in the wake of conflict and the aftermath that remains from cultural tensions, Muslims will increasingly isolate themselves along religious lines.

## ORTHODOXY

> So tear down minarets and mosques
> and kindle the Serbian Yule logs . . .
> I swear to you by the creed of Milos Obilic
> and by the trusty weapons I carry,
> our faiths will be submerged in blood.[50]
> —Petar II, Petrovi-Njegosh

Petar II, the Prince-Bishop (both religious and political Orthodox leader), is often misrepresented by history. Ruler of Montenegro from 1830 to 1851, Njegos, as he is most commonly named, writes in his epic work *The Moun-*

*tain Wreath* of the mass genocide of Islamic converts as a justified action to sustain a battle against Ottoman military forces—who had occupied the Balkans since the fourteenth century.[51] What appears to be, and was, a brutal action taken by a people who believed they were struggling for their own survival belies the Prince-Bishop's own stark assessment of his people. Indeed, if it were not for "ethnic cleansing," there may have been little to nothing that would have united the Montenegrins against the Muslim Turks.

In the Montenegrin example, as Dusko Doder notes, there is "a thin line between freedom and anarchy, as there is between the heroic and the bizarre."[52] In practice, the Montenegrins united *only* when fighting Turks; otherwise, one's true allegiance was to clan and not to the Prince-Bishop. The appetite for violence was also appalling: the Turkish practice of impaling victims was returned in kind by Montenegrins who often competed for carrying home the heads of Turkish warriors to be displayed as trophies in villages and in the capital.[53]

In theory and in legend, at least, such linking of religion and political authority seemed perfectly suitable for Montenegro, the only state in the Balkans to successfully fend off Ottoman advances and maintain centuries of fierce independence, in a place Tennyson named the "rough rock-throne of Freedom." Yet Njegoš came to experience a bitter frustration with his fellow Montenegrins, a frustration observers of the Balkan enigma tend to often ignore: "One may expect anything from such a people. Woe unto him who is their ruler. This is the saddest fate in the world. . . . I curse the hour when this spark rose up from the ashes of Dušan's greatness and into these mountains of ours."[54]

Equally, the Serbian Orthodox Church came to represent the cause of Serbian nationalism under Ottoman occupation. Much like the Catholic Church came to represent the rallying point for Croatian nationalism in World War II, under Marshal Tito's tight socialist control, and in the last Balkan war, so Serbian orthodoxy represented a spiritual, cultural force that could not be detached from the notion of a Serbian national identity over the past six centuries.[55] This linkage has been both the saving grace and the damnation for the Serbian Orthodox Church, an institution that cannot separate its identity from the Serbian nation because it remains so closely aligned with Serbian cultural identity.

For "Western" nations that have forged a secular identity, the linking of state and religious culture may not be viewed as being as important a connection as it truly is in the Balkans. Policy analysts may tend too frequently to associate the Serbian Church with the "Chetnik" movement (the Serbian partisans, monarchists, and nationalist guerrillas of World War II—"eliminated" by Tito in the war's aftermath), while overlooking efforts by the church to act independently when the patriarch and his ecclesiastical synod believed such action necessary.

The church is a powerful force, yet its power and influence vary. Milosevic clearly manipulated the Serbian Church in 1989, ensuring the patriarch was at his side during the six hundredth anniversary of the Battle of Kosovo (where the Ottoman Empire crushed Serbia and destroyed its empire).[56] In 1937, the Serbian Church effectively blocked approval in the Yugoslav parliament of a Vatican Concordat that would have allowed Catholicism greater freedoms within Yugoslavia; this action only returned to haunt the Serbian people four years later in the wake of Nazi invasion and the establishment of death camps for Orthodox Serbs, Jews, homosexuals, and gypsies, with the full cooperation of Croatian *Ustashe*.[57] As early as 1943, strained relations between the Serbian Orthodox Church and the Communist regime in Yugoslavia led directly to the Macedonian Orthodox Church declaring itself autocephalous; to date, the Serbian Church has refused to recognize the schismatic Macedonian Church (and indeed the hierarchs of the church—as do a number of Serbians—consider Macedonians to be nothing less than "south Serbs").

Yet in 1997, despite numerous favors and privileges granted by the regime of Milosevic, the Serbian Orthodox Church turned against the Milosevic regime and declared that local elections of late 1996 had been "rigged," and it proved instrumental in the eventual reversal of the voting results (initially declared "invalid" by the Belgrade government when opposition parties had won overwhelmingly large majorities). The reasons for this decision are simple: "The Serbian Church views itself as identical with the Serbian nation since it considers that religion is the foundation of nationality."[58] In the case of the voting "fraud" of 1996–1997, the Serbian Church believed itself to be defending the nation in turning against the state.

Perhaps more than other ethnic-based orthodox churches, such as the Russian, Bulgarian, Romanian, Greek, and Armenian, the links the Serbian Church bears with the Serbian nation are more critical, and their origins lie in a familiar tale often told when explaining how Serbia takes its greatest pride in its defeat. Such an explanation is not an entirely correct leap of faith. In historical terms, the myth of "defeat" at Kosovo has little importance or connection with fact. (That Bosnian Christians and Albanian Muslims fought alongside Orthodox Serbs in the Battle of Kosovo is a truth often omitted from the legend; equally—as the epic of Kosovo confirms—Serbs also fought on the side of the Ottomans against their brethren.) Indeed, the "history" surrounding Serbia's defeat at Kosovo Polje in 1389 takes on mythical status. There were, after all, no eyewitness accounts, and Serbia did not actually succumb to the Ottomans for fully another seventy years. (The Byzantine empire of Constantinople fell in 1453.)

Six hundred years to the day after the defeat of Prince Lazar, and the day that began the third Balkan war, the President of Serbia, Slobodan Milosevic, stood before a wave of his countrymen on the plain of Kosovo. Slobodan—whose name is a cognomen for "freeman"—pointed one finger to the distance and said, "No one, now or in the future, will ever defeat you again. Look with what ease I have gathered one million Serbs." Where he pointed was in the heart of the crowd, which roared its approval, the place where the knights had been left to rot and the carrion scavengers to feast—the place named Kosovo Polje, in Serbian "The Field of the Black Birds."[59]

In a real and dramatic way, the defeat at Kosovo represented a badge of honor, not shame, for Serbs. The defeat of Lazar represented a call-to-arms for six centuries for Serbs to avenge the defeat of Lazar at Kosovo; in World War I, John Reed noted how with the birth of every Serb peasant male came the greeting: "Hail, little avenger of Kosovo!" Indeed, for Slavophiles such as Dame Rebecca West, the empire of Serbia sacrificed itself for the greater benefit of Europe, essentially living under the yoke of an Ottoman occupation that destroyed both culture and growth and nurtured the status of both myth and legend. Even a cursory study of Balkan history reveals such a claim to be not far from the truth. Ancient Serbia was among the most civilized of European states; Emperor Stefan Nemanja was able to sign his name, while his contemporary Frederick I Barbarossa, Holy Roman Emperor in Germany, could manage only a thumbprint.[60]

Stefan Nemanja's son, Sava, today the most revered of Serbian Orthodox saints, founded the faith of the church—by no accident of chance—in Kosovo. In 1998, in a region dominated by a population of roughly 93 percent ethnic Albanians, Kosovo truly represented a Balkan Palestine. (The sacred church of Gracanica lies only a few kilometers from "The Field of the Black Birds.") Equally, the sharp divisions within Orthodox denominations point to how strong a role religion plays in differences in the Balkans.

Orthodoxy is a religion that grew in the East following the schismatic break with Rome in 1054. Catholicism, Protestantism, and Judaism (as a result of the Diaspora) developed in the West, although the origins of these monotheistic religions, including Islam, are all in the Middle East. Western religions, "even Catholicism, the most baroque of Western religions . . . [are] austere and intellectual"; Orthodoxy, by contrast, emphasizes beauty and magic, a "physical re-creation of *heaven on earth*" [emphasis mine].[61] One need only reference the works of Orthodox clergy to note how such difference of perspective is manifest in the thought, cultural orientation, and attitude of church leaders. Poet and priest Father Stefan Sandjakoski writes in his work *Bogomislie* [The Contemplation of God] of the monasteries of Macedonia, sacred sites embraced by the Holy Spirit for the purposes of contemplation, places where "mysterious spiritual process occurs," where the purpose of monastic life is to "Give blood, take spirit."[62]

Yet with such similarities of religious perspective within Orthodox denominations, it seems all the more surprising that such deep rifts remain within various Orthodox communities. In the Balkans, "regional differences are profound," as former undersecretary of state Matthew Nimetz remarks, "not only between Muslims and Christians, but also between Orthodox and Catholic Christians and among the Orthodox communities themselves."[63] Nowhere is this more true than in Macedonia, where the Orthodox Church itself is not recognized by the Bulgarian, Serbian, or Greek patriarchs.

Given such perspective, it is incorrect to claim Orthodoxy as the exclusive prime mover within the forces of nationalism and violence. To some degree, the church has been a stabilizing element, a cultural touchstone for identity. To a large extent, however, Serbian Orthodoxy was a victim—both of Titoist and Milosevic-ist machinations—as much as it was the aggressor. Because the Serbian Orthodox Church has attempted to act and has portrayed itself "as the most constant defender of the Serbian people and their culture," so it has come to be viewed as responsible for actions it could not control.[64] From another perspective, that taken when cultural fault lines are drawn, it should not be completely surprising to witness a ritual ceremony in which a Serbian priest blesses all of Arkan's Tigers. The church, as institutional force, symbolically endorsed the notion of Serbs as holy warriors, defending not only a nation but a faith as well.

## OTHER RELIGIOUS CULTURAL ELEMENTS

Despite the claim by some that the Balkan Wars took on characteristics of religious struggle, defined by Roman Catholicism, Eastern Orthodoxy, and Islam, there are contradictions with the simplicity of this argument. It was in Bosnia-Herzegovina, after all, torn under the various regimes of Ottomans or Austro-Hungarian occupation, or subsumed within the federation of either Yugoslav monarchy or, later, Tito's Yugoslav "Experiment," where Islam actually thrived and came to represent a religious cultural heartland for an "Eastern" religion in Europe. The Balkans, in truth, have always represented a cultural crossroads where religions have clashed, mingled, and come to interrelate.[65] The Balkans have also given birth, as it were, to unique religious cultural elements found nowhere else.

One such element, largely forgotten outside the region, is the sect of the Bogomils (literally, meaning "One who is dear to God"). The origin of this religion dates to the third century A.D. in the syncretic religious teachings of the Persian Manichæus, combining Zoroastrianism, Gnosticism, and various other elements of Christianity. Although Manichæus was executed, his ideas spread throughout Mesopotamia, and a Bulgarian priest named Bogomil, in the tenth century, began to preach the basic tenets of his religion: the Devil, not God, created the world, and only mankind could redeem itself through overcoming the darkness of the Devil-made world and achieve redemption. In its day, Bogomilism spread as far as southern France, and the Pope is claimed to have sent an army into Bosnia against the heretics. The sect, partially as the result of Ottoman occupation after the fall of the Byzantine Empire, disappeared in the sixteenth century. The Bogomil tombs can be found in Bosnia-Herzegovina today; many of the Bogomil sites are not far from the mass graves that are the remains of the wars of 1992–1995.

Yet Bogomilism did not pave the way, as it were, for the rise of Islam in the Balkans. While it is true that this religion "reflected an inherent tendency towards heterodoxy or towards eclecticism," its "dualistic beliefs" also clashed with fundamental tenets of Islam.[66] Thus, the common assumption that Muslims of Bosnia-Herzegovina are direct descendants of the Bogomil sect is one worthy of serious challenge.[67]

One religious group that exists today in every South Balkan nation, however, and remains—to use the euphemism—"problematic" for various governments is the Pomaks. Most scholars categorize Pomaks as "Slav Bulgarians who speak Bulgarian as their mother tongue and do not understand Turkish," though their religion and customs are Islamic.[68] In Bulgaria, where Muslims comprise about 15 percent of the population, the Pomaks suffered a fate quite different than the relative tolerance Pomaks enjoyed in Yugoslavia: "Bulgarianization" caused government pillaging of Muslim villages, forced the burning of the Koran, and forced Pomaks into detention camps. By 1985, as Sabrina Ramet notes, Muslim culture (Turkish, Pomak, and Tartar populations) was "shattered."[69]

The Pomaks, largely ignored in the last Balkan war by "Western" media, number roughly 200,000 in Bulgaria, 40,000 in Macedonia, 36,000 in Greece, and 120,000 in Albania.[70] The exact count of these figures is controversial, as is the cultural identity of the Pomaks themselves. In Greece, Pomaks are called simply "Muslims," the only recognized minority in the Hellenic Republic under the 1923 Treaty of Lausanne; in Albania, no reliable data exists, though, periodically, various governments have referred to Pomaks as the "Macedonian [that is, a Slavic Macedonian] minority" within Albanian borders; within Turkey, Pomaks have largely assimilated Turkish culture; within Bulgaria, Pomaks are split by a Turkish reluctance to accept them because of their Bulgarian language and a Bulgarian reluctance to accept them because of their Islamic faith.[71]

What stands as significant for groups such as the Pomaks—trapped both within and across cultures by the "fault" of religion and language—is how their significance rises or falls on the play of Balkan tensions. Indeed, as actors and policies outside the Balkans set the conditions for involvement or disengagement from Balkan turmoil, such minority groups tend to fall by the cultural wayside. Yet close study of such groups can prove useful, not only for human rights concerns, but for interest in predicting with accuracy the outbreak of tension—or the potential for conflict.

One of the most useful sources for learning about such tension is the congressionally mandated annual *Country Reports on Human Rights Practices.* These reports contain information gathered by American embassies worldwide and are published by the Department of State. Each report covers practices and abuses within nations, with which the United States has diplomatic relations; often, such information is sensitive, and host governments respond quickly in protest over reports of human rights abuse. In 1992, for example, despite the apparent side-by-side ease with which Islamic and Orthodox communities lived in the former Yugoslav Republic of Macedonia, the *Country Reports* noted potential for conflict based on religious and cultural identities. Specifically, the Macedonian government had placed education and health support restrictions on families with more than three children (Albanians are traditionally Islamic and have both the highest birth and infant mortality rates in Europe).[72] Further, Macedonian authorities had manipulated building codes regarding the height of walls in individual structures, thus allowing the bulldozing of traditional Albanian homes.[73]

## ETHNICITY, RELIGION, AND CIVILIZATIONAL PARADIGMS AS EXPLANATIONS FOR WAR

In late 1993, Huntington provided his first defense of his essay "The Clash of Civilizations?" as "an effort to lay out elements of a post–Cold War paradigm" in an essay titled "If Not Civilizations, What?—Paradigms of the Post–Cold War World."[74] While predictably drawing on Thomas Kuhn's *The Structure of Scientific Revolutions*, suggesting that those who could not understand the "shift" of paradigms were trapped by the structure of previous understandings, his civilizational paradigm, by contrast, provided a theoretical model "better than any alternative" for explaining future behavior and conflict. Arguing for simplicity, Huntington notes that a "paradigm is disproved only by the creation of an alternative paradigm that accounts for more crucial facts in equally simple . . . terms. . . . [T]he civilizational paradigm . . . either accords with reality as people see it or it comes close enough so that people who do not accept have to attack it."[75] In the years between publishing his first essay and the completion of a book that draws on the multitude of events in history since the end of the Cold War, Huntington, in the view of some, only hardened his views. As previously noted in the introductory section of this examination, Said faults Huntington for too easily categorizing "culture" and "civilization" into frameworks by which policymakers and war planners can formulate responses. "Culture" wars, in short, become a new kind of Cold War writ large.[76] Indeed, according to Huntington, religion, as a cultural component, will take on significant meaning in the post–Cold War world. Under his civilizational paradigm, the global religious revival forms "a return to the sacred" and the potential nesting ground for future wars.[77]

What Huntington fails to do, even in his most recent work, is to provide precise definitions for both civilizations and cultures. By his own admission, he avoids precise and "unrealistic" nineteenth-century German attempts to isolate culture and civilization as separate identities.[78] Such blurring of distinctions also allows generalizations that have often proven true in the post–Cold War world. In the Balkans, in particular, the appearance of religious warfare, for some, appears to be the controlling dynamic. Henry Kissinger, for example, has argued that the Bosnian war from 1992 to 1995 was "more akin to the Thirty Years War over religion [than] to political conflict."[79]

Yet the danger of generalization and the lack of clearer understanding about the complexity of culture, as Said points out, can lead to dangerous outcomes.[80] At the least, some definition of culture is necessary. The broadest possible understanding of culture, thus, should be understood as "a set of meanings and values informing a common way of life" and as "the values, norms, institutions, and modes of thinking to which successive generations in a given society have attached primary importance."[81] Second, civilizations should equally be broadly understood as "a space, a 'cultural' area . . . collection of cultural characteristics and phenomena"; "a particular . . . worldview, customs, structures, and culture, . . . [that] forms some kind of historical whole"; a "particular original process of cultural creativity which is the work of a particular people"; "a kind of moral milieu encompassing a certain number of nations, each national culture being only a particular form of the whole."[82]

Finally, the aspect of religion as a cultural component that acts within civilizational forces is perhaps best identified as: (1) a system of symbols which acts to (2) establish powerful, pervasive, and long-lasting moods and motivations in men by (3) formulating conceptions of a general order of existence and (4) clothing these conceptions with such an aura of factuality that (5) the moods and motivations seem uniquely realistic.[83] Thus, even working from such general understandings, Huntington still casts a wide net for explaining the causes for conflict and the cultural biases on actors on the world stage.

With the Balkan example, in particular, Huntington's paradigm may well explain why conflict occurs, but the "remaking of world order," as he terms it, proves unsatisfactory for the prevention of conflict. To the contrary, the remaking of civilization along nine proposed civilizational "alignments," may prove to be, as his critics have argued, little more than self-fulfilling prophecy for disaster.[84] G. John Ikenberry notes that "intercivilizational conflict is by no means inevitable—but it is probably more likely if our leaders take Huntington's thesis to heart."[85]

Yugoslavia died a gradual, methodical, and ineluctable death; it took eleven years following Tito's death for the Federal Socialist Republics of Yugoslavia to implode. Religion, as a component of culture, provided an occasion but was not the singly exclusive cause for the death of Yugoslavia. One could argue more forcefully that it was the "West's" (read, American) reluctance to commit early to preventing the outbreak of conflict that allowed the inevitable collision. It remains a misinterpretation, as observers from Huntington to Kissinger have concluded, to define the most recent conflict in the former Yugoslavia simply as a Balkan "holy war." Prior to the collapse of historical, economic, political, and social ecological factors that led to an inevitable disintegration, Yugoslavia held three major religions within its borders (Catholicism, Islam, Orthodoxy) as well as elements of Judaism, Protestant sects, Jehovah's Witnesses, and Hare Krishnas. Yugoslavs were marked by such culture, and at times, they were proud of their differences. Admittedly, distinctions also often kept them at a permanent distance from each other.

Yet within so-called aligned cultures of the former Yugoslavia, there existed difference. A Serb geographer, Jovan Civic, noted in the late nineteenth century the existence of "cultural" types not only *between* the disciplined "imperial sons" of the Habsburg Military Frontier, but *among* the urban Byzantine Orthodox of Southern Serbia and the patriarchal Orthodox highlanders of Herzegovina and Montenegro, the clergy and burghers of Vojvodina and their kinsmen in the Montenegrin littoral, a Central European belt (Slovenia, northern Croatia, Vojvodina), a Mediterranean belt (the littorals of Albania, Montenegro, Slovenia, Croatia), and a Muslim belt and Orthodox belt inseparably intertwined.[86] Thus, the calls for Serbian "unity" and the fervent appeals of Milosevic for Serbian nationalism drew on a potential fear of *dis*-unity. The cultural diversity within "Serb" culture could quickly lead to cultural fragmentation. In hindsight, this is what happened within Serbian culture in the post-Dayton environment.

The Balkans, there can be no doubt, span a number of rich cultural faults. The continental "crust" of Rome and Byzantium, East and West, meet in a unique way here. Cultures lived with and tolerated each other—even in some ways embraced each other. In Mostar, Herzegovina, before the warlords destroyed it, one was able not too long ago to sip Viennese coffee and read newspapers mounted on wooden frames, listening all along to a muezzin's call in the shadow of a Franciscan church (where the chant was Latinate), and then wander into a fig grove surrounding a Byzantine-style church (where the chant was Slavonic).[87]

Yet the common belief persists that the Balkans are uniquely dangerous, in some ways barbaric, and a region we should avoid for strategic and foreign policy concerns. What *is* unique about the Balkans is that Slavs—the largest ethnic majority in Europe—came to the Balkans in the sixth and seventh centuries A.D. and slowly separated from each other by their physical presence in situ at the crossroads of history. In truth, Balkan Slavs are separated by *multiple cultural overlays*. Yugoslavia was a European nation with an identifiable geography and ethnic composition. Croats, Serbs, Bosnians, Slovenes, Montenegrins, and Macedonians—despite their differences—constitute *one* "ethnos." Yet this recognition is often overlooked. George Kennan, ambassador to Yugoslavia from 1961 to 1963, for instance could claim that Slovenes are not Yugoslavs but "really an alpine people" and Montenegrins have been "effectively subsumed by the Serbian state."[88]

Moreover, the belief persists that involvement in the Balkans is simply not worth the effort, that "the United States runs the risk of its policy being controlled by, rather than controlling events."[89] But politics in the Balkans cannot, in the future, exist independently of religion and other cultural influences, just as, in the past, such factors proved critical to history as it unfolded—or erupted. Without understanding both culture and religion, one can never understand the politics of the so-called Balkan Enigma. The only "Enigma" that exists is in the almost overwhelming dynamics that shape this region of Europe; politics, culture, and religion present daunting, though not insurmountable, challenges that the "West" has chosen, most often at its own peril, to ignore.

Religious difference, cultural diversity, or uneven economic development did not, of themselves, fuel the hostilities of the last Balkan war. Simply put, conflict stemmed from "dissimilar structure and goals of various national ideologies that . . . emerged within the political culture of each of Eastern Europe's national groups."[90] The rise of nationalist ideology found fertile ground in the post–Cold War era and attached to it culture, politics, religion, and beliefs in a complex array that reaped a whirlwind of destruction. There was, and is, no exclusive "War in Religion" in the Balkans. Religion, as a cultural component, contributed to the political culture that saw war as a necessary outcome. Understanding religion, nonetheless, is essential to understanding Balkan culture. At its very least, it serves both structure and understanding (both for the "West" and for the Balkan peoples) as "symbols of intuition and action—that means myth and rites within a social group—[and] has lasting necessity for . . . even the most secularized culture and the most demythologized theology."[91]

Thus, despite a score of antitank mines laid as an assassination attempt on the road to Sarajevo on 13 April 1997, it seems no small event that Pope John Paul II's visit to war-torn Bosnia was welcomed by Orthodox Serbs, Roman Catholics, and Bosnian Muslims alike. In a visit largely ignored by Western media, the Pope delivered a clear message to a people separated by cultural difference but linked by geographic and "civilizational" intimacy: "Let us forgive, and let us ask for forgiveness. We cannot fail to undertake the difficult but necessary pilgrimage of forgiveness, which leads to a profound reconciliation."[92]

## CONCLUSION

History, there can be little doubt, suffers processes of death and renewal in the story of civilization. Some, such as the poet W. B. Yeats, believed these processes of cyclical "gyres" formed the integral core of human evolution. Others, particularly historians such as the skeptical Oswald Spengler in *The Decline of the West*, contend that both cultures and civilizations decline at the moment when both appear to reach apparent peaks.[93] Yet "world history," as Spengler reminds us, "is the history of large cultures."[94] Huntington's civilizational paradigm, especially as it applies to the last Balkan war and the influence of religion on shaping the dynamic for conflict, proves useful for explaining *why* conflict occurs and far less worthwhile for formulating strategies to prevent future tensions from erupting in conflict.

In retrospect, the civilizations paradigm falls short of the claim to be "a useful starting point for understanding and coping with the changes going on in the world."[95] Huntington's paradigm relies on an alignment based solely on cultural identities. As Said has noted in a vigorous objection to Huntington's thesis: The real question is whether, in the end, we want to work for civilizations that are separate, or whether we should be taking the more integrative, but perhaps more difficult, path, which is to see them as making one vast whole, whose exact contours are impossible for any person to grasp, but whose certain existence we can intuit and feel and study.[96]

As concerns the Balkan paradigm and the very specific example of Yugoslav disintegration, why should it come as a surprise that peoples in times of tension and conflict would do nothing less than identify with "faith and family, blood and belief"—and allow themselves to be so ruthlessly manipulated by nationalistic ideologues who only ensured their own destruction?[97]

The danger, of course, is to consider culture the *sole* driving force in human development, to the exclusion of all other human realities. As Liotta and Simons have argued, politics, religion, nationalist ideology, and social relations overlap so tightly in the Balkans region that to privilege any one identity only transforms an analysis of fault line conflict into faulty, incomplete analysis.[98] Indeed, cultures, rather than being monolithic and homogeneous, are enriched by "heterodoxic strands"—aspects of counterculture that can both strengthen and enrich the societies they are part of.[99] The idea and the influence of culture, as with history and religious identity, comprise parts of a complex mosaic of interdependence.

Toynbee once wrote that "the would-be savior of a disintegrating society is necessarily a savior with a sword."[100] Sadly, we remain unsure if intervention by the "West"—the savior with a sword—in attempting to solve the Balkan Enigma, has actually prevented any resolution of the underlying causes for Balkan conflict. The Yugoslav Experiment is dead; the ideals of that experiment, nonetheless, of which religion remains a critical cultural component, are not. In examining the influence of technology upon human realities in the former Yugoslavia, perhaps we should remember how the layers of history were both deep and interdependent, and existed long before, and would perhaps thrive long after most had forgotten the significance of the time known as the Cold War.

Among ancient Greeks, there was no word for culture.[101] There were concepts and ideas that gave the sense of an identity—"civic" and "civility," "polis" and "politic"—but there was no clear distinction, if only because the very understanding of *being* Greek meant to be cultured. The uncultured, the non-Greek, was by definition a "barbarian." Alexander I of Macedonia, for example, was given the title "Philhellene" (by the Greeks)—meaning, friend of the Greek—a title that suggested Alexander was *not* Greek.[102]

Such division between the insider and the outsider is not possible, nor should it be, in the multicultural and multicivilizational world we live in. It remains equally true that elements within civilizations often possess extraordinary cultural diversity: the identity, for example, of Northern and Southern Italians, or Italians and Germans; the differences in the practice of Islam in Kabul versus its uniqueness in Teheran, Jakarta, Riyadh, or in Sarajevo.[103]

Among the ancient Greeks there also existed the sense that a civilization defined itself when a people planted trees knowing that they themselves would never rest in the shadow of its branches. The tensions between culture and civilization, historical difference and religious identity, of course, are locked in a constant battle. At the beginning of the twenty-first century, it seems more relevant than ever to realize how the history of civilization is a palimpsest, not a tabula rasa.

## NOTES

1. Milorad Pavic, *The Dictionary of the Khazars: A Lexicon Novel in 100,000 Words*, translated from the Serbo-Croatian by Christina Pribicevic-Zoric, New York: Alfred Knopf, 1988, 51–52.

2. Alija Izetbegovic, *The Islamic Declaration: A Programme for the Islamisation of Muslims and the Muslim Peoples*, Sarajevo, publisher not indicated, 1970, 22.

3. Izetbegovic 1970, 33.

4. Slobodan Lekic, "Clinton Assures Bosnia Leader," *Washington Post*, March 26, 1997; John Diamond, "Bosnian Leader Visits Pentagon," *Washington Post*, March 26, 1997; Elaine Sciolino, "Bosnia Policy: Shaped by U.S. Military Role," *New York Times*, July 29, 1996.

5. Sabrina Ramet, *Balkan Babel: The Disintegration of Yugoslavia from the Death of Tito to Civil War*, 2d ed. Boulder, Colorado: Westview Press, 1996, 2.

6. Samuel P. Huntington, *The Clash of Civilizations and the Remaking of World Order*, New York: Simon and Schuster, 1996a, 207–208.

7. Misha Glenny, "Carnage in Bosnia for Starters," *New York Times*, July 29, 1993.

8. Kishore Mahbubani, "The West and the Rest," *National Interest*, Summer 1991, 3–13.

9. Edward Said, *Orientalism*, New York: Random House, 1979.

10. Edward Said in *Lecture: The Myth of the Clash of Civilizations*, videocassette produced by Media Education Foundation, 1998.

11. Bernard Lewis, "The Roots of Muslim Rage," *Atlantic Monthly*, January 19, 1999.

12. See review of Bernard Lewis's *Islam and the West* in *Kirkus Reviews*, April 1, 1993; and Robert B. Satloff's review of Bernard Lewis's *The Middle East: A Brief History of the Last 2000 Years*, 1995 in *American Jewish Commentary*, January 19, 1999.

13. Ivo Banac, introduction to Ramet 1996, xiv.

14. Ramet 1996, 1–2.

15. *Keston News Service* 1990, 11.

16. Dame Rebecca West, *Black Lamb and Grey Falcon: A Journey Through Yugoslavia*, London: Macmillan, 1942, 109.

17. Ramet 1996, 136.

18. Aleksa A. Benigar, *Alojzije Stepinac: Hrvatski Kardinal*, Rome: Ziral, 1974, 492.

19. Robert D. Kaplan, *Balkan Ghosts: A Journey Through History*, New York: St. Martin's Press, 1993, 12.

20. Kaplan 1993, 23.

21. Kaplan 1993, 23.

22. Huntington 1996a, 282; Misha Glenny, "Yugoslavia: What Is to Be Done," *New York Review of Books*, March 27, 1993, 16.

23. Pierre Behar, "Central Europe: The New Lines of Fracture," *Geopolitque*, Autumn 1994, 44.

24. Huntington 1996a, 283.

25. Kaplan 1993, 27–28.
26. Ramet 1996, 281.
27. Ramet 1996, 281.
28. "Childe Harold's Pilgrimage," in *Lord Byron—The Collected Works in Verse and Prose,* New York: George Dearborn, 1835, 27. Private collection of the author.
29. Said 1979.
30. Private interview by the author.
31. Huntington 1996a, 271.
32. Dusko Doder, "Letters to the Editor," *Foreign Policy*, Winter 1993/1994, 186–187.
33. Richard Holbrooke, "America: A European Power," *Foreign Affairs*, March/April 1995, 49.
34. Based on remarks made to the visiting students and faculty of the Air War College to the Hellenic Republic, February 1995.
35. Huntington 1996a, 128. Notably, however, Greece's support for Turkey's application to European Union membership cleared the path for accession talks at the EU Helsinki summit in December 1999—obviating Huntington's argument.
36. *Izvestia*, March 6, 1996, 1.
37. Huntington 1996a, 271.
38. Huntington 1996a, 268.
39. Huntington 1996a, 267.
40. Igor Sevostianov, "Islamic Fundamentalism and Extremism Are Not the Same," *International Affairs: A Russian Journal of World Politics, Diplomacy, and International Relations*, vol. 42, no. 3, 1996, 179, 181.
41. Michael Ignatieff, "Unarmed Warriors," *New Yorker*, March 24, 1997, 68.
42. Samuel Huntington, "The West: Unique, Not Universal," *Foreign Affairs*, November–December 1996b, 40–41.
43. West 1942, 915.
44. Michael Menard, "Letters to the Editor," *Foreign Policy*, Winter 1994, 183–185.
45. Ramet 1996, 185.
46. H. T. Norris, *Islam in the Balkans: Religion and Society Between Europe and the Arab World*, Columbia: University of South Carolina Press, 1993.
47. David R. Gress, "Is the West Religious or Secular," *Orbis: A Journal of World Affairs*, Summer 1996, 421.
48. Ramet 1996, 192.
49. Huntington 1996a, 269.
50. Taken from the *Mountain Wreath*, the epic of Montenegro (known in Serbian as "Crna Gora"—for Black Mountain) and Serbia. The text can be found in the original Serbian (with the dialect of nineteenth-century Crna Gora) on the Internet at www.fron.net/nebojsa/njegos/gvijenac.htm.
51. Montenegro lies between Serbia and the Adriatic Sea and formed part of the nominal state known as Yugoslavia from 1991 to 1998. The genocide Njegoš writes of took place in 1702 under the warriors of Metropolitan Danilo Petrovi.

52. Dusko Doder, *The Yugoslavs*, New York: Random House, 1978, 182.

53. As Doder notes (182), the order given by Prince Nikola in the late nineteenth century to abandon this practice went ignored. In later battles, Montenegrins chose the cutting of ears and noses of Turks rather than decapitation.

54. Mark Thompson, *A Paper House: The Ending of Yugoslavia*, New York: Pantheon, 1992, 153.

55. William T. Johnsen, *Deciphering the Balkan Enigma: Using History to Inform Policy*, U.S. Army War College, Carlyle Barracks, Pennsylvania, 1995, 28.

56. From 1991 to 1998, Slobodan Milosevic always attempted to manipulate the Serbian Orthodox Church to his advantage. Long disgruntled by the various ways in which the Yugoslav Communist regime had shunned it, the church immediately warmed to Milosevic's tactical overtures, such as his praising the church in the regime-controlled *Politika* newspaper or replacing Marxism with religious instruction in school curricula.

57. Johnsen 1995, 29.

58. Ramet 1996, 181.

59. Thompson 1992; West 1942; Kaplan 1993.

60. Kaplan 1993, 31.

61. Kaplan 1993, 25.

62. Father Stefan Sandjakoski, *God's Blessing*, Skopje, Macedonia: Metaforum 1993, 198.

63. Mathew Nimetz, "Security in the Balkans," *Mediterranean Quarterly*, Winter 1996, 6

64. Ramet 1996, 165.

65. One of the most extraordinary works to show the influence of Islam, Christianity, and Judaism on the Balkans is, not surprisingly, a work a fiction, a "lexicon" novel that shows the incredible mosaic these religions represent for this region of Europe. The work is Milorad Pavic's *The Dictionary of the Khazars: A Lexicon Novel in 100,000 Words (Male Edition)*, translated from the Serbo-Croatian by Christina Pribicevic Zoric, from which the opening epigraph for this chapter is taken.

66. Norris 1993, 43–44.

67. Mario Apostolov, "The Pomaks: A Religious Minority in the Balkans," *Nationalities Papers*, vol. 24, no. 4, 1996, 727. Apostolov cites a generally authoritative source that claims Bosnian Muslims *are* direct descendants of the Bogomils: Kalman Sass, "Les bogomils," *Dictionnaire des religions*, 2d ed. Paris: Presse Universitaire de France, 1985.

68. Apostolov 1996, 727. Apostolov further cites Hugh Poulton, *Minorities in Bulgaria*, Minority Rights Group Report, no. 87, London: Minority Rights Group, 1988, 7; Alezandre Popovic, *L'Islam balkanique*, Balkanologische Veröffentlichungen, Band 11, Berlin: Osteuropa Institut an der Freien Universität, 1986, 172. The etymology of "Pomak" is unclear; one possible explanation is that it derives from the Bulgarian *pomagam*, after the belief that Pomaks provided aid to the Ottomans during the occupation of Bulgaria. Apostolov suggests that Pomak conversions to Islam took place in the sixteenth and seventeenth centuries as a means to escape the *devshirme* tax (that took

young boys from their families and recruited them into the Ottoman janizary) as well as to escape the *raya*, the practice of cruelty toward non-Muslims.

69. Sabrina Ramet, *Cross and Commissar: The Politics of Religion in Eastern Europe and the USSR*, Bloomington: Indiana University Press, 1987, 35.

70. Apostolov 1996, 728.

71. Apostolov 1996, 732–739. Pomaks are not the only Macedonian religious minority in Albania. Those who live in the village of Dolna Prespa, for instance, are entirely Christian Orthodox. Macedonians refer to Pomaks derogatorily as *torbeshi*—Muslim Macedonian Slavs.

72. *Country Reports on Human Rights Practices for 1988*, 1264.

73. *Country Reports on Human Rights Practices for 1988*, 1264–1265.

74. Samuel Huntington, "If Not Civilizations, What? Paradigms of the Post Cold War World," *Foreign Affairs*, Fall 1993, 56–57.

75. Huntington 1993, 67.

76. Said video, 1998.

77. Ronald Robertson, "Globalization Theory and Civilizational Analysis," *Comparative Civilizations Review*, Fall 1987, 22, quoted in Huntington 1996a, 68.

78. Huntington 1996b, 41.

79. Henry Kissinger, "Limits to What the U.S. Can Do in Bosnia," *Washington Post*, September 22, 1997.

80. Said video, 1998.

81. E. Hillman, C.S.Sp., *Many Paths: A Catholic Approach to Religious Pluralism*, Maryknoll, New York: Orbis Books, 1989, 5.

82. Fernand Braudel, *On History*, translated by Sarah Mathews, Chicago: University of Chicago Press, 1980, 177, 202; Immanuel Wallerstein, *Geopolitics and Geoculture: Essays on the Changing World System*, Cambridge: Cambridge University Press, 1992, 315; Christopher Dawson, *Dynamics of World History*, LaSalle, Illinois: Sheed and Ward, 1959, 51, 402; Emile Durkheim and Marcel Mauss, "Notes on the Notion of Civilization," *Social Research* 1971, 811.

83. Clifford Geertz, *The Interpretation of Culture*, New York: Basic Books, 1973, 90.

84. These civilizational alignments include the West, the Sino, Islamic, Hindu, African, Latin American, Orthodox, Buddhist, and Japanese civilizations.

85. G. John Ikenberry, "Just Like the Rest," *Foreign Affairs*, March/April 1997, 163. In a companion piece titled "Dangerous Conjecture," Tony Smith echoes much the same thought in warning against Huntington's cultural paradigm as little more than self-fulfilling prophecy that ensures disaster. Huntington's nine civilizations in the post-Cold War are Western (Europe and North America), Latin American, African, Islamic, Sinic, Hindu, Orthodox, Buddhist, and Japanese. Of these nine alignments, only Buddhism is a major religion not associated with a major civilization. Judaism, by contrast, though a major cultural force among its people, is, according to Huntington, neither a major religion nor a distinct civilization. This claim, of course, most especially when appended by Huntington's reliance on Toynbee that Judaism is "an arrested civilization which evolved out of the earlier Syriac civilization," is open to debate. See Huntington 1996, 47, 48 n.

86. Ivo Banac, introduction to Ramet 1996, xiv–xv.

87. Banac in Ramet 1996, xiv–xv.

88. Introduction, George F. Kennan, *The Other Balkan Wars*, Washington, D.C.: Carnegie Endowment for International Peace, 1993, 14.

89. Johnsen 1995, 91.

90. Banac in Ramet 1996, xv.

91. Paul Tillich, *The Future of Religions*, New York: Harper and Row, 1966, 82.

92. Paul Homes, "Pope Appeals for Toleration in Bosnia," *Washington Post*, April 14, 1997; Tracy Wilkinson and Richard Boudreaux, "Pope Unfazed by Threats in Sarajevo: Powerful Explosives Found Along Route," *Los Angeles Times*, April 13, 1997.

93. Oswald Spengler, *The Decline of the West*, vols.1 and 2, New York: Alfred A. Knopf, 1926–1928.

94. Spengler, vol. 2, 1928, 170.

95. Huntington 1993, 67.

96. Said video, 1998.

97. Huntington 1993, 67.

98. P. H. Liotta and Anna Simons, "Thicker than Water?: Kin, Religion, and Conflict in the Balkans," *Parameters: The Professional Journal of the U.S. Army War College*, Winter 1998/1999, 12.

99. Said video, 1998.

100. Arnold Toynbee, *War and Civilization*, Oxford: Oxford University Press, 1950, 142.

101. The blurred distinction between culture and civilization exists even today in spoken Greek. See John Lukacs, "Our Enemy, the State," *Wilson Quarterly*, Spring 1996, 115.

102. Peter Green, *Alexander of Macedon, 356–323 B.C.*, Berkeley: University of California Press, 1991, 6–7.

103. Said video, 1998.

# 5

# Economic Aspects of Yugoslavia's Disintegration

*Milica Z. Bookman*

Over a decade has passed since the former Yugoslavia began to unravel. During that time, four republics became sovereign states while one autonomous republic became an international protectorate. To analyze and document these events, a plethora of academic and popular texts have been published. This chapter contributes to that pool with a "ten-year-after" view of an under-researched topic, namely the economic aspects of Yugoslav unraveling. Indeed, the focus in the press, academia, and government circles has been on political change, ethnic cleansing, genocide, and refugees. Significantly less attention has been paid to the fundamental questions of "who gets what": namely, how are scarce resources distributed now, in the twenty-first century, as well as how were they distributed before Yugoslavia broke up. To fill this gap in the literature, this chapter discusses (1) the economic roots of the breakup, (2) the events of the 1990s that had direct bearing on the economies of the region (war, sanctions, transition to capitalism, NATO bombing, etc.), and (3) the current state of the regional economies. In addition to discussing separately the Yugoslav successor states, this chapter concludes with an economic perspective of the entire post-Yugoslav space.

## THE ECONOMIC ROOTS OF YUGOSLAVIA'S DISINTEGRATION

It has been claimed that Yugoslavia disintegrated because of the rise of corrupt leaders, the proliferation of destructive nationalism, the meddling of big powers, the regional differences in political/economic goals, and the mutual intolerance of ethnic/national groups.[1] Each of these causes is indeed a contributing factor. Serbia's Slobodan Milosevic, Bosnia's Izetbegovic, and Croatia's

Franjo Tudjman undoubtedly filled the post-Titoist void by fanning interethnic and international animosities. Western countries, mostly Germany and the United States, contributed by favoring their proteges in the region. The drive by Slovenia to liberalize its economic and political systems placed it at odds with regions where communist tendencies were more entrenched. While all these causes of Yugoslavia's breakup are indeed important, it would be erroneous to omit economic factors, especially *the way in which economic factors affect interethnic relations, tolerance, and conflict.*

In an effort to make the link between economics and ethnicity, three interrelated economic phenomena are discussed below. They are economic competition between ethnic groups, economic decline, and regional inequality. Each is fundamental to ethnic group interactions.

## Interethnic Economic Competition

Ethnic groups compete against each other for economic power.[2] They do this in four ways. First, they compete for scarce resources. The distribution of scarce resources is often the primary source of conflict among ethnic groups. If there is no scarcity, there is no economic source of conflict.[3] According to Van Den Berghe, "Ethnic conflicts, like class conflicts, result from the unequal distribution of and competition for scarce resources."[4] According to Hoetink, "group competition is commonly used if two or more groups try to limit each other's access to scarce resources."[5]

Second, ethnic groups compete for group input in policy making. As a result of their rights to voice concerns and make demands, ethnic groups also obtain economic rewards.[6] Evidence of this was provided by Donald Horowitz, who pointed out that ethnicity is an important factor in the following economic aspects of governmental functioning: development plans, educational controversies, trade union affairs, land policy, business policy, and tax policy.[7] Clearly, if one ethnic group benefits disproportionately from tax laws, business policies, or development projects, then repercussions will permeate throughout the economic, political, and social system with broad ramifications and will further perpetuate the initial advantages of the group in question.

Third, ethnic competition takes place over control over productive inputs. This is especially true if ethnic groups dominate in specific territories and there is some measure of decentralization of power. Under those circumstances, the dominant group exercises control over raw materials, industrial sites, urban developments, and other infrastructure.

Finally, ethnic groups compete over the allocation of economic favors. Favors doled out by ethnic groups include jobs, slots in educational facilities, industrial location, etc.

Given that nationalism is the political expression of ethnic sentiments, its link to interethnic competition is indisputable. Nationalist feelings by definition contain elements of interethnic competition because of the underlying motivation to pursue ends that will enhance a group's overall well-being, position, and advantage within society. A group's well-being is simultaneously political, economic, and cultural (indeed, it is hard to distinguish between the desire for national control of resources among the inhabitants of the tourist-rich Dalmatian coast in Croatia and the pride in their culture and the desire to see their people in power). Thus, nationalism is simply a coherent manifestation of interethnic competition.

## Economic Decline

Economic decline can accentuate feelings of ethnic loyalty and group distinctiveness; in other words, it can stimulate and aggravate feelings of nationalism. There is a consensus among scholars that the relationship between economic decline (or lack of economic development) and ethnic awareness is direct. In other words, the greater the underdevelopment, deterioration, and stagnation of an economy, the greater the efforts of minority ethnic groups to differentiate themselves from the majority or dominant group. (Miroslav Hroch found this in nineteenth-century Europe, Beth Michneck in pre-breakup USSR, Anthony Birch in Bangladesh,[8] and Christine Drake in Sudan, Pakistan, and Indonesia.[9] Interethnic competition increases during economic decline because it unsettles the status quo of interethnic economic relations. It upsets the balance of employment, distribution of resources, education opportunities, and economic advantages that result from changes in economic variables. In the scramble for jobs, ethnic groups may cross over into other group's jobs, causing niche overlap that, according to Susan Olzak, further releases competitive forces.[10] When economic conditions deteriorate, interethnic competition becomes more ferocious and fuels nationalist ideology. Ethnic group differentiation and awareness go hand-in-hand with decline. Macro– and microeconomic problems become exacerbated as interethnic bickering imperils economic functioning and paralyzes economic institutions, contributing to further macro and micro failures. Therefore, it is during times of comprehensive change that political and social competition among ethnic groups for advantages of their members is most acute.

## Regional Inequality

Most states are characterized by inequality between its ethnic groups and its substate regions. When ethnic groups are concentrated in specific regions, as they were in pre-breakup Yugoslavia (Slovenes largely lived in Slovenia, Croats in Croatia, Macedonians in Macedonia, and Montenegrians in Montenegro), then economic competition is pronounced. It is even more pronounced when those regions are unequal with respect to economic growth, development, and potential (numerous studies indicate severe inequality across former Yugoslav regions).[11]

Michael Hechter said that "the uneven wave of industrialization over territorial space creates relatively advanced and less advanced groups, and therefore acute cleavages of interest arise between these groups." As a consequence, "there is a crystallization of the unequal distribution of resources and power between the two groups."[12] This unequal distribution of resources is crucial in perpetuating interethnic competition because it leads to perceptions of economic injustice. Such injustice, perceived by ethnic groups who are not reaping the benefits of economic change, is due to two factors: the objective macroeconomic conditions (such as poverty) as well as policy aimed at rectifying those conditions. However, perception of unjust policies also occurs among ethnic groups who have been advantaged by economic change. Indeed, policy aimed at rectifying the unequal distribution of resources across ethnic groups/regions is often perceived as unjust because it can result in the following: above-average contribution to the national budget by some groups, insufficient benefit from the national budget by some groups, unfavorable terms of trade resulting from price manipulation (that affects some groups and not others), unfavorable regulation pertaining to investment and foreign inflows of resources (affecting selected regions and peoples), and so on. It is clear that perceptions of economic injustice may be experienced by groups in regions that are more or less developed relative to the nation, as is evident in the former Yugoslavia (Slovenia as well as Macedonia). The high-income, subnational regions such as Slovenia experienced tax revolts, reflecting dissatisfaction with what they perceived to be unfair drainage of their resources. At the same time, the less developed regions lobbied for increased "spread effects" of national development, as well as a change in the redistributive policy. Either of these motivate ethnic populations to mobilize their energies and increase interethnic competition for resources.[13]

In the former Yugoslavia, interethnic competition, economic decline, and regional inequality all came together during the 1980s. At this time, the Yugoslav economy was in decline (indeed, the Yugoslav GDP per capita fell by 5 percent during this period). Such a decrease in the size of the total economic pie also implied that the slice of each republic/autonomous region also declined. The ensuing competition for resources that took place among ethnic groups has been the underlying source of conflict in the Yugoslav wars of 1991 to 1994.

Interethnic competition, economic decline, and regional inequality also led to the formulation of demands by segments of the Yugoslav population. Such demands varied in scope and tenacity. In some cases, they were simply demands for increased favoritism by the center toward a region or a targeted segment of the population (such as the Slavic Muslims of Sandzak). Alternatively, they were demands for a dramatic change in the participation of a region in the central and state affairs (such as in Vojvodina). Finally, they were such that nothing short of severance of preexisting economic and political ties with the center would be acceptable. The latter demand is referred to by Leslie as the "we want out" demand, while Bremmer called it the "exit option."[14] This is exactly the demand that Slovenia, Croatia, Macedonia, and Bosnia made in the early 1990s.

## THE 1990S: POLITICAL ACTIONS, ECONOMIC REPERCUSSIONS

Yugoslav disintegration did not take place in a vacuum. The regions did not split apart without any *a priori* or *a posteriori* linkage effects. Instead, the period before and after the breakup was a time when destructive nationalism unleashed violence of a magnitude unexpected in contemporary Europe. Warfare, on shifting stages, resulted in several hundred thousand deaths. Involuntary population movements resulted in the displacement of several million people. Physical capital, including infrastructure and property, was destroyed; and human capital was decimated, as millions emigrated, the educational system collapsed, and pervasive unemployment de-skilled the skilled. The economic transformation from socialism to capitalism, which so effectively transformed Poland, Hungary, and the Czech Republic, was stalled or even reversed in most of the former Yugoslavia. The sanctions imposed on the Federal Republic of Yugoslavia (FRY: Serbia and Montenegro) wreaked economic havoc that spread beyond their boundaries. Throughout the region, the legal and security structures collapsed and a corrupt mafia emerged, one that profited handsomely from the overall chaos. The accumulation of these events drew the attention and involvement of Western leaders, Muslim countries, and international organizations such as NATO.

Each of these events had economic repercussions, both on individual new states as well as on the post-Yugoslav space as a whole. Some of these are discussed below.

### The Economic Repercussions of War

The wars of Yugoslav succession have brought on billions of dollars of damage, devastated lives, created some two million refugees, dried up external financing, and resulted in a major economic setback for the entire Balkan region. They broke out in earnest in July 1991 in Croatia, and by the spring of 1992, the location of the fighting had shifted to Bosnia-Herzegovina, where it proved to be more devastating than in Croatia. The waging of these wars entailed direct changes in the economies of Croatia and Bosnia-Herzegovina. While the war did not take place in Serbia or Montenegro at this time, these regions nevertheless exhibited characteristics of a war economy: war was waged at its borders, aid in various forms was siphoned to Serbs in the warring zones, and refugees became a burden to the economy. As a result of the wars, the economies of Croatia, Serbia, Montenegro, and Bosnia-Herzegovina underwent partial conversion of a civil economy to a war economy. This took place in several ways, including diverting production for war needs, displacing competitive processes, reshuffling the labor force, and the financing of the war effort. These are discussed below.

With respect to production, Bosnia suffered the most pervasive cessation of civil production and the channeling of scarce resources into military production.[15] Production of strategic goods, secondary to the war effort, were also encouraged.[16] In the 70 percent of Bosnia controlled by Bosnian Serbs, all industry was put under military control in early 1994.[17] The FRY economy also altered production to accommodate the war it was indirectly aiding by introducing state control over key sectors in the economy, such as food, medicine, and energy. In the agricultural sector, at various periods during the mid-1990s, there was compulsory procurement of foodstuffs and some raw materials used as inputs in further production. Moreover, strategically important companies were taken over by the state in an effort to control production, thus making FRY the only country in Eastern Europe that moved into, not out of, large-scale military production during the 1990s.[18]

With respect to the displacement of competition by the war, there is no doubt that the authorities in FRY, Croatia, and Bosnia extended state control of various aspects of their respective economies. Indeed, war forced the introduction of a command economy similar to what Yugoslavia experienced in the aftermath of World War II, including the renationalization of banks and numerous firms. The displacement of competition by war also affected the process of price liberalization, trade liberalization, and currency convertibility. Indeed, in all countries affected by war, these were discontinued at various times in the early 1990s (with the exception of Bosnian territory under Muslim control, where the utter confusion and disruption of communication lines prevented the exertion of government power). In addition, price controls and price freezes were introduced, as well as rationing of essential goods (namely, flour, sugar, oil, and detergent).

The Yugoslav wars have depressed the labor markets of Bosnia, Serbia, and Montenegro, where decreases occurred in both the supply and demand for labor. The supply of labor decreased because, first, many workers were drawn into the conflict (army or expanding police force), leaving their enterprises short of skilled labor. Second, workers emigrated out of the warring states in order to escape both a possible draft and dire economic conditions. Very significant has been the exodus of the skilled population (brain drain), which affected Serbia especially harshly (it is estimated that some 100,000 to 150,000 professionals left Serbia in 1992 alone).[19] Third, the war created refugees, as people became involuntarily displaced from their homes. These population movements caused shortages of labor in some locations and an overabundance of labor in others. On the demand side, given the deteriorating aggregate demand and the plummeting economic production, large numbers of workers were laid off. There also emerged large-scale, disguised unemployment, as workers were asked to take indefinite paid vacations.

Finally, with respect to financing the war effort, it was to be expected that the regions directly involved in the war, namely, Bosnia and Croatia, should experience rising spending on military. What is more interesting is the extent to which the FRY, not directly involved, experienced similar increases in expenditure. (According to one estimate, such support constituted 20 percent of gross domestic material product of Serbia in 1992.[20] When coupled with the fact that the Serbian budget for 1993 was altered to include an allocation of 75 percent to the military, it points to serious siphoning of funds for the war effort.)[21] In all states affected by war, the government budgets were supplemented when authorities froze individual and enterprise foreign currency holdings, which they "borrowed" to finance the war effort. (Estimates of this amount are hard to come by, although one source puts it at $12 billion in private hard currency accounts.)[22] Moreover, authorities were often compelled to print money in order to finance expenditure. All these measures were necessary in light of the decrease in government tax revenue due to the disintegration of the tax base: income taxes were lost due to the overall impoverishment of the populations, import duties were lost due to the cessation of trade, business taxes were decreased due to the lack of money in nonproducing enterprises, and the sales tax dried up due to the low consumption rate.

## The Economic Repercussions of Sanctions

Sanctions were imposed on FRY in 1992 (under UN Resolution 757) for its involvement in the Bosnian war. While these sanctions underwent several modifications over the years, they remained in effect until 2000. Some outer sanctions continue to be in place at the time of writing.

While the Yugoslav sanctions have affected all countries in the Balkans, they unequivocally contributed to the devastation of the FRY economy during the 1990s. After only one year of sanctions, the loss of revenue was estimated to be some $25 billion, and the per capita national income has dropped by an order of ten, from around $3000 to $300 (cumulative statistics for the entire sanctions period are discussed below). In one year, the price of bread has increased 800 times, while the price of milk increased over 1000 times. GNP dropped by $12 billion in that year, the value of foreign trade fell by $9 billion, industrial output fell by 40 percent in the first five months of 1993 over the same period in 1992, and one half of the labor force is unemployed. According to the Belgrade Economic Research Center, 97 percent of the population fell to the poverty level in the early 1990s. Moreover, it takes three and a half monthly salaries to purchase the same bundle of goods that could have been purchased with one month's salary in 1990. In Montenegro, sanctions were responsible for a loss in revenue of $277 million, and businesses lost $130 million in exports, $90 million in tourism, and $57 million from shipping in the first year alone.

## The Economic Repercussions of the Breakup

Among the numerous economic effects of the Yugoslav breakup, the most salient, with respect to their effect on the individual economies, are the loss of markets and the cessation of interregional flows of capital.[23]

With respect to the loss of markets, all Yugoslav successor states had to adjust to the transformation of what was previously internal trade into international trade. Those regions that depended on Yugoslav markets for the sale of their output and the purchase of their inputs found themselves having to compete in international markets, expend foreign currency, and trade with the enemy. In some regions, this was not a big issue. Contrary to the Soviet experience in trade dependency, Yugoslav republics had highly fragmented markets (especially from 1974 to 1991). Empirical studies by Bicanic, Ocic, Ding, and Bookman all indicate extremely low levels of interregional trade.[24] Some former Yugoslav republics had trade relations with foreign countries independent of the federal center. In some cases this accounted for 30 percent of its trade. Slovenia and Croatia had lower trade dependency than Kosovo and Bosnia.

With respect to interregional flows, those regions that were net recipients suffered more from the redrawing of boundaries than those that were net losers. In the former Yugoslavia, the less developed regions (Kosovo, Montenegro, Bosnia, and Herzegovina) contributed less to the center than they received; Slovenia, Croatia, and Serbia proper contributed more. An earlier study by the author shows that, in fact, Serbia contributed the most to the Federal Fund,[25] while Kosovo and Montenegro contributed the least.[26] Ding appraised the fiscal burden of each republic relative to the strength of its economy and found that, by this measurement, Serbia ranked the highest.[27]

### The Economic Repercussions of the Transition to Capitalism

Economic reforms aimed at the transition to a market economy in Yugoslavia began at the federal level in the late 1980s. Following the breakup of Yugoslavia, each successor state took steps toward reform that were determined by its particular political and economic conditions (for example, FRY had to contend with sanctions, Bosnia with war, Macedonia with the Greek embargo, etc.). Efforts at privatization and price liberalization were made, with differing levels of enthusiasm, in all states. Efforts at decreasing government budgets and public expenditure as well as stabilizing the macroeconomy were also not consistent across regions.

### The Economic Repercussions of the NATO Bombing

In March 1999, NATO forces, led by the United States, began a bombing campaign against the FRY. After 78 days and 23,000 bombs, NATO stopped bombing, the Serbian police withdrew across provincial borders between Kosovo and Serbia proper, and some 650,000 Albanian refugees returned to their homes. The repercussions of the NATO intervention are great and continue to reverberate in the area. In addition to raising questions about sovereignty, humanitarian intervention, and self-determination, they also include economic costs of destruction of homes, infrastructure, and livelihoods as well as human capital costs associated with the involuntary displacement of populations.

In Serbia proper, the NATO bombing destroyed industries and infrastructure, crippling the economy. The magnitude of the damage differs according to source, but one number that keeps coming up is $4 billion. It also produced the inflow of some 100,000 Serbs and 80,000 Gypsies from Kosovo, adding to some 700,000 to a million refugees from Croatia and Bosnia, forming Europe's biggest refugee population.[28]

## THE CURRENT STATE OF THE REGIONAL ECONOMIES

How did the above events and processes play themselves out in the individual states and regions that make up the post-Yugoslav space? How are these regions and their economies faring in the early 2000s? In order to answer these questions, it is useful to telescope in on the individual economies. In doing so, we find large differences in how the events of the 1990s were experienced.

## Slovenia

Slovenia is a success story, par excellence. After a difficult beginning, Slovenia's economy has been mostly robust and healthy during the 1990s. It continues to enjoy the highest GDP per capita of the transitioning economies of the region ($10,900).[29] In 1999, its growth rate of 3.5 percent was high, its rate of inflation was manageable, and its 7.1 percent unemployment was being addressed. While privatization and capital market reforms are not yet completed, Slovenia has made significant strides toward transforming its economy. It undoubtedly benefited from its political isolation from the remaining post-Yugoslav space. Indeed, it did not suffer the economic ramifications of the wars, population displacements, and sanctions that engulfed its neighbors. Instead, it has been successful in retaining its human capital and attracting foreign investment. Its economy is export oriented, and its trade is mostly with western states, principally the EU.[30] As a result, in comparison to other former Yugoslav regions, Slovenia is said to be "the one who got away."

But that is not surprising, given Slovenia's economic position during the Titoist era. Slovenia was on one end of the bell-shaped curve, while Kosovo was on the other. It enjoyed higher rates of growth over sustained periods; it experienced a greater structural transformation of its economy; and it had the lowest trade dependency on the rest of the Yugoslav regions.[31] It should therefore not come as a surprise that, a decade after the breakup of Yugoslavia, Slovenia continues to be the most developed state in the region.

In addition to its economic development, Slovenia has been at the forefront of political liberalization. According to Ramet, Slovenia's success in democratization clearly placed the country among the Western community of states.[32] These political changes, coupled with economic successes, made Slovenia the only Yugoslav successor state invited to join negotiations for EU membership.

## Croatia

Before the dissolution of Yugoslavia, the Republic of Croatia was the most prosperous and industrialized region after Slovenia, with a per capita output about one-third above the Yugoslav average. During the 1990s, its economy suffered setbacks due to the wars in Croatia and Bosnia (military expenditure as well as destruction of bridges, power lines, factories, and buildings). It also suffered setbacks due to the inflow of refugees as well as extensive corruption and nepotism among the authorities. Moreover, while Croatia did not share Serbia's pariah status, it did face some international isolation due to the policies of its leader, Franjo Tudjman, especially with respect to refugee issues and cooperation with the war criminal extradition effort. That resulted in fewer international loans and less foreign investment than was expected.

The result was a devastated economy. Its banking system became prone to crony lending, and its privatization process stalled as enterprises were sold off to the mafia and then bled dry.[33] The recession that began at the end of 1998 continued through most of 1999, and the GDP growth for the year was flat. Now, inflation is low and the kuna is stable, although the unemployment rate is 20 percent.[34] The good news is that Croatia was successful in some reforms; macroeconomic stabilization policies, after a difficult start, helped the economy rebound and partially successful privatization and banking reforms occurred. [35]

The Croatian economy would have suffered even more if it did not have its traditional links to Germany, which provided both financial and political protection. Moreover, it was the western gateway into Bosnia, so its economy benefited from linkage effects associated with activities of international organizations.

Croatia lagged behind Slovenia with respect to political reforms. While it introduced a multiparty system and general elections, civil liberties and political rights were not up to Western standards. The death of President Tudjman in December 1999 and the defeat of the ruling Croatian Democratic Union in parliamentary and presidential elections in January 2000 ushered in a new era. Not only was there a sense of a loosening political noose, but there was also a renewed commitment to economic reform. The policies of the new government are clearly focused on putting the past decade behind them as rapidly as possible and moving toward Western Europe, using Slovenia as a model.

## Macedonia

Macedonia was the poorest republic in the former Yugoslavia (while Kosovo was the poorest region). As a result, the breakup of the country and the disruption of inter-republic relations were a major blow to the Macedonian economy. It lost key protected markets and large transfer payments from the center. Currently, the economy can meet its basic food needs but depends on outside sources for all of its oil and gas and most of its modern machinery and parts. Growth in 1999 was low (some 2.5 percent), due to the effects of the Kosovo conflict. Unemployment is very high, 35 percent.[36]

Macedonia is heavily dependent on foreign assistance. It has been supported and protected by the West, and especially by the United States and NATO during and after the intervention in Kosovo. It is also awash in NGOs.[37] As a result, its economy has stayed afloat. Until recently, the Western presence was also instrumental in ensuring that the potentially explosive relations between the Albanian population and the Macedonians did not escalate.[38]

There is a way in which it might be argued that Macedonia, as Slovenia, got away. However, two fundamental differences exist between the two successor states. In the former, both economic and political harmony are artificially bolstered by the West, while in the latter, there has been an institutionalization of democracy and economic liberalization. It is likely that, in the absence of Western resolve, Macedonia would fare poorly. It has little physical and human capital, it is not rich in resources, and it does not provide a lucrative terrain for foreign investment. Moreover, while Slovenia is ethnically homogeneous, Macedonia contains a large Albanian minority. It is estimated that anywhere between 20 to 40 percent of the population is Albanian, many of them rural and uneducated. The volatility of the interethnic relations threatens Macedonia's long-term prognosis.

Duncan Perry has said that Macedonia is "finding its way."[39] That way currently consists of walking a thin line between success and failure on the way to becoming a European state. However, it is unclear whether it can maintain its current status among the Yugoslav successor states without continued Western intervention and the cooperation of its Albanian minority.

## Serbia

Referring to the political changes in Belgrade in the fall of 2000, Misha Glenny said "the revolution [of October 2000] was the easy part."[40] His observation is undoubtedly shared by Miroljub Lablus and other economists in Vojislav Kostunica's government who inherited an economy in shambles. It is a third of its size in 1989 and has contracted by 20 percent in mid-1999 to mid-2000. Unemployment, while officially at 27 percent, is closer to 50 percent. Average wages are some $45 per month. Inflation is 50 percent,[41] and foreign debt is estimated at $16 billion.[42] Moreover, numerous institutions are in a state of disarray, including the judiciary, social security, education, and police. Corruption in the economy has become widespread due to years of state-sanctioned mafia activities and crony privatization. According to Milan Nikolic, 70 percent of the economic transactions take place in the gray zone, free from regulation and taxation.[43]

There are many reasons why the Serbian economy went into a free fall. The collapse of the Yugoslav federation in 1991 resulted in the breakup of important inter-republic trade flows. Like most other former Yugoslav republics, Serbia depended on its sister republics for large amounts of energy and manufactures. The war in Croatia and Bosnia siphoned scarce resources, and the NATO bombing destroyed infrastructure and economic capacity. International sanctions isolated the country and prevented trade and investment. The paucity of reforms placed Serbia behind its neighbors in the race to transform the economy. Some 700,000 to one million refugees from Croatia, Bosnia, and Kosovo, Europe's biggest refugee population,[44] add to the competition for resources. Government mismanagement of the economy further accentuated the above problems. The cumulative financial impact of the above is estimated at $30 billion.[45]

While the economic challenges facing Serbia today are greater than those in Bosnia, its prospects for renewal are also greater. This is due, at least in part, to those same factors that enabled it to be at the Yugoslav average before the breakup. It is rich in natural resources, and it has a concentration of industry, albeit now somewhat incapacitated. Due to its former position in the federation, Serbia is a center for communications, transportation, and energy, all of which only await repair. Serbia's biggest obstacle to reconstruction and development is in the area of human capital. It has lost highly skilled and educated workers (according to Pesakovic, 67 percent of all registered researchers, working in research and development, left the country during 1990 to 1993),[46] while the refugees that it gained are at low levels of education.

Serbia's potential for change is further bolstered by the political changes that have occurred since the fall of 2000. A decade of progressively more repressive and corrupt policies kept Slobodan Milosevic in power, despite international isolation. Political changes were a slow and laborious task, often consisting of one step forward and two steps back. Sekelj called Yugoslav's political changes "change without transformation," indicating the lack of fundamental liberalization.[47]

### Vojvodina

In discussing Vojvodina and Kosovo, the two formerly autonomous regions within Serbia, a word of caution is warranted. Given the turbulence of the past decade, statistical collection has become unreliable. Moreover, most data in the FRY are no longer disaggregated by region, making economic assessments of Vojvodina and Kosovo difficult. As a region within Serbia, Vojvodina (and to a lesser extent Kosovo) has shared its economic and political fate during the past decade.[48] According to secondary evidence, Vojvodina continues to outperform the FRY economic averages while Kosovo lags behind (see discussion below).

### Montenegro

The economy of Montenegro exhibited the same free fall as Serbia since they are the only two republics remaining in the federation. As a result, the pro-independence President, Milo Djukanovic, attempted to distance himself from Serbia both politically as well as economically. With respect to the former, he simultaneously flirted with secession and sought an independent *rapprochement* with the West. With respect to the latter, he attempted to isolate Montenegro from the economic disaster in Serbia by engaging in independent economic policies, such as the introduction of the German mark.

Before the breakup of Yugoslavia, Montenegro was a relatively poor region with few resources and little infrastructure. It was the recipient of net transfusions from the central coffers.[49] While it did get some preferential treatment from the West during Milosevic's rule, that benefit is unlikely to continue as long as democratization continues in Belgrade. If Montenegro is forced to rely on its own resources and capacities, its trade and capital dependency on the outside will continue to be large.

## Kosovo

Before 1991, Kosovo was the poorest region of Yugoslavia. It was not rich in resources, had little productive capacity, and tended to rely on agriculture, small-scale trade, and extractive industries. It was a net economic beneficiary of its ties to the federation. After a decade of boycott of Yugoslav institutions, the establishment of a parallel government, repression of independence efforts by Serbian authorities, and mutually destructive interethnic violence, NATO intervened on behalf of the Albanians in 1999 with a bombing campaign against the Serbs.

Today, Kosovo has a paradoxical status. It is a western Protectorate, managed by the United Nations and patrolled by NATO troops. The UN has taken an active role in its economic affairs. It has introduced the German mark as legal tender, it has begun to create a fiscal system for Kosovo (by collecting excise and customs taxes at border crossings and by developing government budgets), and it is developing a new legal system. These are all signs of independence. Yet Kosovo remains a part of a sovereign state, Yugoslavia, that effectively has no jurisdiction over its territory. This paradox is clearly visible in economic policy. It is also visible in the growing problem of unresolved claims of Serbian property and business interests.

Despite the infusion of assistance and international attention, Kosovo continues to have a dysfunctional economy, heavily dependent on the outside. This is most clear in the emergence of an economy based on trade rather than production. Little is produced, since industrial facilities cannot operate, and there is lack of key personnel, lack of electrical power, and years of inadequate maintenance. There is small-scale retail trade and a lot of smuggling. Together with Bosnia, this region has become a center for illegal trade in goods and people. To attract foreign investment and provide jobs, Kosovo must privatize and reform its economy, which has been crippled. Foreign assistance has been distributed to local populations who often invested it in provision of services (such as food establishments and property rentals) that cater to foreigners. Indeed, the plethora of aid workers, journalists, and UN, NATO, and EU personnel have demands that the entrepreneurial local population rushed to satisfy. However, such economic activity does not constitute the basis of long-term development. When foreign workers leave, local demand cannot sustain such production. The economic implications of the foreign presence in Kosovo led the then shadow president Rugova to say, in 1999, that, as far as he was concerned, the UN could remain in Kosovo forever because the chances of the region standing on its own in the future was remote.[50]

Political liberalization in Kosovo has been retarded first by the Serbs and then by the Albanian leaders. During the 1990s, Serb police repressed expressions of dissatisfaction, especially in the aftermath of the reversal of Kosovo's autonomy. The NATO intervention brought the KLA leadership to power and a different form of repression began. It is only with the election of Ibrahim Rugova's moderate party in municipal elections in the fall of 2000 that political and civil liberties might have a chance to prosper.

### Bosnia

In the former Yugoslavia, Bosnia was ranked below average by numerous economic indicators. Its economic prospects were not helped by the breakup of the country, the war that broke out in 1992, and the continued interethnic animosities that have followed. During 1990 to 1995, production plummeted by 80 percent, and while a recovery did take place in 1996 to 1998, GDP remains below its 1990 level.[51] There continues to be much black market activity and much corruption in the economy. Bosnia has a huge and unsustainable trade deficit, virtually no domestic investment, overblown budgets, massive unemployment, and semi-corrupt and inefficient institutions. While there currently is macroeconomic stability, it is artificial, due to heavy doses of foreign assistance.[52] Indeed, the aid package for Bosnia was many times the relative size of the Marshall Plan. The country has received an infusion of $5 million in the five years since the Dayton Peace Accords were signed. Despite this, Bosnia continues to be ranked low among the Yugoslav successor states.

The process of political liberalization has been stalled by the persistent nationalism of the three contending ethnic groups. As a result, Western scholars have said that Bosnia experienced failed democratization.[53]

Thus, Bosnia is a less developed state, lacking solid institutions and permeated with political distrust and outside dependency. Pessimism about its future has been very strong among the population, as expressed in a recent survey that indicated 62 percent of the young people would leave the country if they had a chance.[54]

## THE PERSISTENCE OF REGIONAL DISPARITIES: IMPLICATIONS FOR THE POST-YUGOSLAV SPACE

Among the many conclusions that can be drawn from the above economic assessment, the most glaring has to do with the regional discrepancies that continue to dominate the post-Yugoslav space. It is clear that, in most cases, the changes over the past decade cemented each region's relative position vis à vis the others. Indeed, one decade after the biggest war and population displacement in Europe in half a century and the largest per capita transfusion of assistance Europe has ever experienced, the regional inequality among the units emerging from the former Yugoslavia has not changed significantly. Indeed, Slovenia continues to be the best off, followed by Croatia. Kosovo continues to be worst off, and Bosnia continues to lie close to the bottom of the ranking.

Does this imply that Kosovo and Bosnia, despite massive Western assistance, are just doomed to perpetual inferiority and low standards of living? Not necessarily! A positive and constructive approach to development across the post-Yugoslav space is rooted in the realpolitik view that a gap between regions will always exist, there will always be richer and poorer regions; however, that inequality may be the source of development.

Indeed, it is as a result of regional inequalities that the economic impact of the demonstration and the multiplier effects is maximized. The former draws on the fact that Yugoslav successor states, given that they were part of the same country in the recent past, cannot but compare themselves to each other. In Slovenia, liberalizing trends in economics and politics have led to a high degree of Westernization. Its example reverberates throughout the Yugoslav space, as all successor regions share the goal of joining Europe. In their desire to emulate the successes of Slovenia, other successor states will absorb, through the demonstration effect, its lessons. They will be nudged further in that direction by international pressure (such as the conditions set by the EU for acceptance into the union).

The multiplier effect will also reverberate throughout the Yugoslav successor states as economic growth, though trade and exchange, ripples throughout the area. During pre-war Yugoslavia, interregional trade patterns were set in large part by the differing levels of development. For example, Slovenia exported manufactured goods to Bosnia and Kosovo while Macedonia exported agricultural products to Croatia and Slovenia. Such trade patterns, determined and enabled by regional inequalities in both consumer capacity and producer capability, are likely to reemerge. This inequality was the reason why these regions traded in the first place (during a decentralized Yugoslavia), and it is the reason they will trade in the future.

Thus, despite their current animosities, Yugoslav successor states and regions are likely to have economic interactions as a result of the persistent regional inequalities. Paradoxically, the continuing inequalities in the post-Yugoslav space can stimulate economic growth in the less developed regions.[55]

Thus, this chapter concludes with a maverick perspective. In the literature, it is no longer fashionable to study the Yugoslav successor states as a group, since their paths have diverged, and thus, it is argued, their futures have become unrelated. In contrast, this chapter takes the opposite view, contending that a strong justification exists to study these new entities together, namely, geography. It is likely that, over time, the economic links between the successor states will expand rather than contract, irrespective of their political arrangements. It is myopic to ignore that economic possibility simply on the basis of current animosities. Therefore, rather than being outdated, the economic study of the cumulative post-Yugoslav space is forward looking.

## NOTES

1. Numerous attempts have been made to distinguish between the population groups of the former Yugoslavia in a definitive way. Sometimes the distinguishing factor is religion, alternatively it is nation or ethnicity. While there is no consensus as to which classification is most appropriate, for the sake of simplicity, the term ethnicity will be used in this paper. For an elaboration of this classification debate, see Milica Zarkovic Bookman, *The Demographic Struggle for Power*, London: Frank Cass, 1997, chapter 3.

2. Bookman, *Demographic Struggle*, chapter 2.

3. If there is no scarcity, then there is no problem. While there is scarcity in all goods in society, there must be limited access and attainability. Hoetink describes this condition as competition that comes from scarcity, in both the objective and subjective sense; it is not only that all economic goods are scarce (in the objective sense), but members of society must perceive them as such (subjective). Harmannus Hoetink "Resource Competition, Monopoly, and Socioracial Diversity" in Leo Despres (ed.) *Ethnicity and Resource Competition in Plural Societies*, The Hague: Mouton Publishers, 1975, p. 10.

4. Pierre L. Van Den Berghe, "Ethnicity and Class in Highland Peru" in Despres, *Ethnicity*, p. 72.

5. Hoetink, "Resource Competition," p. 9.

6. These rewards, and the lack thereof, are the subject of a study by Susan F. Feiner, *Race and Gender in the American Economy*, Englewood Cliffs, New Jersey: Prentice Hall, 1994.

7. Donald L. Horowitz, *Ethnic Groups in Conflict*, Berkeley: University of California Press, 1985, pp. 8–12.

8. Miroslav Hroch, *Social Preconditions of National Revival in Europe*, Cambridge: Cambridge University Press, 1985; Beth Michneck, "Regional Autonomy, Territoriality, and the Economy," paper presented to the American Association for the Advancement of Slavic Studies, Washington, D.C., October 1990; Anthony Birch, *Nationalism and National Integration*, London: Unwin Hyman, 1989.

9. Christine Drake, *National Integration in Indonesia: Patterns and Policies*, Honolulu: University of Hawaii Press, 1989, p. 145.

10. Niche overlap releases competitive forces. At the same time, competition causes niche overlap. Susan Olzak, *The Dynamics of Ethnic Competition and Conflict,* Stanford, California: Stanford University Press, 1992, pp. 26–27.

11. Baletic and Marendic calculated that Slovenia was approximately three fourths above the national average by various development indicators. It was followed by Vojvodina and Croatia, both of which were above the national average by approximately one fifth. Serbia proper was slightly below the national average, whereas Macedonia, Montenegro, Bosnia, and Herzegovina were about one third below the national average. Kosovo, by far the least developed region by all indicators, was some forty percent below the national average. Z. Baletic and B. Marendic, "The Policy and System of Regional Development," in Rikard Lang, George Macesich, and Dragan Vojnic, (eds.), *Essays on the Political Economy of Yugoslavia*, Zagreb: Informator, 1992, p. 251. In addition, Flakierski contends that, overall, Yugoslavia had larger discrepancies among its republics than any socialist country, including Czechoslovakia and the Soviet Union (Henryk Flakierski, *The Economic System and Income Distribution in Yugoslavia*, Armonk, New York: M.E. Sharpe, 1989). Also, Gros and Steinherr calculated the coefficient of variation in regional disparities among European countries and found that it was highest in Yugoslavia (51 percent) (Daniel Gros and Alfred Steinherr, *Winds of Change, Economic Transition in Central and Eastern Europe*, London: Longman, 1995, p. 338). These findings of regional inequality were supported by Bookman and Ding, both of whom used them as a starting point to assess the viability of regions in the case of an eventual breakup (Milica Zarkovic Bookman, "The Economic Basis of Regional Autarchy in Yugoslavia," *Soviet Studies* 42, no. 1, 1990; Milica Zarkovic Bookman, *The Economics of Secession*, New York: St. Martin's Press, 1992; Wei Ding, "Yugoslavia: Costs and Benefits of Union and Interdependence of Regional Economies," *Comparative Economic Studies* 33, no. 4, 1991).

12. Michael Hechter, *Internal Colonialism*, Berkeley: University of California Press, 1975, p. 39.

13. Unless they take another path: when perceptions of economic injustice influence the valuation of relative costs and benefits of belonging to a national union, and when costs outweigh benefits, economic factors are then mingled with ethnic, religious, or cultural factors to form a set of demands that may include leaving the union (namely, secession).

14. Peter Leslie, "Ethnonationalism in a Federal State: The Case of Canada," in Joseph Rudolph and Robert Thompson (eds.), *Ethnoterritorial Politics, Policy and the Western World*, Boulder, Colorado: Lynne Rienner Publishers, 1989, p. 47; Ian Bremmer, "Fraternal Illusions: Nations and Politics in the USSR," paper presented to the American Association for the Advancement of Slavic Studies, Miami, 1991, p. 47.

15. In the Muslim territories, the Bratstvo plant in Novi Travnik, the Slavko Rodic plant in Bugojno, and the Igman plant near Konjic were all actively engaged in production of military equipment and supplies. These areas of central Bosnia were the source of 55 percent of arms production in Bosnia before the war. Production today includes howitzers, mortars, antitank missiles, explosives, hand grenades, and ammunition. *Philadelphia Inquirer*, April 21, 1994.

16. For example, in the Bosnian Serb territories, the Birac factory in Zvornik began producing aluminum oxide and granulated zeolite. *Ekonomska Politika* #2177, December 27, 1993, p. 12.

17. This is due in part to concerns about the future of subsidies from the FRY given the new monetary policy introduced in Belgrade, which entails a reduction of public spending (*Economist*, February 5, 1994, p. 54).

18. Indeed, the factory Crvena Zastava had decreased its automobile production but continued producing small arms, M-84 tanks, and unguided and guided missiles, while a machine building factory in Valjevo had been converted to aircraft engine production. *RFE/RL Research Report*, vol. 2, no. 41, October 15, 1993, p. 35.

19. *RFE/RL News Brief*, December 28–January 8, 1993, p. 14.

20. *Ekonomska Politika*, July 19, 1993, p. 23, cited in REF/RL Research Report, vol. 2, no. 34, August 27, 1993, p. 22.

21. *FRE/RL Daily News*, June 16, 1993.

22. Sabrina P. Ramet, "War in the Balkans," *Foreign Affairs* 71, no. 4 1992, p. 91.

23. A comprehensive discussion of the economic effects of the breakup is included in Bookman, *Secession*.

24. Bookman, "Regional Autarchy"; Ivo Bicanic "Fractured Economy," in Dennis Rusinow, *Yugoslavia, A Fractured Federalism*, Washington, D.C.: The Wilson Center Press, 1988; C. Ocic, "Integracioni i Dezintegracioni Procesi u Privredi Jugoslavije," *Marksisticka Misao* 4, 1983. The study by Ding uses data compiled from the Yugoslav press to show that trade with other republics accounts for roughly one-third of Slovenia's trade. Wei Ding, "Yugoslavia: Costs and Benefits of Union and Interdependence of Regional Economies" *Comparative Economic Studies* 33, no. 4, 1991, p. 22.

25. This fund is part of the federal spending, which also included military spending, administrative spending, and miscellaneous expenditures. Payment into the fund comes from individual republics, which is one of the three sources of funds for the federal government (the other two are federal sales taxes and import duties).

26. Bookman, *Secession*, chapter 4.

27. In per capita terms, this translated into the following: Slovenia $360, Croatia $188, Vojvodina $178, and Serbia $132. Ding, "Yugoslavia," p. 8.

28. Carl Bildt, "A Second Chance in the Balkans," *Foreign Affairs*, January/Febuary 2001, p. 153.

29. www.odci.gov/cia/publications/factbook/geos/si.html, accessed February 19, 2001.

30. See evidence of Slovenia's trade patterns in Stefan Bojnec, "Restructuring and Marketing Strategies at Macro and Micro Levels: The Case of Slovenia," *Europe-Asia Studies* 52, no. 7, 2000, pp. 1335–37.

31. Bookman, *Secession*, pp. 72–73.

32. Sabrina Petra Ramet, "Democratization in Slovenia—the Second Stage," in Karen Dawisha and Bruce Parrott (eds.), *Politics, Power and the Struggle for Democracy in South-East Europe*, Cambridge: Cambridge University Press, 1997.

33. Bogdan Denitch, "Post-Tudjman Croatia: Time to Rethink Western Policy" *East European Studies Newsletter*, Spring 2000, p. 5.

34. www.odci.gov/cia/publications/factbook/geos/hr.html, accessed February 19, 2001.

35. Ivo Bicanic, "The Croatian Economy: Transition and Stabilization," in Joint Economic Committee Congress of the United States, *East Central European Economies in Transition*, Washington, D.C., 1994.

36. CIA Factbook, Macedonia, www.odci.gov/cia/publications/factbook/geos/mk.html, accessed February 19, 2001.

37. See Alice Ackermann, *Making Peace Prevail: Preventing Violent Conflict in Macedonia*, Syracuse, New York: Syracuse University Press, 2000.

38. Rebels from Kosovo, emboldened by some successes in Serbia Proper, have begun incursions into Macedonia (*New York Times*, February 25, 2001).

39. Duncan M. Perry, "The Republic of Macedonia: Finding Its Way," in Dawisha and Parrott, *Politics, Power and the Struggle for Democracy*, p. 226.

40. *New York Times*, October 7, 2000.

41. *New York Times*, October 8, 2000.

42. *Miami Herald*, October 9, 2000.

43. *New York Times*, October 7, 2000.

44. Carl Bildt, "A Second Chance in the Balkans," *Foreign Affairs*, January/February 2001, p. 153.

45. *New York Times*, October 8, 2000.

46. Gordana Pesakovic, "Pauperization of a Nation: Effects of Economic Sanctions Upon Health, Education, Social Welfare and Income Distribution in Yugoslavia," paper presented to the International Studies Association meetings in Chicago, February 24, 2001.

47. Laslo Sekelj, "Parties and Elections: The Federal Republic of Yugoslavia—Change Without Transformation," *Europe/Asia Studies* 52, no. 1, 2000, p. 57.

48. Vojvodina lost its autonomous status at the same time as Kosovo, in 1989.

49. Bookman, *Secession*, pp. 78–79.

50. *Wall Street Journal*, November 2, 1999.

51. CIA Factbook, Bosnia, www.odci.gov/cia/publications/factbook/geos/bk.html, accessed on February 19, 2001.

52. Steven Rattner, *Promoting Sustainable Economies in the Balkans*, New York: Council on Foreign Relations, 2000, p. 12.

53. Steven Burg and Paul Shoup, *The War in Bosnia and Herzegovina*, Armonk, New York: M. E. Sharpe, 1999; Robert M. Hayden, *Blueprints for a House Divided*, Ann Arbor: University of Michigan Press, 1999.

54. Bildt, "A Second Chance in the Balkans," p. 152.

55. The international community might also participate in this growth process in two ways: by providing foreign assistance and by integrating the region into the globalizing economy through investment and trade. In the short run, it is assistance that will jump-start their economies, since direct foreign investment will be slow in coming and domestic savings slow in growing. However, in the long run, international integration and participation must supercede foreign assistance as the principal form of infusion.

# 6

## International Policy in Southeastern Europe: A Diagnosis

*Gordon N. Bardos*

**SUMMARY**

Ten years of intensive international engagement have failed to stabilize southeastern Europe. Ethnic cleansing has not been prevented (or entirely reversed), wars have not been averted, and democratic transitions are far from consolidated. Much of the explanation for this state of affairs lies in misguided policies adopted by the "international community" to deal with the breakup of the former Yugoslavia. International policies have failed to differentiate between what can influence political actors in the short term with what is detrimental to the economic and social stability needed for democratic polities in the long term. Economic development is crucial for stability and democratization in the Balkans, yet many aspects of international engagement in southeastern Europe disrupted the normal flow of trade through the region or destroyed the productive capacities of perhaps the most crucial strategic and economic power in the region, Serbia. This article attempts the following: (1) to describe the conventional western paradigm for understanding the disintegration of Yugoslavia; (2) the policy implications that result from such an understanding; and (3) to provide an alternative understanding of the forces at work in driving recent Balkan history.

After a decade of intensive engagement in the Balkans, international policy in the region has far to go to achieve its stated policy objectives of creating multiethnic democracies with market economies within stable borders. Yet during a decade of tragedy and bloodshed in the states of the former Yugoslavia, rather than fostering the development of stable multiethnic democracies, the international community has instead assisted (albeit unwittedly) perhaps) in the creation of either dysfunctional international protectorates or monoethnic independent states. Instead of reversing the results of ethnic cleansing, successive U.S. and EU policies have legitimated them. Instead of easing the transition to a market economy for the states of southeastern Europe, international policies toward the region have retarded the transition. And instead of weakening Slobodan Milosevic's regime, international policy, arguably, consistently helped make his grip on power stronger throughout the 1990s.

How policies adopted by the EU and the United States achieved, as Michael Mandelbaum dubbed the Kosovo conflict, such a "perfect failure,"[1] is due to a fundamental misdiagnosis of the prerequisites for stabilizing southeastern Europe. Much of international policy over the past decade has been akin to swatting flies with a sledgehammer, in that actions taken to thwart the alleged actions of one man (or a small group of men) have done considerable long-term damage to the region. The problems with international policy are now painfully obvious. Slobodan Milosevic is sitting in The Hague and former Croatian president Franjo Tudjman is now dead, yet the problems of Bosnia-Herzegovina, Kosovo, Macedonia, Montenegro, and the Presevo Valley continue to disrupt regional stability. Without major changes in the international approach to southeastern Europe, the prospects for establishing stable democracies in the region are limited.

## CONVENTIONAL EXPLANATIONS

Perhaps the most popular explanation for the disintegration of the former Yugoslavia places the blame on a small group of malevolent politicians and leaders who deliberately adopted policies leading to the disintegration of the state and led their respective populations into war to keep themselves in power. Richard Holbrooke, for instance, claimed that "Yugoslavia's tragedy was not foreordained. It was the product of bad, even criminal, political leaders who encouraged ethnic confrontation for personal, political, and financial gain."[2] Similarly, Warren Zimmerman has argued that "Yugoslavia's death and the violence that followed resulted from the conscious actions of nationalist leaders who coopted, intimidated, circumvented, or eliminated all opposition to their demagogic designs. Yugoslavia was destroyed from the top down."[3] A rather confused version of this argument is provided in a recent survey of the post-Milosevic Balkans by the International Institute for Strategic Studies (IISS) which argues, "Although terrorist incidents and localized violence will continue [in the Balkans], the Balkan wars, which repeated themselves with terrifying monotony during the last century, are now over."[4]

Here is a perfect example of muddled reasoning: now that Milosevic is gone, there will be no more war in the Balkans, even though these wars repeated themselves "with terrifying monotony" for at least eighty-five years before Milosevic came to power.

A succinct summary of much of the thinking of this school of thought can be found in a recent report on the November 2000 elections in Bosnia-Herzegovina produced by the International Crisis Group (ICG):

> Despite five years and five billion US dollars of international community investment in Bosnia, the 11 November Bosnian elections demonstrated once again that international engagement has failed to provide a sustainable basis for a functioning state, capable of surviving an international withdrawal. The elections highlighted once again the near complete failure—in the face of determined nationalist extremism—of an international approach that places emphasis on hope that moderate, cooperative Bosnian partners will come to power through elections. The elections also revealed the complete unsuitability of the present Dayton constitutional structures, as well as the international community implementing structures and policies. . . . Many in the international community had naively hoped that democratic change in Zagreb and Belgrade would translate into change among Bosnia's Croats and Serbs. To the contrary, these democratic victories appear to have energized Bosnia's ethnic extremists.[5]

A careful reading of the above suggests that these "ethnic extremists" must have almost superhuman abilities. Neither the passage of time nor the expenditure of billions of dollars can defeat their agenda. They are able to defy the will of the international community and have found ways of sabotaging or subverting constitutional arrangements designed by the brightest minds at the U.S. State Department. They are impervious to positive democratic changes in Bosnia's immediate environment. They are even able to waylay the will of the people, as expressed in elections organized, supervised, and paid for by the international community.

Of course, echoes of this debate over the role of elites in nationalist conflict can be heard within the scholarly community as well. The "constructivist school" of ethnic identity formation, as Alexander Motyl points out, claims that nations are "constructed, invented, or imagined in the age of nationalism" by self-conscious elites. Motyl goes on to point out that

> if elites can create nations, they should also be able to pull off, as most strong constructivists would indeed grant, the far less complicated task of whipping them up into a nationalist frenzy. But if such omnipotent and prescient elites can create nations and whip them up, they must be no less capable of "whipping down" nations, and indeed, of "un-creating" them.[6]

Much of international policy in the Balkans over the past decade has indeed been focused on replacing or toppling individuals or elites held responsible for "whipping up" nations, and on finding counter-elites willing to "whip" them back down. The implications of such views, however, are not encouraging for those who hope to consolidate democratic transitions in the region. The belief that entire societies can be manipulated in such ways, as Rogers Brubaker points out, reduces the general population to being "passive dupes, vehicles or objects of manipulative designs" instead of "active participants" and "political subjects in their own right."[7] But if the average citizen in Southeastern Europe is indeed a "passive dupe," perhaps we should reconsider the extent to which it is worth the effort to foster Jeffersonian-style democracy in the region.

There is another problem with this line of reasoning, which has had direct consequences for international policy in the region. Arguably, international (and especially American) policy in the region for much of the past decade has been using sledgehammers to kill mosquitos. The hallmarks of international policy in the Balkans—economic sanctions, international isolation, experiments in state and nation building, and military interventions—were designed to deal with the machinations of a small group of individuals who allegedly destroyed a state and plunged a region into war. Yet these same policies, intended to produce short-term policy results or modifications in elite behavior, instead resulted in long-term damage to the region. If the true goal of international policymakers over the past decade has been to foster the social and economic development needed to sustain stable democratic polities, then the policies used throughout the 1990s and beyond can only have been counterproductive. What follows is a deconstruction of these policies, and an examination of their effects.

## SANCTIONS

One of the primary weapons the international community used in its effort to topple the Milosevic regime, or to force it to moderate its policies, has been the use of economic sanctions. A related policy has been the use of international isolation: cutting diplomatic ties and minimizing a state's (and society's) contacts with the outside world, such as by prohibiting national sports teams from participating in international competitions. During the Bosnian war, it was argued that the sanctions would so weaken the Federal Republic of Yugoslavia (FRY) that Milosevic would sue for peace. After the Bosnian war, a so-called outer wall of sanctions (prohibiting the FRY from gaining access to international financial institutions) was unilaterally imposed on the

FRY by the United States until it made substantial progress on liberalization within the country and resolution of the situation in Kosovo.

In the end, the sanctions regime achieved none of these goals. The war in Bosnia continued for some forty months after the imposition of sanctions on the FRY in May 1992. Similarly, the sanctions did not force Milosevic to liberalize political conditions within the FRY, nor, of course, to seek a political settlement with the Kosovo Albanians.

Given the failure of similar punitive policies against Cuba or Iraq, however, the failure of economic sanctions to produce their intended results should not come as a surprise; as one recent study found, "economic sanctions have little independent usefulness for pursuit of noneconomic goals."[8] In fact, from a variety of perspectives a powerful argument can be made that the sanctions were counterproductive. Ethicists have long argued that economic sanctions, which inflict a disproportionate amount of suffering on the weakest members of society, are morally unacceptable.[9] But apart from the questionable morality of using sanctions as a policy weapon, however, international isolation and economic sanctions often work to the detriment of civil society in authoritarian regimes. Minimizing a state's contacts with the outside world only makes authoritarian regimes more powerful vis-a-vis their own societies. Groups arguing for more political liberalization and more space for civil society are thereby isolated from their natural supporters in the outside world. As the Croatian writer Slavenka Drakulic has noted, "No dictator wants his country to be part of something bigger. On the contrary: The more isolated we are, the safer they (i.e., dictators) feel."[10] Jiri Dienstbier, the former United Nations Special Rapporteur on Human Rights for Yugoslavia, has expressed similar views. As Dienstbier notes, dissidents behind the Iron Curtain during the Cold War favored as much openness and contact with the outside world as possible, realizing the impact that this would have on weakening the communist regimes.[11] Indeed, it was Gorbachev's reforms and the greater openness he allowed in Soviet society and toward the outside world that ultimately brought down the Iron Curtain. If the Soviet experience is any guide, it would have been better to try to undermine the Milosevic regime with a policy of "glasnost imposed from outside."

In fact, far from weakening the Milosevic regime, the sanctions increased the regime's control over the economy by increasing the importance of state-owned businesses or those allied with the regime. Meanwhile, smaller privately owned firms failed, effectively reducing the social and financial support available to regime opponents.[12] Opposition to the regime was also weakened by the demographic and social upheaval that occurred in Serbia over the past decade. Serbian society suffered from a brain drain of significant proportions in the 1990s, as younger, better-educated, and more liberally minded individuals—the demographic groups that sociological surveys repeatedly showed were the most opposed to the Milosevic regime—left the country in increasing numbers.[13] As a result, older people, the lesser-educated, the poor, the rural peasantry, and refugees and displaced persons—the same demographic groups that were the most likely supporters of the Milosevic regime and/or the extreme nationalist Serbian Radical Party—assumed increased importance in Serbian political life.

Moreover, the extremely negative impact of the sanctions regime affected not only the FRY, but also became a regional problem, feeding the growth of large criminal syndicates throughout the Balkans that made huge profits off of sanctions-busting and illegal trade with the FRY. In Albania, for instance, the sanctions regime against the FRY was cited as a major cause of the rise in criminality in northern parts of the country. Similar sanctions-busting criminal organizations developed in Bulgaria, Montenegro, Macedonia, and Romania. Yet international officials now claim that these very same criminal syndicates are at present the greatest threat to democratization in the region. As Ambassador Robert Barry, former head of the OSCE's (Oragnization for Security and Cooperation in Europe) mission in Bosnia-Herzegovina recently noted,

> Organized crime and corruption are a more serious threat to security and stability than military forces. The growing nexus between extremist politicians, organized crime and the former communist intelligence services is becoming ever stronger, and this is the single greatest obstacle to democratic reform, economic investment and membership in Euro-Atlantic institutions. Rolling back the mafia must be a central goal of the Stability Pact, NATO, the EU, and the OSCE.[14]

Apart from providing the fertile ground in which these criminal organizations thrive, the sanctions had other negative economic effects throughout the region. Because of the FRY's key strategic position as a transportation hub and major market for goods from neighboring states, economically isolating Yugoslavia effectively held back the economic development of all of southeastern Europe. According to one estimate, the cost to neighboring countries of the international sanctions regime on the FRY from 1992–1996 was some $35 billion.[15] For Macedonia, the sanctions regime meant the loss of its main trading partner, along with the increase in ethnic tensions associated with declining living standards. At a protest by workers in Macedonia's capital, Skopje, one trade union leader claimed, "We have a right to send a powerful message to the international community and Europe that Macedonia cannot overcome its economic crisis with all of these barriers and blockades."[16] Bulgaria was losing an estimated $2 billion per year after 1992 as a result of the sanctions regime.[17] Due to the West's refusal to rebuild damaged bridges on the Danube, the Romanian shipping industry was crippled, losing $100 million and laying off 80 percent of its workforce.[18] Almost a year after the end of the Kosovo conflict, the prime ministers of Bulgaria and Romania jointly attacked the international community for refusing to provide funds for rebuilding destroyed bridges over the Danube, claiming "Romania and Bulgaria have suffered more than the Belgrade regime" from the Danube's closure.[19] Other regional leaders, such as Croatian president Stipe Mesic, argued that a more effective strategy against Milosevic would have been lifting the sanctions and allowing the Serbian economy to "get back on its feet."[20]

In light of all of these problems caused to Serbian society, and indeed throughout the region, were there better policy options available? Richard Haass and Meghan L. O'Sullivan have recently argued that, instead of economic sanctions, a more advantageous policy for dealing with problem states is adopting a policy of either conditional or unconditional engagement: it can help build the private sector and other non-state elements in the target countries, widen the base of support for engagement with the international community, or build a constituency supporting adherence to international norms in general.[21]

Ironically, engagement was in fact the favored approach of the Clinton administration in dealing with other "problem countries." In public remarks on the passage of legislation allowing China into the World Trade Organization, Bill Clinton claimed,

> By this agreement, we will also export more of one of our most cherished values, economic freedom. Bringing China into the WTO and normalizing trade will strengthen those who fight for the environment, for labor standards, for human rights, for the rule of law. . . . [A]t this stage in China's development, we will have more positive influence with an outstretched hand than with a clenched fist.[22]

Obviously, if economic integration and international engagement could have such a beneficial impact on a country of more than one billion people, it could have had a decisive impact on one of only ten million.

One of the most widely accepted tenets in the study of politics holds that the establishment and maintenance of a democracy requires a significant degree of economic prosperity and social stability. As the authors of a recent study note,

> Few concepts in political science have been as widely accepted (particularly in the Western world) as the idea that socio-economic well-being is the crucial foundation of a sound democracy. The formation and growth of a middle class through robust economic development is considered to be the bulwark of democratic stability.[23]

But the long-term economic consequences of the sanctions policy, in the form of the increasing impoverishment of ever greater numbers of the Serbian population and the demographic shifts that have resulted from this impoverishment, have made any eventual transition to a stable democratic system in the FRY much more difficult. Far from fostering the creation of a middle class capable of sustaining a democratic polity, the purpose of the sanctions regime, according to a high-ranking State Department official, had been to "de-civilize Serbia."[24] Unfortunately, "de-civilized" countries seldom become stable democratic ones.

## ELECTIONS/CONSTITUTIONS

Much of the international community's policy in the Balkans over the past ten years has been premised on bringing new leaders to power. Former U.S. Secretary of State Madeleine Albright, for instance, claimed that "Democracy is the key to our strategy throughout southeastern Europe. Democratic governments are more stable internally, more likely to encourage ethnic tolerance and more interested in establishing closer economic and political ties with their neighbors and the West."[25]

Yet the belief that elections will result in greater degrees of ethnic tolerance was repeatedly proven unfounded in the Balkans in the 1990s. Paradoxically, in many newly independent and democratizing states, elections can increase ethnic tensions and the potential for violence.[26] This was repeatedly true in the Yugoslav case throughout the 1990s, where elections held at the wrong time or under the wrong circumstances often derailed democratic transitions instead of advancing them. Thus, the former Yugoslavia's first democratic elections in 1990 brought to power all of the nationalist leaders the West has so frequently criticized. Yet despite a decade of conflict, destruction, and economic decline, in 1999 all of these leaders were still in power, often after several rounds of elections.

In Bosnia-Herzegovina, in the various sets of elections held in the country since 1996, voters have repeatedly voted along ethnic lines, consistent with the historical pattern Xavier Bougarel has pointed out, noting that "All elections held in Bosnia since 1910 have been dominated by national parties."[27] Moreover, one can validly ask whether elections have any real meaning or legitimacy in post-Dayton Bosnia when the international High Representative—essentially an international bureaucrat with no democratic mandate or domestic popular accountability to the people of Bosnia itself—has the authority to remove publicly elected officials from office, a power he has used to dismiss both the president of Republika Srpska in 1998 and the Croat member of the joint state presidency in 2001, along with several dozens of other lesser officials. In Macedonia, despite the existence of an uneasy ruling coalition government between Macedonian Slav and ethnic Albanian parties, few observers see a promising future for the country, and the massive vote fraud that took place in Albanian populated areas in the 1999 elections did much to polarize the political situation there,[28] as has the Albanian political parties' support for the "National Liberation Army." In Montenegro, EU and U.S. officials strongly supported Milo Djukanovic from 1998 to 2000 as an alternative to Slobodan Milosevic, despite his more or less open ties to various smuggling operations and organized crime syndicates in the Balkans. With Milosevic's overthrow, Djukanovic no longer enjoys the support of the international community, and the ethnic Albanian and Muslim Slav support that Milo Djukanovic's government currently receives would quickly evaporate should Montenegro declare its independence, as the rationale for what keeps his coalition together—limiting Belgrade's influence in the republic—would disappear. Albanians have already begun demanding greater autonomy for Albanian-populated municipalities in Montenegro, re-creating an explosive political dynamic that had tragic consequences in Bosnia, Croatia, and Kosovo.[29]

In January 2000, the Croatian electorate brought moderates to power but only after the nationalist agenda—the creation of an essentially monoethnic Croatia through the forced expulsion of the local Serb population, and recognition as an independent state[30]—had been achieved. Moreover, despite promises of greater readiness to accept Serb refugees, the actual return of these refugees has been held up from a combination of local obstruction and lack of funding from the international community.[31]

If, however, international officials insist on claiming the Croatian election results as a victory for their policies in the region, then the policy that was vindicated was one of constructive engagement. Despite Croatia's abysmal record on a range of issues—its extensive involvement in the Bosnian conflict, unwillingness to cooperate with the ICTY (International Criminal Tribunal for the former Yugoslavia), the ethnic cleansing of its Serb population, its active involvement in the obstruction of the Dayton Peace Accords in Bosnia, its refusal to facilitate the return of refugees, and even Croatia's refusal to accept election results in various parts of the country—U.S. and EU policies that were intended to show their disapproval of Tudjman's policies often amounted to little more than slaps on the wrist. Thus, even as ICTY prosecutor Carla del Ponte was charging Croatia with noncompliance with her investigations, the World Bank agreed to extend Croatia a $29 million loan—its eighteenth such loan since 1993.[32] Croatia also received over $550 million in U.S.-approved IMF loans between 1994 and 1997.[33]

## WAR/INTERVENTIONS—WHAT PRICE VICTORY?

The most damaging manifestation of Western engagement in the Balkans, of course, has come in the form of military intervention; specifically, NATO's seventy-eight-day bombing campaign against the FRY in the spring of 1999. But its antecedents go back further, to mistaken lessons learned during the war in Bosnia. Despite the popularity of the strategy of "diplomacy backed by force," a strong argument can be made that it has often been bad diplomacy during the Balkans crises that has made the use of force (according to some) indispensable. Von Klausewitz notwithstanding, if a state resorts to military action, its diplomacy has already failed.[34]

The most severe manifestation of this problem came in 1993, when perhaps the best chance to end the war in Bosnia, the Vance-Owen Peace Plan, was effectively derailed by the Clinton Administration on the grounds that it did not provide sufficiently strong guarantees for the war's principal (but not only) victims, the Bosniacs.[35]

As a result, the war dragged on for another two and a half years. The conventional wisdom now holds that the NATO bombing campaign against the Bosnian Serbs brought the conflict to a halt. But the reality is considerably different. In fact, it was the Clinton Administration, which made significant political concessions to the Bosnian Serbs *before* the bombing campaign started, that made the peace agreement negotiated at Dayton possible. As Carl Bildt notes,

> A major shift in US policy came in the first days of August. . . . For the first time, the White House committed itself not only to recognizing the Bosnian Serb entity, *Republika Srpska* (RS), but also to a territorial deal far more likely to obtain Serb support than the previous Contact Group maps. The core of the new US approach, closely following the lines recommended by the Europeans during the summer, was in fact endorsed by the Bosnian Serb parliament before the NATO bombings began in September 1995. . . . Popular mythology gives credit mainly to NATO's bombing efforts. But the key events were political rather than military; the US recognition of the RS was far more important than the air campaign.[36]

The lesson to be drawn is obvious: better-informed and more realistic diplomacy saves lives and time. Unfortunately, it was a lesson left unlearned by many Western diplomats by the time of the next Balkan crisis.

In 1998, the conflict between the Kosovo Liberation Army (KLA, a group Timothy Garton Ash once memorably described as a "bunch of farmyard Albanian ex-Marxist-Leninist terrorists")[37] and Yugoslav government forces had constituted a fairly typical guerrilla war and counterinsurgency campaign, with all of the excesses common to such warfare; as Istvan Deak notes, "history has still to show a police or military force that did not grow ruthless when attacked by fighters dressed as civilians."[38] Indeed, KLA brutality led the top U.S. Balkans envoy at the time, Robert Gelbard, to claim that the KLA "is without any question a terrorist group."[39] Prior to the NATO attack, the fighting in Kosovo had been confined to areas in which the KLA had been active, while Kosovo's major urban areas, such as Pristina, Djakovica, and Kosovska Mitrovica, and large parts of eastern and southern Kosovo, had seen little or no fighting. As even supporters of NATO's attack on Yugoslavia now admit, "there was no humanitarian crisis in Kosovo in 1997, or in 1998, or in most of 1999, in any conventionally understood sense of the term."[40]

But instead of accepting the complexity of the conflict in its historical and strategic contexts, Western leaders tried to reduce the problem in Kosovo to the workings of a single individual. As NATO Secretary-General Lord George Robertson claimed on one occasion, "The 19 democratic nations of the Alliance did not commit an act of aggression against the Yugoslavian (sic) people. We did not have anything against them. We acted against Milosevic."[41]

Thus, instead of engaging in the painstaking diplomacy required to prevent an escalation of the conflict—such as has characterized the American approach to the conflicts in the Middle East or northern Ireland—U.S. policymakers opted for a different strategy—designing a "peace plan" for the Kosovo conflict to be rejected by the FRY. Consider, for instance, Appendix B, Paragraph 8, of the Rambouillet Accords:

> NATO personnel shall enjoy, together with their vehicles, vessels, aircraft, and equipment, free and unrestricted passage and unimpeded access throughout the FRY including associated airspace and territorial waters. This shall include, but not be limited to, the right of bivouac, maneuver, billet, and utilization of any areas or facilities as required for support, training, and operation.[42]

This clause, obviously, was a deal breaker no sovereign country could accept. As Barry R. Posen has noted, "Serb agreement to such a clause would have essentially been an abdication of sovereignty to NATO. NATO officials could have exploited this unconstrained military access to pursue Serb officials accused of war crimes, and to assist other potential secessionist movements in Serbia."[43] Indeed, former Clinton Administration officials have now publicly admitted that the Rambouillet negotiations were never intended to produce a settlement to the Kosovo conflict. As former Assistant Secretary of State Jamie Rubin recently claimed, "*our internal goal was not to get a peace agreement at Rambouillet*. . . . [Rambouillet] was never intended to be another Dayton."[44]

NATO's subsequent decision to begin a bombing campaign dramatically escalated both the scale and the nature of the fighting in Kosovo between Albanians and Serbs; as Misha Glenny notes, "Instead of preventing a humanitarian catastrophe, NATO's decision contributed to a flood of biblical proportions."[45] Nevertheless, as the civilian Albanian population was being expelled from its homes and villages, NATO did nothing to protect it from the military reaction that was completely predictable. As Douglas Macgregor notes, "Faced with a population that concealed and supported the KLA, the Yugoslav forces did exactly what U.S., French, and British forces have done in counterinsurgency operations: they expelled the population and removed the insurgency's base of support."[46]

Moreover, since June 1999, when Yugoslav forces withdrew from Kosovo, forty thousand NATO troops have failed to prevent what has become perhaps the most comprehensive ethnic cleansing campaign yet seen in the Balkans. During the NATO-monitored ethnic cleansing of Kosovo, over two hundred fifty thousand people—Serbs, Roma, Turks, Gorani, Bosniacs, Croats, and the Jews of Pristina—have been driven from their homes, amidst a widespread campaign of murder, arson, and intimidation, *since NATO moved into Kosovo*. Yet in the UN's first five months in Kosovo, despite the more than four hundred murders that had been committed, only four people had been brought to trial.[47]

UN Secretary-General Kofi Annan has called the new ethnic cleansing of Kosovo "orchestrated" while a top U.S. official has labeled it as being "systematic."[48] Perhaps the most serious rebuke of NATO's efforts, however, has come from Carla del Ponte, the chief prosecutor for the ICTY, who recently claimed that "What is currently happening (in the Serbian province) is as serious as what happened there before" NATO's intervention.[49] That is, what is happening in NATO's Kosovo is as bad as what was happening in Milosevic's Kosovo.

Consequently, the success of facilitating the return of Albanian refugees to their homes (many of whom had, in any case, already been in their homes before NATO began its bombing campaign) has been negated by the NATO-monitored ethnic cleansing of Kosovo. As Dennis McNamara, the UN High Commissioner for Refugees (UNHCR) special envoy for the Balkans noted,

> We got nearly a million (ethnic Albanian) people back and a quarter of a million new ones (Serbs and other minorities) left. . . . [T]hat is a refugee cycle that we don't need and the region doesn't need, and it is continuing. It is a destabilizing factor and it makes it difficult to see how, in regional terms, a stability pact for southeastern Europe, which is predicated on population stability, can go very far until we can deal with that refugee problem.[50]

Apart from failing to prevent the original expulsion of Kosovo's Albanian population during the war, and failing to prevent the expulsion of Kosovo's non-Albanian population after NATO moved into Kosovo, what the NATO campaign also did not do, as is now evident, is inflict any significant damage on Yugoslav military forces. A preliminary NATO review of its performance in Kosovo concluded that Operation Allied Force "had almost no military effect," and that Milosevic agreed to terms in early June only after Moscow had withdrawn its diplomatic support from Belgrade.[51] According to a secret U.S. military assessment leaked to the press, 38,000 sorties (including the use of 31,000 rounds of radioactive depleted uranium shells) over seventy-eight days of bombing managed to destroy only fourteen tanks and an insignificant number of armored personnel carriers and artillery pieces.[52]

What the NATO campaign did do, however, is have an exceedingly negative impact on political and economic conditions in the region. The greater strategic uncertainty in the Balkans in the aftermath of the Kosovo conflict has allowed security services and the militaries of the frontline states to begin playing more important roles in policy making—and these, obviously, are not the institutions that are the greatest supporters of democracy. The KLA's success in Kosovo has encouraged its wings in Serbia proper and Macedonia, where the so-called National Liberation Army and other splinter groups have brought Macedonia's ever fragile existence to the breaking point. Indeed, the depth of the failure of the U.S. alliance with the KLA became painfully obvious in July 2001, when President George W. Bush signed an Executive Order which, among other things, noted that the activities of several leading members of the KLA in Kosovo, Macedonia, and southern Serbia "constitute an unusual and extraordinary threat to the national security and foreign policy of the United States."[53]

In economic terms, in Yugoslavia alone, the number of people living below the poverty line doubled in the immediate aftermath of the Kosovo war.[54] In the seven countries of southeastern Europe (Albania, Bosnia-Herzegovina, Bulgaria, Croatia, Romania, Macedonia, and the FRY), after a modest 1998 increase in GDP growth (1.3 percent), in 1999 the region as a whole moved into recession (with a 3 percent decline in GDP).[55] As a recent report by the European Commission/World Bank found, the post-Kosovo economic situation negatively affected the economies of southeastern Europe in numerous ways. Foreign investors' confidence in the region was shaken, resulting in increasing risk premiums on capital market borrowings. The disruption to trade meant significant losses in export earnings. The countries of the region will have higher debt-servicing costs and, as a result, wider balance of payments gaps. Lower incomes and the disruption to customs collection resulted in lost governmental fiscal revenues and increasing budgetary gaps. Larger budget deficits, in turn, mean cuts in social spending on health, education, and pensioners. And all of these problems combined will delay the structural reforms needed for sustained economic development.[56]

Unfortunately, NATO countries have been distinctly unwilling as of yet to invest as much money into rebuilding the region as they put into the bombing campaign. One estimate of the cost of the NATO operation in Kosovo was $40 billion.[57] This figure stands in sharp contrast to the annual budget for the United Nations Mission in Kosovo (UNMIK), which amounts to less than half of the cost of one-day's bombing.[58] Or, put another way, the G17 Institute, a group of independent economists in the FRY, has estimated that the NATO bombing of Yugoslavia resulted in some $30 billion worth of damage to Yugoslavia's economy and infrastructure.[59] In July 2001, by contrast, an international donor's conference for the FRY raised a total of approximately $1.3 billion for the country.

In July 1999, Romanian President Emil Constantinescu summed up the views of many Balkan leaders when he claimed, "We really have had enough of your nice words, while you do nothing to stop our losses, which grow bigger each day."[60]

## ELEMENTAL, INEVITABLE NECESSITIES AND THE DIALECTICS OF REGIONAL INTEGRATION

In contrast to what can be considered the reigning conventional wisdom regarding the Balkans conflicts over the past decade, with its emphasis on the culpability of individuals, an alternative explanation involving more of a historical and comparative perspective would view the Balkans conflicts over the past decade as the last part of a long European historical process of nation and state building. This process began with the transformation of European politics in the eighteenth and nineteenth centuries from a series of wars over dynastic succession (e.g., the War of the Spanish Succession, the War of the Austrian Succession, etc.) to a series of conflicts over the fate of peoples (for example, the "Polish Question," the "Irish Question," and, indeed, the "Eastern Question"). As Gale Stokes has described this process,

> Remapping state boundaries onto ethnic lines is one of the major threads of post-French Revolutionary European history. The process began with the unifications of Italy and Germany, ran through the creation of new states at the end of World War I, and had its most catastrophic outcomes at the end of World War II with the Holocaust and the expulsion of the Germans from Eastern Europe. . . . [T]he wars of Yugoslav succession are not some aberrant Balkan phenomenon; they are the last stages of a process of European redefinition that has been going on since the French revolution.[61]

Indeed, as Istvan Deak adds, "the creation of nation-states has been so much a part of modern European history as to allow us to call it inevitable."[62]

Moreover, as Ernest Gellner argues, the political principle driving this process, nationalism (defined as the belief that political and national units should be congruent), is a "necessity" given modern productive methods and the organization of society they imply.[63] For better or worse, nationalism has been a particularly potent force in Eastern Europe for much of the past two hundred years. As Ivo J. Lederer observed in 1969,

> The eastern European "way of life" is akin to a stream made up of a variety of tributaries of which nationalism is only one, but nationalism has run so deep and strong that it has appeared to possess an elemental, almost gravitational, quality. Time, location, and circumstances have, of course, altered its flow, as have war, revolution, social-economic transformation, ideology, perhaps even some of the brave efforts at emancipation from the bonds of historical fancy. Still nationalism has been the fundamental fact of life for nearly two hundred years. Nowhere has this been so clear and agonizingly the case as in the case of the Yugoslavs.[64]

Nor has the "Age of Nationalism" appeared to have run its course, either in Europe or elsewhere around the world, Eric Hobsbawm nothwithstanding.[65] As Rogers Brubaker notes,

> the spectacular reconfiguration of political space along national lines in Central and Eastern Europe and Eurasia has suggested that far from moving beyond the nation-state, history—European history at least—was moving back to the nation-state. The "short twentieth century" seemed to be ending much as it had begun, with Europe entering not a post-national but a post-multinational era through the wholesale nationalization of previously multinational political space. . . . Everywhere, political space has been reconfigured along putatively national lines.[66]

There are, of course, numerous other explanations for why this "spectacular reconfiguration of political space," a result of "elemental" and "inevitable" "necessities," has taken place, apart from the very powerful popular appeal of nationalism. By the late twentieth century, the international environment had become very conducive to the emergence of small states due to changes in the international economic order and security system. Traditionally, mercantilism had argued that only large states had the economies of scale and the internal markets necessary to generate the internal capital required for successful competition in the international economy. In terms of security, small states with little armies had little chance of surviving in an era dominated by great powers.

By the 1980s and 1990s, however, most of these conditions no longer held. In the nuclear age, superpowers eclipsed great powers, and small states could satisfy their defense requirements in collective security alliances. Changes in the international economy also proved favorable for the creation of small states. Institutions such as the World Bank and the International Monetary

Fund made investment capital available to smaller states, and the liberalization of international trade allowed small states to carve out their own niche in the international economy by exploiting their comparative advantages in various sectors.[67]

Yet much of international policy over the past decade in the Balkans, designed to stymie the designs of "evil leaders," has essentially ignored many of these phenomena or considered them irrelevant; as Timothy Garton Ash has noted, international policy in the Balkans has attempted to "freeze history."[68]

This effort to "freeze history" has manifested itself in the attempts to prop up dysfunctional international protectorates in Bosnia-Herzegovina, Kosovo, and (perhaps in the not-too-distant future) Macedonia as well, where these states obviously lack the popular legitimacy to survive on their own. Often, the effort is based on a belief that the Balkan peoples should behave more like "Europeans." In the Bosnian context, for instance, the above-cited report by the International Crisis Group calls "on Bosnia's Serbs, Bosniacs, and Croats . . . to move away from narrow ethnic politics and begin to move toward European integration."[69]

Yet "narrow ethnic politics" have far from disappeared in other parts of Europe. As Walker Connor noted in his classic article "Nation-Building or Nation-Destroying?" some thirty years ago, "Western Europe is held up as a model of something it is not, as proof that something can be achieved elsewhere that is in fact far from achieved there."[70] Indeed, British opposition to adopting the Euro (reportedly by up to two-thirds of the population as of December 2001)[71] and widespread opposition to joining the European Union in many parts of East-Central Europe suggest that "narrow ethnic politics" is a much more powerful force than many Euro-optimists believe.[72] Alexander Motyl is probably closer to the mark when he states that

> nationalism is not some atavistic premodern phenomenon that is slated to disappear with the growing modernity of the world. To the contrary, many trappings of modern life promote nations, states, and thus nation-states. . . . We can, in sum, expect nationalism to grow in intensity as modern states become even more modern and unmodern states embark on the road to modernity. Besides huffing and puffing, postmodernists and globalizers can do little about this.[73]

Instead of "huffing and puffing" against the competing nationalisms of the Balkan peoples, developing a more useful approach to promoting regional integration and peace in southeastern Europe requires a proper understanding of the path "Europe" itself took to reach its present state. Europe's (somewhat) successful post–World War II effort at political and economic integration has been based on the emergence of viable democratic nation-states enjoying large measures of popular legitimacy. As Ash has described this process,

> we in Western Europe have long since been molded into nation-states, in a process that lasted from the Middle Ages to the early twentieth-century. . . . It's precisely on this basis of clear separation into nation-states that we have been getting together in the European Union, as well as becoming more ethnically mixed again, through immigration.[74]

In a later essay, Ash developed this idea further:

> This separating out into small states or sub-state units with clear ethnic majorities, driven though it has been by manipulative and often cynical post-communist nationalism, nonetheless has powerful precedents and counterparts in the rest of Europe. Elsewhere in Europe, too, people generally prefer to be ruled by those they consider somehow "of their own kind." Only once thus constituted, in some version of a nation-state, are they prepared (up to a point) to come together in larger regional and all-European units. A realistic liberal internationalism for the twenty-first century needs to take on board the insights of liberal nationalists from the nineteenth.[75]

Given *this* European historical experience and reality, does this mean that the best option for the international community would be to simply carve up the Balkans into relatively homogenous nation-states? Given the moral implications of such a policy, the answer is undoubtedly no. But we should also ask whether it is possible to control or halt this process? For what is indisputable is that such a carving up into more or less ethnically homogenous areas has already de facto taken place throughout the former Yugoslavia over the past decade. Since the breakup of the truly ethnically heterogeneous Yugoslavia in 1991 to 1992, the successor states and statelets have become progressively more monoethnic. Consider the demography of the former Yugoslavia today.[76] Slovenia is now approximately 90 percent Slovene. Croatia, thanks to the forced expulsion of much of its Serb population between 1993–1995, is well over 80 percent Croatian. Bosnia-Herzegovina is divided into three ethnically controlled areas, each of which is approximately 90 percent ethnically "clean," and postwar efforts to resettle refugees and internally displaced persons has not met with remarkable success. Macedonia, as a result of the current conflict, is quickly becoming a state of two clearly delineated ethnically homogeneous areas. Kosovo, as we have seen, witnessed a massive NATO-monitored ethnic cleansing of non-Albanian ethnic groups after June 1999. The FRY is perhaps the only truly multiethnic state left among the successor states of Tito's Yugoslavia, but even here, the loss of Kosovo, together with the outflow of significant numbers of Hungarians and Croats from Vojvodina and the influx of some six hundred thousand Serbs from Croatia, Bosnia-Herzegovina, and Kosovo, has made the FRY a much more monoethnic state than it was only a few years ago.

Clearly, international policies of the past decade have been unable to stop or reverse the Balkan experience of an all too bloody European historical process of nation and state building. They have also, as argued above, seriously damaged the possibilities for stable democratic transitions in the region.

Yet there are still glimmers of hope that the problems of the past decade can be laid to rest. For perhaps the first time in history, all of the states of southeastern Europe have the same domestic and foreign policy agendas—creating market economies and democratic political systems and joining the European Union and NATO. The European Union, for its part, now realizes that Balkan instability significantly threatens its own interests and is devising ways to integrate the region into the common market. In 2000, the EU authorized autonomous trade preferences to provide free entry of goods for over 95 percent of merchandise exports from southeastern European countries to the EU. In June 2001, representatives of Albania, Bosnia-Herzegovina, Bulgaria, Croatia, the FRY, Macedonia, and Romania signed a Memorandum of Understanding aimed at establishing what is essentially a Balkan free trade zone by the end of 2002 through the negotiation of a series of bilateral free trade agreements.[77] And, as Susan Woodward has recently argued, the overthrow of Milosevic in October 2000 has removed what was in many ways an artificial obstacle to progress in the region, giving southeastern Europe and international policymakers a "second chance" to deal with *real* problems rather than bogeymen.[78]

Despite these few encouraging moves, however, international policy toward southeastern Europe still has far to go to make up for the mistakes of the past decade. Although it is probably too extreme to claim, as R. W. Seton-Watson did some seventy years ago, that "All the troubles in the Balkans for a century past were due to foreign interference, especially from the Great Powers," the record of the recent past shows that the "international community" has often made a bad situation in southeastern Europe worse.[79] All too often, policymakers have believed that removing a few troublesome individuals, or a donor's conference that raises one billion dollars, or a barrage of cruise missiles, can solve the problems of the Balkans in the three to four years between American presidential campaigns. With Franjo Tudjman dead and Slobodan Milosevic in The Hague, it will be increasingly difficult to maintain these illusions.

## NOTES

1. Michael Mandelbaum, "A Perfect Failure: NATO's War Against Yugoslavia," *Foreign Affairs* 78 (September/October 1999), pp. 2–8.

2. Richard Holbrooke, *To End a War* (New York: Random House, 1998), pp. 23–24.

3. Warren Zimmerman, *Origins of a Catastrophe* (New York: Times Books, 1993), p. vii.

4. "Healing the Wounds in the Balkans," *Strategic Survey* (2000/2001), p. 124.

5. *Bosnia's November Elections: Dayton Stumbles* (Sarajevo/Brussels: International Crisis Group Report No. 104), 18 December 2000, Executive Summary.

6. Alexander J. Motyl, *Revolutions, Nations, Empires: Conceptual Limits and Theoretical Possibilities* (New York: Columbia University Press, 1999), p. 91.

7. Rogers Brubaker, *Nationalism Reframed: Nationhood and the National Question in the New Europe* (Cambridge: Cambridge University Press, 1996), p. 72. Brubaker's comments were made in reference to the Krajina Serbs in the period 1990 to 1991.

8. See Robert Pape, "Why Economic Sanctions Do Not Work," *International Security* 22 (Fall 1997), p. 93.

9. For a discussion of the morality of economic sanctions, see Joy Gordon, "A Peaceful, Silent, Deadly Remedy: The Ethics of Economic Sanctions," *Ethics and International Affairs* 13 (1999), p. 124.

10. "The Revolution to Come," *Wall Street Journal Interactive Edition*, 25 October 1999.

11. See "Svet je zatvorio Srbiju, a zatvaranje pomaze vladarima protiv opozicije," *Danas* (Belgrade), 29 June 2000, available at www.danas.co.yu.

12. For an extended discussion of these topics, see Eric Gordy, *The Culture of Power in Serbia: Nationalism and the Destruction of Alternatives* (University Park: Pennsylvania State University Press, 1999), pp. 192–198.

13. Of course, a large number of young men eligible for military service also left the country at this time to avoid conscription.

14. See the commentary by the OSCE Chief of Mission in BiH, Ambassador Robert Barry, in the *Frankfurter Allegemiene Zeitung*, 20 July 1999.

15. *Unfinished Peace: Report of the International Commission on the Balkans* (Washington, DC: Carnegie Endowment for International Peace, 1996), p. 8.

16. See the remarks by Zivko Tolevski, President of the Macedonian Alliance of Unions, "Thousands Attend Macedonian Union Rally," *Reuters* (Dateline Skopje), 1 March 2000.

17. Misha Glenny, *The Balkans 1804–1999: Nationalism, War, and the Great Powers* (London: Granta Books, 1999), p. 639.

18. "Romania Loses $100 Million Over Danube," *Associated Press*, 19 March 2000.

19. "Romania and Bulgaria Call for Rapid Clear-Up of the Danube," *Agence France Presse*, 3 April 2000.

20. See Mesic's interview in *Der Spiegel* (Hamburg), 3 April 2000, pp. 180–185.

21. See Richard N. Haass and Meghan L. O'Sullivan, *Engaging Problem States*. The Brookings Institution Policy Brief, no. 61, June 2000.

22. "Remarks by the President on Passage of Permanent Normal Trade Relations With China By the House of Representatives," The White House, 24 May 2000. The *New York Times* would claim that, by supporting this legislation, Clinton "cemented in place the post–cold war experiment of using economic engagement to foster political change among America's neighbors and its potential adversaries." David E. Sanger, "Rounding Out a Clear Clinton Legacy," *New York Times*, 25 May 2000.

23. Stefano Bianchini and Marko Dogo, foreword to *The Balkans: National Identities in a Historical Perspective,* Stefano Bianchini and Marco Dogo, eds. (Ravenna: Longo Editore, 1998), p. 16.

24. The comments were made by a State Department official during a gathering of Balkans scholars and policymakers at Princeton University on 2 December 1999.

25. Nadia Rybarova, "Albright Announces Aid to E. Europe," *Associated Press* (Dateline Prague), 7 March 2000.

26. Jack Snyder, *From Voting to Violence: Democratization and Ethnic Conflict* (New York: W. W. Norton, 2000). For an interesting analysis of this point from the perspective of the democratization process in Croatia, see Vesna Pusic, "Dictatorships with Democratic Legitimacy: Democracy versus Nation," *East European Politics and Societies* 8 (Fall 1994), pp. 383–401.

27. See Xavier Bougarel, "Bosnia and Herzegovina: State and Communitarianism," in D. A. Dyker and I. Vejvoda, eds., *Yugoslavia and After: A Study in Fragmentation, Despair, and Rebirth* (London: Longman, 1996), p. 87.

28. See Mark Almond's report on his observations of Macedonia's November 1999 elections in the *Economist* (London), 4 December 1999, p. 6.

29. Rade Stanic, "Albanci u Crnoj Gori: Autonomaski Sok," *Reporter* (Banja Luka), no. 102, 5 April 2000, available at www.reporter.co.yu.

30. A point made in the International Crisis Group report "State of the Balkans." Sarajevo: 4 November 1998.

31. "Croatian Serbs Criticize Government over Lack of Results," *Agence France Presse*, 16 June 2000; "Not Enough Money for Balkans Refugees Return," *Agence France Presse*, 21 June 2000; and "Return of Croatian Serbs Obstructed on Local Level," *Agence France Presse*, 30 June 2000.

32. RFE/RL Newsline, 6 October 1999.

33. *New York Times*, 1 February 1998, p. 8 BU.

34. A point frequently made in the lectures of the late Edwin H. Fedder, former Director of the Center for International Studies, University of Missouri–St. Louis.

35. For the Clinton Administration's role in scuttling the Vance-Owen Peace Plan, see David Owen, *Balkan Odyssey* (New York: Harcourt Brace & Company, 1995). The Clinton Administration's own peace plan to end the Bosnian conflict, the Dayton Peace Accords negotiated by Richard Holbrooke, provided far fewer guarantees for an effective state in Bosnia-Herzegovina and put the Bosniacs in a much less favorable position vis-à-vis the Croats and Serbs. It also came some thirty months later, a

period during which tens of thousands of people were killed and hundreds of thousand more forced from their homes.

36. Carl Bildt, "Holbrooke's History," *Survival* 40, no. 3 (Autumn 1998), p. 188.

37. See Timothy Ash, "Kosovo: Was it Worth It?" *The New York Review of Books*, 21 September 2000, p. 53.

38. See Istvan Deak, "Out of the Past," *The New Republic*, 8 June 1998.

39. As quoted by Chris Hedges, "Kosovo's Next Masters?" *Foreign Affairs* (May/June 1999), p. 36. Indeed, several top KLA leaders are now believed to be under investigation by the International Criminal Tribunal for the Former Yugoslavia (ICTY) for war crimes committed during 1998–1999 before the NATO attack began. See, for instance, Tom Walker, "KLA Faces Trials for War Crimes on Serbs: Inquiry Turns on Albanians," *Sunday Times* (London), 3 September 2000, and Chris Hedges, "Kosovo's Rebels Accused of Executions in the Ranks," *New York Times*, 25 June 1999.

40. David Rieff, "Kosovo's Humanitarian Circus," *World Policy Journal* 17 (Fall 2000), p. 27.

41. See Yuri Pankov's interview with Robertson, "Dialogue, Not Confrontation," in *Krasnaya Zvezda* (Moscow), 20 February 2001.

42. *Interim Agreement for Peace and Self-Government in Kosovo*, appendix B, paragraph 8.

43. See Barry Posen, "The War for Kosovo: Serbia's Political-Military Strategy," *International Security* 24 (Spring 2000), p. 80.

44. Rubin made his statement during an interview on the Charlie Rose show, which aired on 18 April 2000, transcript #2663. Emphasis added.

45. Misha Glenny, *The Balkans, 1804–1999: War, Nationalism, and the Great Powers* (London: Granta Books, 1999), p. 658. It is important to note that the U.S. State Department's own report on this period essentially agrees with this version of events. As the State Department notes, "In late March 1999, Serbian forces *dramatically increased* the scope and pace of their efforts, moving away from selective targeting of towns and regions suspected of KLA sympathies toward a sustained and systematic effort to ethnically cleanse the entire province." See *Erasing History: Ethnic Cleansing in Kosovo* (Washington, DC: U.S. Department of State, May 1999). Overview section. Italics added.

46. See Douglas Macgregor, "The Balkan Limits of Power and Principle," *Orbis* 45 (Winter 2001), p. 100. It should be pointed out that, during the Kosovo war, Colonel Macgregor was chief of strategic planning and director of the Joint Operations Center, Supreme Headquarters Allied Powers Europe.

47. Figures according to Bernard Kouchner, the head of the UN Mission in Kosovo. *Agence France-Presse*, 25 January 2000.

48. "Report of the Secretary-General on the United Nations Interim Administration in Kosovo," S/2000/538, 6 June 2000. The comments by the U.S. official, James O'Brien, can be found in George Jahn, "Anti-Serb Violence Condemned," *Associated Press*, 8 June 2000.

49. "UN Tribunal Awaiting Arrests of Warcrimes Suspects Karadzic, Mladic," *Reuters*, 18 July 2000.

50. "Refugee Cycle Threatens Balkan Stability-UNHCR," *Reuters*, 20 March 2000.

51. Daniel Goure and Jeffrey Lewis, "The Strained U.S. Military: Evidence from Operation Allied Force," *National Security Studies Quarterly* 6 (Winter 2000), pp. 21–42.

52. John Barry and Evan Thomas, "The Kosovo Cover-Up," *Newsweek*, 15 May 2000.

53. "Executive Order Blocking Property of Persons Who Threaten International Stabilization Efforts in the Western Balkans" (Washington, DC: The White House, 27 June 2001). See also "UN Suspends Five Top Members of Kosovo Civil Corps," *Agence France-Presse*, 6 July 2001.

54. "U.N. Says Yugoslav Poverty is Soaring," *New York Times*, 5 November 1999.

55. *Economic Survey of Europe* (United Nations Economic Commission on Europe), no. 1, 2000, p. 6.

56. The statement is available at www.seerecon.org/WarImpact/WarImpact.htm.

57. Michael R. Sesit, "Cost of Kosovo War Could Hit $40 Billion," *Wall Street Journal*, 29 July 1999, p. A11.

58. Misha Glenny, "The Muddle in Kosovo," *Wall Street Journal*, 23 February 2000.

59. See the G17 report, "Ekonomske posledice NATO bombardovanja: procena stete i sredstava potrebnih za ekonomsku rekonstrukciju Jugoslavije," available at www.g17plus.org.yu.

60. Bianca Guruita, "The Price of Acquiescence," *Transitions OnLine* (October 1999).

61. Gale Stokes, "The Unpalatable Paradox," *Nationalities Papers* 27 (June 1999), pp. 327–329.

62. Istvan Deak, "A Somewhat Pessimistic View of Charles Ingrao's 'Understanding Ethnic Conflict in Central Europe,'" *Nationalities Papers* 27 (June 1999), p. 320.

63. Ernest Gellner, *Nations and Nationalism* (Ithaca, NY: Cornell University Press, 1983), p. 129.

64. Ivo J. Lederer, "Nationalism and the Yugoslavs," in *Nationalism in Eastern Europe*, Peter F. Sugar and Ivo J. Lederer, eds. (Seattle: University of Washington Press, 1969), p. 396.

65. On this note, it is clear that analyses of recent history from the Marxist perspective have fallen wide of the mark. See, for instance, Eric Hobsbawm's *Nations and Nationalism since 1780: Programme, Myth, Reality* (Cambridge: Cambridge University Press, 1990), especially Chapter 5.

66. See Rogers Brubaker, *Nationalism Reframed: Nationhood and the National Question in the New Europe* (Cambridge: Cambridge University Press, 1996), pp. 2–3.

67. Many of these themes are discussed in detail in Susan L. Woodward, *Balkan Tragedy: Chaos and Dissolution After the Cold War* (Washington, DC: Brookings Institution, 1995).

68. See Timothy Ash, "Cry, the Dismembered Country," *The New York Review of Books*, 14 January 1999, p. 32.

69. *Bosnia's November Elections: Dayton Stumbles*, op. cit., p. 2.

70. Walker Connor, "Nation-Building or Nation-Destroying?" *World Politics* 24 (April 1972), p. 350.

71. Alan Cowell, "For Britain, Euro Is Invasion It May Have to Invite," *New York Times*, 9 December 2001, p. A3. Cowell cites a telling conversation with a butcher in the town of Battle explaining why local residents were against adoption of the Euro: "They don't like it because they think Europe is taking over. They feel they fought a world war and now everything is being taken away." If one takes note of the reluctance of "modern" and "progressive" citizens of Western Europe to embrace European integration efforts fifty-five years after a bloody war, it makes it easier to understand the resistance to forced integration efforts of populations in southeastern Europe significantly less than a decade after similarly bloody conflicts with their neighbors.

72. In a recent poll among East Europeans, only 49 percent of Poles, 48 percent of Lithuanians, 47 percent of Czechs, and 38 percent of Estonians expressed their support for joining the EU. *RFE/RL Newsline*, 8 November 2001.

73. Motyl, *Revolutions*, pp. 110–113.

74. Ash, "Cry, the Dismembered Country," p. 32.

75. Timothy Ash, "Anarchy and Madness," *The New York Review of Books*, 10 February 2000, p. 53.

76. All references to percentages of the population according to ethnicity are based on those in *The World Factbook* (Washington, DC: Central Intelligence Agency, 2001). These numbers, however, are based on figures from the last Yugoslav census of 1991; consequently, I have made approximate estimates of what these numbers are today in light of the population dislocations of the past decade.

77. *Memorandum of Understanding on Trade Liberalization and Facilitation*, Stability Pact Working Group on Trade Liberalisation and Facilitation, 27 June 2001.

78. See Susan L. Woodward, "Milosevic Who? Origins of the New Balkans," *The Hellenic Observatory, London School of Economics Discussion Paper No. 5*, July 2001.

79. See R. W. Seton-Watson, "King Alexander's Assassination: Its Background and Effects," *International Affairs* 14, no. 1, pp. 20–47.

# II

# WARS, WAR CRIMES, AND INTERNATIONAL LAW

# 7

# Wars, Humanitarian Intervention, and International Law: Perceptions and Reality

*Raju G. C. Thomas*

## WARS AND INTERNATIONAL STABILITY

### World Security under Pax Americana

The collapse of the Soviet Union caused a systemic transformation in the global power relationships. The origins of its disintegration may be traced to the policies of *glasnost* (openness) and *perestroika* (reforms) under Mikhail Gorbachev in the late 1980s. The process culminated in the failed military coup against Gorbachev in August 1991, resulting in a greatly weakened Soviet military. A series of declarations of independence by the Soviet Union's constituent federal units followed, beginning with Georgia and the Baltic republics. This transformation contributed to the fate of Yugoslavia.

The sudden displacement of the Cold War military balance by a unipolar world where no countervailing power existed between the United States and the new Russia—at least in the new qualitative high-tech weapons in America's arsenal—changed the rules of Great Power relations. In particular, fears of getting sucked into a Vietnam-type military quagmire was over for America. The United States was capable of inflicting enormous death and destruction on other states in the pursuit of what it sees as moral and humanitarian causes while suffering insignificant or no casualties. There were other factors that strengthened the West. The Berlin Wall fell in 1989, and in the following year, Germany was united and powerful again, thereby adding to the power of the Western alliance. On the other hand, the Russian economy was crippled and dependent on the West for survival. Now that the Cold War was over, Washington believed that an expanding American-led NATO alliance system, faced with no threats to itself, was a good thing for the world. Peace, security, and justice for all would prevail under the new Pax Americana.

This belief in a U.S.-dictated system of hegemonic stability, whether it applies to global security or the world economy, has some merit. In a study undertaken by Professor A. F. K. Organski of the University of Michigan on the European balance of power over several centuries, he concluded that balance of power politics was likely to generate instability and wars, while a preponderance of power was more likely to produce peace and stability.[1] According to Organski, under conditions of military preponderance, the weaker state dare not attack, while the stronger state need not attack, and therefore there was peace. Especially when the dominant state or group of states is considered to be benevolent, just, and without territorial ambitions, a noncompetitive military preponderance of power may be the most desirable condition for world peace.[2]

However, the underlying problem in the immediate post–Cold War era is that mutual nuclear deterrence among existing nuclear powers cannot deter a conventional attack by a hegemonic state against third party states, especially where there is no balance of conventional military power between the nuclear weapons states. Such a situation prevailed between the United States and Russia in the 1990s. Russia may be able to deter NATO military intervention over human rights violations in Chechnya, but it could not deter such intervention against Serbia over violations in Kosovo. Balance of power theory in Western strategic literature taught that only a system of countervailing power could ensure the sovereignty and independence of states, both large and small.[3] While American leaders and observers argue that world peace and justice have a better chance without a prevailing global balance of military power, they are unwilling to accept such preponderance in regions where it does not advance American foreign policy goals, for example, South Asia and the Middle East.[4]

Germany's reunification was not expected to threaten the rest of Europe outside NATO, although the first action of a united Germany was to push for the secessions of Slovenia and Croatia. Likewise, at the end of the Cold War, preserving NATO without much military opposition was not enough. The expansion of NATO to make it even more powerful was now the American objective. At the Conference on Security and Cooperation in Europe (CSCE) meeting in December 1994, Russian president Boris Yeltsin condemned American efforts to project Russia as a future threat in order to justify NATO's expansion. According to Yeltsin: "We hear explanations to the effect this allegedly is the expansion of stability just in case there are undesirable developments in Russia."[5]

The late Amos Perlmutter, an Israeli who taught at the American University in Washington, drew a parallel between the behavior of imperial Austria in the Balkans just before it attacked Serbia in 1914 and the behavior of imperial America in the former Yugoslavia just before its decision to attack Serbia in 1999:

> U.S. ambassadors Richard Holbrooke, Christopher Hill and William Walker have surrogated for the Ottoman governor, the kaymakam, for settling disputes in what used to be provinces of the Ottoman and Austro-Hungarian Empires. Some argue that American-NATO-U.N. and OSCE ambassadors and negotiators have replaced the Austro-Hungarian rulers. Bosnia is an American-NATO creation. . . . Furthermore, the United States is responsible for the creation, training, equipping and modernization of the Muslim army of Croat-Muslim Bosnia. It has given military aid to Croatia. This was not even done by the Austro-Hungarian Empire. The American kaymakams Christopher Hill and William Walker are separately creating a new entity out of Kosovo in the name of negotiating with Yugoslavia over its autonomous province.[6]

U.S. military dominance, backed by the ability to threaten economic punishments or to promise economic rewards to those who oppose or support American policies, has changed the character of the United Nations. The UN system has been reduced to an obedient organization of the United States and the West, a return to the early years of the UN when its membership did not include the emerging independent Afro-Asian bloc of states. With the collapse of the Soviet Union and the Warsaw Pact alliance, voting in the Security Council in the 1990s was almost always unanimous in favor of U.S. policies with an occasional abstention or negative vote.[7] States with veto powers, including Russia and China, have rarely ventured to veto U.S.-sponsored or -supported UN resolutions. In the Iraq and Yugoslav crises of the 1990s, the unusual phenomenon of what Stephen Walt has called "bandwagoning" with the dominant power—instead of "balancing"—was evident.[8] Even more disturbing was that NATO showed itself to be a docile group of states following the wishes of American leadership. The collapse of the Soviet Union and the end of the Cold War has allowed the United States and NATO to assume the role and responsibilities of the "international community."

In 1998, when faced with the threat of Russian and Chinese vetoes in the Security Council, the United States twice bypassed the United Nations within a space of six months. First, the United States and Britain launched attacks on Iraq in December 1998 because the chief UN weapons inspector, Richard Butler, chose to pull out, complaining of lack of cooperation from Iraq. And then a U.S.-led NATO launched a massive attack on Yugoslavia from March to June 1999, in violation of the UN Charter that authorizes force only in self-defense, because Belgrade rejected Western terms at the negotiations at Rambouillet.

Yet, NATO's military actions against two sovereign states produced no international censure at the UN. Other states have simply jumped on the American bandwagon in this new U.S.-dominant global system. The United States provides effective NATO military power, and NATO now serves as the gendarme of the United Nations. There is no NATO without U.S. military capabilities, and there can be no UN "collective security" action without NATO. Military actions are now undertaken in the name of the United States, NATO, and the UN, an unholy and dangerous trinity. Even more troubling is the fact that U.S. policy is shaped increasingly by its media and powerful public relations firms representing favored ethnic groups.

One of the basic problems with Organski's preponderance theory is that under these conditions, the preponderant power is not supposed to initiate a war against a weaker state. NATO's massive and full-scale assault on tiny Serbia in 1999, bypassing the UN Security Council and violating a slew of international laws, demonstrated the weakness of the "preponderance-equals-peace" theory and the strength of the arguments underlying the need to maintain a balance of power among states to preserve the territorial integrity and sovereignty of states.

Thus, there was some initial speculation and moves in India and China on how to counterbalance NATO's unrestrained power. Reflecting the widespread strategic sentiment in India regarding the new unipolar security environment, a 1999 *Times of India* editorial written at the height of NATO's attack on Serbia noted the dangerous new American-dominant world, the American development of new missile defense systems, the legitimization of wars of intervention abroad on self-determined moral grounds, and being able to fight them with very few or no American casualties because of the new high-tech weapon systems.

> In these circumstances two major trends are likely to emerge. Independent powers like Russia and China are bound to develop their own military capabilities to deter US dominance to the extent possible and to defend their own national interests and sovereignty. In this, the nuclear weapons and long range missiles are bound to play a crucial role. Secondly, the deep resentment against US hegemonism is bound to unleash various terrorist activities by nonstate actors against US interests and personnel in various parts of the world. India has to take note of these developments and formulate its own national security strategy to safeguard its strategic autonomy. That calls for the country to accelerate its acquisition of a credible minimum deterrent, programme of ballistic and cruise missiles.[9]

Some Chinese military strategists responded to the prevailing absence of a level playing field by proposing new rules of "unrestricted war," which would include the resort to terrorism, ecological destruction, cyber-warfare through the spread of computer viruses, and trafficking in drugs to undermine the enemy's population from within, thereby bringing destruction into the heart of the Western countries, especially the United States.[10] According to Colonels Qiao Liang and Wang Xiangsui, the authors of *Unrestricted War*, this strategy was the only viable method of balancing unequal military states. "Unrestricted War is a war that surpasses all boundaries and restrictions. . . . It takes nonmilitary forms and military forms and creates a war on many fronts. It is the war of the future." In an interview, Colonel Wang declared: "We are a weak country. So do we need to fight according to your rules? No. War has rules, but those rules are set by the West. But if you use those rules, then weak countries have no chance. But if you use nontraditional means to fight, like those employed by financiers to bring down financial systems, then you have a chance." According to John Pomfret of the *Washington Post*, the Chinese military strategists saw a direct connection between Kosovo and Taiwan and Tibet. According to Colonel Wang, "If today you impose your value systems on a European country, tomorrow you can do the same to Taiwan or Tibet."

NATO's use of force against Yugoslavia without sanction from the UN Security Council brought about several countermoves among Russia, China, India, and Indonesia.

*Russia and China*. In July 2001, Russia and China signed the familiar Cold War era-type "treaty of friendship and cooperation," the first such treaty since the era of Stalin and Mao. It bound the two former communist giants for the next twenty years, "committing them to oppose jointly much of the framework for international security that the United States is seeking to erect after the Cold War."[11] "The Chinese-Russian treaty is a nonaggression pact whereby both parties agree to keep the peace on their shared frontier so that they can focus their attentions elsewhere. The treaty obligates both parties to refrain from using force or economic pressure in their relations and eventually reduce the military forces stationed on the border."[12] However, the security connotations of the treaty is diluted by the fact that China had a trade volume with the U.S. of $115 billion in 2000, compared with less than $10 billion with Russia.[13]

*India and China*. On June 14, 1999, a week after the hostilities ended in the Balkans, India and China established a "Security Dialogue," which was stated by their respective foreign ministers to be a response to NATO's actions.[14] In November 2000, Ms. Zhang Qiyue, a Chinese Foreign Ministry spokesperson, told an Indian delegation that China did not see India as a rival or threat to itself but as a partner in maintaining global stability and peace.[15] In January 2001, Indian Prime Minister Atal Bihari Vajpayee and Chinese leader Li Peng agreed to complete the process of clarification of the Line of Actual Control "as soon as possible."[16] Vajpayee stated that "As two great civilizations and neighbors, India and China are engaged in the process of resolving, and putting behind us, past differences and forging a new and dynamic relationship for the 21st century for the benefit of our two countries and the world."

*India and Russia.* In early 1999, during NATO's bombing, there was some Indian interest in the call by then Russian premier Yvgeny Primakov to forge a counter alliance against NATO among Russia, China, and India. A China-India-Russia "anti-NATO axis" had started to evolve by the fall of 1999 to check the new unbridled use of American military power.[17] Russian-Indian cooperation took on more concrete shape during President Vladimir Putin's visit to India in October 2000, when a limited strategic partnership was established between India and Russia. Prime Minister A. B. Vajpayee stated that the two countries shared common concerns and interests, and that "the history of the last five decades demonstrates that close Indo-Russian understanding is essential to peace and stability in Asia and the world. This is what makes India and Russia strategic partners. Our friendship is not based on short-term calculations, but transcends the twists and turns of history and politics."[18] Putin claimed that a multipolar world was a safer world, and that the Indo-Russian strategic partnership would contribute to this desirable global condition. The central and immediate feature of the partnership was an immediate $3 billion defense deal, with a further $2.5 billion military of sophisticated weapons.[19] In June 2001, a protocol was signed between the two countries whereby Russia would supply $10 billion worth of weaponry and other military hardware over the coming decade.[20]

*India and Indonesia.* The threat of Western dominance and the right of humanitarian intervention also drew Indonesia and India closer together. During an exchange of visits by Prime Minister A. B. Vajpayee and President Abdurrahman Wahid in January 2001, both the Indonesian president and Defense Minister, Mr. Mahfud, proposed a quadrilateral alliance of Russia, China, India, and Indonesia.[21] Five Indo-Indonesian agreements were then signed in Jakarta, including the formation of a joint commission for defense cooperation. Indonesia's desire for such an alliance is understandable. It had just suffered the loss of East Timor through Western diplomatic humanitarian intervention. Referring to what appeared to be a new appreciation of each other's bilateral concerns, Vajpayee declared that "as multi-ethnic, multi-religious and diverse societies, both our countries support each other's unity and territorial integrity."[22] Most significantly, President Wahid supported India's territorial integrity, which presumably included Kashmir.

These moves toward counterbalancing NATO were restrained by the economic dependency of all four countries on the United States and the European Union, and it suddenly came to an abrupt end after Al-Qaeda's terrorist attack on the United States on September 11, 2001. Russia, China, and India joined the United States' war on international terrorism, which included diplomatic support for the U.S. war in Afghanistan against Al Qaeda bases and their Taliban hosts that ruled Afghanistan.

## Humanitarian Intervention in a Western Dominant System

NATO's war over Kosovo was declared the first major "humanitarian war" to prevent Serbian "ethnic cleansing" and "genocide" of Albanians. Underlying the morality of humanitarian intervention are two varying philosophies. First, that the use of military force that is not for self-defense may be justified to advance moral principles and the pursuit of a just cause whatever the consequences. Second, the resort to military force on moral grounds that leads to greater immoral consequences cannot be justified. This distinction may be found in the writings of the German philosopher Immanuel Kant, as against that of the utilitarian writings of the British philosopher Jeremy Bentham. Western foreign policy, especially that of the new-wave liberals under Democratic President Bill Clinton and Labor Prime Minister Tony Blair, has taken on a Kantian approach in dealing with the various crises in the former Yugoslavia, the issue of East Timor in Indonesia, and sanctions on Iraq, which, directly or indirectly, caused the deaths of more than a million civilians. Political opportunism and moral zealotry have prevailed over political prudence and moral pragmatism in the new Anglo-American foreign policy conduct.

U.S. behavior since the collapse of the Soviet Union resembled that of an all-powerful monarch in a feudal setting, where rewards and punishments are advanced according to personal judgments and where the justice system becomes subordinated to personal whims and self-interests. The ruler remains above the rule of law, or ensures that the enforcers of the law work to prevent any prosecution of himself. The selective manipulation of the international justice system and process has become one of the means of conducting U.S. foreign policy. The U.S.-sponsored and -supported creation of the International Criminal Tribunal for the Former Yugoslavia (ICTY) is an illustration of such a system of biased justice where the main goal is to indict Serbs while preventing any indictment of NATO leaders and minimizing those against Croats and Muslims. Indeed, the United States has rejected the right of any international legal body to try U.S. citizens and refused to adhere to the new International Criminal Court that went into effect on July 1, 2002.[23]

The new "humanitarians" in the United States and the West have declared that the sovereignty of states is now virtually obsolete, the era of the Westphalian state has come to an end, and concepts of realism and neorealism, which emphasize the pursuit of state power or security, can no longer be sustained. These new rules of the game have been declared by American leaders, journalists, and scholars as essential for world peace and security and for the promotion of individual rights and human dignity. However, the undermining of the sovereignty of states beyond voluntary multilateral economic and military agreements (such as the World Trade Organization, the Non-

Proliferation Treaty, the Biological Weapons Convention, and the Chemical Weapons Convention) could lead to more "Yugoslavias" in the rest of the world as more ethnic groups resort to insurgency and terrorism to secede from existing multiethnic states with the expectation of political and military support from the West.

The rising tide of insurgency and terrorism in Chechnya in Russia, Xinjiang in China, and Kashmir in India, all Muslim majority areas no different from Kosovo in Yugoslavia, is indicative of the problem. As noted in my earlier chapter, the dislodging of East Timor from Indonesia in the fall of 1999, and its eventual independence in 2002 have since provoked other violent secessionist movements in Aceh, Ambon, and the Moluccan Islands. If the Kosovo Liberation Army could be reclassified so easily by the U.S. State Department from terrorist organization and drug traffickers to freedom fighters, then other terrorist separatist groups may hope for the same. Thus, for example, there were some fears in India that the "international community" may now generate a similar outcome in Muslim-majority Kashmir in predominantly Hindu India, where a violent secessionist movement has raged since 1989. Writing in the *New York Times* on October 22, 1999, Barbara Crossette advised that the United States now turn its attention to Kashmir following the successful severance of Kosovo from Serbia and East Timor from Indonesia. Against such American tendencies, Prem Shankar Jha, a leading Indian journalist and former adviser to Prime Minister Inder Kumar Gujral, noted in the *Hindustan Times* on November 5, 1999, that "two days ago, the Congress of the United States began a hearing on human rights. It was not an enquiry into the state of human rights in America but in Kashmir, in a country that did not elect them, over which it does not have the remotest jurisdiction, and where even the most calamitous events would not affect America's political or economic well-being."[24]

## The United States and the United Nations[25]

NATO's assault on Yugoslavia beginning March 24, 1999, after bypassing the Security Council, undermines the relevance and credibility of the United Nations. Though not of the same magnitude or likely outcome, some parallels may be seen in the fate of the League of Nations in the 1930s. The League was destroyed by three of its members, Japan, Italy, and Germany, who eventually forged a triangular alliance known as the "Axis Powers." Like the United States, Britain, and Germany operating under the NATO alliance today, the Axis powers either disregarded international norms and the clauses of the League's Covenant, or bypassed the League altogether, or claimed they were acting in accordance with the Covenant. None of them publicly declared that they were acting illegally or immorally, although Mussolini's Italy came close to declaring that the League and international laws did not matter when it attacked and annexed Ethiopia without provocation in 1935. Japan's earlier attack and annexation of the Chinese province of Manchuria in 1932 was claimed to have been undertaken within the boundaries of international law and the League Covenant. Japan claimed it was acting in self-defense to enforce its extraterritorial rights in Manchuria, although the belated Lytton Commission of Inquiry determined otherwise.[26]

When Hitler's Germany annexed the Sudetenland region of Czechoslovakia in 1938—the prelude to World War II—the protests by this small state were determined by Britain to be unreasonable considering that mostly Germans lived there anyway. Thus, the parallel is not that Milosevic is like Hitler, but that Kosovo is to Serbia in 1999 as the Sudetenland was to Czechoslovakia in 1938, despite ethnic minority populations constituting the majority in those regions. The assumptions in the West, that Milosevic's Serbia was the equivalent of Hitler's Germany and that NATO's military onslaught was similar to the determined action of allied forces during World War II to end evil, are misplaced. Serbia did not invade (say) Hungary in 1999 the way Germany invaded Poland in 1939. First, the Serbs sought to retain Serbs and territory within the disintegrating Yugoslavia and, failing that, to keep their historic and religious territory, Kosovo, which was indisputably part of Serbia. There was nothing evil about carving out a "Greater Serbia" from the territories of Yugoslavia, something they could have had at the end of World War I.

The events that led up to World War II were the result of a collapsing League of Nations and the rising arrogance of the Axis powers, while the other major powers, Britain, France, and America, offered feeble resistance. Similarly, the 1999 crisis that led to NATO's assault on Yugoslavia was the result of a weakening United Nations and the rising arrogance of power of the NATO alliance, while the other major powers, Russia, China, and India, could offer only verbal resistance. Moscow, Beijing, and New Delhi protested vehemently but to no avail.[27]

Fifty years of reasonable orderliness between 1950 and 2000 at the global level, if not at the regional level, was because of three institutional factors: (1) the United Nations system provided a general forum for discussing territorial disputes and political differences, although it failed miserably as a collective security organization; (2) a system of international laws were largely and voluntarily obeyed by all states because of the mutual benefits perceived to accrue to all; and (3) a system of countervailing military power between East and West, represented by NATO and the Warsaw Pact countries, ensured that neither side would destroy each other's friends and allies.

Regional confrontations and military imbalances in the Far East, Southeast Asia, South Asia, and the Middle East were adjusted, modified, or regulated by the overall global military balance. However, with the collapse of the Soviet Union in 1990, there is no countervailing military power to an aggressive, unrestrained, expanding, and morally self-righteous NATO. NATO has usurped the authority of the UN, and the U.S. has usurped that of NATO.

Perhaps the argument could be advanced that the old nuclear balance of terror still exists between the United States and Russia or China based on mutual nuclear retaliatory strike capabilities. But this is precisely the problem. While Russia and China may still be able to deter nuclear and conventional attacks on themselves by an expanding and threatening NATO, the failure of Russia to be able to deter an attack on its close ally, Serbia, holds lessons for the rest of the world. That the attack was launched without consulting Russia, and when the Russian prime minister, Ivgeny Primakov, was halfway across the Atlantic to beg Americans for more IMF loans, is an indication of the dependency and powerlessness of Moscow.

With the United Nations largely a bystander, an onlooker, and even a conspirator in NATO's assault on Serbia, other states anxious about their own security may either have to move up to a higher level of military capability by acquiring their own nuclear deterrent, as India has done, or they may have to move down to a lower level of an anarchic and quasi-military capability by engaging in terrorist attacks against Americans and others, thereby taking the war to the heart of NATO member countries, as some radical Islamic groups have done. Indeed, the irony is that, while Clinton and Blair were bombing Saddam Hussain's Iraq to halt his drive to procure weapons of mass destruction, that bombing probably justified—in Iraq's eyes—its search for nuclear, chemical, and biological weapons. There is no other defense or deterrence against the new high-tech conventional weapons that the United States now possesses.

The behavior of states at the end of the twentieth century reflects the natural response to a dominant but mainly benevolent state with no territorial ambitions against others. On the civil war in the former Yugoslavia (defined as "Serbian aggression" by the United States), there were no negative votes in the Security Council on a series of resolutions that were introduced between 1991 and 1997, despite serious reservations by some members on some of those resolutions sponsored by the United States and its newfound Muslim and Third World "allies" in the Security Council and General Assembly. By late 1994, after expressing several grave misgivings, Russia finally vetoed a Security Council resolution sponsored by the United States to embargo Serbian oil to the Bosnian and Krajina Serbs.[28]

When the United States sought to lift the arms embargo to the former regions of Yugoslavia in order to enable arms to flow to the Muslims in the Bosnian civil war, it appeared that four vetoes may have been cast by the remaining four permanent members of the Security Council. But that never happened and was unlikely to have happened despite all the informal disagreements that were expressed. However, to avoid embarrassing the other permanent members of the Security Council, all of whom were opposed to the lifting of the arms embargo to the Bosnian Muslims in 1994, the United States took the case to the General Assembly in November, where it got its nonbinding resolution passed by the margin of ninety-seven votes in favor, sixty-one abstentions, and without a single negative vote being cast.[29] Surely, every one of those sixty-one countries who abstained also disagreed with the UN resolution in varying degrees, and yet none dared or cared to vote against the United States. It is pertinent to note that Canada and the European nations, including Germany, abstained. Such voting in the UN defies credibility.

During the bombing of Yugoslavia, a similar vote was passed in the UN Commission on Human Rights on April 23, 1999.[30] Here a draft resolution introduced by the Russian Federation called simply for an immediate cessation of hostilities and violation of human rights and called on parties to the conflict to find peaceful solutions through negotiations while maintaining the territorial integrity of the Federal Republic of Yugoslavia. This harmless resolution calling for an end to hostilities was defeated by a roll-call vote of eleven in favor, twenty-four against, and eighteen abstentions. The countries in favor of the Russian resolution were China, Colombia, Cuba, Ecuador, India, Mexico, Peru, Russia, Sri Lanka, Uruguay, and Venezuela. Those opposed included nine NATO members of the Commission, including Germany, France, Italy, UK, and the U.S., five would-be NATO members, five Muslim members, the largest being Pakistan and Bangladesh, and two key American allies in Asia, Japan and South Korea. The abstentions included Argentina and Chile, which meant that nearly all of Latin America was opposed to NATO's bombing, with some unwilling to put this is on the official record. Nearly all of the key African countries abstained as well as Indonesia, the largest Muslim state. This would indicate that more than half the world's population opposed NATO's war, and half of the remaining half preferred (according to my guess) not to alienate the sole superpower.

A demonstration that what the United States wants it gets at the UN may be seen in the American prevention of Boutros Boutros Ghali from seeking a second term as Secretary-General. Then Ambassador to the UN and, at the time, Secretary of State Madeleine Albright carried a personal dislike and antagonism towards Boutros Ghali. According to the *Washington Post*, "It was she, sources say, who crafted and pushed the plan to dump the U.N. secretary-general."[31] She wished to replace him with the Ghanian, Kofi Anan. Fourteen out of fifteen members of the Security Council voted in November 1996 to renew

Boutros Boutros Ghali's term. The United States vetoed Boutros Ghali's appointment and eventually got its man, Kofi Anan, appointed to the position. No state, not even France, who earlier opposed the United States on this issue, was prepared to object. If the above described UN voting patterns were to occur within any country that claimed to be a free and democratic society, it would invite skepticism and derision. Thus, Kofi Anan, having first declared NATO actions in violation of the UN and NATO's own charters on March 25, was quickly persuaded by the United States to withdraw his views by early April. We now have a UN that is pliant to Western interests and a Secretary-General that is compliant to U.S. demands.

## WARS, AGGRESSION, AND WAR CRIMES

### NATO and International Law

In attacking Serbia over Kosovo, which is part of a sovereign independent state, in 1999, the United States and NATO violated several international laws. American legal specialists have claimed that NATO actions constitute an evolving system of international laws. The reality was that NATO made up the laws as it went along to rationalize its actions. Indeed, the United States has declared itself the prosecutor, judge, and executioner of whatever laws it chooses to make up to advance its policy agenda. The following are some of the main violations of international laws committed by NATO.

(1) NATO actions constituted a violation of Chapter I, Article 2 (4) of the UN Charter, which states: "All Members shall refrain in their international relations from the threat or use of force against the territorial integrity or political independence of any state, or in any other manner inconsistent with the purposes of the United Nations." Chapter VII, Article 39 states: "The Security Council shall determine the existence of any threat to the peace, breach of the peace, or act of aggression and shall make recommendations, or decide what measures shall be taken in accordance with Articles 41 and 42, to maintain or restore international peace and security."

Efforts to justify these actions through earlier resolutions or Chapter VII of the Charter are acts of distortion and convenience. Article 51 of Chapter VII states that "Nothing in the present Charter shall impair the inherent right of individual or collective self-defense if an armed attack occurs against a Member of the United Nations, until the Security Council has taken measures necessary to maintain international peace and security." The problem is that Yugoslavia did not attack any neighboring states outside its sovereign borders, let alone a NATO member. Instead, Yugoslavia was attacked by NATO. The Security Council did not sanction the use of force here. NATO bypassed the

Security Council to attack Yugoslavia illegally because a resolution calling for military action would certainly have been vetoed by Russia and China.

(2) The bombing of Yugoslavia was a violation of NATO's own charter, which claims it is a defensive organization and is only committed to force if one of its members is attacked. No member of NATO was attacked. The relevant sections of NATO's basic purpose reads as follows: "It provides deterrence against any form of aggression against the territory of any NATO member state. It preserves the strategic balance within Europe."[32] When communist rule ended in Europe and the Warsaw Pact was dismantled, presumably these rationales for NATO's existence also ended. An alliance usually posits an enemy in advance, and the enemy lies outside of the alliance system. A commonly perceived external enemy is, after all, the main reason for forging an alliance, not for some vague eventuality that a powerful enemy may arise in some distant future.[33] Without an external enemy there would not be sufficient consensus and motivation to keep the alliance together. There is no strategic balance in Europe to keep. NATO is dominant and international laws have become inconvenient.

No doubt, maintaining an alliance without predetermined external threats may serve notice to nonmembers that the security interests of the alliance countries would be protected. But a single military alliance without the prevalence of countervailing military power would be perceived as a serious threat to other states and would provoke them to seek appropriate military counterbalancing measures. Subsequent to the bombing, there were moves among Russia, China, and India to forge a strategic partnership, until the terrorist attack on the United States on September 11, 2001. Having experienced terrorism by extreme Islamic groups themselves in Chechnya, Kashmir, and Xinjiang, all three states immediately joined the U.S.-led campaign against global terrorism.

However, the purpose of NATO's existence remains controversial as it constitutes a standing provocation to the rest of the world. It is an alliance in search of an enemy, or needing to create one, in order to justify its existence.[34] In 1999, NATO discovered a new mission—as absurd as it may sound to normal people except NATO enthusiasts—in pulverizing eight million impoverished Serbs into the ground through twenty-four-hour-a-day aerial bombardment over seventy-eight days. Meanwhile, Russia was not supposed to feel threatened by an expanded NATO and the attack on Serbia, a condition which the United States would not contemplate in reverse, including a similar hypothetical Russian attack on Canada.

(3) The so-called Rambouillet Agreement (Serbia did not agree to it) was a violation of Articles 51 and 52 of the 1980 Vienna Convention on the Law of Treaties. Article 51, entitled "Coercion of a Representative of a State," declares: "The expression of a State's consent to be bound by a treaty which has been procured by the coercion of its representative through acts or threats directed

against him shall be without legal effect." Article 52, entitled "Coercion of a State by the Threat or Use of Force," reads: "A treaty is void if its conclusion has been procured by the threat or use of force in violation of the principles of international law embodied in the Charter of the United Nations."

First, Serbia was threatened with force in order to coerce it to sign the Rambouillet "Agreement," and when that failed, Serbia and its entire population were subjected to massive terror bombing in order to bring about submission to NATO *diktats*. The Rambouillet "Agreement" was not negotiated with Yugoslavia but presented as a fait accompli. There were no discussions between Serbs and Albanians. The Albanians were persuaded to sign only because they were given to understand that, once they got immediate de facto independence, within three years it would automatically become *de jure*. Besides, they would get to see Serbia bombed into a premodern era, an offer they could hardly refuse. Yet Serbia accepted the political terms of the *diktat* only insisting that it would not accept a NATO military presence in Kosovo. Indeed, the military annex of the Rambouillet *diktat* was far reaching, requiring that Yugoslavia allow NATO forces unhindered access to all of its territory at no cost to NATO. The military annex was sneaked in on the last day of the talks without the Russian representative's knowledge. Milosevic or no Milosevic, no state or statesman could have accepted these humiliating terms. It was a deliberate setup to invite rejection so as to proceed with the bombing.[35]

> *Section 6 (a):* NATO shall be immune from all legal process, whether civil, administrative, or criminal. (b) NATO personnel, under all circumstances and at all times, shall be immune from the Parties' jurisdiction in respect of any civil, administrative, criminal, or disciplinary offenses which may be committed by them in the FRY. The Parties shall assist States participating in the Operation in the exercise of their jurisdiction over their own nationals.

> *Section 8:* NATO personnel shall enjoy, together with their vehicles, vessels, aircraft, and equipment, free and unrestricted passage and unimpeded access throughout the FRY including associated airspace and territorial waters. This shall include, but not be limited to, the right of bivouac, maneuver, billet, and utilization of any areas or facilities as required for support, training, and operations.

The following exchange between NATO spokesman Jamie Shea and a reporter reveals the embarrassing terms of the "Agreement" with respect to the West.[36]

> *Question:* The Rambouillet Accords, appendix B in particular . . . called for the occupation of all of Yugoslavia. . . . Unrestricted passage throughout [its] air space, territorial waters, rail, airports, roads, bridges, ports without payment, the electromagnetic spectrum and so on. Was not the Rambouillet accord, which

[Slobodan] Milosevic refused to sign, in fact, a desire to occupy all of Yugoslavia and not just simply Kosovo?

*Jamie Shea:* No, absolutely not. . . . We were looking . . . to be able to deploy an international security force, and that means, of course, being able to deploy the assets for that security force. . . . At the moment, all of our predeployed elements in the former Yugoslav Republic of Macedonia have come in by the Greek port of Thessaloniki. And for that, obviously, one has to have an agreement with the Yugoslav government to be able to have access to those roads, those rail systems, the air space for the business of setting up an international security presence, and therefore NATO personnel who may have had at the time . . . to transit temporarily through Yugoslavia will have had to enjoy those kinds of immunities. . . .

*Question:* That's simply not the language, sir. It's "free and unrestricted passage," the ability to detain people, for example, . . . and total use of electromagnetic spectrum, sir.

*Jamie Shea:* I was not a negotiator at Rambouillet . . . but my understanding, sir, is that it refers to, as you say, passage, exactly transit. And that's the point I've made.

(4) NATO's objective in Kosovo was a violation of Clause IV of the Declaration of Principles Guiding Relations Between Participating States of the Helsinki Accords Final Act of 1975 which guarantees the territorial frontiers of the states of Europe. As noted in my first chapter, according to this agreement: "The participating states will respect the territorial integrity of each of the participating states. Accordingly, they will refrain from any action . . . against the territorial integrity, political independence, or the unity of any participating state."

The former Yugoslavia was a party to this agreement, not the new states, such as Croatia and Bosnia, which subsequently invoked the Helsinki territorial principles to preserve their boundaries that were carved out from the old state. Ironically, while attempts by Serbs of Croatia and Bosnia to remain part of Yugoslavia were denied, and their declarations of independence rejected in order to maintain the territorial integrity of Croatia and Bosnia, which had never existed under modern international law, the right of the Kosovo Albanians to secede was encouraged. What this so-called Rambouillet peace plan offered was (a) the severance of Kosovo through NATO bombing with immediate effect; or (b) the severance of Kosovo through NATO occupation three years later. The Serbs chose option A.

(5) As noted in my first chapter, if the sequel to the bombing is recognition of Kosovo as an independent state, this will violate international law that prohibits recognition of provinces that unilaterally declare independence against the wishes of the federal authorities.

The illegality of Unilateral Declarations of Independence (UDI) was established by the British when Rhodesia's Ian Smith unilaterally declared independence when the British still ruled that state (now Zimbabwe). No doubt, the policies regarding UDI have been inconsistent. The formal secession of the Turkish Republic of Northern Cyprus in 1981, a de facto functioning state, has not been recognized although the secession of Bangladesh in 1971 under similar circumstances was recognized. The UDI of Biafra from Nigeria in 1971, Punjab from India in the mid-1980s, Abhkazia from Georgia in 1994, and Chechnya from Russia in 1995 have not been recognized. Clearly, Palestinians have a right to declare themselves an independent state because it is not even a part of Israel but is a group of illegally occupied territories since the Arab-Israeli war of 1967. Yet Israel has warned that it would not recognize the threatened UDI by Yasir Arafat in May 1999.

(6) The destruction of many Serbian religious and historical sites by NATO's bombing was a violation of the 1954 Hague Convention for the Protection of Cultural Property in the Event of Armed Conflict. This Convention was adopted in the light of experience during two world wars when there was wanton destruction of cultural and historical property in Europe. It was first mooted during World War II by President Woodrow Wilson and British Prime Minister Asquith. Keith Eirinberg noted that "Some 80 years later, the destruction of cultural property, this time on the territory of the former Yugoslavia [by the former Yugoslavs themselves], again shocks the world."[37] But the United States could do little to protest these actions by Serbs and Croats because Washington had failed to ratify the 1954 Hague Convention, perhaps with good reason since it has engaged in such actions from the air itself in Iraq and Yugoslavia.

No doubt, the extent of the damage to Serbian and Byzantine cultural and religious sites in Kosovo was much less than had been assessed during the bombing. But we do know that NATO deliberately targeted military and civilian buildings in Serbia. Historic bridges over the Danube were destroyed. The presidential palace, a place of historic value as the residence of the historical figure Josip Broz Tito, and previously the royal residence of the Serbian monarchy, was deliberately destroyed. The Banovina palace in Novi Sad, the ramparts of the fifteenth-century fort in Belgrade, and much of the historic city of Pec were destroyed. NATO arrogated to itself the role of determining what is and what is not a military site. Given the fact that it had run out of military targets, its definitions had become pretty lax. As Simon Jenkins of the *Times* (London) put it, NATO waged vandalism, not war. If Milosevic committed crimes against humanity, NATO committed crimes against civilization.[38]

(7) The 1949 Geneva Convention (IV) Relative to the Protection of Civilian Persons in time of War specifically prohibits deliberate attacks on civlians. Part II, Article 13 states: "The Provisions of Part II cover the whole populations of the countries in conflict, without any adverse distinction

based, in particular, on race, nationality, religion or political opinion, and are intended to alleviate the sufferings caused by war."[39] The Geneva Conventions Act (amended 1995) of the United Kingdom specifically states that "civilians shall not be the object of attack" (Schedule 5, Article 52.1) and that "civilians shall enjoy protection unless they take a direct part in hostilities" (Schedule 6, Article 13.3).[40] The attack on the Serbian radio and TV station at night when it was inhabited only by civilians, leading to the deaths of sixteen civilians and serious injury to many more, constituted an intentional attack on civilians. To claim that the fault lay with Milosevic for not evacuating the facility knowing that it was likely to be bombed by NATO because it was declared to be a Serbian war propaganda machine, cannot justify the bombing, no more than Serbia—if it had the capability—would have had the right to bomb CNN headquarters in Atlanta killing its journalists because CNN was perceived to be spewing NATO propaganda.

(8) Beyond the above, there were several other environmental international regulations that were violated by the attacks on chemical plants, fuel storage, and refineries. The 1976 Convention on the Prohibition of Military or Other Hostile Use of Environmental Modification Techniques, and the 1977 Protocol I Additional to the Geneva Conventions, article 55 states: "Care shall be taken in warfare to protect the natural environment against widespread, long-term and severe damage. This protection includes a prohibition of the use of methods or means of warfare which are intended or may be expected to cause such damage to the natural environment and thereby to prejudice the health or survival of the population."[41]

Other conventions include the Vienna Convention for the Protection of the Ozone Layer (1985, UNEP), the Montreal Protocol on Substances that Deplete the Ozone Layer (1987), and the United Nations Framework Convention on Climate Change (1992).[42] A *Times of India* editorial noted:

> In Yugoslavia, oil refineries and chemical plants have been attacked. . . . Every attack on a chemical plant is likely to produce a Bhopal, big or small. While NATO authorities claim to have successfully attacked and destroyed chemical plants, they do not enlighten the world about the ecological consequences of such assaults, on the long-term impact on human beings and unborn children. The so-called "Gulf War Syndrome" focused much concern on the US veterans exposed to the chemicals released during the last days of the war against Iraq in 1991. But there is ominous silence about the ecological impact of bombing oil refineries and storages, chemical plants and high rise buildings employing highly flammable synthetic materials. It is cynical in the extreme to pretend that the air strikes against Yugoslavia have exclusively targeted military installations and the civil population has not been affected. This is sheer propaganda and undermines the credibility of NATO authorities in other statements they make.[43]

## International Military Intervention to Halt State Aggression

Parallel to NATO's justification of the right of humanitarian intervention in Yugoslavia to halt human rights abuses in Bosnia and Kosovo was the claim to the right of military intervention to halt "Serbian aggression." When fighting continues among peoples and armies that were once part of the old state, does this constitute a "civil war," or is it "aggression"? The situation becomes particularly confusing if the old federal armed forces or the localized parts of the military are involved in the fighting in what have suddenly become new states. Articles I and II of the General Assembly Resolution No. 3314 of the United Nation defines "aggression" as follows: [44]

> *Article I:* Aggression is the use of armed force by a State against the sovereignty, territorial integrity or political independence of another State, or in any other manner inconsistent with the Charter of the United Nations, as set out in this definition. . . .
> *Article II:* The first use of armed force by a State in contravention of the Charter shall constitute prima facie evidence of an act of aggression although the Security Council may, in conformity with the Charter, conclude that a determination that an act of aggression has been committed would be justified in the light of other relevant circumstances, including the fact that the acts concerned or their consequences are not of sufficient gravity.

Simply put, aggression occurs when one country attacks or invades another country, especially when there has been no significant or immediate provocation or where the state attacked posed no threat to the attacker. Italy's invasion and annexation of Ethiopia in 1935 and Iraq's invasion and annexation of Kuwait in 1991 were clear-cut cases of aggression. There was little or no provocation. Neither Ethiopia nor Kuwait constituted a threat to Mussolini's Italy or Saddam Hussain's Iraq, respectively. However, even when two established states go to war, it is difficult to say that the side that attacked first is the aggressor given prior periods of prolonged simmering conflict, frequent border skirmishes, and sometimes the need for preemption to gain military advantage. Israel initiated the lightning attack against Arab forces in the seven-day war in June 1967, but this was military action that followed months of Arab provocations, especially along the Lebanese border, the Golan Heights, and the Gulf of Aqaba. Often, external states involved in wars beyond their own territory claim they were invited by the local governments, and therefore their military intervention does not constitute aggression: for example, American forces in Vietnam and Soviet forces in Afghanistan.

In legal parlance, "internal conflicts are those occurring within a state and in which there is no lawful involvement by another state in the sense of a breach of Article 2(4) [of the UN Charter] or [breach of] the duty of nonintervention. In this type of conflict there is, basically, no right of intervention for any outside power and no occasion for any exercise of a right of self-defense."[45] The principle of the sovereignty and equality of states has generally prescribed that outside powers have no right of intervention on any side, although arguments have been made for intervention in civil wars on humanitarian grounds.[46] In more informal parlance, a civil war occurs when armed conflict occurs within an existing state whether it involves the military, newly formed militias, or civilians. Civil wars are often uncontrollable, disorganized, and not responsive to formal rules of interstate warfare. "Just War" theory was not constructed and geared to address civil wars, although there could be such a thing as just civil wars and unjust ones. The precise origins of a civil war and determining which side is to blame for the outbreak of hostilities remain even more ambiguous than determining the aggressor state between two warring states. If "who fired the first shot?" is difficult to establish in interstate wars, the same question may appear totally irrelevant in civil wars. The ambiguity and confusion between civil wars and wars of aggression may be seen in some of the following cases.[47]

Although the West recognized the right of the former Soviet republics to secede and become independent states, Russian attempts to crush the unilateral declaration of independence by the Muslims of Chechnya was declared to be an internal matter and, therefore, a civil war. However, as the war continued, doubts began to rise as to whether this was war or civil war. As with the other Soviet republics, Georgia seceded from the Soviet Union without attempts by Moscow to prevent it. However, the armed violence that erupted following the attempt by Muslim Abkhazians to secede from Georgia was considered to be civil war even after the Abkhazians were able to set up a de facto independent state. Abkhazia was not recognized.

The brief civil war that broke out in Yemen in May 1994 was triggered by the declaration of independence by the south. The north proceeded to crush the secession through armed force. But, the merger of the north (Yemen Arab Republic) and the south (the Peoples Democratic Republic of Yemen) had taken place just four years earlier. In 1870, the north was occupied by the Turks, who relinquished control after World War I. The south was occupied by the British in 1839 and granted independence in 1967.[48] For over a hundred years, the two Yemens had no common history or political experience. Yet, there were no allegations of "aggression" against the north in its attempt to crush the secession of the South, which had agreed to a union only a few years earlier. Indeed, there were no allegations of aggression when the forces of Nasser's Egypt and Saudi Arabia fought on the sides of the republican and royalist forces, respectively, during the civil war in the Yemen Arab Republic in the mid-1960s. And when India seized the Portuguese territory of Goa in 1961 by force and Indonesia seized the former Portuguese territory of East

Timor in 1974, also by force, neither of these two major Asian countries considered their acts to be aggression, but the rightful fulfillment of national-territorial objectives that had been subverted by Portuguese colonial occupation. The United States in Vietnam and the Soviet Union in Afghanistan did not see their prolonged military operations in Vietnam and Afghanistan as acts of aggression.

The blurring between civil war and aggression is clear in the case of the former Yugoslavia. War in the former Yugoslavia would appear to be a "civil war" that suddenly became a "war of aggression" following Western recognitions of Slovenia, Croatia, and Bosnia. Thus, while the military suppression of secessionist forces by federal forces within one of the provinces of an independent sovereign state would classify as a "civil war," the recognition of that province attempting to secede as an independent state by the international community would instantly reclassify it as a "war of aggression" by what was once federal forces attempting to crush or reverse that secession.

The crucial dividing line between civil war and aggression in the Balkan conflict was the recognition of new states. For instance, the hypothetical international recognition of Chechnya, Tibet, or Kashmir as independent states would make Russia, China, and India's efforts to suppress Chechen, Tibetan, and Kashmiri secessionist movements (from the point of recognition onward) instant wars of aggression. The recognition of an independent consolidated Kurdistan incorporating the Kurdish areas of Iraq, Turkey, Iran, and Syria would generate instantly Iraqi, Turkish, Iranian, and Syrian aggression, provided their federal forces are still involved in crushing the various Kurdish separatist movements. If an independent Palestine state on the West Bank and Gaza had been recognized soon after Israel occupied these territories following the 1967 Arab-Israeli war, then Israeli security operations there over the last thirty-five years would have constituted a war of aggression against an independent Palestinian state. Indeed, the Israeli acceptance of Palestinian autonomy in 1994 would imply that all Israeli military operations from hereon on the West Bank and Gaza constitute aggression.

International policy in the former Yugoslavia on the question of aggression following the breakup of a state was different from virtually all other similar situations in the past and the present. In the hasty recognition of Slovenia and Croatia, even the Yugoslav Army's inevitable presence in Slovenia, where there was a feeble attempt to prevent secession, was considered to be "Serbian aggression." In reality, a token contingent of the Yugoslav army already stationed there suddenly found themselves trapped on "alien" Slovenian soil and were immediately declared to be "aggressors." Since there were few Serbs in Slovenia, the Serb-dominated Yugoslav army units there were seeking ways to get out of Slovenia. Strangely, this phenomenon was portrayed by American politicians and the media as a case of brave and good Slovenians who stood up to the military might of the evil Serbs, an example which should be followed by good Croats and Muslims—if only the arms embargo could be lifted. Surely, the Yugoslav Army, if it chose to do so, could have crushed Slovenia's secession within a month. Indeed, the power of the Serb-dominated Yugoslav Army was such that it could have crushed all the secessionist movements by Slovenes, Croats, Muslims, Macedonians, and Albanians in due course of time: that is, if only there were no restrictions on the application of full and unrestrained force, Western media allegations of genocide and crimes against humanity, and Western military intervention.

Thus, the repeated claims that Yugoslavia lost four wars in Slovenia, Croatia, Bosnia, and Kosovo are not factual. The marginal Yugoslav federal forces withdrew from Slovenia giving little or no resistance for lack of interest in that province. After an initial rampage in Croatia in 1991, federal forces were withdrawn, leaving an insignificant, weak, and demoralized Krajina Serb army to fend for themselves against a Croatian army trained by Military Professional Resources Incorporated (MPRI) of Virginia, an organization composed of retired U.S. military officers. MPRI provided training and logistical support to Croatian forces while U.S. intelligence agencies provided satellite-based intelligence and information.[49] The surprise lightning strike by Croatian forces in 1995 produced no resistance by the ragtag Krajina Serb forces, causing the flight of much of the Serb population from Croatia. Yugoslav federal forces were not involved in this war. Likewise, Yugoslav federal forces were withdrawn from Bosnia by the fall of 1992 amidst cries of Serbian aggression and genocide, although some assistance continued to be channeled by Belgrade to the Bosnian Serb army. And, as noted subsequently in this chapter, Serbian forces were unaffected in Kosovo despite the massive seventy-eight-day bombing campaign by NATO. They withdrew by mutual agreement when UN Security Council Resolution 1244 met Serbia's two demands that Kosovo remain part of Serbia and that NATO would not occupy the rest of Serbia. NATO's capitulation to Serbia's demands, which were initially made at Rambouillet, brought an end to this war, not the other way around.

In particular, the classification of the war in Bosnia as one of "Serbian aggression" makes even less sense, since the war in Bosnia was fought mainly by Bosnian Serbs who have lived there for centuries. True, supplies came from Serbia, and there have been members of the Yugoslav Army and other militia from Serbia fighting on the side of the Bosnian Serb forces. It is commonplace for various sides in civil wars to gain such military supplies from sympathetic outside powers. And, invariably, outside forces get involved.

The American Civil War in the 1860s and the Spanish Civil War in the 1930s were no exceptions in this respect. Civil wars in Korea, Vietnam, and Afghanistan had the Great Powers directly or indirectly involved, making these wars essentially international wars of proxy. The civil war between Greeks and Turks in Cyprus in the 1970s drew the Turkish armed forces directly into the conflict in 1974, dividing up Cyprus. The Indian military intervened with tremendous force during the Pakistan civil war in its eastern province in 1971. The problem of distinguishing between altruistic actions of intervention and prejudicial actions in favor of one side in the civil war becomes difficult. Turkish military intervention in Cyprus and Indian military intervention in East Pakistan also carried self-serving political objectives.[50] The problem in the Balkans was complicated by the fact that the Serbs spread through the new states of Serbia, Bosnia, Montenegro, and Krajina are indistinguishable from each other except by place of residence. They were all once citizens of the same state. The Croats of Bosnia and Croatia were all also once part of the same South Slav state.

Thus, it would appear inevitable that large numbers of Croatian forces from the newly independent state of Croatia would be involved on the side of the Bosnian Croats in the war in Bosnia against Serbs and Muslims. This was never declared to be "Croatian aggression." And, as in civil wars nearly everywhere, outside forces become involved. Sizeable numbers of Muslim "Mujahideen" from Arab lands, Chechnya, Iran, Pakistan, and Afghanistan were also involved in the fighting in Bosnia. Perhaps this was inevitable and justifiable since the Bosnian Serbs possessed overwhelming military advantage. The Bosnian Serbs' ability to obtain a relatively superior military machine was partly because they were once a significant part of the Yugoslav Army, and many of the armament factories and military storage depots were located in Bosnia, which the Serbs seized. Undoubtedly, the war in Bosnia was an uneven war between Serbs and Muslims, but do wars have to be among equal military forces to be classified as "civil wars" instead of "aggression"?

## War and Civilian Casualties

The American definition of aggression received further enhancement in 1995. A finding by the Central Intelligence Agency that its satellite-based aerial cameras had irrefutably established that "Serbs carried out at least 90 percent of the ethnic cleansings in Bosnia" was interpreted by the *New York Times* as follows: "The report makes nonsense of the view—now consistently put forward by western European governments and intermittently by the Clinton Administration—that the Bosnian conflict is a civil war for which guilt should be divided between Serbs, Croats and Muslims rather than a case of Serbian aggression."[51] It is dubious whether satellite cameras orbiting in outer space can identify the ethnicity of peoples in Bosnia and whether CIA data collection was conducted in a fair and impartial manner. Indeed, reports of the

United Nations High Commissioner for Refugees in 1994 indicated that there were at least 750,000 Serbian refugees in Serbia, Montenegro, and Serb-held territories of Bosnia and Krajina, constituting about 35 percent of the two million refugees in the former Yugoslavia. But the more intriguing aspect of the new American distinction between civil war and aggression in the former Yugoslavia was the claim based on the "percentage" of atrocities committed by the Serbs.

The greater numbers of innocent civilians killed deliberately by Serbian forces became another reason for classifying the Balkan wars as Serbian aggression. However, the alleged numbers of civilians killed and women raped by Serbs have been grossly exaggerated while crimes committed by the other ethnic groups underestimated. This is not to suggest that Serb forces did not commit massacres and atrocities between the breakup of Yugoslavia and the end of the war in Kosovo.

General Satish Nambiar, the first UNPROFOR commander in the former Yugoslavia, told me that, in Bosnia, he and his deputy, General Lewis MacKenzie, had twenty-eight thousand soldiers under them and were in constant contact with personnel from the UN High Commission for Refugees and the International Red Cross. Apart from some killings here and there, neither of them witnessed any genocide. It was at the end of General Nambiar's tenure as commander in March 1993 that the figure of two hundred thousand killed in Bosnia became an established "fact" through repetition in the media. Both Nambiar and MacKenzie had determined that the "breadline massacre" of May 1992 (in which mainly poor Serbs queuing for food were killed) was staged by the Muslims. That massacre, which was attributed to the Serbs, triggered sanctions against Serbia in May 1992, sanctions that were lifted only in November 2000 after Milosevic was overthrown by the Serbs themselves. In their American Political Science Association award-winning book, *The War in Bosnia-Herzegovina*, Steven Burg and Paul Shoup have questioned, documented, and rejected alleged Serb responsibility for the "Three Massacres," namely, the "breadline" massacre on May 27, 1992, the first Markale massacre on February 5, 1994, and the second Markale massacre on August 28, 1995.[52]

In his book *To End a War*, Richard Holbrooke's first sentence in his "Note to the Reader" states, "Between 1991 and 1995, close to three hundred thousand people were killed in the former Yugoslavia." Presumably, those killed were mainly Muslims and Croats by Serbs.[53] This is an impossible figure. At the end of the 1991–1992 war in Croatia, the death toll was declared to be about ten thousand. After the Markale Market massacre in February 1994 (for which Serbs have denied responsibility), the killing of sixty-eight civilians was claimed to be the worst such incident in a single day of the war. But if we take the highest figure of sixty-eight killings per day and multiply it by seven hundred days of war, that would add up to 47,600 fatalities. But the highest figure of sixty-eight civilians killed did not occur every day of the war. The toll of Muslims killed at Srebrenica began at ten thousand and eventually settled at about six thousand. But if a "Srebrenica" occurred every month for the forty-month duration of the war in Bosnia from May 1992 to August 1995, the total death toll should be 240,000. But a "Srebrenica" did not occur every month. Indeed, between the large-scale killings in Vukovar in Croatia by Serb forces at the beginning of the Yugoslav conflict and the Srebrenica massacre in Bosnia toward the end of the conflict, relatively little of such magnitude happened.[54]

George Kenney, the former State Department official who headed the Yugoslav desk, has protested these figures repeatedly. In an article in the *New York Times*, he stated: "In 1995, lacking the bodies, the charge of Genocide has worn thin. It seems to have almost become sensationalism for its own sake. . . . As long as the world tosses around words like 'genocide' so loosely, the present tragedy will revolve endlessly. Counts count."[55] And again, in 1997, he wrote in response to a leader in the *Guardian* of London:[56]

> You associate me with efforts to "rewrite history." What history? Surely you cannot mean that journalistic accounts accurately reflected events. I could offer dozens of examples that exerted at critical times debilitating influence over policy, but take one: the number killed. Starting in mid-1993, using statistics given by Bosnian officials, virtually every large media organization published a boilerplate figure of 200,000–250,000 killed and they continue to do so. But the respected Stockholm International Peace Research Institute in its 1996 Yearbook estimates 30,000-50,000 total by the end of the war, on all sides. Which is most likely to be right? . . . Hysterical journalists, especially revved up visions of Nazi concentration camps and the killing field of Cambodia? Bosnia was not at all like that. When journalists brand as "Serb apologists" those who call for dispassionate analysis of what has happened, something has gone badly wrong with the public debate.

As regards rape, allegations began with one hundred thousand women raped, which then came down to sixty thousand, then forty thousand, and finally twenty thousand. But the actual recorded number of alleged rapes with the ICTY based on affidavits were fewer than one thousand over a three-year period of war and chaos, much of them amounting to criminal activity.[57] To put this in context, compare this with an annual record of about one hundred thousand rapes in the United States as reported to the police, and much more that probably are not reported. When the allegation of sixty thousand rapes was first made against the Serbs in Bosnia in 1992, the recorded rape statistics in the United States was 109,060 for that year.[58] Diana Johnstone observed:[59]

> Today the public is largely convinced that mass rape as a deliberate Serbian war strategy of ethnic cleansing is a proven fact. This past March [1997] a group of nine U.S. women senators sent a letter to President Clinton demanding tougher prosecution of Serbian war criminals and claiming that "investigators have documented rapes of over 50,000 women and girls." Yet the oft-repeated figure of 50,000 is not based on any documentation. The commission to investigate war crimes in the former Yugoslavia set up by the Security Council to prepare the documentary basis for the I.C.T.Y. received reports of more than 1,600 cases of rape, and interviewed 223 victims who reported up to 4,500 cases. But at the conclusion of its work in May 1994, the commission had gathered 575 affidavits with precise identifications. . . . In testimony before a Senate committee in August 1995, commission chairman Bassiouni said 20,000 rapes was a "sustainable projection." Indeed, all larger figures are "projections" based not on victims' complaints, but on hearsay, from a conflict where rumors and vivid accusations have been every bit as much as a "weapon of war" as was rape, and no doubt more so.

In the case of Kosovo, the justification for NATO's military assault on Serbia in 1999 was that Milosevic and the Serbs were about to commit genocide, and it had to be prevented before they did. But estimates made during the war by U.S. Defense Secretary William Cohen, British Defense Secretary Geoffrey Hoon, and other officials and reporters that some one hundred thousand Albanians may have been killed by Serb forces proved fraudulent. Prime Minister Tony Blair had assessed that the final figure may be greater. Estimates were then reduced to ten thousand at the end of the war. Three years later, less then five thousand bodies on all sides were found. But the perverse hope still abounds that more will be found. More importantly, there was no evidence of any planned systematic genocide. Richard Gwyn observed:

> No genocide of ethnic Albanians by Serbs, therefore: No "human catastrophe." No "modern-day Holocaust." . . . All of those claims may have been an honest mistake. Equally, they may have been a grotesque lie concocted to justify a war that NATO originally assumed would be over in a day or two, with Milosevic using the excuse of some minimal damage as a cover for a surrender, but then had to fight (at great expense) for months. . . . No genocide means no justification for a war inflicted by NATO on a sovereign nation. Only a certainty of imminent genocide could have legally justified a war that was not even discussed by the U.N. Security Council. . . . Even more questionable is the West's continued punishment of the Serbs—the Danube bridges and the power stations remain in ruins—when their offence may well have been stupidity rather than criminality.[60]

A German doctor who had spent the war in a refugee camp in Macedonia noted the unusual craving by the Western media to find genocide committed by the Serbs. There was almost a desperate hope to find that all the Albanian men of military age in Kosovo had been murdered by Serbs. He told *Die Welt*: "It was very surprising that a large number of journalists either could not or would not perceive the majority of the people in the refugee camps were men of military age. It was always represented as if there were no men in the camps at all. Even when the journalists were told this they refused to take account of it."[61] The media and many in academia were determined not to be cheated out of their genocide.

Related to the problem of aggression is the question of Serbian "irredentism," that is, Serbian efforts to create a "Greater Serbia." "Irredentism" occurs when a country seeks to annex parts of neighboring countries because the particular ethnic group of the first country inhabits parts of these other countries or because that ethnic group believes that, during historical times, some of these areas were once part of their country or their empire. Irredentist policies and actions may be seen in Germany's claim to parts of Poland and Czechoslovakia in the 1930s or China's claim to the territories of its old Manchu and earlier empires, which at one time or another included Tibet and the northern parts of India, Burma, and Vietnam. Similarly, if Hungary today sought to annex by force Vojvodina or parts of Romania and Slovakia because Hungarian minorities lived there, or because these areas were once part of the Austro-Hungarian empire, this would constitute Hungarian aggression and irredentism.

The situation in the former Yugoslavia was different. In Yugoslavia, a sovereign, multiethnic, independent state that had existed for over seventy years was abruptly taken apart through the Western policy of diplomatic recognition. Serbs, who had lived together since 1918, were separated suddenly into three different states against their wishes. Thus, the Serbian struggle to remain united within the old state of Yugoslavia does not quite fit the terms "aggression" or "irredentism" in the usual sense. Indeed, the conceived "Greater Serbia," which had already existed within the larger Yugoslavia from 1918 to 1991, would appear to be no greater than Italy, France, Germany, Iran, or Japan, where most of an ethnic group live in the boundaries of a single state. The drive for uniting the Serbs and the integration of territory considered to be Serbian-inhabited, which was spread through the Ottoman and Austro-Hungarian empires, began about the same time as the drive for the unification of the Italian and Germanic peoples in the 1860s and 1870s into what would be called today as a "Greater Italy" and a "Greater Germany."

The quest for a "Greater Serbia" was achieved at the end of World War I at tremendous Serbian sacrifice fighting on the side of the Entente powers, Britain, France, and Russia. According to John Keegan:

> Germany, though it lost the largest number of counted dead—those of Russia and Turkey remain uncounted with any exactitude—was not the worst proportionate sufferer. That country was Serbia, of whose pre-war population of five million, 125,000 were killed or died as soldiers, but another 650,000 civilians succumbed to privation or disease, making a total of 15 percent of the population lost, compared with something between two and three percent of the British, French and German populations.[62]

The Serbs eventually settled for the Kingdom of Serbs, Croats, and Slovenes under a Serbian monarch since this new state encompassed their historic goal of a Greater Serbia. With the German- and American-induced secessions of Croatia, Bosnia, and Macedonia, Yugoslavia and Greater Serbia within was yanked right out from under the feet of Serbs living in the Yugoslav territories of Croatia and Bosnia. Part of the problem of "Serbian aggression" can be traced to the refusal of the West to redraw the internal boundaries of the former Yugoslavia so as to provide for the continuation of a unified Serbian state.

Of course, redrawing boundaries frequently caused bloodshed and refugee flows, as the partition of India in 1947 demonstrated. In the division of Punjab and the redrawing of boundaries, about one million civilians lost their lives in a massive slaughter by all sides. Whether it was the Muslims, Sikhs, or Hindus who killed the most seemed almost irrelevant given the enormity of the bloodshed. Within two months, ten million Muslims, Sikhs, and Hindus, caught on the wrong side of the new international frontiers of newly divided Punjab, were forced to flee to the other side. By the end of 1947, there were virtually no Sikh or Hindu Punjabis left in Pakistan Punjab and no Muslim Punjabis left in Indian Punjab, despite the fact that all Punjabis had lived peacefully side by side before the partition of India. Similarly, in the case of Cyrpus, the de facto partition into Greek and Turkish Cyprus left no Turks on the Greek side and no Greeks on the Turkish side. Nearly two hundred thousand Greeks out of a population of six hundred thousand were forced from the Turkish side to the Greek side. Redrawing of boundaries would not have avoided bloodshed. Events in the former Yugoslavia show parallels. The population of Bosnia, in particular, was too mixed and scattered, and Serbian efforts to create an ethnically pure Serbian Republic of Bosnia was bound to be bloody, no less than the efforts by the Croats of Bosnia and of Croatia to create ethnically pure states. But at least some boundary readjustments and the protection of newly created minorities should have been attempted before Croatia and Bosnia were recognized.

## Did NATO Commit Aggression? Did It Win?

The actions of NATO displayed confusion about its role. Set up as an alliance to defend against attacks on Western Europe by communist Warsaw Pact countries, it was geared to tackle conventional and nuclear forces and not interethnic warfare, where the battle lines are unclear and changing. Moreover, NATO's threat to intervene on the side of the Bosnian Muslims against the Bosnian Serbs, and then Serbia itself, suggested that it was not acting as a military alliance anymore but as a regional collective security organization. Since all the former Warsaw Pact states have become, or seek to become, members of NATO, and with the forging of the NATO-Russia Council in 2001, the Cold War alliance's rationale has disappeared. The problem was that NATO's political and military organizational structure did not provide it with the will and ability to respond to the type of violent interethnic conflict in the former Yugoslavia involving regular armed forces, militia, and civilian snipers. Indeed, similar interethnic warfare raged in Afghanistan, Tajikstan, in Ngorna-Karabakh and Georgia, but there was no talk about military interventions to stop the killings in these wars, neither by NATO nor by any other international force.

The decision to attack Serbia had everything to do with the failure of Belgrade to submit to an ultimatum presented at Rambouillet in February 1999. However, the United States considered these Serbian requests unreasonable. This was virtually a replay of Austria's ultimatum to Serbia in 1914 following the assassination of the Archduke Ferdinand of Austria and his wife by Gavrilo Princip, a Bosnian Serb, in Sarajevo. Although it was clear that Serbia had nothing to do with the assassination, and although it agreed to virtually all the terms of the Austrian ultimatum, Austria proceeded to go to war against Serbia anyway. For Austria, the example of Serbian nationalism could not be allowed to spread to other Slavs in the Austro-Hungarian empire. Similar to Vienna's ultimatum to Serbia in 1914 following the assassination of the Archduke of Austria by a Serb, Washington used the Racak massacre in Kosovo in January 1999 (which it blamed on Milosevic and the Serbian government) to issue an ultimatum to Serbia. Like Austria, which refused to accept Serbia's compliance to its ultimatum and attacked anyway, the U.S. ultimatum was designed to be rejected in order to go to war to teach Serbia a lesson. One American official stated that the bar was raised deliberately at Rambouillet because the United States felt that the Serbs "needed a little bombing." As in the case of Austria in 1914, Serbian defiance of the United States undermined the credibility of the sole superpower, which was politically intolerable.

Eventually, the "humanitarian war," directed mainly against Serbia's civilian infrastructure in order to terrorize civilians into poverty and despair, was halted because NATO leaders agreed to both of Serbia's demands: an international military presence with some NATO component to be deployed in Kosovo alone and the acceptance of Serbia's territorial integrity, which would include Kosovo. This was approximately what Serbia had demanded at the

Rambouillet negotiations and is now embodied in the UN Security Council Resolution 1244. Indeed, the word NATO is barely mentioned in the terms of the cease-fire defined by the UN.

Despite all the Western media and governmental spins about NATO's glorious victory, there was no NATO victory. A settlement negotiated by Russia ended the war. If the war had lasted another month, NATO's unity might have collapsed. The excitement and enthusiasm of the offshore English-speaking governments of NATO—the United States, Canada, and Britain—for pulverizing the Serbs was not shared by the other non-English speaking members on the European continent, especially Italy, Greece, Germany, and Spain. Besides, there was little left to bomb that could be considered remotely military without making it obvious that the intended targets were civilian in order to terrorize the Serbian civilian population into submission.

Walter J. Rockler, a prosecutor at the Nuremberg War Crimes trial, observed of NATO's bombing:

> We have engaged in flagrant military aggression, ceaselessly attacking a small country primarily to demonstrate that we run the world. . . . As a primary source of international law, the judgment of the Nuremberg Tribunal in the 1945–1946 case of the major Nazi war criminals is plain and clear. The International Court declared, "To initiate a war of aggression, therefore, is not only an international crime, it is the supreme international crime diferring only from other war crimes in that it contains within itself the accumulated evil of the whole."[63]

Rockler continued:

> From another standpoint of international law, the current conduct of the bombing by United States and NATO constitutes a continued war crime. Contrary to the beliefs of our war planners, unrestricted air bombing is barred under international law. Bombing the "infrastructure" of a country—waterworks, electricity, plants, bridges, factories, television and radio locations—is not an attack limited to legitimate military objectives. Our bombing has also caused an excessive loss of life and injury to civilians, which violates another standard. . . . The notion that humanitarian violations can be redressed with random destruction and killing by advanced technological means is inherently suspect. This is mere pretext for our arrogant assertion of dominance and power in defiance of international law. We make the nonnegotiable demands and rules, and implement them by military force. It is all remindful of Henrik Ibsen's: "Don't use that foreign word 'ideals.' We have that excellent word 'lies.'"

The claim of humanitarian intervention was dishonest since there was no humanitarian crisis until after NATO launched its attack. The Albanian refugee crisis was caused by NATO's massive and relentless bombing campaign. That such massive bombing causes refugee crises was demonstrated again in October 2001 at the commencement of the U.S. bombing of Afghanistan, causing a similar humanitarian catastrophe.[64] According to a BBC report, "The US is taking military action against the ruling Taliban in Afghanistan for harbouring Osama Bin Laden, chief suspect for the 11 September terror attacks on New York and Washington. But the UN has warned that as many as 1.5 million people may be displaced if the military action continues, with as many as 300,000 Afghans seeking refuge in Pakistan this year alone."[65] However, all the borders across into Pakistan and Iran were closed so that these human masses who fled their homes because of U.S. bombing were classified as internally displaced people rather than refugees.

The United States and Britain have ensured that there will be no indictment of NATO leaders for war crimes by the "independent" prosecutors for the ICTY, despite the relentless bombardment of Yugoslavia's civilian infrastructure that carried no military purpose. It is no accident that NATO's bombardment left the Serbian military unscathed in much of Kosovo and all of Serbia. Statements by U.S. Generals Wesley Clark and Michael Short during the war made amply clear that the bombing was intended to terrorize and subjugate the Serbian population. In a May 24, 1999, interview with the *Washington Post*, U.S. Air Force Lieutenant General Michael Short explained the strategy:

> If you wake up in the morning and you have no power to your house and no gas to your stove and the bridge you take to work is down and will be lying in the Danube for the next 20 years, I think you begin to ask, "Hey, Slobo, what's this all about? How much more of this do we have to withstand?" And at some point, you make the transition from applauding Serb machismo against the world to thinking what your country is going to look like if this continues.[66]

In similar fashion, NATO spokesman Jamie Shea warned: "If President Milosevic really wants all of his population to have water and electricity, all he has to do is accept NATO's five conditions and we will stop this campaign." The executive director of Human Rights Watch, Kenneth Roth, said such statements made clear that the targets were deliberately civilian in the hope they would put pressure on their government to abandon its resistance to NATO attacks.[67] Yet NATO was not indicted for aggression or war crimes.

In Eugene Davidson's account of the Nuremberg Trials of 1945–1946, Mr. Justice Jackson's clause on aggression defined the chief "Crime Against Peace" for which indictments against the Nazi political leaders were prepared: (a) Planning, preparation, initiation, or waging war of aggresion, or war in violation of international treaties, agreements, or assurances; or (b) Participation in a Common Plan or Conspiracy for the accomplishment of any of the foregoing.[68] An application of this definition to NATO's actions against

Serbia shows criminal U.S. culpability that calls for its own separate war crimes trial. Indeed, the UN human rights chief Mary Robinson warned that NATO, too, could be tried by the International Criminal Tribunal for the Former Yugoslavia (ICTY). Robinson pointed out that large numbers of civilians have been "incontestably" killed, civilian installations were targeted, and "NATO remains the sole judge of what is or is not acceptable to bomb."[69]

In the end, Serbian forces that marched out of Kosovo looked as fresh and clean as the NATO forces that marched in, and with nearly all their weapons intact. Only about a dozen Serbian tanks and a few more artillery pieces were destroyed or damaged. William Pfaff noted in the *International Herald Tribune*:

> Last year [1999] NATO claimed that it had destroyed 120 tanks, 220 armored personnel carriers and 450 artillery pieces in 744 "confirmed" air strikes. In Washington, Secretary of Defense William Cohen said these attacks had "severely crippled [Serbian] military forces in Kosovo by destroying more than 50 percent of [their] artillery and one-third of the armored vehicles." The reality, according to the new air force report, is that NATO destroyed 14 tanks, 18 armored personnel carriers and 20 artillery pieces—more or less what the Serbian government said at the time, which was dismissed by NATO as Serbian "disinformation."[70]

This is in contrast to the claim of "Army Gen. Wesley Clark, who oversaw the NATO air war as Supreme Allied Commander Europe, [who] reported last fall that the Air Force concluded it struck 93 Serb tanks and 153 armored personnel carriers."[71]

Much of NATO and U.S. policy toward Serbia and the Serbs appears to be based on the Munich Syndrome and the domino theory.[72] Parallels have been drawn between Prime Minister John Major's conciliatory policy toward Milosevic's Serbia and Prime Minister Neville Chamberlain's appeasement policy toward Hitler's Germany in 1938. Many Western, and especially American, analysts were convinced that if "Serbian aggression" was not stopped and reversed in Croatia and Bosnia, there would be dire consequences for the rest of the world. It may not mean that Milosevic's alleged Nazi-like state would overrun the rest of Europe and the world. The Milosevic-Serbian threat to the world was perceived to be based on a new and grand domino theory that would appear to surpass all previously existing domino theories. Thus, if Milosevic got away with carving up Croatia and Bosnia, aggressive nationalists everywhere else would take heart and seek to do so the same. The problem would be especially acute in the former Soviet Union, where Russians find themselves trapped in new states as minorities. These minorities would appeal to Russian nationalists who would then seek to establish a "Greater Russia" by military intervention in the Baltic States, Ukraine, Uzbekistan, and Kazakhstan, where sizeable Russian minorities still live.

The Munich Syndrome and the domino theory may make for great historical theater and grandiose strategic analysis, but they do not appear convincing in reality. As regards allegations of appeasement and the dire consequences that may follow, Fareed Zakaria observed that "if a demonstration of American force in one country chills the blood of would-be aggressors in another, why did the Persian Gulf War not deter the Serbians, Azeris, Sudanese, Georgians and Somalis?"[73] Note that, apart from Laos and Cambodia, which, along with Vietnam, were part of French Indochina, dominoes did not fall even after the fall of Saigon in 1974. There were no additional threats to American security, and there were no Communist takeovers among the group of states that constitute the Association of South-East Asian Nations (ASEAN). Instead, war broke out among the Communist states themselves following American withdrawal: Vietnam against Cambodia and China against Vietnam.[74]

Rather than invoke images of Munich and falling dominoes, it may make more sense to face the reality that NATO is the only military alliance left in the world facing no predesignated external military threat. And when NATO (which in reality means the United States) can fight wars without casualties, the likelihood of military interventions against weaker and defenseless states will increase. Alliances are usually forged among states who perceive common military threats from outside of the alliance group. Thus, NATO, set up to counter the communist threat, was not geared to deal with potential Greek-Turkish conflict, since both Greece and Turkey are members of NATO. NATO after the Cold War may serve a useful purpose in policing Europe as a collective security organization. A collective security organization, like the League of Nations and the United Nations, does not denote the external enemy in advance. However, its members agree that they will come to the defense of one of its members if it is attacked by another one of its members. But, this means that all those states that NATO insists on policing and protecting must also preferably be members of the collective security organization—which the states of the former Yugoslavia were not.

## Lessons and Prospects

In the twentieth century, it became a habit for the victors of war to claim that God and morality were on their side and that they were incapable of committing crimes during war. Only the vanquished are war criminals deserving of all the punishment. In the Versailles Peace treaty of 1919 at end of World War II, Germany was punished severely through the imposition of economic reparations and was compelled by France to accept a "guilt clause." Antonio Cassese, the former Independent Prosecutor of ICTY, informed a packed audience at Yale Law School's conference on the Dayton Agreement, which was held on its first anniversary in November 1996, that several thousand soldiers were identified as war criminals at the end of World War II, of which the Kaiser was the most prominent. However, the then proposed war crimes tribunal was scuttled by immoral realists. If those trials had taken place back then, war crimes may not have taken place twenty years later. From the floor, when I asked how many of those several thousand alleged war criminals were British, French, Russians, and Americans, he admitted that there were none. They were all Germans and Austrians.[75]

The atomic bombing of Hiroshima and Nagasaki, the firebombing of Tokyo and Yokohama, the demolition of Dresden along with its civilians, and the expulsion of fifteen million Germans from Poland, Czechoslavakia, and elsewhere amidst widespread killings and rape were not subject to war crimes trials. The destruction of the people and land of Vietnam over a period of ten years in the name of freedom have now been forgotten. A collective amnesia about the destruction of Vietnam descended on the American nation. There were no apologies made or compensations paid, but instead, the Vietnamese were subjected to American economic sanctions for the next twenty years for having defeated U.S. forces in defense of their homeland.

NATO's claims during the Yugoslav conflict between 1991 and 1999 were no different. And when the powerful victors emerge and proclaim themselves without sin, the rest of the world rushes to jump on their bandwagon. Those who once condemned NATO's attack may soon be expected to concede that it was the right thing to do in the name of the greater good of mankind. The losses and grievances of the defeated become buried permanently. Moreover, history is written by the victors, a history of self-serving lies and distortions. NATO and its supporters have flooded global information outlets with their version of events in order to overwhelm all opposing viewpoints.

All the basic principles of Just War—necessity, proportionality, and discrimination—were violated by NATO, whatever their apologists and spinmeisters in the media and academia may argue. There was no necessity for this war since the final terms for ending the war embodied in UN Resolution 1244 were essentially what Serbia had asked for at Rambouillet. The attack was launched to save NATO's face after having given an ill-advised ultimatum expecting Serbia to capitulate. There was no proportionality in the near total destruction of Serbia's civilian infrastructure and the livelihood of its people. And there was not even the pretense of discrimination between military and civilian targets. Almost all the targets hit deliberately in Serbia were civilian structures, even if civilians themselves were not directly targeted.

With the fall of President Milosevic in Yugoslavia in October 2000, Bill Clinton and his Secretary of State, Madeleine Albright, and Tony Blair and his Foreign Secretary, Robin Cook, felt vindicated. The *New York Times* claimed that it was the tenacity of Madeleine Albright that brought this about. Cook claimed that bombs and sanctions worked. If it were not for the bombing of Kosovo, Milosevic would still be in power. Robert Hunter, a former U.S. Ambassador to NATO during much of the crisis, declared: "A one-two punch by the North Atlantic Treaty Organization and the European Union has again led to success in Eastern Europe. This time, the two institutions provided the backdrop for the Serbian people to cast off the last communist autocrat in the Balkans. NATO stopped the Serbian state's aggression; the EU held out hope of a better future."[76]

However, Simon Jenkins of the *Times* (London) observed,

> No, it was not the bombing, the sanctions and the posturing of NATO politicians. It was not the "fall of the last Communist dictator." It was certainly not the British Foreign Secretary, Robin Cook, endlessly lecturing the Serbs on "what they should do" and "what we want to create in Yugoslavia." Nor is the Yugoslav question answered. It will begin again. Despite NATO's efforts to bomb Slobodan Milosevic from power, indeed to kill him in his house, he was toppled by a self-inflicted, democratic miscalculation. Tony Blair presented him as a dictator akin to Hitler. But Mr. Milosevic was elected President of Serbia in 1989 and as President of Yugoslavia in 1997.[77]

## NOTES

1. See A. F. K. Organski, *World Politics*, New York: Knopf, 1958; and A. F. K. Organski and Jacek Kugler, *The War Ledger*, Chicago: University of Chicago Press, 1980.

2. The conclusion reached in the study of this issue by James Schampel was that "parity predicts war" more than preponderance. See James H. Schampel, "Parity or Preponderance: One more Look," *International Studies Notes* (of the International Studies Association), vol. 19, no. 3, Fall 1994, 1–6. Note that there is a growing belief that the spread of democracies produce peace irrespective of whether there exists a military balance or military preponderance. The empirical observation here is that democracies have not gone to war against each other. However, the spread and rise of democracies has been a more recent phenomenon and this observation may have limited value. For a discussion of this theme, see Christopher Layne, "Kant or Cant: The Myth of Democratic Peace," and David E. Spiro, "The Insignificance of the Liberal Peace" and "How Liberalism Produces Democratic Peace," all in *International Security*, vol. 19, no. 2, Fall 1994, 5–125.

3. One of the more persuasive arguments for balance of power conditions was made by Inis L. Claude Jr., in *Power and International Relations*, New York: Random House, 1962. See pages 41–66 and 88–93.

4. A report and analysis about the growing Russian resentment toward American domination may be found in Fred Hiatt, "Whose New World Order? Russia is Won-

dering Who Left the US in Charge of Everyone Else," *Washington Post: National Weekly Edition*, November 14–20, 1994.

5. *New York Times*, December 6, 1994. See also Daniel Williams, "The Cold Peace between America and Russia," *Washington Post National Weekly Edition*, December 19–25, 1994.

6. Amos Perlmutter, "Designated Realm of Yugoslavia," *The Washington Times*, January 6, 1999.

7. The need for a power balance in the manipulations at the United Nations is provided by Inis L. Claude Jr., "The Management of Power in the Changing United Nations," in Richard A. Falk, Samuel S. Kim, and Saul H. Mendlovitz, eds., *The United Nations and a Just World Order*, Boulder, Colorado: Westview Press, 1991, 143–152.

8. Stephen Walt, "Alliances: Balancing and Bandwagoning," in Robert Art and Robert Jervis, eds. *International Politics*, New York: Addison Wesley Longman, 2000, 110–117.

9. See *Times of India* editorial, "Securing Our Future," April 3, 1999.

10. See John Pomfret, "China Ponders New Rules of 'Unrestricted War'," *Washington Post Foreign Service*, August 8, 1999.

11. See Patrick E. Tyler, "Russia and China Sign 'Friendship' Pact," *New York Times*, July 17, 2001.

12. From Bruce A. Elleman and Sarah C. M. Paine, "Security Pact with Russia Bolsters China's Power," *International Herald Tribune*, August 6, 2001.

13. Figures are from Tyler, "Russia and China Sign 'Friendship' Pact."

14. See Seema Guha, "China, India to Set Up Security Dialogue," *Times of India*, June 15, 1999.

15. "India's Development Not a Threat: China," *Hindu*, December 1, 2000.

16. See "India, China Decide to Stop Fencing Over Boundary," *Times of India*, January 16, 2001.

17. Tyler Marshall, "Anti-NATO Axis Poses Threat, Experts Say," *Los Angeles Times*, September 27, 1999. According to Marshall, U.S. analysts were warily eyeing the evolving post-Kosovo China-India-Russia coalition intended to check American military power.

18. Quoted from Press Trust of India report of October 4, 2000, in the *India Network News Digest*, October 4, 2000, vol. 12, issue 170.

19. See Dinesh Kumar, "India, Russia Ink $3bn Defence Deals," *Times of India*, October 5, 2000. See also Vladimir Radyuhin, "Secrecy on Defence, Nuclear Deals," *Hindu*, October 6, 2000.

20. "See Russia and India Consolidate Military Ties," and "The Indo-Pakistan Military Balance," *BBC World/South Asia*, February 13 and July 4, 2001.

21. Amit Baruah, "Wahid Supports Vajpayee Position on Kashmir," *India Network News Digest*, January 12, 2001, vol. 13, issue 8.

22. From Baruah, "Wahid Supports Vajpayee Position on Kashmir."

23. For reports of the new International Criminal Court and U.S. refusal to accept its jurisdiction, see Marlise Simons, "Without Fanfare or Cases, International Court

Sets Up," *New York Times*, July 1, 2002; Serge Schmemann, "U.S. Vetoes Bosnia Mission, Then Allows 3-Day Reprieve," *New York Times*, July 1, 2002, and his "U.S. vs. U.N. Court: Two Worldviews," *New York Times*, July 2, 2002.

24. Prem Shankar Jha, "The Making of a Rogue State," *Hindustan Times*, November 5, 1999.

25. This section and the following section are extracted from Raju G. C. Thomas, "NATO, the UN and International Law," *Mediterranean Quarterly*, vol. 10, no. 3, Summer 1999, 25-30; and Raju G. C. Thomas, "The U.S., NATO and the U.N.: Lessons from Yugoslavia," *Global Dialogue*, vol. 2, no. 2, Spring 2000, 53-64.

26. See Sara R. Smith, *Manchurian Crisis: Tragedy in International Relations*, New York: Columbia University Press, 1948.

27. For some protests in India, see report "Indian [Defense] Minister [George Fernandeds] Praises Yugoslav Resistance to NATO," *Agence-France Presse*, Friday, December 31, 1999; T. V. Rajeswar, "A Warning to All," *Hindustan Times*, May 1, 1999; former Foreign Secretary of India A. P. Venkateswaran, "The Arrogance of Power," *Hindustan Times*, April 1, 1999; K. Subrahmanyam, "Clear and Present Danger: US Path to Unipolar Hegemony," *Times of India*, May 3, 1999; Siddharth Varadarajan, "NATO on a Dangerous and Illegal Course," *Times of India*, March 29, 1999, and his "Ruses for War: NATO's New Strategic Concept," *Times of India*, May 10, 1999; former Foreign Secretary of India Mukchund Dubey, "The NATO Juggernaut: The Logic of an Indian Defence Deterrent" *Times of India*, April 8, 1999; C. Raja Mohan, "Kosovo: The Liberals War," *Hindu*, April 6, 1999; and Lt. General Satish Nambiar, "NATO Celebrates Its Fiftieth Anniversary by Destroying Yugoslavia," *Mediterranean Quarterly*, vol. 10, no. 3, Summer 1999, 15–24.

28. *New York Times*, December 4, 1994.

29. *New York Times*, November 4, 1994.

30. UN Press Release, HR/CN/99/54, April 23, 1999.

31. See Thomas W. Lippmann and John M. Goshko, "Madeleine Albright's High-Risk Boutros-Ghali Strategy," *Washington Post National Weekly*, January 13, 1997, 14–15.

32. *NATO Handbook*, Brussels: NATO Office of Information and Press, 1992, 13.

33. Throughout 1994, major American newspapers have argued for the continuation of NATO. A direct reference that Russia is expected to be the future threat may be found in William Safire, "Strategic Dilemma," *New York Times*, December 1, 1994. Safire provides two "mindsets," as he calls it. On the one hand, he claims that "Within the next decade the Russian bear will become strong and hungry and will growl again, so we must strengthen and extend the Western alliance to avert a test by war. Deep geothinkers like Kissinger and Brzezinski support this mindset with historical sweeps: Russia is authoritarian at heart and expansionist by habit." On the other hand, he claims that "If allies are not prepared to pull their weight in an alliance, let them go it alone."

34. See, for instance, Ted Galen Carpenter, *A Search for Enemies: America's Alliances after the Cold War*, Washington D.C.: CATO Institute, 1992.

35. For the text of treaty, see www.state.gov/www/regions/eur/ksvo_rambouillet_text.html.

36. From a NATO press conference at the National Press Club Monday with spokesman Jamie Shea. *Washington Post*, April 28, 1999.

37. See Keith W. Eirinberg, "The United States Reconsiders the 1954 Hague Convention, *International Journal of Cultural Property*, vol. 3, no. 1, 1994, 27–35.

38. Simon Jenkins, "Vandalism, Not War," *Times* (London), May 7, 1999.

39. From W. Michael Reisman and Chris T. Antoniou, eds. *The Laws of War: A Comprehensive Collection of Primary Documents on International Laws Governing Armed Conflict*, New York: Vintage Books, 1994, 235.

40. This information was obtained from a letter to the *Independent* (London) by Sam Harry, April 25, 1999. In the same collection of letters, Lieutenant-Colonel John Woodhouse (Retired) wrote: "Nato targeted and hit the Serb TV station in Belgrade knowing it was on air and staffed by civilians. The deaths that resulted are surely not collateral damage but murder."

41. Reisman and Antoniou, *Laws of War*, 68–69.

42. This information was part of an appeal and a statement published in the *Times of India*, among other Indian newspapers, from the Institute of Public Health of Belgrade and Concerned Scientists at the University of Belgrade, April 1999.

43. *Times of India*, April 21, 1999.

44. See Reisman and Antoniou, *Laws of War*, 10.

45. Derek W. Bowett, "The Interrelation Theories of Intervention and Self-Defense," in John Norton Moore, ed., *Law and Civil War in the Modern World*, Baltimore: Johns Hopkins University Press, 1974, 41.

46. See Ian Brownlie, "Humanitarian Intervention," and Richard B. Lillich, "Humanitarian Intervention: A Reply to Dr. Brownlie and a Plea for Constructive Alternatives," in Moore, *Law and Civil War*, 217–251.

47. See John W. Burton's discussion on "Intervention and Aggression Reconsidered," in his chapter "The Relevance of Behavioral Theories in the International System," in Moore, *Law and Civil War*, 99–101.

48. See Fred Halliday's short description of Yemen in Joel Krieger, ed., *The Oxford Companion to the Politics of the World*, New York: Oxford University Press, 1993, 996–997.

49. A *Newsweek* investigation revealed that U.S. intelligence cooperation with Croatia during the Balkan wars was extensive. Croat forces, with the help of U.S. surveillance images of Serb troop positions, were able to counterattack Serb forces in Krajina. Images by surveillances planes were passed on to General Ante Govina during and after the 1995 "Operation Storm." According to Miro Tudjman, son of the late President Franjo Tudjman: "All our [electronic] intelligence in Croatia went on line in real time to the National Security Agency in Washington. We had a de facto partnership." Subsequent to the operation, General Govina was indicted by the UN war crimes tribunal for the murder of 150 Krajina Serbs, the ethnic cleansing of "as many as 200,000 others, and the torching of thousands of homes." *P.R. Newswire*, August 19, 2001. Also found on *Newsweek*'s news releases at: www.Newsweek.MSNBC.com.

50. There have been several interventions between the Napoleonic wars and World War I, all undertaken to save people. See Richard B. Lillich, "Humanitarian Intervention: A Reply," in Moore, *Law and Civil War*, 232.

51. See *New York Times*, March 9, 1995.

52. See Steven Burg and Paul Shoup, *The War in Bosnia-Herzegovina: Ethnic Conflict and International Intervention*, Armonk, New York: M.E. Sharpe, 1999, 164–169.

53. Richard Holbrooke, *To End a War*, New York: Random House, 1998, xv.

54. These figures remind me of the allegations during the struggle for an independent Bangladesh in East Pakistan in 1971. According to Indian and Bengali assessments, during the passions of war, the West Pakistani army slaughtered three million Bengalis and drove ten million of them as refugees into India. While claims regarding the ten million refugee population were probably right, the three million killed would appear to be exaggerated at least threefold.

55. George Kenney, "The Bosnia Calculation," *New York Times Magazine*, April 23, 1995, 43.

56. Letter to the *Guardian* (U.K.), April 17, 1997.

57. See Diana Johnstone, "Selective Justice in the Hague," *Nation*, September 22, 1997.

58. See the annual *World Almanac and Book of Facts: 1994*, Mahawah, New Jersey: Funk & Wagnalls, 1994, 964.

59. Johnstone, "Selective Justice in the Hague."

60. See Richard Gwyn, "No Genocide, No Justification for War on Kosovo," *Toronto Star*, November 3, 1999. See also Ben Barber, "Kosovo, East Timor Figures Inflated," *Washington Times*, November 10, 1999; John Pilger, "Kosovo Killing Fields?" *New Statesman*, November 15, 1999; Andrew Alexander, "Lets Kill the Lies About Kosovo," *Daily Mail*, November 10, 1999.

61. Quoted by John Laughland in "The Massacres that Never Were," *Spectator*, October 29–November 3, 1999.

62. John Keegan, *The First World War*, New York: Alfred A. Knopf, 1999, 7.

63. Walter J. Rockler, "War Crimes Law Applies to U.S. Too," *Chicago Tribune*, May 23, 1999.

64. For the sudden flight of Afghans during the first ten days after the bombing commenced, see John Pomfret and Edward Cody, "Afghans Flee Heavy Airstrikes," *Washington Post*, October 19, 2001; and Douglas Frantz, "Chaotic Border and Words of Grieving," *New York Times*, October 22, 2001.

65. See "Refugees Force Their Way Into Pakistan," BBC World, Monday, October 22, 2001, 16:47 GMT 17:47 UK.

66. From *Fairness & Accuracy in Reporting*, Media Action Alert: "*Washington Post* a 'Useful Tool' for NATO? Paper's Coverage Distorts Facts about Kosovo War Crimes," fair-l@listserv.american.edu.

67. See letter by Kenneth Roth, Director of Human Rights Watch, to the *Guardian* (London), January 12, 2000.

68. See Eugene Davidson, *The Trial of the Germans: An Account of the Twenty-Two Defendents before the International Military Tribunal at Nuremberg*, New York: The Macmillan Company, 1966, 19.

69. *Agence France Presse*, April 30, 1999.

70. See William Pfaff, "After NATO's Lies About Kosovo, It's Time to Come Clean," *International Herald Tribune*, May 11, 2000. See also Robert Fisk, "Serb Army Unscathed by Nato," *Independent* (London), June 21, 1999; and Paul Beaver, Jane's Information Group, "How Yugoslavia Hid its Tanks," BBC online, World Edition, Europe, June 25, 1999.

71. See Associated Press report, "Postwar Review Found Far Fewer Serb Weapons Hit in Kosovo," in the *Washington Post*, May 9, 2000. A recent book that supports NATO's claim of victory is provided by Benjamin Lambeth, "NATO's Air War for Kosovo: A Strategic and Operational Assessment," Santa Monica, California: RAND, 2001.

72. See Stanley Hoffmann, "What Will Satisfy Serbia's Nationalists: Ethiopia, Munich and Now Bosnia," *New York Times*, December 4, 1994.

73. Fareed Zakaria, "Bosnia Explodes Three Myths," *New York Times*, September 26, 1993. Cited by Ted Galen Carpenter in his "The Balkan Crisis."

74. See George Donelson Moss, *Vietnam: An American Ordeal*, Englewood Cliffs, New Jersey: Prentice-Hall, 1990, 371.

75. I write this from memory. I was in attendance at the Dayton Accords' first anniversary conference at the Yale Law School in November 1996.

76. Robert Hunter, "Peacekeepers in Yugoslavia Need to Stand in Place," *Milwaukee Journal-Sentinel*, October 15, 2000.

77. Simon Jenkins, "This is Serb Business—And It's Still Unfinished," *Times* (London), October 7, 2000.

# 8

# The Use of Refugees as Political and Military Weapons in the Kosovo Conflict

*Kelly M. Greenhill*

What motivated Slobodan Milosevic to launch a massive ethnic cleansing campaign as part of his spring 1999 offensive in Kosovo? What did he hope to achieve, and when did he decide large-scale ethnic cleansing was a viable way to accomplish his goals?[1] With the world's most powerful military alliance arrayed against him, why did he believe he could succeed? Finally, why in the end did his gambit fail? The most widely promulgated history of the conflict suggests that Milosevic's ethnic cleansing campaign—purportedly dubbed "Operation Horseshoe" by the Serbs—was a premeditated plan designed to empty the province of its Albanian majority and reestablish Serb dominance,[2] which had already been inaugurated when NATO's bombing campaign commenced.[3] As characterized by U.S. government sources, confronted with a "humanitarian crisis of staggering proportions," NATO was compelled to respond to "rescu(e) and relocat(e) more than one million refugees,"[4] thereby "preventing starvation and ensuring, ultimately, that the Kosovars could return safely to their homes."[5] In short, it is alleged that Milosevic was already engaged in, or at least committed to, ethnically cleansing all or large portions of Kosovo when NATO intervened to stop him.[6]

Though it is a compelling story, the facts do not support it. While the "facts" as presented are not strictly wrong, they are simplistically rendered and somewhat distorted. As I shall attempt to demonstrate, neither the signals emanating from Belgrade prior to (and during) NATO's bombing campaign,[7] nor the conduct of Yugoslav forces on the ground, nor the timing and patterns of refugee flows out of Kosovo during the course of the conflict[8] support the proposition that Milosevic's ethnic cleansing campaign was part of a preplanned mass expulsion that was to be executed no matter what NATO did,[9] that is, whether or not the alliance bombed the Federal Republic of Yugoslavia (FRY).[10] Instead, using the tenets of coercion theory as a touchstone, I shall argue that, rather than the wholesale expulsion of the province's Albanian population and/or partition of the province, the primary objective of Milosevic's spring campaign was the destruction of the separatist Kosovo Liberation Army (KLA).[11] Moreover, while the evidence is not conclusive, it suggests that Milosevic's preferred strategy for achieving his aim was a two-pronged coercive effort designed to simultaneously crush the KLA and deter NATO from interfering with this endeavor. Only after deterrence failed—and NATO air strikes commenced—did the Serb offensive escalate into a full-scale ethnic cleansing campaign, with the dual intent of compelling NATO to cease its attacks, while annihilating the remnants of the KLA.

I will further argue that—unable to compete militarily against the world's most powerful alliance—Milosevic attempted to exploit the West's well-documented fear of refugee flows as an "asymmetric" means of influencing NATO's behavior.[12] In short, while NATO was actively seeking to deter, and then to compel Milosevic to cease his spring offensive through the use of air strikes, Milosevic was likely engaged in his own intensive game of counter-coercion against NATO and its allies. However, for Milosevic, refugees, rather than bombs, were the political and military weapons of choice. [13]

*Politically*, it appears that Milosevic initially attempted to deter a NATO attack by raising the specter of the destabilizing consequences of refugee outflows, and he did so as early as February 1999, following the collapse of talks at Rambouillet.[14] Already visible fissures in the facade of NATO unity likely gave Milosevic reason to believe that he might succeed in deterring the alliance from attacking. After deterrence failed, he persisted in trying to fracture the alliance and cultivate fear within those neighboring countries supporting the NATO war effort in an attempt to convince the alliance to end its bombing campaign and to do so on terms more favorable than those offered at Rambouillet.[15]

Likewise, the available evidence indicates Milosevic also sought to use refugees militarily: first, to gain tactical advantage against the KLA insurgents through the frequently employed strategy of population displacement; and second, to impede NATO operations by flooding neighboring states (and NATO staging areas) with refugees. As a military weapon, population displacement is a common strategy, designed to sever rebel supply and communications lines and to reduce insurgents' capacity to hide among civilians. As such, some displacement would surely have occurred as a direct consequence of the Yugoslav campaign against the KLA, even in the absence of NATO action.[16] However, once the bombing began, any restraint based upon fear of NATO reprisals vanished, leading Milosevic to pursue a larger and more destructive campaign than was originally planned.[17] Moreover, as tactical weapons designed to disrupt NATO operations, the intent of the refugee flood appears to have been twofold: designed in part to directly undermine NATO's ability to launch offensive operations[18] and in part to overwhelm the alliance's (and recipient states') logistical capabilities.

While it appeared for a time that Milosevic's refugee gambit would succeed, in the end it failed for three key reasons. First, because NATO had staked so much of its prestige on the success of the mission, the alliance could not afford to back down, even in the face of massive refugee outflows. Thus any negotiating leverage Milosevic might have hoped to gain through initiating a prodigious, multifront refugee crisis did not materialize. Second, the costs (at least to the alliance) of the conflict were perceived to be low and limited to the Balkans, as the vast majority of refugees were contained within the region and the number of NATO casualties remained small. Thus domestic and, for the most part, international support for the mission remained relatively stable, despite Milosevic's attempts to undermine it. Third, and most importantly, through the use of a dexterous public relations campaign—and ubiquitous media coverage of the outflows—NATO was able to exploit the crisis generated by Milosevic as a political weapon of its own.[19] NATO used the refugee crisis to cement alliance cohesion under a period of great stress, effectively turning the refugee weapon back on Milosevic and finally convincing him that it was time to make a deal.[20]

## BACKGROUND TO THE CONFLICT

A short review of the key events that led up to the March offensive is necessary to set the stage for the argument that follows.[21] The proximate cause of the 1999 Kosovo conflict was the rise of the Kosovo Liberation Army (KLA) in the mid-1990s. This rise followed the perceived failures of the nonviolent activism of Ibrahim Rugova and his Democratic League of Kosovo (LDK) and their efforts to improve the plight of the oppressed Albanian minority in Kosovo. Frustrated with the trifling results of Rugova's efforts on behalf of Kosovo's beleaguered Albanians, the previously nascent KLA began to actively engage in terrorism, targeting ethnic Serb officials and police, prominent Serb civilians, and Kosovar Albanians perceived to be Yugoslav loyalists.[22] Albania's economic and political collapse in 1997—in the wake of failed pyramid investment schemes—further catalyzed development of the KLA. During this period, large quantities of Albanian army weaponry found their way to Kosovo.[23] As the KLA became better armed and equipped, its effectiveness increased. In response to the rise in terrorist incidents, Serb security forces cracked down on suspected KLA members, and as the spiral of attacks and reprisals swelled, the situation within Kosovo grew more violent. On January 4, 1998, the KLA proclaimed itself "the armed forces of the Kosovar Albanians and that the armed struggle for the independence of Kosovo and its unification had begun."[24]

By late winter in 1998, the KLA reportedly controlled about half of the province. In an attempt to crush the expanding insurgency, the Serb government launched a massive and brutal counteroffensive, which, by March 1998, had achieved considerable success.[25] However, the cost for the Kosovar Albanians was high; many villages were razed and civilian casualties mounted. The Serbs' tactics were brutal but militarily effective. In response, in late spring 1998, the European Union (EU) and the United States publicly condemned the Serb offensive and stepped in to mediate the conflict. However, Western diplomatic efforts resulted in little progress; and as the West was either unwilling or unable to augment its diplomatic efforts with credible threats of military action, it failed to persuade the Serbs that it was serious about protecting the Kosovar Albanians. Shortly thereafter the Serbs renewed their offensive, and by September 1998, the KLA had been largely—albeit only temporarily—neutralized as a military force.

The renewed Serb offensive generated several hundred thousand additional refugees and internally displaced people (IDPs), many of whom fled to western Europe seeking asylum. Alarmed by this turn of events, again the West intervened diplomatically in an attempt to curb Serbian military attacks in Kosovo, this time with the threat of air strikes. After a series of meetings that October, U.S. Balkan envoy Richard Holbrooke and President Milosevic came to terms over the province, thus averting air strikes on Serbia and permitting the vast majority of those displaced during the offensive to return to their homes, a fact generally ignored by those who promulgate the "Operation Horseshoe" theory. In exchange, the Serbs agreed to a ceasefire and were enjoined to reduce their forces in Kosovo to pre-March 1998 levels.[26] They also agreed to the presence of Organization for Security and Cooperation in Europe (OSCE) cease-fire monitors. For its part, Holbrooke reportedly promised that NATO would secure KLA compliance with the cease-fire, even though the KLA was not party to the agreement,[27] a shortcoming that some argue likely crippled the agreement from the outset.[28]

However, the partial withdrawal of Serb forces was met not by compliance but by immediate KLA advances and a concomitant rise in terrorist attacks, which were well documented by the OSCE and KDOM observers on the ground.[29] By early 1999, large areas of Kosovo were again occupied by KLA forces. The Serbs saw a return to the situation they faced before the offensive a year earlier. Convinced that the West was unwilling to hold up its end of the bargain—that is, ensuring that the KLA would adhere to the ceasefire and, in fact, was probably aiding the KLA[30]—the Serbs responded brutally and effectively. According to OSCE observers, Yugoslav and Serbian security forces seized the initiative in mid-December, attacking suspected KLA strongholds, including the village of Racak,[31] where the apparent massacre of forty-five civilians in mid-January 1999 re-galvanized Western efforts to mediate the conflict.[32] Halfhearted peace plans were offered up at Rambouillet and in Paris, but, as many acknowledge, there was little in these "agreements" for the Serbs.[33] It soon became clear that there was no longer a peace for the OSCE monitors to verify, and they withdrew.[34] Shortly thereafter the spring offensive began apace, NATO air strikes commenced, and ethnic cleansing began in earnest.

## ATTEMPTED DETERRENCE: KNOW THINE ENEMY

### Milosevic Seeks to Exploit Western Fears of Refugees and the Spread of Conflict

In his seminal work on coercion, Thomas Schelling argued that "the coercive use of the power to hurt is the very exploitation of enemy wants and fears."[35] It is clear that Milosevic understood exactly what the West feared most—that is, large-scale refugee flows and regional destabilization—because its key representatives told him. For instance, when asked whether bombing might simply accelerate the rate of ethnic cleansing in Kosovo, Richard Holbrooke responded, "That is our greatest fear by far."[36] Moreover, Holbrooke's statement was hardly the first inkling Milosevic had gotten of Western apprehension over refugees.[37]

As Milosevic was no doubt aware, refugees have come to be most unwelcome sights, since the numbers of asylum applicants to Western Europe began a steep and prolonged ascent in the mid-1980s. Since that time, fear and distrust of foreigners more generally has risen as well.[38] As early as 1992, even before the first Balkan outflows began in earnest, public opinion polls indicated that 78 percent of Germans thought that immigration was their country's most pressing problem.[39] Five years later, an EU-wide survey uncovered a disturbing level of racism and xenophobia within its member states, with nearly 33 percent of those interviewed openly describing themselves as "quite racist" or "very racist."[40] More than 71 percent of those interviewed said "there was a limit to the number of people of other races, religions, or cultures that a society can accept." And 65 percent said that this limit had already been reached in their country and that "if there were to be more people belonging to these minority groups we would have problems."[41] Moreover, additional refugees from the Balkans may have been viewed as particularly unwelcome.[42] For instance, one British study found that 80 percent of the Kosovar refugees that fled to the United Kingdom between 1997 and 1999 were subjected to hostility from sections of the British public and the press.[43] The existence of this antipathy toward minority groups, particularly immigrants, would not have been lost on Milosevic, nor would its potential effects on the political fortunes of European leaders. Both sides would have been aware of the potential dangers of large-scale refugee flows, particularly since they had already begun to affect, albeit in a limited way, the political makeup of the continent.[44]

Moreover, Milosevic also probably realized that many Western leaders view refugee flows as a danger from a security standpoint as well as from a political standpoint, and he may have bargained that he could exploit the fears of those countries likely to suffer more acutely than others, as well as fears of those certain to suffer if the crisis spread beyond the Balkans.[45] In particular, Milosevic might have bargained that Italy would try to forestall a bombing campaign, especially after the pyramid scheme scandal that toppled the Albanian government in 1997 and created large refugee flows across the Adriatic. Memories of the situation would have been sharpened by reflection on the weak support provided by Italy's allies during that crisis. To staunch the outflows and stabilize the situation, the Italian government had unilaterally launched Operation Alba.[46] Britain and Germany quickly vetoed their own involvement and that of the EU as a whole. In addition, NATO, the UN, and the OSCE all agreed not to "touch Albania" until they were satisfied that one country bore full responsibility for the enterprise.[47] With that historical backdrop in mind, Italian Prime Minister Massimo D'Alema met with President Clinton in early March 1999 and reportedly asked skeptically about contingencies if NATO air strikes failed to subdue Milosevic. "The result, Mr. D'Alema said, would be 300,000 to 400,000 refugees passing into Albania and crossing the Adriatic into Italy. 'What will happen then?' Reportedly the Clinton Administration's only answer was, 'We'll keep on bombing.'"[48] Such an answer could have provided small comfort to the Italian leader.[49]

Other countries' leaders were also clearly concerned about the consequences of another flood of refugees from the Balkans. For instance, given their propinquity, the Greeks were particularly alarmed about the prospect of NATO bombing and its possible effect on refugee outflows. As one official preciently stated in late February 1999, "up to now, the Serbs have held back for fear of provoking a NATO attack. 'Once bombing starts, they could lose all restraint.'"[50] And Germany, after having taken in 350,000 Bosnians during the last Yugoslav war—more than all the other EU member states put together—feared it would also bear the brunt of a full-scale crisis in Kosovo.[51] Thus while the failed Rambouillet talks were underway in France, Germany was hosting its own unsuccessful summit, this one (futilely) aimed at generating support for European refugee burden-sharing initiatives.[52]

## Messages Sent but Not Received . . . or Simply Not Believed?[53]

Milosevic would surely also have been aware of the underlying disagreements within NATO about the right tack to pursue in Kosovo, which were regularly noted in the press during the lead-up to the conflict.[54] He appears to have attempted to intensify intra-alliance discord by fueling the unease that existed within some European countries about the militant stance taken by the United States. For instance, as the Serbian state-run TANJUG News Service reported in the aftermath of Rambouillet, "it could be clearly seen that 'the Americans and the English' stick fast, and completely to a military, militant option, while, on the other hand, considerable wavering has arisen, above all, among the Italians. But it was observable also with the Frenchmen and Germans."[55]

Similarly, it appears that Belgrade sought to sow divisions between the United States and its European allies by emphasizing that the Europeans had a better appreciation of the possible refugee-generating consequences of NATO action than did the Americans. The West had broadcast its fears about the consequences of refugee flows to Milosevic, and he, members of his government, and press representatives responded with vague and not-so-vague promises of fulfilling them. An open letter by a Serbian columnist, published in a state-owned newspaper in early March, is illustrative.[56] The columnist began by noting that "there are not only cracks in the Contact Group but fundamental differences in opinion on the crisis and the possible solution" and proceeded to argue that:

> the perspective on Albanians can't be the same from Washington where they arrive with pockets full of dollars intended for certain senators and other individuals, and the perspective from let's say Rome where you can see boats full of desperate and aggressive Albanian immigrants along with Shiptar mafia, which is according to the documentation of Italian authorities already overpowering some Sicilian clans. The situation is similar in Germany, France and even Great Britain where . . . *The Economist* reports under the alarming headline "Tirana on Thames" that Albanians organized by their narco-bosses are flooding the "Proud Albion" under the pretext of political asylum.[57]

The columnist took aim at the FRY's more immediate neighbors as well,[58] noting that Europeans should be "concerned because Americans support Albanians and their extreme demands thus *creating grounds for a permanent crisis that could easily spread to Macedonia, Greece and trigger Turkish involvement in the Balkan boiling pot.*"[59] A day earlier, another columnist in another state-run newspaper offered similar warnings:

> It's not a question of ordinary local conflicts or instability that they are provoking in Yugoslavia. It's about *a real possibility of expanding the war beyond Yugoslav borders*. In this conflict between ethnic groups and religious elements, the essential part have political games in the process which are also included [*sic*] NATO, so-called Contact Group [France, Great Britain, Italy, Germany, Russia] and one actor in the group that is acting for its own benefit: USA. . . . Within all that, what is noticeable is that a military disposing [*sic*] is underway, and somebody will have to pay for it one day. . . . [The] failure of the discussion in Rambouillet is *an introduction to the new migration wave, which benefits to regional disintegration as well as to stimulating xenophobic elements present in the conflict.*[60]

The columnist continued by warning that "Kosovo represents a strategic zone of terrorism and drug trade. . . . It is well known that this terroristic internal structure was supported by Albanian communist leader Enver Hoxha . . . [and] if we add to all this the fact that the terrorists are mostly Moslems, it seams [*sic*] that things are getting to quite another dimension." [61] This was a masterful piece of fear mongering, custom-tailored to push the buttons of anxious western European politicians, that is, the threat from Kosovo is not only refugees but Communist, drug-trading, Muslim, terrorist refugees.

The federal government in Belgrade also offered more direct warnings of impending humanitarian disaster and the conflict's potential spreadability. On March 20 (the day OSCE observers withdrew from Kosovo), the government published an open letter in the state-run press indicating that "all those threatening to use force against our country must face the responsibility for the *consequences of humanitarian problems, which might arise* as a result of the use of such force."[62] The letter went on to suggest that the "build-up of foreign troops on the border of the FRY as well as the public threats of NATO aggression against our country . . . *could pose a threat to peace and security in the wider region* of South Eastern Europe,"[63] a fear that had been publicly enunciated and was widely shared in the West.[64] A day earlier, a letter from the FRY's foreign minister prevailed upon the then President of the UN Security Council to call for the withdrawal of NATO troops from the FRY's borders, which would "contribute to the reduction of tensions and the elimination of *unforeseen threats to peace and security in the region*."[65]

Milosevic himself issued some warnings probably intended to have a deterrent effect. For instance, we now know that Milosevic told German Foreign Minister Joschka Fischer in early March 1999 "that he could empty Kosovo within a week."[66] And on the day before bombing started, Milosevic threatened in an open letter that "anyone who tries to impose solutions by force will have to take the responsibility for actions against the policy of peace and *face the ensuing consequences*."[67]

Thus it appears that, between the end of the Rambouillet Conference on February 22 and the beginning of the bombing campaign on March 24, Belgrade did attempt to signal to the West that it would respond with force if provoked and would be inclined to do so in a way designed to create fear and provoke panic in potential refugee-receiving states, including several members of NATO. Granted, some of the threats as issued were vague, and others could have been easily construed as swagger or domestic propaganda; and to be fair, observers would have had to be paying close attention to understand what was at stake.[68] However, it is also true that Milosevic would have also realized that such threats could have real resonance, at least in certain NATO capitals and neighboring countries. And it appears that some leaders *did* understand these signals. For instance, we now know that President Kucan of Slovenia and President Gligorov of Macedonia warned NATO that Milosevic might resort to mass expulsions.[69]

Even the independent Yugoslav media seemed to understand that Milosevic had an appreciation for the power of expulsions. On March 27—three days after the bombings started—journalist Braca Grubacic wrote in his column:

> Milosevic will try to destabilize the entire southern Balkans and expand the conflict to Macedonia, Bosnia, and Albania in order to scare his adversaries in NATO. *He intends to expel a large number of Albanians from Kosovo in order to provoke a reaction from Western Europe*, which already does not know what to do what the masses of Albanian refugees and fake asylum seekers.[70]

In addition, General Clark—at least after the fact—claims that, by Rambouillet those in Washington began to ask "the right questions," including, "What if the Serbs follow through on threats to take revenge on Albanian civilians?"[71] This statement by Clark implies two key things: first, that Milosevic (or his proxies) had articulated their threats in a transparent enough manner that at least some people in Washington recognized that he was trying to influence their behavior; and second, that at the end of February 1998 civilian-directed attacks had not yet begun in a concerted way.

## Lack of Response Belies Claims That Intervention Was Launched After Cleansing Started

Nevertheless, despite a variety of threats and admonitions from Belgrade, worried queries from potential receiving states, and direct warnings from Yugoslavia's neighbors, NATO failed to prepare for the possibility that Milosevic might use refugees as a weapon in any concerted fashion. As UNHCR's (United Nation's High Commissioner for Refugees) Nicholas Morris notes,

> Like almost every Western decision maker and commentator, and indeed like most Kosovan Albanians, UNHCR did not predict the mass expulsion of the majority of the ethnic Albanian population of Kosovo. That we were in such company is no excuse. However, in the days before the exodus began, the international community, particularly the Western governments, were banking on peace, and urging UNHCR to get prepared for the early implementation of the Rambouillet Accords.[72]

"There were a lot of Milosevic watchers who said a few bombs might do it (that is, lead him to capitulate). . . . What was not assumed, and not postulated was that he would try to empty the country of its ethnic majority, another senior NATO official acknowledged."[73] And the forewarned Joschka Fischer later said "he regretted not having taken Milosevic seriously" when he said he could empty Kosovo in a week.[74]

In the end, the fact that the West was so unprepared for the outflows belies post hoc claims about foreknowledge of "Operation Horseshoe"[75] and its purported objectives.[76] If, as has been alleged, NATO had reason to anticipate a prodigious outflow associated with a premeditated mass expulsion, why were no preparations made to accommodate large numbers of refugees in potential receiving states and/or in NATO staging areas, either by the military or by the relevant humanitarian assistance organizations? In the absence of any such preparations, retrospective claims that the bombing campaign was launched to stop a premeditated massive ethnic cleansing campaign designed to ethnically reengineer Kosovo, and which NATO knew about *ex ante*, simply do not make sense. Thus while Milosevic was sending messages that he would generate a crisis if provoked, most in the West did not believe him. However, and ironically, once the bombing began, and Milosevic followed through on his promised threats, NATO seized upon the cleansing that was just beginning to justify the bombing already in progress.

## DETERRENCE BEGETS COMPELLENCE

### Why the Campaign Expanded After Bombing Began

Moreover, despite Western claims to the contrary, the bombing campaign likely provided motivation and opportunity for wider and more savage operations by Yugoslav forces than were originally envisioned.[77] Though the Serbs did intensify their offensive against the KLA during the interval between the withdrawal of OSCE monitors and the onset of air strikes, all available evidence suggests they did not engage in widespread ethnic cleansing until after bombing began. Unable to deter NATO, it seems plausible that Milosevic switched tacks and tried to compel the alliance to stop bombing by forcing upon it a dose of what it purportedly feared most. Milosevic likely calculated that once the bombing started his best chance of success was to push forward with great alacrity to his primary objective, that is, to crush the KLA—recognizing that doing so would generate a fair number of refugees—and then to sue for peace and bargain from a position of relative strength.[78] (As the analysis that follows indicates, the patterns and timing of refugee outflows are consistent with such a strategy.) He probably gambled that by that time discord and conflict arose within NATO (and in the court of public opinion), it would entice the alliance to deal.[79]

Nevertheless, in reality, Milosevic's task became even more difficult once the NATO bombing campaign commenced, as the stakes and the costs of backing down had changed for both sides. Exacting the desired response through compellence is, as a rule, more difficult than through deterrence because the costs of complying with the other side's demands rise significantly. To be successful, compellence demands a visible shift in behavior in response to an equally visible and forceful initiative by another.[80] In contrast to deterrent threats, compellent actions more directly engage the prestige and passions of the put-upon states. Thus Milosevic failed to appreciate the magnitude of the task he set before himself because he did not or could not fathom the new and complex interplay that would be born of compellence. While NATO's myopia may have led to a failure of deterrence, Milosevic's mistaken gamesmanship led to a conflict of greater ferocity than either side foresaw at the outset.

## TIMING, SPEED, AND PATTERNS OF REFUGEE FLOWS

### When Did the Expulsions Begin?

The assertion that Milosevic's campaign shifted to ethnic cleansing—in which he unleashed "demographic bombs" against NATO staging areas in Macedonia and Albania—only after aerial bombing commenced is borne out by several facts. First, on March 22—two days *before* the alliance launched its airstrikes—in tacit acknowledgment that cleansing had not begun in earnest, NATO officials asked the KLA "to desist from terrorist attacks against Serbs in Kosovo so as to not give Belgrade a pretext to engage in ethnic cleansing."[81] Second, the first reports of mass expulsions began to emerge only *after* bombing had been under way for several days.[82] Third, significant numbers of refugees did not appear on the borders of Albania and Macedonia until several days after the bombing began.[83] For instance, two days after the bombing began, the UNHCR's representative in Tirana gave a briefing to diplomats, local UN staff, and the Director of the Albanian government's Office for Refugees. They discussed the few recent arrivals (of which there had been none that day) and the state of the organization's preparedness. No one present expressed concerns or indicated they believed an impending crisis was brewing.[84] Fourth, the pattern and timing of these arrivals indicate that the expulsions were dictated (at least at the beginning of the war) by strategic and tactical requirements, as the following analysis indicates.

### Speed of the Outflows

Some observers have suggested that, even if documentation of "Operation Horseshoe" does not exist,[85] the speed and "organized" nature of the outflows demonstrate that a centrally orchestrated, mass expulsion plan must have been in place even before NATO's bombing commenced. But this claim is problematic on several fronts. First, history offers numerous examples of large-scale exoduses at least as fast and "efficient" as what happened in Kosovo, but not necessarily centrally orchestrated. For instance, during Pakistan's counterinsurgency campaign in Bengali East in 1971, over ten million fled to India between April and December 1971. And within the first month, nearly a million had entered India, at an average daily rate of 100,000 per day.[86] Moreover, most crossed the border on foot, which slowed them down relative to many of those who fled Kosovo in motor vehicles and on tractors. Likewise, in the aftermath of the Rwandan genocide, more than 250,000 Rwandans crossed the border into Tanzania in a single day; again, virtually all on foot.[87] Second, the history of ethnic cleansing in the Balkans did not necessitate central planning to convince people to leave. Consider that, without the need for much prodding, in early August 1995 alone, between 150,000 and 200,000 Serbs fled the Krajina in a matter of days as Croat forces seized the region during Operation Storm. Finally, as the Serbs were engaged in a counterinsurgency campaign, the Yugoslav Army would surely have formulated some contingency plans for emptying the province.[88] Nonetheless, the fact that such plans likely existed does not mean they were being carried out. However, it does mean that, even without orchestration, central planning, and execution, massive ethnic cleansing of an area as modestly sized as Kosovo—with a population predisposed to flee in the face of conflict—would have been relatively facile.

### Patterns of Refugee Outflows

Statistical analyses of the patterns of refugee outflows during the crisis clearly demonstrate that they occurred in three distinct pulses separated by periods of relatively light activity:[89] Phase One, from March 24–April 6, when most refugees came from western and southwestern Kosovo; Phase Two, April 7–April 23, during which most refugees fled from the northern and central municipalities; and Phase Three, April 24–May 11, when most refugees hailed from the western and southern municipalities.[90] (Again, it should be noted these patterns of outflows are inconsistent both with the alleged "Operation Horseshoe" plan, as it has been described,[91] and with alleged plans to partition the province.)[92]

### *Phase One*

The first refugee pulse—which started on March 24 (when the bombing started) and ran until April 6 (when Milosevic unilaterally declared his "Orthodox Easter cease-fire")—included the heaviest flow of the entire conflict, with migration concentrated in the Pec-Prizren corridor.[93] The nature of Phase One flows offers strong circumstantial evidence that Milosevic's initial campaign was directed at the KLA, first and foremost. NATO perhaps inadvertently acknowledged as much at the end of this phase, since it accused Milosevic of continuing to "conduct counterinsurgency sweeps" in spite of his unilaterally declared cease-fire.[94] Outflows were particularly heavy in the municipalities of Djakovica, Orohovac, Suva Reka, Pec, Decani, and Prizren.[95] These municipalities were areas of strategic significance (along the Albanian border), many were also known KLA strongholds, and they were all heavily targeted.[96]

In addition, as noted previously, sending refugees across the borders to potential NATO staging areas was surely also a tactical objective of Milosevic during this initial pulse of expulsions.[97] FRY forces effectively emptied two cities (Pec and Prizren) and more than five hundred square miles of territory. This greatly surprised and unnerved NATO and the FRY's neighboring states, including Macedonia, which shut its border until the alliance promised to airlift out of the region almost one hundred thousand refugees and provide it with significant financial and logistical assistance.

### *Phase Two*

By the middle of Phase Two, which ran roughly from April 7 through April 23, it is harder to interpret exactly what was happening. But evidence suggests that Milosevic was still manipulating outflows in a tactically, if not strategically, significant way. During this phase, flows were greatest from Kosovska Mitrovica and its southern neighbors, Vucitrn and Srbrica, as well as Kosovo Polje, Lipljan, and Istok, slightly further south and west. Migration was concentrated most heavily in the northern and central municipalities, though significant movement of peoples continued in areas previously targeted, that is, in the southwest.[98] Many of the municipalities targeted in Phase Two also hosted significant KLA presence, particularly Srbrica in the central Drenica region, which, according to the OSCE, had been "a heartland" of KLA activity since its inception.[99]

However, not all of the major expulsions in Phase Two took place in areas of KLA strength. How to account for this? In light of unequivocal NATO rejection of cease-fire overtures, FRY forces may have decided to "up the ante" and actively alter the ethnic balance in those areas with larger Serb populations.[100] Nevertheless, to be clear, the pattern of expulsions does not support the assertion that Milosevic sought to partition the province as many predicted he would.[101] Nevertheless, cleansings in the north—particularly in Kosovo Polje and Kosovska Mitrovica, which Serbs refer to as "Serbia's Kuwait" and many view as the most valuable Balkan real estate—were consistent with an attempt to gain uncontested control of the province's major economic and strategic assets.[102] In light of NATO's rejection of Milosevic's Orthodox Easter ceasefire overture, FRY forces may have also engaged in mass ethnic cleansing without strategic motivation, in contrast to their behavior in Phase One and earlier. Though evidence is sparse, this seems to be borne out by the condition of the refugees crossing the border after the initial onslaught against the KLA. As a rule, counterinsurgency operations are intensive and violent. The cleansing that frequently accompanies such operations is bruising to the civilian population that survives. However, observers on the ground reported that, in general, the state of the refugees who crossed the border in Phase Two was markedly better than those who had crossed earlier.[103] At the same time, it appears that Serb forces began to engage in more random, retributive behavior.

### *Phase Three*

By the beginning of Phase Three—which ran from roughly April 24 (which coincided with NATO's fiftieth anniversary summit and the expansion of NATO's target, set to include Milosevic personally) to May 11 (when Milosevic lost his most important ally, Russia)—Milosevic would likely have realized that the refugee gambit was going to fail, particularly since the NATO summit provided persuasive evidence that the alliance was not going to crumble, at least not imminently. During Phase Three, refugees came primarily from areas in the south and southwest and included particularly heavy flows from Prizren, although flows were more modest than they had been previously, probably in large part because so many people had already fled. It is difficult to analyze the pattern of expulsions in this period because almost 50 percent of those who crossed the border in this period had left their homes before April 24.[104]

## Pattern of Killings

During the conflict, it was frequently asserted that Milosevic's goal was the genocide of the Kosovar Albanian population. But evidence does not support this claim.[105] First, postwar investigations indicate that instead of large-scale massacres, the pattern of killing was less extensive and more purposeful than expected. Investigators have discovered what they refer to as "ethnic cleansing light," which they acknowledge was probably designed to root out and undermine the KLA.[106] Even human rights researchers now say that most killings occurred in areas where the KLA had been most active or in urban streets that backed into rural areas where the KLA could infiltrate.[107] They argue that the FRY aimed to clear out areas of KLA support, using "selective terror, robberies, and sporadic killings."[108] Second, OSCE findings support such conclusions and identify a pattern of displacement that "suggests a kind of military rationale for the expulsions, which were concentrated in areas controlled by the insurgents and along likely invasion routes."[109] Finally, no reports have surfaced indicating that the large Albanian population of Belgrade or other parts of Serbia were mistreated during the conflict;[110] this observation, too, is consistent with ethnic cleansing motivated by strategy and tactics, not genocide.

Furthermore, anecdotal evidence also suggests that, viewed in totality, Serb behavior in Kosovo, while undoubtedly contemptuous, was more humane and restrained than it had been during the Bosnian war. This loosely supports the proposition that the preponderance of activities in Kosovo were directed at crushing the KLA rather than at targeting the entire population. For instance, unlike in Bosnia, electricity and water remained on in most cities, and Serb forces did not destroy all of the mosques in the province (though, notably, key sites in Pec and Djakovica were severely damaged).[111]

## Timing of Outflows

The timing of observed population movements in Kosovo provide evidence that the FRY controlled the migrations to a large extent, starting and stopping them when necessary and in an attempt to compel NATO to halt the bombing.[112] For instance, Phase One began with the start of the NATO bombing campaign and ended concomitantly with Milosevic's self-declared Orthodox Easter cease-fire, at which time the ebbing flow of refugees was stanched by the surprise closure of the border. As suggested earlier, Milosevic may have hoped that NATO would accept a compromise at this point, having been unable to stop FRY forces and to save the Kosovar Albanians from large-scale expulsions.[113]

Following the reopening of the border on April 10,[114] Milosevic reinforced the perception that he controlled targeted "demographic bombs" in the form of groups of refugees occasionally released for the final trek to a border crossing.[115] Observers on the ground sensed that there was "clear management of the flow of refugees."[116] FRY forces marched them around Kosovo in seemingly random patterns. As part of this herding, it is likely that refugees were used as human shields to protect FRY forces and materiel and to keep open communication routes.[117] However, this management makes it difficult to analyze the precise timing of flows after Phase One.[118] In addition, many people who left Kosovo were not expelled directly but fled preemptively, of their own volition.[119] This is a key point that should not be underestimated but is one that makes analysis of flows more problematic.[120] (Though it is unclear exactly what percentage of people fled without directly being pushed, Physicians for Human Rights interview data suggests that at least one-third of those who fled did so at their discretion.)[121]

Finally, though evidence is circumstantial, it is worth noting that no significant flows occurred after early May, which, for numerous reasons, is about the time that it had likely become clear to Milosevic that it was time to make a deal.[122] First, the G-8 talks during the first week in May had generated the broad outlines of a settlement that both Russia and the West were willing to consider.[123] Second, even the humiliating bombing of the Chinese Embassy on May 7 had failed to crack NATO's unity and resolve. Third, on May 13 President Yeltsin replaced Prime Minister Primakov—a staunch supporter of the Serbs—which sent a signal to Milosevic that he had lost a major ally. Fourth, on the same day, though a heated battle took place inside the Bundestag, Germany stood fast as a NATO partner. (As did Italy when domestic turmoil arose within its government several days later.) Fifth, and perhaps most tellingly, the second week in May saw a rush of new offers from Europe's governments to accept refugees, which made it clear to Milosevic that the refugee gambit had decisively failed.[124] In short, by early May it had likely become clear to Milosevic that NATO unity would not be shattered, Russia was backing away from its role as Milosevic's ally, and neither refugees nor domestic dissent were going to lead the Europeans to defect. Accordingly, after May 11–12, refugee flows remained low until the end of the conflict in June.[125]

### Accounting for Anomalies

Clearly, not all outflows and acts of brutality were consistent with a counterinsurgency campaign directed at crushing the KLA. However, general patterns of expulsions and killings seem to support this proposition. How then to account for the outliers? Three key factors may explain a great deal. First, it appears that the Serb police, militia groups, and army may have been pursuing different strategies. As one Belgrade-based journalist noted,

> there were differences between the police and the army. The police were in favour of expulsions because they could steal money from people. The intelligence guys were against it because they said it was bad for us. There were vague ideas about expulsions but I doubt there was a real Horseshoe plan. I think that when the bombing started they just did it. The worst were paramilitaries and locals. Before the bombing, it was common knowledge that they would expel Albanians, but it was more a case of "we'll f—k 'em if they start."[126]

This disparity in the conduct of operations could explain why some areas, not known to be KLA strongholds, were targeted and why money and valuables were often all that was demanded before people would be sent on their way.[127] Second, one should not underestimate revenge for NATO bombings as a motivator for seemingly random acts of violence and brutality.[128] As one former member of the militia gang, Lightning, noted, "early on, the Serbian secret police were transporting Albanians safely to the border by hiding them in the trunks of cars. They charged them $2,700. . . . Later after the NATO bombing got worse I wouldn't bother taking (them) to the border. I'd just take their money and kill them."[129] Third, and relatedly, some expulsions may just have been driven by spite, that is, expulsions just for the sake of expulsions. Though, given the overall pattern of outflows, such activity appears to have been only sporadic. Fourth, and finally, as was noted previously, many people seem to have fled without being pushed, a common phenomenon in wartime, in general, and one that has a long history in the Balkans.[130]

## WHY DID MILOSEVIC'S GAMBIT FAIL?

Successful coercion requires making the cost of noncompliance sufficiently high that the object of coercion will be willing to accept the lower cost of backing down. Milosevic's attempted coercion via the use of refugees was doomed to fail because, in this case, the costs of backing down actually rose over time. In the end, NATO's (real or perceived) costs of backing down far exceeded those of continuing the campaign for two completely contrary reasons. First, the alliance ratcheted up its own costs of backing down by leveraging much of its prestige on the success of its efforts. Second, and conversely, NATO was able to mitigate the pain inflicted by Milosevic's demographic bombs—that is, effectively lowering the costs of noncompliance—by (a) keeping these costs largely hidden from Western audiences and (b) by forcing some of these costs back upon Milosevic via the use of a massive and extremely effective public relations and media campaign.

## The Importance of Preserving NATO

For much of the 1990s, NATO sought to redefine itself as the core of an enlarged security community and a tool for managing conflict within Europe and around its periphery.[131] It emphasized its ability—even its obligation—to maintain stability and safeguard human rights and democracy as key reasons for its continued existence. Perhaps Jamie Shea summed it up best when he stated that "NATO feels that Kosovo is a defining moment for the future of the alliance in showing NATO's determination to uphold values in the wider Europe."[132] Thus it was widely believed that if NATO failed in Kosovo, against a foe no better than a "schoolyard bully" commanding an army of "thugs," its new *raison d'être* would be undermined, its credibility destroyed, and a dangerous precedent set. As Tony Blair asserted during the NATO summit, "many of our problems have been caused by two dangerous and ruthless men—Hussein and Slobodan Milosevic. . . . [Thus] one of the reasons why it is so important to win the conflict is to ensure that others do not make the same mistake in the future."[133] And even before the bombing started, General Clark reportedly told Madeline Albright that they would have to go ahead even though they knew the consequences could be dire for Kosovar Albanians, because they had "put NATO's credibility on the line. [They had] to follow through and make it work. There [was] no real alternative."[134] In the end, NATO could not accept failure because it had so entwined its whole reason for being with the success of its mission in Kosovo. In essence, it made the reputational costs of backing down impossibly large.

Though many of NATO's European members resented their military reliance on the United States and frequently grumbled about its heavy-handed dominance of the alliance,[135] they were clearly wholly unprepared to let it collapse.[136] Even Jacques Chirac, a frequent and vocal critic of NATO, proclaimed at the anniversary summit, "Unity and determination, total and unanimous."[137] The possibility that a real or perceived NATO failure in Kosovo could spell the death knell for the alliance led its European members to stifle (at least publicly) their criticism of the conduct of the war and to forego all opportunities to defect from NATO's stated strategy. The Europeans considered the possibility that they might be left to fend for themselves too risky, particularly given that they still perceive themselves as incapable of going it alone militarily. Though the EU is highly effective in determining and implementing common aid and trade policies, it remains neither a unified nor a credible diplomatic actor. Moreover, it is poorly equipped to deal swiftly and effectively with out-of-area crises, and it has a vastly underdeveloped military force projection capacity.[138] Whatever the costs of sticking with a U.S.-driven alliance, the Europeans obviously viewed them as lower than shouldering future costs alone.

## Alleviating the Pain of Coercion

### *The Value of Troops in Albania and Macedonia*

When Milosevic launched demographic bombs against Albania and Macedonia, he likely hoped that—in addition to impeding KLA and NATO military operations—the refugees would overwhelm the local infrastructure and possibly destabilize the region.[139] Given how few preparations the West had made to accommodate the massive flows that emerged, this was a reasonable gamble. And, for a time, it appeared that it might work. When the refugee crisis along the Macedonian border crossing near Blace "increased the potential costs of collaboration, key figures in the (Macedonian) government threatened to publicly criticize the air strikes and ask NATO forces to leave the country."[140] This led the U.S. embassy to intensify its efforts to solve the refugee crisis at Blace and placate the Macedonian government.[141]

However, in the end, here, too, Milosevic's gambit failed. Over ninety thousand refugees were temporarily evacuated from the region, thus reducing pressures at the Macedonian border.[142] In addition, after promises of significant financial aid and logistical support were forthcoming, the Macedonians did reopen their border. And tens of thousands of NATO troops, in conjunction with UNHCR and the NGO community, provided relief to the refugees that remained, thereby further mitigating the pain Milosevic hoped to inflict on NATO and its neighbors. Thus, although a week into the crisis it was claimed that "without international relief assistance, starvation [was] expected within 10 days to two weeks," catastrophe never struck.[143] Ironically, therefore, though ground troops were never sent into battle against Milosevic, effectively they degraded his refugee "weapons" capabilities.

### *Localizing the Pain*

The containment of the vast majority of refugees to the Balkans and the relatively small number of NATO casualties also helped dampen the domestic costs of continuing the conflict. An examination of polling data is illustrative in this regard. For example, though in mid-April 1999 87 percent of the British people polled still widely favored NATO action to protect Kosovar Albanians, only 15 percent of them were willing to accept any Kosovar refugees into Britain. Moreover, 56 percent of those polled said they would not sacrifice the life of a single British soldier to save the lives of Kosovar Albanians.[144] Similarly, a poll in *Der Spiegel* in late March indicated that, while 64 percent of those in the western part of Germany supported air attacks on the FRY, only 33 percent would support the addition of ground troops to the operation. (The numbers for the eastern part of Germany were even lower.)[145] Though this evidence is hardly conclusive, it suggests that, as long as the costs of NATO action appeared to be negligible to domestic audiences, support would hold.[146] As Michael Ignatieff noted in *Virtual War*, Kosovo was a "virtual conflict" in which, while people suffered and died on the ground, the foreigners who became involved were able to view the war as if watching a sporting event on television, in which they were able to root for their team—the "good guys"—and then change channels. "And even though the game was in deadly earnest, the deaths were mostly hidden, and above all, they were someone else's."[147] If, however, either refugees with suitcases or the good guys' soldiers in body bags had started appearing at home, support likely would have plummeted.

### *Domestic Containment Policies*

A slick and dexterous NATO public relations campaign cum media machine further aided the effort to make the costs of the campaign *appear* negligible to Western audiences. For several months, NATO members also neutralized domestic opposition to the bombing campaign and sidestepped questions about whether it had inflamed the crisis through the work of spokespeople who likened Kosovo to Cambodia under Pol Pot and likened FRY activities to "the Great Terror."[148] Tearful accounts by refugees, accompanied by pictures of clogged border crossings, filled Western television screens.

It is clear, at least in retrospect, that much of the coverage generated by the NATO media machine was exaggerated, misleading, or just plain wrong.[149] For instance, a report released by the State Department—and widely disseminated—claimed that one hundred thousand Albanian men had been herded into a Pristina soccer stadium and held against their will. However, when one French journalist went to see for himself, he found the stadium empty.[150] Nevertheless, the propaganda campaign was extremely effective. And it was instrumental in permitting NATO to turn the refugee weapon back onto Milosevic, convincing the world that he alone was responsible for the tragedy that had unfolded and effectively neutralizing any benefit he had hoped to derive from the export of refugees.[151] In short, the triumph of NATO's propaganda campaign was thrusting the costs associated with the refugee crisis, which Milosevic sought to impose on the West, back onto him. (It is worth noting that Milosevic's brutal behavior during the earlier Bosnian war helped make the propaganda offered up during the Kosovo campaign more credible than it might otherwise have been.)

Moreover, ironically, in the end NATO was actually able to use the refugees to sustain support for its intervention. It fixed upon them and succeeded in portraying their existence as the key reason for the intervention, though that only became the mission's defining goal well after the bombing began.[152] As one close observer of the conflict suggested, "Western public opinion would have turned against the bombardment, had it not been for the wrenching scenes of refugees pouring over the borders. The question would have been asked, 'How can we bomb a small country—whatever we think of its government—because it refuses to sign an agreement about the future of part of its territory?'"

### And A Dash of Luck for Good Measure

In spite of the success of NATO's media campaign, after several months of bombing, NATO's rationalizations had grown threadbare in some circles, and it appears that the tide may have been turning. For instance, by late May, even in the United States—where support for NATO's bombing campaign had been consistently strong—human rights and peace groups began to mobilize against it, insisting that the bombing campaign had failed to protect civilians targeted by FRY troops. The groups admitted that concerns about alleged Yugoslav atrocities had "made some of us think twice about what to do," but that, by mid-May, they believed they should agitate for a new approach.[153] Demonstrations were planned throughout the country, which were to culminate with a rally in the capital on June 5. Luckily for the Administration, Milosevic agreed to the G-8 deal on June 3.

## CONCLUSIONS

### About Coercion

As Schelling has said, "a certain death may stun (a man), but it leaves him no choice."[154] When NATO presented Milosevic with the terms of the Rambouillet

Accords, it dictated what probably seemed like certain death, and, thus, coercion failed. However, NATO was saved from total failure because its shortsightedness, borne of indifference, was matched by Milosevic's substantial miscalculation of Western resolve, resilience, and resourcefulness. In the end, Kosovo offers several lessons for those who might engage in coercion. First, there must be something in the bargain for the other side, or it's no bargain. Second, effective coercion requires that threats issued must be credible, and they must be understood. Third, if one's adversary can neutralize the costs of noncompliance, the power to coerce rapidly evaporates. Finally, before one opts to raise the costs of one's own compliance to prohibitive levels, one ought to be sure the option of noncompliance is really the preferable one.

### About the Use of Refugees as a Weapon

In the end, Milosevic's gambit failed. But close examination of the course of events demonstrates that, at least for a time, he came close to succeeding. This fact alone ought to give us pause, because along with all of the purported "lessons" keen observers and future adversaries may glean about the limits of coercion and the power of propaganda, they may also learn a thing or two about the potential firepower of demographic bombs. Rising xenophobia in Europe and around the world may still make the refugee game worth playing for some. Moreover, cases where one country faces a crisis alone (for example, Italy in 1997) are likely to be more common than those where a nineteen-member coalition comprises the opposition, particularly since NATO may not wish to put its credibility to a test again soon.

Conversely, NATO's intervention in Kosovo may encourage other groups to manipulate international opinion (via their own propaganda campaigns). By provoking attacks upon themselves by their own governments, these groups may seek assistance with their bids for self-determination or the overthrow of "undemocratic" governments.[155] If Tony Blair's notion is taken seriously, of when the principle of noninterference in others' internal affairs may be unacceptable—that is, whenever oppression produces massive flows of refugees that unsettle neighboring countries—it could provide a "virtual blank check" for future interventions.[156] Such a proactive stance by NATO may present a powerful incentive for those struggling for independence, something we can not afford to dismiss lightly.

## NOTES

I wish to thank Robert Art, Aleksa Djilas, Michael Glosny, Charles Keely, Alan Kuperman, Sarah Lischer, Ian Lustick, Barry Posen, Chuck Spinney, Benjamin

Valentino, Stephen Van Evera, and several anonymous reviewers for valuable comments and criticisms on earlier versions of this work, which was first presented at the American Political Science Association (APSA) Annual Meeting in Washington, D.C., in August 2000. I also wish to thank the MacArthur Foundation and the Social Science Research Council for their generous financial support of this research.

1. This is not meant to suggest that ethnic cleansing or using refugees as weapons was Milosevic's only, or even his primary, tool in the spring 1999 offensive. Nevertheless, this phenomenon deserves more attention than it has heretofore been given, particularly since, historically, refugees have been used coercively with greater frequency than is generally recognized. See, for instance, Kelly M. Greenhill, "People Pressure: Strategic Forced Migration as an Instrument of Statecraft and the Rise of the Human Rights Regime," M.I.T. Ph.D. dissertation, forthcoming.

2. See, for instance, General Klaus Naumann's statement to the U.S. Senate in *Lessons Learned from the Military Operations Conducted as Part of Operation Allied Force*, p. 2, cited in Ivo Daalder and Michael O'Hanlon, *Winning Ugly: NATO's War to Save Kosovo* (Washington, D.C.: Brookings Institution, 2000), p. 292, fn. 137. Surprisingly this version of events persists, even after a retired general in the German Army (among others) admitted "claims of a plan [that is, Operation Horseshoe] were faked from a vague intelligence report in order to deflect criticism in Germany of the bombing." From Human Rights Watch, *Under Orders: War Crimes in Kosovo* (New York: HRW, 2001), p. 59. See also John Goetz and Tom Walker, "Serbian Ethnic Cleansing Scare Was a Fake, Says General," *Sunday Times*, April 2, 2000; and Stephen Gowans, "The Truth on Trial: Charges against Slobodan Milosevic Mask the War Crimes of NATO," *Ottawa Citizen*, April 18, 2001, p. A19. (It was the Germans who announced the existence of Operation Horseshoe.)

3. See, for instance, *Joint Statement on the Kosovo After Action Review*, U.S. Department of Defense, October 14, 1999, pp. 1–3, found at www.defenselink.mil:80/news/Oct1999/b10141999_bt478-99.html and *Report to Congress: Kosovo/Operation Allied Force After-Action Report*, January 31, 2000, p. xvii, for the U.S. government position. See also Daalder and O'Hanlon, *Winning Ugly*, pp. 58–69 and 194–95; Michael Ignatieff, *Virtual War: Kosovo and Beyond* (New York: Metropolitan Books, 2000), p. 122; and William M. Arkin, "Operation Allied Force: The Most Precise Application of Air Power in History," in Andrew J. Bacevich and Eliot A. Cohen (editors), *The War Over Kosovo: Politics and Strategy in a Global Age* (New York: Columbia University Press, 2001), p. 2.

4. Ibid. See also Hearing of the Senate Armed Services Committee, "Lessons Learned from Military Operations and Relief Efforts in Kosovo," October 14, 1999.

5. *Report to Congress: Kosovo/Operation Allied Force After-Action Report*, p. 4.

6. It has been argued that NATO needed to cling tightly to such an interpretation in order to justify its actions. Timothy Garton Ash, for instance, claims that "western European leaders stressed the motive of averting 'humanitarian disaster' so strongly because this was the only way in which taking military action without the sanction of a UN Security Council resolution—something they had recoiled from doing for the best part of a year—might possibly be justified in international law. This legal expedient had been suggested by a British Foreign Office memorandum circulated to Britain's

NATO allies as early as October 1998." From Timothy Garton Ash, "The War We Almost Lost: Was NATO's Kosovo Campaign a Legitimate Response to a Humanitarian Catastrophe—or Did It Cause One?" *The Guardian*, September 4, 2000, p. 2.

7. I surmise that these signals may be loosely interpreted as Milosevic's intentions, particularly when backed up by corresponding behavior. While we cannot know for certain what Milosevic intended until the archives in Belgrade are opened, or unless Milosevic decides to tell us, perhaps during his war crimes trial. Barring such a disclosure, analysis of his rhetoric and his actions offer the best available proxy.

8. Daalder and O'Hanlon claim that Milosevic set out to put Operation Horseshoe into effect in November 1998 and that the "coordinated attack (was to) involve a broad swath of territory in the shape of a horseshoe, moving from the northeast down to the west and back to the southeast of Kosovo." From Daalder and O'Hanlon, *Winning Ugly*, p. 58. However, this depiction of Serb intentions is wholly at odds with the *actual* pattern of outflows during the crisis. See in particular Patrick Ball, "Policy or Panic?: The Flight of Ethnic Albanians from Kosovo, March–May 1999" published online by the AAAS Science and Human Rights Program at hrdata.aaas.org/kosovo/policyorpanic/, which offers a comprehensive statistical analysis of the pattern of refugee outflows and which demonstrates that the preponderance of outflows did not occur as Daalder and O'Hanlon describe. Rather, during the three refugee "pulses" identified by Ball, the *most significant flows* commenced in the west and southwest of the province, then increased in the north-central portion of the province, and finally moved back to the south/southwest of the province, as the report's maps of flow concentrations indicate.

9. See, for instance, R. Jeffrey Smith and William Drozdiak, "Serbs' Offensive Was Meticulously Planned," *Washington Post*, April 11, 1999, p. A1, who argue that the Serbs would have pursued Operation Horseshoe in any event. However, they offer no evidence to support this claim.

10. Furthermore, the actual chronology of events undermines the claim that NATO's bombing campaign was launched *in response to* Milosevic's on-going ethnic cleansing campaign, namely, because it did not begin in earnest until after the bombing commenced, a fact that many have just recently begun to acknowledge. See, for instance, Joseph Lelyveld, "The Defendant: Slobodan Milosevic's Trial, and the Debate Surrounding International Courts," *New Yorker*, May 27, 2002; and Human Rights Watch, *Under Orders*, p. 4.

11. To be clear, this paper is not a test of coercion theory. Instead it is a case study of Milosevic's attempt to use refugees as weapons, which employs the tenets of coercion theory merely as a blueprint for understanding Milosevic's strategy and tactics, motivations, and objectives.

12. It is worth keeping in mind that (1) NATO's aggregate gross domestic product (GDP) was about nine hundred times that of the FRY (2) their defense budgets were three hundred times greater than the FRY's; and (3) their population was approximately seventy times greater than the FRY's. Barry R. Posen, "The War for Kosovo: Serbia's Political-Military Strategy," *International Security*, vol. 24, no. 1 (Spring 2000) p. 49.

13. This proposition has been echoed by others, including recognized refugee expert Bill Frelick of the U.S. Committee on Refugees. See, for instance, the program transcript for the Center for Defense Information's America's Defense Monitor for the

documentary *Refugees as Weapons of War*, which can be found at www.cdi.org/adm/1306/Frelick.html. In his interview, Frelick says, "Initially in 1998 I think that the Serbian strategy was a counter-insurgency strategy. They were provoked by the KLA. At various points the KLA was seeking independence. They were trying a sort of Boston Tea Party, or to provoke the Redcoats, so to speak. And the Yugoslav army and the Sebian police overreacted, hitting civilian populations. But essentially it was directed at the KLA at that time. I don't think that the strategy, at that time was ethnic cleansing per se. That changed dramatically with the bombing campaign that NATO embarked upon on March 24, 1999." Frelick believes that, once NATO bombing commenced, the Serbs saw an opportunity to cleanse the province and set about doing it. See also Lelyveld, "The Defendant," p. 85.

14. For a discussion of rising xenophobia and fear of refugee flows in Europe, see, for instance, Sandra Lavenex, *Safe Third Countries: Extending the EU Asylum and Immigration Policies to Central and Eastern Europe* (Budapest: Central European University Press, 1999).

15. The stipulations of the Rambouillet Accords would have allowed NATO troops unimpeded access to all of the FRY—not just Kosovo—something that many on both sides of the political spectrum acknowledge no sovereign country would willingly accept. See, for instance, Henry Kissinger, "The Wrong Invasion," *Ottawa Citizen*, February 22, 1999, p. A13, and William E. Ratliff, "Madeline's War and the Costs of Intervention," *Harvard International Review*, vol. 22, issue 4, (Winter 2001), pp. 70–76, as well as Robert Hayden, "Humanitarian Hypocrisy," *Kosovo and Yugoslavia: Law in Crisis*, a presentation of JURIST: The Law Professor's Network, 1999, found at www.jurist@law.pitt.edu. Even the Prime Minister of Slovenia, who believes the United States pursued the right tack at Rambouillet—given Milosevic's past behavior—acknowledges that "the Rambouillet talks were not 'negotiations,' as the term is usually understood. Both sides . . . were presented with a take-it-or-leave-it proposal." From Janez Drnovsek, "Riding the Tiger: The Dissolution of Yugoslavia," *World Policy Journal*, vol. 17, no. 1 (Spring 2000). Likewise, the British House of Commons' Foreign Affairs Committee concluded " whatever the actual impact of the Military Annex, NATO was guilty of a serious blunder in allowing a Status of Forces Agreement into the package which would never have been acceptable to the Yugoslav side, since it was a significant infringement of its sovereignty." From the *House of Commons' Select Committee on Foreign Affairs Fourth Report*, May 23, 2000, available online at www.parliament.the-stationery-office.co.uk/pa/cm199900/cmselect/cmfaff/28/2802.htm.

16. In the midst of counterinsurgency campaigns, population displacement frequently occurs even when the forces involved are less disposed to brutality than the Serbs. Consider, for instance, that U.S. search-and-destroy tactics in Vietnam *during the spring of 1965 alone* generated over four hundred thousand refugees. From Robert B. Asprey, *War in the Shadows: The Guerrilla in History* (New York: William Morrow and Company, 1994), p. 832. See Asprey's book as well for a number of other examples of the civilian externalities of counterinsurgency campaigns.

17. Interestingly, Greek diplomats predicted as much about a month before the bombing began. See Paul Wood, "Regional Tensions: Greece Fears the Balkans Could Ignite and Drag Her into Conflicts of the Past," *Independent*, February 21, 1999, p. 20.

18. It has been argued, for instance, that to "protect their forces on the ground and confound targeting, Serb units intentionally operated among civilian refugees, in villages, and near prohibited targets such as churches." Arkin, "Allied Force," p. 15. See also DOD/JCS, *Joint Statement on the Kosovo After Action Review*, October 14, 1999.

19. NATO was aided on this front by the KLA, which "was not in a position to fight a straight out battle between standing armies, [and thus] used their civilian population as part of its tactic to win international support and to really bring the international community as an ally in their struggle against the Serbs," according to Bill Frelick. See again *Refugees as Weapons of War* program transcript. Found at: http://www.cdi.org/adm/1306/transcript.html. See also Alan J. Kuperman, "False Hope Abroad: Promises to Intervene Often Bring Bloodshed," *Washington Post*, June 14, 1998, and Greenhill, "People Pressure."

20. To be clear, Milosevic's decision to deal was driven by a number of factors, of which this was but one. However, by the time he agreed to negotiate with NATO, it was abundantly evident that the refugee weapon was not going to fracture the alliance, despite early indications that it might.

21. For a more detailed chronology, see "A Kosovo Chronology," which may be viewed on the PBS Frontline website at www.pbs.org/wgbh/pages/frontline/shows/kosovo/, as well as Tim Judah, *Kosovo: War and Revenge* (New Haven, Conn.: Yale University Press, 2000), chapters 4–8; and Daalder and O'Hanlon, *Winning Ugly*, chapter 2.

22. Though the KLA claims to have launched its first attack in 1993, most observers focus on the period between 1996 and 1998 as key to understanding Serb fears regarding their growing strength and the growing scope and scale of their operations. Consider that there were thirty-one documented KLA attacks in 1996, fifty-five in 1997, and sixty-six in just the first two months of 1998. See Chris Hedges, "In New Balkan Tinderbox, Ethnic Albanians Rebel Against Serbs," *New York Times*, March 2, 1998. See also Human Rights Watch, *Under Orders*, chapter 2.

23. See, for instance, Judah, *Kosovo*, pp. 128–29.

24. Cited in William Hayden, "The Kosovo Conflict and Forced Migration: The Strategic Use of Displacement and the Obstacles to International Protection," *Journal of Humanitarian Assistance* at www.jha.sps.cam.ac.uk/b/b597.htm. (Hayden's article preceded the March 1999 conflict and contains an interesting viewpoint on why it would not have been in the Serbs' interest to opt for massive ethnic cleansing of Kosovo, at least until after the West had intervened.) See also *RFE/RL Newsline*, vol. 1, no. 188, (January 5, 1998), part 2.

25. On February 23, 1998, during a visit to Pristina, U.S. special envoy Robert Gelbard announced that the United States "condemned very strongly terrorist actions in Kosovo. The UCK (KLA) is, without any question, a terrorist group." Cited in Judah, *Kosovo*, p. 138. It is widely acknowledged that Milosevic interpreted this statement—obviously incorrectly—as a green light from the United States to act against the KLA.

26. See, for instance, Daalder and O'Hanlon, *Winning Ugly*, pp. 45–62, General Wesley Clark, *Waging Modern War* (New York: Public Affairs, 2001), pp. 131–61, and Judah, *Kosovo*, pp. 183–89.

27. See again fn 11. Moreover, Major General John Drewienkiewicz declares as much when discussing the Serb reaction to KLA advances in late 1998–early 1999.

"Because the Serbs said to us, well hang on, the deal was that we withdraw from these things, and you were going to police the agreement. So can you just get these Kosovo Liberation Army (sic) out of the trenches that we were in a month ago?" From Alan Little, "Moral Combat: NATO at War," transcript of a BBC2 special, broadcast on March 12, 2000; on-line version available from the BBC website at: http://news.co.uk/hi/english/static/events/panorama/transcripts/transcript_12_03_00.txt.

28. See, for instance, Daalder and O'Hanlon, *Winning Ugly*, pp. 57–59; and Timothy W. Crawford, "Pivotal Deterrence and the Kosovo War: Why the Holbrooke Agreement Failed," *Political Science Quarterly* (Fall 2001).

29. Both OSCE and KDOM monitors on the ground verify that the KLA was undermining the ceasefire almost as soon as it was signed. See *Kosovo/Kosova: As Seen, As Told, Part I*, pp. 26–30, and chapter 5, pp. 163–401, which contains information about the security situation and levels of violence in each of Kosovo's municipalities, as well as *KDOM Daily Report*, October 31, 1998, cited in Daalder and O'Hanlon, *Winning Ugly*, p. 292, fn 133, in which KDOM monitors noted that "KLA (UCK) presence is growing in those areas where Serb troops and police have departed, having established its own checkpoints on secondary roads in the Drenica, Podujevo, and Malisevo areas." See again Crawford, "Pivotal Deterrence," pp. 512–17.

30. In appears they were correct. Some U.S. and British intelligence agents now confirm that they helped train the KLA before NATO's bombing of Yugoslavia. See, for instance, Tom Walker and Aidan Laverty, "Ready for War: The KLA Was Given Covert Assistance by the CIA before NATO Began Its Bombing Campaign," *Sunday Times* (London), March 12, 2000, and Allan Little, "Moral Combat."

31. Even Hashim Thaci, head of the wartime KLA, acknowledges that "a key KLA unit was based in the area" around Racak. See Alan Little, "Moral Combat."

32. Most believe that of those killed at Racak, at least some—if not all—were innocent civilians. However some contend that those killed were battle deaths and the apparent massacre was a hoax perpetrated by the KLA, in an attempt to galvanize Western support for action against the Serbs. They cite as evidence the fact that the Finnish forensic investigative team that examined the site reported that "most of the 45 Racak dead had been shot at long range, not execution-style." From Peter Worthington, "The Hoax That Started a War," *Toronto Sun*, April 1, 2001.

33. See again Judah, *Kosovo*; Posen; and fn. 16. For his part, State Department spokesman James Rubin now acknowledges that "obviously, publicly we had to make clear we were seeking an agreement, but privately we knew the chances of the Serbs agreeing were quite small." From Alan Little, "Moral Combat." See also James Rubin, "A Very Personal War: Countdown to a Very Personal War," *Financial Times* (London), September 30, 2000, p. 9.

34. To provide some context as to where things stood at this point—that is, just before the advent of the NATO campaign—consider the following. Most sources agree that, to this point, there had been a total of only one to two thousand conflict-related deaths between the start of the first Serb offensive in March 1998 and the withdrawal of the OSCE observers in mid-March 1999. In this same period, UNHCR figures suggest that perhaps two to three hundred thousand persons had been displaced from their homes, most victims of what was "essentially a temporary rural displacement resulting from government operations against villages suspected of sympathizing with

guerrillas . . . many of [whom] returned to their damaged homes over the course of the year." From Michael Barutciski, "Western Diplomacy and the Kosovo Refugee Crisis," *Forced Migration Review*, vol. 5 (August 5, 1999), p. 9. In fact, Daalder and O'Hanlon note that after the October agreement was signed "all displaced persons inside Kosovo had either returned to their villages or had found temporary shelter elsewhere." From Daalder and O'Hanlon, *Winning Ugly*, p. 49; see also fn 93 on p. 289. Some fled again once the ceasefire had definitively broken down, but as UNHCR spokesman Fernando Del Mundo put it, "last summer people were fleeing for their lives. Now they are being displaced because of fear." This implies that in early 1999 civilians were not yet being pushed out but rather were fleeing preemptively. From Jonathan S. Landay, "Make-or-Break Time for Kosovo," *Christian Science Monitor*, February 25, 1999, p. 6.

35. From "The Diplomacy of Violence," in Thomas Schelling, *Arms and Influence* (New Haven, Conn.: Yale University Press, 1966); reprinted in Robert J. Art and Robert Jervis (ed.), *International Politics* (New York: Harper Collins, 1996), p. 169.

36. Bronwen Maddox et al., "The 80 Days War," *Times* (London), July 15, 1999.

37. Western fears about the consequences of Kosovar refugee flows had been appearing in the press since at least the start of the March 1998 offensive when Strobe Talbott said, "one of the greatest fears in Washington about Serbian brutality against ethnic Albanians in the province of Kosovo is that violence could spread into Albania and neighboring Macedonia." See Jane Perlez, "US Official Asks Restraint by Albanians. Talbott Seeks Limit On Kosovo Conflict," *New York Times*, March 17, 1998.

38. See, for instance, "Austria, Switzerland, and the Politics of Nationalism," Global Intelligence Update: Weekly Analysis, November 1, 1999, www.stratfor.com, as well as Jeanette Money, *Fences and Neighbors: The Political Geography of Immigration Control* (Ithaca, N.Y.: Cornell University Press, 1999). Consider as well the recent rise in popularity of anti-immigration parties throughout western Europe (for example, France, the Netherlands, and Norway).

39. This same poll indicated that over 60 percent of Germans wanted immigration reduced or stopped altogether. From Philip Martin, "Germany: Reluctant Land of Immigration," in Wayne Cornelius et al. (eds.), *Controlling Immigration* (Stanford, Calif.: Stanford University Press, 1994), p. 189.

40. "Racism and Xenophobia in Europe," *Eurobarometer Opinion Poll*, no. 47.1 (December 1997). Ironically, the results of this survey were first presented at the Closing Conference of the European Year Against Racism, held in Luxembourg, December 18–19, 1997.

41. Ibid., pp. 5–6

42. Some argue that fears associated with immigration from Central Europe are the key driver of current initiatives in EU immigration policy. See again Lavenex, *Third Countries*.

43. One national tabloid featured an article about migrants from Slovakia and Kosovo seeking asylum in order to exploit Britain's generous welfare provisions and displaying threatening behavior when good housing was not available. From Alice Bloch, "Kosovan refugees in the UK: The Rolls Royce or Rickshaw Reception?" *Forced Migration Review*, vol. 5 (August 5, 1999), p. 24.

44. The victory of Jorg Haider's Freedom Party is but one example. Extreme right parties have been present in Europe for some time, notably in France, Italy, and Switzerland.

45. As British Prime Minister Tony Blair proclaimed in the midst of the Kosovo conflict, "when oppression produces massive flows of refugees which unsettle neighboring countries then they can properly be described as 'threats to international peace and security.'" See Tony Blair, "Doctrine of the International Community," transcript of a speech given before the Chicago Council of Economists, April 23, 1999.

46. Andrew Gumbel, "Italy Ready for Mission Impossible; Intervention in Albania Could Bring Instability to Rome," *Independent*, April 7, 1997, p. 15.

47. Andrew Gumbel, "Albanian Mission Puts Italy's Government to the Test," *Independent*, April 8, 1997, p. 15. Ironically, the decision to undertake Operation Alba and increase political stability in Albania almost led to the fall of the reigning Italian government.

48. Elaine Sciolino and Ethan Bronner, "The Road to War: How a President, Distracted by Scandal, Entered Balkan War," *New York Times*, April 18, 1999, p. A1.

49. It also appears that Milosevic might have viewed Italy as particularly vulnerable to these tactics in that in the first weeks of the war—during Milosevic's self-declared ceasefire—an open letter to the Italian government was published in the state-run newspaper, entreating the Italians to "show they were better than fascists" and renounce the "military aggression" being pursued by "American-NATO." From "Open letter to Scalfaro, D'Alema, and Dini," *TANJUG News Service*, April 9, 1999, www.serbia-info.com/news.

50. See again Paul Wood, "Regional Tensions." The article goes on to note that the Greeks believed that it was believed that bombing "would send refugees into Macedonia and Albania, filling camps with dispossessed ethnic Albanians bent on revenge. Albania is already highly unstable. Problems there, especially given the availability of weapons, would add to a separatist campaign by ethnic Albanians in Macedonia. Diplomats fear that such a conflict could see neighbouring states revive territorial claims: the Greeks to southern Albania, the Serbs to northern Macedonia and the Bulgarians to western Macedonia. It is not simply Kosovo which is at stake."

51. Ibid. As one diplomat put it: "Germany feels that the rest of Europe is not pulling its weight. It wants its partners to see this as a European problem, not as a German problem." Unfortunately for Germany, its "partners" did not share its view.

52. Joint burden-sharing proposals presented by the European Commission were rejected by France, the UK, and Spain. From Emma Tucker, "Bonn Fears It May Be Left to Shoulder Burden of Refugees: German Pleas To Treat Expected Balkans Exodus as a European Problem Are Falling on Deaf Ears," *Financial Times* (London), February 16, 1999, p. 2.

53. It is evident that the Serbs engaged in textual analysis of documents and therefore could have expected the West would do the same, thereby actually "getting" the messages it seems Belgrade attempted to send. For instance, one article in the state-run paper attempts to deconstruct NATO's Joint Statement about operations in Kosovo and notes, "It is interesting in this unusually long statement, they permanently speak about innocent Kosovo civilians." In previous NATO documents, in each sentence they used

the term "ethnic Albanians." See "NATO Ministers Free Themselves of a Responsibility by Lies," *TANJUG News Service*, April 13, 1999, www.serbia-info.com/news.

54. See, for instance, Arkin, "Allied Force."

55. "Seselj: Contact Group's Goals Not Reached," *TANJUG News Service*, February 28, 1999; found online at www.serbia-info.com/news.

56. I am making a logical jump here in assuming that a column in the state-run press can reasonably be seen to be reflecting the views and attitudes of the government.

57. Dusko Vojnovic, "American and European View on Kosovo and Metohia—Reasons for Differences and Disputes," *TANJUG News Service*, March 5, 1999, www.serbia-info.com/news.

58. Some of which themselves have simmering ethnic tensions. For instance, Macedonia is divided between ethnic Slavs and ethnic Albanians, who make up a third of the population. Fears that large-scale influxes of Albanians would upset the ethnic balance were widespread and probably justified.

59. See again Vojnovic, "American and European View on Kosovo and Metohia."

60. Juan Pablo Cordoba Elias, "The Reform: US Political games on Kosovo and Metohia," *Politika*, March 4, 1999; found on-line at www.serbia-info.com/news. Elias goes still further and warns that "Kosovo represents a strategic zone of terrorism and drug trade . . . (and) it is well known that this terroristic internal structure was supported by Albanian communist leader Enver Hoxha . . . (and) if we add to all this the fact that the terrorists are mostly Moslems, it seams (sic) that things are getting to quite another dimension."

61. Ibid.

62. "Yugoslav government condemns NATO threats of aggression," *TANJUG News Service*, March 20, 1999; found online at www.serbia-info.com/news.

63. Ibid.

64. See again Perlez, "US Official."

65. "Minister Jovanovic writes to Security Council and OSCE," *TANJUG News Service*, March 19, 1999; found online at www.serbia-info.com/news.

66. Lara Marlowe, "War and Peace Revisited," *Irish Times*, March 25, 2000, p. 68.

67. "Milosevic Receives Holbrooke, Hill, Petritsch, and Mayorsky," *TANJUG News Service*, March 23, 1999; found online at www.serbia-info.com/news.

68. Nevertheless, given the number of diplomats, policymakers, and analysts tracking the Kosovo situation, it seems reasonable that somebody should have entertained the possibility that Milosevic was sending genuine and serious signals.

69. See, for instance, Ash, "The War We Almost Lost," p. 2.

70. Cited in Judah, *Kosovo, p.* 242.

71. Clark, *Waging Modern War*, p. 164.

72. Nicholas Morris, "UNHCR and Kosovo: a personal view from within UNHCR," *Forced Migration Review*, vol. 5, August 5, 1999, electronic version. This view of events is supported by the fact that, only one week into the bombing, the alliance was running short of cruise missiles and found its stockpiled food aid—in Kosovo—behind "enemy lines." See, for instance, Mary Dejevsky, "Will America Crack? While the US Stands High in Military Might, on the Human Front It Is Finitely Vulnerable," *Independent* (London), April 2, 1999, p. 5.

73. Elaine Sciolino and Ethan Bronner, "The Road to War: How a President, Distracted by Scandal, Entered Balkan War," *New York Times*, April 18, 1999, p. A1.

74. Lara Marlowe, "War and Peace Revisited."

75. Then Secretary of Defense Cohen alleges, for instance, that "we knew from the beginning that the use of allied military force could not stop Milosevic's attack on Kosovar civilians, which he had planned in advance and had deployed forces to carry out. . . . We knew it would take time. We knew that the Yugoslav military was not an insignificant foe. We knew we'd have to deal with significant refugee flows." From the "Hearing of the Senate Armed Services Committee: Lessons Learned from Military Operations and Relief Efforts in Kosovo," October 14,1999.

76. Further questions about the authenticity of the so-called Operation Horseshoe master plan have been raised by a variety of skeptics, who ask why no concrete evidence of this plan has surfaced since the conflict ended. They also appropriately ask why some key figures, including Chief Prosecutor of the UN Criminal Court for Yugoslavian Affairs in the Hague Louise Arbour and NATO commander General Wesley Clark were apparently unaware of such a plan and why OSCE monitors did not report any widespread expulsions before departing shortly before the bombing commenced. Ms. Arbour has said, "As to Operation Horseshoe, I have my doubts as to its capacity to prove anything. If it were a document with cover, date, and signature, it would be fantastic. But mostly such things look more like verbal descriptions and conclusions." See *Der Spiegel*, no. 17/1999, April 27, 1999, p. 152. See also "Important Internal Documents from Germany's Foreign Office Regarding Pre-Bombardment Genocide in Kosovo," April 28, 1999, and "The Aftermath of the Publication of the German Government Documents," both translated from the German by Eric Canepa, and found on www.zmag.org/crisecurevts/germandocs.htm and www.zmag.org/crisecurevts/germandocsmore.htm.

77. As has been pithily noted, "Contrary to what NATO planners seem to believe, enemies often react when shot at." See Carnes Lord, "What Milosevic Really Wants," *Boston Globe*, April 4, 1999.

78. "BETA Examines Milosevic's Kosovo Options," *BETA News Service*, March 4, 1999, offers a precient echo of this theory of Serb strategy, although the author also predicted that Milosevic would attempt to partition northern Kosovo at this point, which did not happen.

79. The timing of Milosevic's Orthodox Easter ceasefire supports this proposition.

80. Robert Art, "The Functions of Force," reprinted in Art and Jervis (eds.), *International Politics*, p. 159.

81. Cited in Christopher Layne, "Collateral Damage in Kosovo," *NATO's Empty Victory* (Washington, D.C.: The CATO Institute, 2000), pp. 52–53. See also Steven Erlanger, "US Issues Appeal to Serbs to Halt Attacks in Kosovo," *New York Times*, March 23, 1999.

82. See again Layne, "Collateral Damage," as well as Paul Watson, "Airstrikes May Be Triggering New Massacres," *Los Angeles Times*, March 27, 1999, p. Al; Jane Perlez, "White House Tells of Reports of a Forced March in Kosovo," *New York Times*, March 27, 1999, p. A1; and Jane Perlez, "US Stealth Fighter is Down

in Yugoslavia As NATO Orders Attacks on Serb Army Units: 'Ethnic Cleansing,'" *New York Times*, March 28, 1999, p. A1.

83. Also the OSCE cites UNHCR figures indicating that there were only 69,500 refugees throughout the region before March 24, when the bombing began, but a total of 247,000 a week later, and 450,000 four days after that. From *Kosovo/Kosova: As Seen, As Told, Part I*, p. 99

84. See Judah, *Kosovo*, pp. 239–40.

85. In *Virtual War*, Ignatieff says that the Germans and Austrians provided Louise Arbour, Chief Prosecutor of the UN Criminal Court for Yugoslavian Affairs in the Hague, with evidence of Operation Horseshoe; yet Arbour has stated publicly that the evidence was not convincing. See, for instance, *Der Spiegel*, no. 17/1999, April 27, 1999, p. 152. For its part, the Independent International Commission on Kosovo concluded that the issue of whether Horseshoe existed at all and "what relevance it had" remains an open question. From Independent International Commission on Kosovo, *The Kosovo Report: Conflict, International Response, Lessons Learned* (Oxford: Oxford University Press, 2000), p. 88. One could reasonably argue that Daalder and O'Hanlon, Ignatieff, and others may have adopted a different stance regarding the authenticity of Operation Horseshoe had their books been written after publication of the Independent Commission's report, particularly since Ignatieff was a member of said commission. Nevertheless, even analyses and journalistic accounts published subsequent to the report's release continue to treat Horseshoe as fact. See, for instance, Arkin "Allied Force," above, as well as Anthony Weymouth and Stanley Henig (eds.), *The Kosovo Crisis: The Last War in Europe* (London: Reuters, 2001), which cites only one reference to the Albanian-American newspaper, *Illyria*, to support such a claim, as well as Christian Jennings, "Village Still Haunted by Screams of the Dying," *Daily Telegraph*, June 30, 2001, p. 5; Peter Beaumont, Ed Vulliamy, and Nick Thorpe, "Milosevic to Face Justice: End of the Line for the Butcher of Belgrade," *Observer*, June 24, 2001, p. 18; and Carol J. Williams, "Walls are Closing in on Milosevic," *Los Angeles Times*, July 11, 2001, p. A4. The Williams piece first states explicitly that evidence of Horseshoe was intercepted by the Germans but then notes that it remained unclear "whether [German] forces were able to put their hands on actual documents attesting to Operation Horseshoe and its author." (To this author's knowledge, as of May 2002, no concrete evidence that Horseshoe actually existed had been made public, nor was it included in the indictment against Milosevic in his trial before the International Criminal Tribunal for the Former Yugoslavia.)

86. UNHCR, *State of the World's Refugees: Fifty Years of Humanitarian Action (2000)* (Oxford: Oxford University Press, 2000), pp. 59–61.

87. Ibid., p. 247.

88. See again Asprey, *War in the Shadows*, on the use of population displacement in counterinsurgency operations.

89. This analysis is roughly consistent with my own impressionistic assessment of the flows, derived from an examination of a variety of U.S. and European news sources, State Department, UNHCR, and OSCE documents, and a number of reports from human rights organizations.

90. See Patrick Ball, "Policy or Panic?"

91. See again Daalder and O'Hanlon, *Winning Ugly*, pp. 58–9, which describes a "coordinated attack . . . in the shape of a horseshoe, moving from the northeast down to the west and back to the southeast of Kosovo along the Albanian and Macedonian borders."

92. Which presumably would have concentrated principally on the wholesale cleansing in the north and those portions of the province that were Serb-dominated and economically most significant.

93. Ibid. Other areas were also targeted—in particular, Kosovo Mitrovica and Pristina—though less intensively.

94. See Thomas W. Lippman, "NATO Expands Fleet of Aircraft; Refugees Reappear At Kosovo Borders; NATO to Expand Fleet of Warplanes," *Washington Post*, April 11, 1999, p. Al.

95. Pec, Djakovica, and Prizen all sit on the border with Albania, and the main road through southwest Kosovo flows through Suva Reka. Djakovica, Orohovac, Suva Reka, and Pec were also known to have strong KLA presences. Prizren did not, though its strategic significance, straddling both the Albanian and Macedonian borders, made control of this municipality critical for the Serbs. Moreover, it is possible that a number of Prizren's residents may have fled the KLA rather than the Serbs, as the OSCE recorded numerous KLA attacks against perceived Serb loyalists. See *Kosovo/Kosova: As Seen, As Told*, chapter 5.

96. NATO (perhaps inadvertently) acknowledged that this was the intent of the cleansing when it accused Milosevic of continuing to "conduct counterinsurgency sweeps" in spite of his unilaterally declared ceasefire for Orthodox Easter. See Lippman, "NATO Expands Fleet of Aircraft."

97. In fact, one could make an argument that this was really the only intent of the expulsions. The refugees were only meant to be used as a mindless spoiler, designed to impede KLA and NATO military operations, as well as to tax their infrastructures. There is clearly some truth in this line of argument, and I do believe Milosevic sought to use refugees this way. However, the evidence suggests this was not the refugees' only purpose, that is, it appears they were used as "smart weapons," not just "dumb bombs." For instance, the expulsions were, for the most part, not random but rather targeted KLA strongholds and supposed sympathethizers. Moreover, they appeared to be in large part orchestrated movements—they ebbed and flowed, shifted trajectories and concentrations—not simply an uncontrolled flood across the border.

98. See "Policy or Panic?" part 2.

99. See *Kosovo/Kosova: As Seen, As Told*, chapter 5.

100. While Serbs made up only 10 percent of Kosovo's total population, in Kosovo Polje, they made up 24 percent of the population, while in Kosovo Mitrovica municipality they made up 20 percent, and in Mitrovica town, Serbs represented 29 percent of the population. See *Kosovo/Kosova: As Seen, As Told, Part I*, chapter 5.

101. See, for instance, Carlotta Gall, "Serbs' Fear Put Segregation Back on the Table in Kosovo," *New York Times*, August 26, 1999, p. A1, and "BETA Examines Milosevic's Kosovo Options," *BETA News Service*, March 4, 1999.

102. Mitrovica is Kosovo's second city and main industrial center, bordering on the Trepca mining complex, an area twenty-five miles long and ten miles wide. It also provides much of the electricity for Kosovo, Montenegro, Macedonia, and southern Serbia, giving it significant strategic and economic importance. See Carol Hodge, "'Serbia's Kuwait' Is the Prize as Partition of Kosovo Moves Ever Closer to Reality," *Scotsman*, September 11, 1999, p. 12. Kosovo Polje is also a major industrial area, which contains coal mines, a major power plant, and the Pristina airport. See *Kosovo/Kosova: As Seen, As Told, Part I*, chapter 5.

103. "Unlike those who left earlier the most recent refugees appeared not to have been abused physically and they were allowed to retain their identity papers and other personal documents. 'It appears to be a civilized cleansing,'" said Owen O'Sullivan, an OSCE monitor on the Albanian border. From Lippman, "NATO Expands Fleet of Aircraft."

104. Ball, "Policy or Panic?" part 2.

105. Nor does the ICTY indictment include such a charge.

106. See, "Where are Kosovo's Killing Fields?" Published by stratfor.com, October 17, 1999; found on the web at www.stratfor.com. See also Daniel Pearl and Robert Block, "Body Count: War in Kosovo Was Cruel, Bitter, Savage; Genocide It Wasn't," *Wall Street Journal*, December 31, 1999, p. A1.

107. For instance, Holly Burkhalter, Washington director of Physicians for Human Rights, now concedes, "I was wrong. . . . but if you wait until it (genocide) is proved to you six ways to Sunday, you haven't prevented it, have you?" From Pearl and Block, "Body Count."

108. Ibid.

109. *Kosovo/Kosova: As Seen, As Told, Part I*, chapter 5, p. 100.

110. Barutciski, "Western Diplomacy," p. 10.

111. Maddox et al., "The 80 Days War."

112. See, for instance, Thomas W. Lippman and Bradley Graham, "NATO Takes New Look At Options for Invasion; 20,000 Kosovo Refugees to Be Allowed into US," *Washington Post*, April 22, 1999, p. A1.

113. As one observer noted when evaluating the state of play during this period, with help from Russian Prime Minister Primakov, "Milosevic has begun a diplomatic counteroffensive aimed at making himself appear reasonable, even moderate. It is a measure that can hardly fail to sap NATO's already uncertain resolve. And for good measure, he has made a new friend in Iraqi President Sadaam Hussein—a leader well schooled in the art of turning military defeat into political triumph." See again Carnes Lord, "What Milosevic Really Wants."

114. See Ball, "Policy or Panic?" part 2 and John Gaps, "Allies Add Air Power; 600 Jets Deployed; More Refugees Flee," *Chicago Sun-Times*, April 11, 1999, Sunday News Section, p. 1.

115. See again, Ball, "Policy or Panic?" part 2.

116. Ibid., p. 110.

117. See, for instance, *Kosovo/Kosova: As Seen, As Told, Part I*, especially pp. 104–11.

118. However, one incident in particular is suggestive. A surge in outflows did occur almost immediately (circa April 14) after news broke of a NATO airstrike on a

refugee convoy near Djakovica, which killed sixty people. See Thomas Lippman and Charles Babington, "Allies Confirm Civilian Attack; Clinton Defends Air Campaign," *Washington Post*, April 16, 1999, p. A1. It is possible that Milosevic anticipated an upsurge in public outrage after the NATO bombing and sought to take advantage of it by ratcheting up the pace of cross-border expulsions. (It should be noted that many of those who crossed during this peak period had left their homes sometime earlier; they just did not cross the border until mid-April.) See Ball, "Policy or Panic?" part 2. This escalation subsided again after a few days, such that four or five days later, "only a handful" of refugees crossed into Macedonia, while the Albanian border "remained essentially closed." From Lippman and Graham, "NATO Takes New Look."

119. A report by Natasa Kandic of the Belgrade-based human rights group the Humanitarian Law Center is instructive. She reports that on March 30 she drove around downtown Pristina and into a part of town where everyone was Albanian. There she "'encountered groups of people discussing what to do: should they make their way to the border or stay until the police ordered them out of their homes?' She then joined a column of cars heading for the border, apparently without having been coerced." Cited in Judah, *Kosovo*, p. 242.

120. See, for instance, Lippman and Babington, "Allies Confirm Civilian Attack."

121. See again Physicians for Human Rights, *War Crimes in Kosovo*, p. 40, which reports that, of those interviewed, nearly one quarter (23 percent) of respondents left Kosovo "because they feared Serb forces" and 9 percent gave no reason—or cited non-Serb-related reasons—for leaving, thus indicating that about one-third of those who fled self-reportedly left voluntarily. (This is not to suggest that they had no reason to fear the Serbs, only that they left without actually being pushed. This distinction is important in that such displacements complicate analysis of expulsion patterns.)

122. On May 10, Milosevic announced an end to attacks on the KLA, claiming that some units of the army and police were being withdrawn. NATO, however, disputed this claim.

123. "Bombs over Belgrade, Diplomatic As Well As Military," *Economist*, May 8, 1999, p. 49.

124. Offers included one from normally refugee-allergic Britain, which said it would take one thousand a week, and from Italy, which said it would take ten thousand more as well as ferry more aid to the camps in Macedonia. See "Guns or Refugees—An Unequal Alliance?" *Economist*, July 3, 1999, p. 50. Several weeks earlier, the United States had also reversed its policy and offered to take twenty thousand refugees, while Canada agreed to take five thousand. See Lippman and Graham, "NATO Takes a New Look."

125. "Policy or Panic?" part 1.

126. Cited in Judah, *Kosovo*, pp. 241–42.

127. The fact that most reports of extortion and robberies are associated with the police is consistent with the theory that the police and army pursued different strategies. See *Kosovo/Kosova: As Seen, As Told*, especially pp. 103–4 and pp. 110–12, as well as reports from different municipalities in part 1, chapter 5, in which most looting, robberies, appropriation of automobiles, and profiteering, that is, gouging those

attempting to buy transportation out of the province, is connected with the police and paramilitaries rather than the army.

128. The paramilitaries in Kosovo were particularly savage and would taunt people with queries about, "where were their NATO saviors now when they needed them?" See again *Kosovo/Kosova: As Seen, As Told, Part I*, especially p. 105, as well as reports from different municipalities in chapter 5.

129. American Radio Works, "Kosovo: The Promise of Justice," interviews with militia members, found at www.americanradioworks.org/features/kosovo/more.htm.

130. A Carnegie Endowment for International Peace report from 1913 is instructive on this point. "Thus generally speaking, the army of the enemy found on its way nothing but villages which were either half deserted or entirely abandoned. To execute the orders for extermination, it was only necessary to set fire to them. The population, warned by the glow from these fires, fled in all haste. There followed a veritable migration of peoples." From Carnegie Endowment for International Peace, *Report of the International Commission to Inquire into the Causes and Conduct of the Balkan Wars* (Washington, D.C., 1914), pp. 151. See also Barry Posen, "Military Responses to Refugee Disasters," *International Security*, vol. 21, no. 1, (Summer 1996), pp. 72–111, for an insightful typology of the reasons people flee their homes during conflicts.

131. See, for instance, Joseph Legvold, "NATO's Post-Cold War Collective Action Problem" *International Security*, vol. 23, no. 1 (Summer 1998), pp. 78–106.

132. Lippman, "NATO Expands Fleet of Aircraft."

133. Tony Blair, "Doctrine of the International Community." President Clinton also publicly put NATO on the hook, so to speak. See, for instance, William Jefferson Clinton, "A Just and Necessary War," *New York Times*, May 23, 1999, p. 17.

134. General Wesley Clark, *Waging Modern War* (New York: Public Affairs, 2001), p. 171. Albright reportedly responded, "Yes, I think so, too." See again p. 171.

135. See William Drozdiak, "European Allies Balk At Expanded Role to NATO," *Washington Post*, February 22, 1998, p. A27.

136. As Philip Gordon has pointedly asked, "If the [first] Yugoslav crisis on Europe's periphery—combined with a US policy that was erratic, uncertain, and domineering at the same time—was not enough to motivate . . . [adoption of] common security policies and military integration, what will?" See Philip Gordon, "Europe's Uncommon Foreign Policy," *International Security*, vol. 22, no. 3 (Winter 1997/1998), p. 76.

137. Doyle McManus, "Nineteen Countries Speak with One Voice," *Los Angeles Times*, April 24, 1999.

138. See again Gordon, "Europe's Uncommon Foreign Policy."

139. Certainly some of the threats issued from Belgrade implied as much. And refugee expert Kathleen Newland contends that "Milosevic very consciously directed refugee flows from Kosovo toward Macedonia rather than toward Albania because Macedonia had a much more complicated ethnic mix, was politically more fragile, and had its own problems with its own ethnic Albanian population." See again *Refugees as Weapons of War* program transcript.

140. From Michael Barutciski and Astri Suhrke, "Lessons from the Kosovo Refugee Crisis: Innovations in Protection and Burden-Sharing," *Journal of Refugee Studies*, vol. 14, no. 2 (2001), p. 101.

141. Ibid.

142. Ibid. See Richard Caplan, "Kosovo: The Implications for Humanitarian Intervention," *Forced Migration Review*, vol. 5, (August 5, 1999), p. 7 (inset box), for a breakdown of the locations to which the 91,000 Kosovars were transported during the Humanitarian Evacuation Program (HEP).

143. Holger Jensen, "New Dangers Now Arise in Kosovo Crisis," *Denver Rocky Mountain News*, April 1, 1999, p. 2A. "The bilaterals, as the NATO armies came to be known, were hugely important in the relief effort, not only providing the logistical support traditionally associated with the role of the military, but also setting up and managing refugee camps on behalf of the governments that they represented," From Toby Porter, "Coordination in the Midst of Chaos: The Refugee Crisis in Albania," *Forced Migration Review*, vol. 5, (August 5, 1999), electronic version.

144. See www.gallup.hu/gallup/self/polls/Kosovo/bombings.htm. To be fair, not all polling results are equally grim. Some European states strongly supported hosting refugees, even if only for a limited period.

145. *Der Spiegel*, March 29, 1999. This level of support was replicated in many NATO countries, including Britain, France, and the Netherlands, where, throughout the early part of the war, support for the bombing—but not for the introduction of ground troops—was strong. See, for instance, Richard Boudreaux, "Europeans Hardened by Reports of Serb Atrocities," *Los Angeles Times*, April 1, 1999, p. 8.

146. Reportedly, on the eve of the NATO summit, Clinton urged Blair to stop talking about the possibility of introducing ground troops into the campaign because "it caused domestic problems for allies." From Dana Priest, "A Decisive Battle That Never Was," *Washington Post*, September 19, 1999, p. A1.

147. Michael Ignatieff, *Virtual War* (New York: Metropolitan Books, 2000), introduction.

148. Holger Jensen, "New Dangers Now Arise in Kosovo Crisis," *Denver Rocky Mountain News*, April 1, 1999, p. 2A.

149. For instance, as one NATO official put it: "'We were all hamstrung.' As the war dragged on, he says, 'NATO saw a fatigued press corps drifting towards the contrarian story: civilians killed by NATO's bombs. NATO bombs. [In response], NATO stepped up its claims about Serb 'killing fields.'" From Pearl and Block, "Body Count." In the same vein, refugee reports that Serb soldiers used rape to drive expulsions "went from an assertion to an assumption of a systematic pattern in the span of a day." From Frank Bruni, "Dueling Perspectives: Two Views of Reality Vying on the Airwaves," *New York Times*, April 18, 1999, p. 8. See also Katherine Butler, "War in the Balkans: Briefings' NATO Spokesman Accused of Exaggerations by the French," *Independent*, April 10, 1999, p. 3.

150. Butler, "War in the Balkans."

151. One illuminating example is offered by Jamie Shea's response to criticism of NATO after the bombing of the refugee convoy near Djakovica. Shea turned the argument on its head and asserted that the blame for the refugees' deaths lay with Milosevic, not with the pilots who make mistakes "in the heat of bombings." After all, "why was a refugee convoy escorted by Serb military vehicles on the Prizren-Djakovica road

at 3:00 yesterday afternoon in the first place?" From Lippman, "Allies Confirm Civilian Attack."

152. Thomas Lippman, "NATO Commits Troops, Aircraft to Help Feed, Shelter Refugees, Allies Discuss a Force to Ensure Safe Return," *Washington Post*, April 4, 1999, p. A1.

153. Norman Kempster, "Peace Organizations Set to Take on Clinton," *Los Angeles Times*, May 21, 1999, p. A24.

154. Schelling, *Arms and Influence*, p. 170.

155. As the KLA now readily admits it did.

156. Ted Galen Carpenter, "Perils of the New NATO," *NATO's Empty Victory* (Washington, D.C.: The CATO Institute, 2000), p. 178. Also see again Blair speech, "Doctrine," April 1999.

# 9

## Propaganda System One: From Diem and Arbenz to Milosevic

*Edward S. Herman*

The way in which the mainstream media have handled the turning of Milosevic over to the Hague Tribunal once again reinforces my belief that the United States is not only number one in military power but also in the effectiveness of its propaganda system, which is vastly superior to any past or present state-managed system. The main characteristic of the U.S. model is that, while offering diversity on many subjects, on core issues—like "free trade" and the need for a huge "defense" establishment—and on the occasions when the corporate and political establishment needs their service—as in legitimating George W. Bush's presidency in the wake of an electoral coup d'etat, or supporting the "sanctions of mass destruction" on Iraq—the media can be relied on to expound and propagandize what would be called a "party line" if done in China. They do sometimes depart from the official position as regards tactics, arguing, for example, that the government is not attacking the enemy with sufficient ferocity (Iraq and Yugoslavia), or that the cost of the enterprise is perhaps excessive (the Vietnam War, from 1968), but that the enemy is truly evil and the national cause meritorious is never debatable. The debates over tactics helpfully obscure the agreement on ends.

A further important feature of the U.S. system is that this propaganda service is provided without government censorship or coercion, by self-censorship alone, with the truth of the propaganda line internalized by the numerous media participants. This internalization of belief makes it possible for media personnel to be enthusiastic spokespersons in pushing the party line, thereby giving it a naturalness that is lacking in crude systems of government-enforced propaganda.

A third feature of the system is that the party lines are regularly supported by nongovernmental and self-proclaimed "nonpartisan" thinktanks like the

American Enterprise Institute and Independent International Commission on Kosovo, nongovernmental organizations like the Open Society Institute and Human Rights Watch, and assorted ex-leftists and liberal and left journals that, on particular subjects, "see the light." These organizations are commonly funded by interests (and governments) with an axe to grind, and they serve those interests, but the media feature them as nonpartisan and give special attention to the ex-leftists and dissidents who now see the light. This helps firm up the consensus and further marginalizes those still in darkness.

A final feature of the U.S. system is that it works so well that a sizable fraction of the public doesn't recognize the media's propaganda role and accepts the media's own self-image as independent, adversary, truth-seeking, and helping the public to "assert meaningful control over the political process" (former Supreme Court Justice Lewis Powell). This public bamboozlement is aided by the facts that the media are fairly numerous, are not government controlled, have many true believers among their editors and journalists (the second characteristic), are supported by NGOs and elements of the "left" (the third feature), and regularly proclaim their independence and squabble furiously with government and among themselves. Even those who doubt the media's claims of truth-seeking are often carried along, or confused, by the force and self-assurance of the participants in this great propaganda machine.

## PARTY LINE CONSENSUS

An important operational characteristic of the system, which facilitates general adherence to the party line without overt coercion, is the assurance and speed with which the line is established as a consensus truth, so that deviations and dissent quickly take on the appearance of foolishness or pathology, as well as suspiciously unpatriotic behavior. Noam Chomsky and I found that the very asking of questions about the numerous fabrications, ideological role, and absence of any beneficial effects for the victims in the anti–Khmer Rouge propaganda campaign of 1975–1979 was unacceptable and was treated almost without exception as "apologetics for Pol Pot."

That "free trade" is beneficial and in the "national interest" whereas "protectionism" is hurtful and a creature of "special interests" is a consensus party line of the mainstream media today that profoundly biases their treatment of trade agreements and protests against corporate globalization at Seattle, Washington, D.C., Quebec City, and Genoa.[1] The consensus around a party line is very quickly established in dealing with international crises. Once an enemy is demonized—from Ho Chi Minh in Vietnam and Jacobo Guzman Arbenz in Guatemala in the early 1950s to Slobodan Milosevic in the 1990s and up to today—the media display a form of hysteria that helps mobilize the public in support of whatever forms of violence the government wishes to carry out. They become a virtual propaganda arm of the government, joining with it in the common fight against "another Hitler." Under these conditions, remarkable structures of disinformation can be built, institutionalized, and remain parts of historic memory even in the face of ex post confutations, which are kept out of sight. Let me give a few short illustrations before showing how this exceptional propaganda service applies to the Milosevic/Tribunal case.

## RED THREAT AS PARTY LINE: VIETNAM AND GUATEMALA

In the Cold War years, propaganda service and mobilization of the public was commonly framed around the Red Threat. This general demonization of the target produced the requisite hysteria and media identification with "us" and complete loss of critical capability. When the U.S.-imported puppet to South Vietnam, Ngo Dinh Diem, won a plebiscite in 1954 with over 99 percent of the votes, an outcome that would elicit much sarcasm if realized in an enemy state, this was not news here. And from then onward, U.S. support of a government admittedly lacking an indigenous constituency, relying on state terror and U.S. financial and military aid, was treated in the mainstream media as entirely reasonable and just.

The self-deception and patriotic biases internalized by media personnel were displayed in their 100 percent inability, from 1954 to today, to call the U.S. intervention and ultimate direct invasion of Vietnam either an "invasion" or "aggression." It was also beautifully illustrated in James Reston's Orwellian statement of 1965 that the United States, which from beginning to almost the very end believed it could impose its preferred rulers by virtue of its superior military power, was in Vietnam to establish the "principle . . . that no state shall use military force or the threat of military force to achieve its political objectives."

Another remarkable case of propaganda service occurred as the United States destabilized Guatemala's democratic government in the years 1950–1953 and then removed it by means of a U.S.-organized "contra" invasion in 1954. U.S. hostility began when this government passed a law in 1947 allowing the organization of unions, and active destabilization followed and accelerated upon its attempt to engage in moderate land reforms, partly at the expense of the United Fruit Company. From 1947 the search was on for "communists" to explain the reformist policies and to rationalize the hostile intervention. The U.S. mainstream media became completely hysterical over this Red Threat from 1950 onward, very worried that Arbenz would not allow elections to take place in 1951—this same media had not been bothered by the Ubico dictatorship, 1931–1944, and was entirely unconcerned with the absence of democracy from 1954 onward—and featured a stream of alarming reports on Red influence in that country and an alleged "reign of terror." There were endless headlines in the *New York Times* like "Soviet Agents Plotting to Ruin Unity, Defenses of America" (June 22, 1950); "Guatemalan Reds Seek Full Power" (May 21, 1952); "How Communists Won Control of Guatemala" (March 1, 1953), and even *The Nation* ran a sleazy putdown of the democratic government under attack (March 18, 1950).

This was all hysterical nonsense—even court historian Ronald Schneider, after reviewing the documents seized from the Reds in Guatemala, concluded that the Reds had never controlled Guatemala, and that the Soviet Union "made no significant or even material investment in the Arbenz regime" and paid little attention to Central America—but it was effective in making the overthrow of an elected government acceptable to the U.S. public. And the media's propaganda service was completed by their long cover-up of the hugely undemocratic aftermath of the successful termination of the brief democratic experiment.[2] No government-managed propaganda system could have done a better job of mobilizing the public on the basis of systematic disinformation; and the achievement here is especially impressive given the fact that it was all done with the aim and effect of ending a liberal democracy by violence and installing a terror state.

## BULGARIAN CONNECTION

Another illustration of outstanding, even remarkable, propaganda service, and one pertinent to the ongoing Milosevic-Tribunal drama because it involved a judicial proceeding, was the "Bulgarian Connection." The Reagan administration had been anxious to demonize the Soviet Union in the early and mid-1980s, and the assassination attempt against Pope John Paul II in May 1981 provided an opportunity to pin the attempt on the KGB and their Bulgarian client. The Turkish fascist Mehmet Ali Agca, who had shot the Pope, had spent time in Bulgaria (as well as in ten other countries).

After seventeen months in prison in Italy, and after numerous visits by secret service, judicial, and papal personnel, who had admittedly offered him inducements to "confess," he claimed that he was on the Bulgarian-KGB payroll, had cased the joint with Bulgarian officials in Rome, and had visited one of them in his apartment. Although the case was laughably implausible, the U.S. mainstream media bought it with enthusiasm and failed to acknowledge their gullibility and propaganda role even after CIA professionals told congress during the CIA confirmation hearings on Robert Gates in 1991 that they knew the Connection was false because, among other reasons, they had penetrated the Bulgarian secret services.

A very important feature of the media's treatment of the Bulgarian Connection, very similar to that which they apply now to the Hague Tribunal in its pursuit of Milosevic, was their pretense that the Italian judiciary, police, and political system were only seekers after truth and justice, even a bit fearful of finding the Bulgarians guilty. The *New York Times* even editorialized that the Reaganites were aghast at the implications of a Soviet involvement in the assassination attempt ("recoiled from the devastating implication that Bulgaria's agents were bound to have acted only on a signal from Moscow," Oct. 30, 1984), a propaganda lie confuted by the CIA professionals in 1991, who explained that their own doubts were overruled by the Reaganite leaders of the CIA who insisted on pushing the Connection as true. The Bulgarian Connection can be well explained by the exceptional corruption of the Italian system and the service of this manufactured connection to the Cold Warriors serving the Italian state (and their U.S. parent). This explanation was expressed often in the Italian media during the 1980s, but not in the U.S. mainstream media where, with only insignificant exceptions, the propaganda line functioned without a hitch.[3]

## HAGUE TRIBUNAL: SERVING US, SO NO AWKWARD QUESTIONS, PLEASE!

In the case of the Hague Tribunal also, the mainstream media portray it as a presumably unbiased judicial body seeking justice with an even hand, despite the massive evidence that it is a political and propaganda arm of the United States and other NATO powers. Its ultimate propaganda service was performed in May, 1999, when the prosecutor of the International Crimes Tribunal for the former Yugoslavia (ICTY), Louise Arbour, announced the indictment of Yugoslav president Milosevic and four associates for war crimes. This was done, hastily, at a time when NATO was increasingly targeting the civilian infrastructure of Yugoslavia in order to hasten that country's surrender. NATO needed this public relations support as a cover for its own war crimes—the Sixth Convention of Nuremberg prohibits and makes a war crime the targeting of civilian facilities not based on "military necessity"—and the ICTY provided it, with the indictment quickly greeted by Albright and James Rubin as justifying NATO's bombing policy.

To my knowledge, the U.S. mainstream media have never once suggested that this indictment servicing the NATO war discredited the Tribunal as an independent judicial body. *The New York Times*'s Steven Erlanger even explained to Terry Gross that this indictment displayed Arbour's independence, as she was allegedly fearful that Milosevic would escape punishment in a political deal if she didn't move quickly! (Fresh Air, National Public Radio, July 12, 2001). Erlanger was not alone in offering this imbecile analysis, which not only failed to recognize the indictment's service to NATO's immediate policy needs, but also ignored other evidence of Arbour's and the Tribunal's deference to U.S. and NATO desires. The media also failed to raise any questions about Arbour's statement of May 24, 1999, that, although people are "entitled to the presumption of innocence until they are convicted," she was issuing the indictment because "the evidence . . . raises serious questions about their suitability to be guarantors of any deal, let alone a peace agreement"—that is, she found them guilty before they were convicted and thought that on this basis she should interfere with any possible political settlement.

On the other hand, Arbour and her successor, Carla Del Ponte, have never found allies of the NATO powers or the NATO powers themselves worthy of indictment, even when they did exactly the same things for which the NATO targets were indictable. Thus, Serb leader Milan Martic was indicted for launching a rocket cluster-bomb attack on military targets in Zagreb in May 1995, with the very use of cluster bombs cited by the Tribunal as showing the aim of "terrorizing the civilians of Zagreb." But NATO's cluster-bomb raids on Nis on May 7, 1999, far from any military target, and the forty-eight-hour Croat army shelling of civilian targets in the city of Knin during the August 1995 Croat Operation Storm, produced no indictments. Operation Storm, supported by U.S. officials and helped by U.S.-related professional advisers, resulted in large-scale expulsions and the killing of many Serb civilians, but neither Croat leader Tudjman nor the supportive U.S. officials were indicted, and Croat military officials also escaped indictment till Del Ponte recently claimed several in an effort to show her "balance" in the context of the bringing of Milosevic to The Hague.

This double standard, which makes a mockery of justice, has been of absolutely no interest to the U.S. mainstream media; and in his long session with Terry Gross on July 12, when asked "What Americans might be brought to stand trial before an international court?" Steven Erlanger failed to come up with a single name for any actions in the Balkans (and Gross did not follow up on his nonresponse).

Under pressure to address NATO's wartime activities, which had resulted in the deaths of many Serb civilians—estimates run from five hundred to three thousand—Tribunal prosecutor Carla Del Ponte issued a report in June 2000 that declared NATO not guilty. But the document supporting this conclusion was not based on any investigation by the Tribunal, and it openly acknowledged a heavy dependence on NATO sources, asserting "that the NATO and NATO countries press statements are generally reliable and that explanations have been honestly given." Canadian legal scholar and expert on the Tribunal Michael Mandel asks: "Can you imagine how many indictments would have been issued against the Serb leadership if the Prosecutor had stopped at the FRY press releases?" But this remarkable Del Ponte report was of no interest to the mainstream media.

Also of no interest to the media is the fact that the Tribunal has been described by John Laughland in the *Times* (London) as "a rogue court with rigged rules" (June 17, 1999). As normal practice, it violates virtually every standard of due process: it fails to separate prosecution and judge; it does not accord the right to bail or a speedy trial; it has no clear definition of burden of proof required for a conviction; it has no independent appeal body; it allows a defendant to be tried twice for the same crime; suspects can be held for ninety days without trial; confessions are presumed to be free and voluntary unless the contrary is established by the prisoner; and witnesses can testify anonymously, with hearsay evidence admissible. These points are almost never mentioned in the U.S. mainstream media or considered relevant to the legitimacy of the Tribunal or the likelihood that Milosevic will get a fair trial.

The Tribunal's biased performance follows from the fact that it was organized by the United States and its close allies, is funded by them and staffed with their approval, and depends on them for information and other support. The Tribunal's charter requirements that its expenses shall be provided in the UN general budget (Article 32) and that the Prosecutor shall act independently and not take instructions from any government (Article 16) have been systematically ignored. Gabrielle Kirk McDonald, former president of the Hague Tribunal—before that a director, and now "Special Counsel to the Chairman on Human Rights," of Freeport-McMoRan Copper & Gold Inc., a notorious human rights violator working in Irian Jaya with the cooperation of the Indonesian army—stated in 1999 that Tribunal personnel regard Madeleine Albright as the "mother of the tribunal." NATO public relations man Jamie Shea pointed out in a May 17, 1999, press conference in Brussels that Arbour will investigate "because we will allow her to"; that the NATO countries are the ones "that have provided the finance to set up the Tribunal"; that they are the ones who do the leg work "and have been detaining indicted war criminals"; and that when she "looks at the facts she will be indicting people of Yugoslav nationality" and not folks from NATO.

But neither this open admission that the NATO powers controlled the Tribunal nor the evidence of serious abuses of the judicial process that has characterized its work have been of interest to the mainstream media. As with the prosecution of the Bulgarian Connection, the Hague Tribunal is servicing the U.S. government and its aims, and the media therefore regard any bias or political service as reasonable and take them as givens. Because of their internalized belief that their country is good and would only support justice, the media can't even imagine that any conflict of interest exists. This is deep bias.

Also, no questions come up in this context as to why there are no tribunals for Suharto, Wiranto (the Indonesian general in charge of the destruction of East Timor in 1999), or Ariel Sharon. These are our allies, even if major state terrorists, who received and still receive our support, so that, in a well-managed propaganda system, the failure to mention their exclusion from a system of global enforcement of the new ethical order opposed to ethnic cleansing and human rights violations is entirely appropriate.

## DISINFORMATION AS CONSENSUS HISTORY: MILOSEVIC AND THE BALKANS

From the time the U.S. government decided to target Milosevic and the Serbs as the root of Balkan evil in the early 1990s, the U.S. propaganda system began its work of demonization of the target, enhanced atrocities management, and the necessary rewriting of history. The integration of government needs and media service was essentially complete, and was beautifully symbolized by the marriage during the crisis years of State Department public relations chief James Rubin and Christiane Amanpour, CNN's main reporter on the Kosovo war, whose reports could have come from Rubin himself. More recently, in connection with Milosevic's transfer to The Hague, Amanpour entertained Richard Holbrooke on the subject, and the two, speaking as old comrades-in-arms, congratulated one another on a joint success, just as a policy-enforcing official might express mutual congratulations with a public relations officer (Holbrooke applauded Amanpour's "fantastic coverage of the war throughout the last decade").[4]

It should be noted that Holbrooke visited Zagreb two days before Croatia launched Operation Storm in August 1995, almost certainly talking over and giving U.S. approval to the imminent military operation, reminiscent of Henry Kissinger's visit to Jakarta just before Indonesia's invasion of East Timor in September 1975. As Operation Storm involved a major program of killings and expulsions, with killings greatly in excess of the numbers attributed to Milosevic in the Tribunal indictment of May 22, 1999, an excellent case can be made that Holbrooke should be tried for war crimes. We may also be sure that Christiane Amanpour's "fantastic coverage" of the wars in Yugoslavia did not deal with Operation Storm or mention Holbrooke's and the U.S. role in that butchery and massive ethnic cleansing.

As NATO prepared to go to war, which began on March 24, 1999, the media followed the official lead in focusing heavily on Serb atrocities in Kosovo, with great and indignant attention to the Racak massacre of January 15, 1999. The failure of the Rambouillet Conference they blamed on Serb intransigence, again following the official line. During the eighty-seven-day bombing war, the media focused even more intensively on atrocities (Serb, not NATO) and passed along the official estimates of one hundred thousand Kosovo Albanian murders (U.S. Defense Secretary William Cohen) and other estimates, smaller and larger. They also accepted the claim that the Serb violence that followed the bombing would have taken place anyway, by plan, so that the bombing, instead of causing the escalated violence, was justified by its occurrence ex post.

In the post-bombing era, a number of developments have occurred that have challenged the official line. But the mainstream media have not let them disturb the institutionalized untruths. Let me list some of these and describe the media's mode of deflection.

1. *Racak Massacre.* The only pre-bombing act of Serb violence listed in the Tribunal indictment of Milosevic on May 22, 1999, was an alleged massacre of Albanians by the Serbs at Racak on January 15, 1999. The Serbs had carried out this action with invited OSCE representatives (and AP photographers) on the scene, but on the following day, after KLA reoccupation of the village, some forty to forty-five bodies were on display for the U.S.-OSCE official William Walker and the media. The authenticity of this massacre, which follows a long pattern of convenient but contrived atrocities to meet a PR need—well described in George Bogdanich's and Martin Lettmayer's brilliant film *The Avoidable War*—was immediately challenged by journalists in France and Germany, but no doubts whatever showed up in the U.S. media. Christophe Chatelet of *Le Monde* was in Racak the day of the "massacre" and left at dusk, as did the OSCE observers and Serb police, without witnessing any massacre. The AP photographers and on-the-scene OSCE representatives have never been available for corroboration or denial, and the forensic report of the Finnish team that examined the bodies at the behest of the OSCE has never been made public. The issue is still contested, but a very strong case can be made that the Racak "massacre" was a staged event.[5]

But the strong challenging evidence has been effectively blacked out in the U.S. mainstream media, and the "massacre" is taken as an established and unquestioned truth (e.g., Amanpour and Carol Lin, CNN Live at Daybreak, July 3, 2001; Steven Erlanger in his July 12 interview with Terry Gross). Why didn't the Serb army remove the incriminating bodies, as the propaganda machine claimed, then and now, that they were doing as a matter of policy directed from above? As in the case of the analyses and evidence in the 1980s that Agca might have been coached to implicate the Bulgarians and KGB, the U.S. mainstream media refuse to burden a useful party line with inconvenient questions and facts. Also, while giving heavy, uncritical, and indignant attention to Racak, the media have never allowed the far larger and unambiguous massacre of civilians at Liquica in East Timor on April 6, 1999– three months after Racak—to reach public consciousness. This was a massacre by the U.S. ally Indonesia, U.S. officials did not feature it, and the media therefore served national policy by giving it short shrift.

2. *U.S. and NATO Opposition to Serb "Ethnic Cleansing" and "Genocide" as the Basis of the NATO Bombing.* The official and media propaganda line is that the United States and NATO powers were deeply upset by Serb violence in Kosovo and eventually went to war to stop it. But there are problems with this view. For one thing, evidence has turned up showing that Washington, through its own agencies or hired mercenaries, actually aided and trained the KLA prior to the bombing, and in this and other ways encouraged them in provocations that stimulated Serb violence.[6] The postwar publication by the NATO Parliamentary Assembly, *General Report: Kosovo Aftermath*, noted that "Under the influence of the Kosovo Verification Mission the level of Serbian repression eased off" in late 1998, but "on the other hand, there was a lack of effective measures to curb the UCK [KLA]" which had an interest in "worsening the situation." In short, U.S. policy before the bombing encouraged violence in Kosovo. The evidence for this has been made public abroad, but it has not yet surfaced in the U.S. mainstream media.

A second problem is that NATO supplied greatly inflated estimates of Serb killings and expulsions in Kosovo, quite obviously trying to prepare the ground for bombing. The claim that Serbian policy constituted "ethnic cleansing" and even "genocide" has long been confuted by OSCE, State Department, and human rights groups' findings of limited and targeted Serb violence, and by disclosure of an internal German Foreign Office report that even denies the appropriateness of the use of "ethnic cleansing" to describe Serb behavior.[7] These contesting points of evidence, even though coming from establishment sources, are not only off the screen for the mainstream media, they are ignored, and the old lies are repeated by Christopher Hitchens in *The Nation*.[8] A third problem is: how could this humanitarian motive be driving Clinton and Blair in Kosovo when they had both actively supported Turkey's far larger-scale ethnic cleansing of Kurds throughout the 1990s? The mainstream media dealt with this and similar problems by not letting the issue be raised.

3. *NATO Reasonableness, Serb Intransigence at Rambouillet.* On the question of negotiations versus the use of force, the official line has been that the NATO powers made reasonable negotiating offers to the Serbs, trying to get "Serbia and the Kosovo Albanians to come to a compromise" (Tim Judah), but that the Serb refusal to negotiate led to the bombing war. This line was demonstrated to be false when it was disclosed that NATO had inserted

a proviso demanding full occupation by NATO of all of Yugoslavia, admitted by a State Department official to have been a deliberate "raising of the bar" to allow bombing.[9] This disclosure has been comprehensively suppressed in the mainstream media, allowing the propaganda lie to be repeated today (Judah's repetition of the lie was on June 29, 2001).

4. *Serb Genocide by Plan during the NATO Bombing*. Three big lies expounded during the NATO bombing war were that (1) the Serbs were killing vast numbers; (2) they were doing this and expelling still larger numbers in a process of "ethnic cleansing" and "genocide"; and (3) that they had planned mass killing and expulsions anyway, so that these could not be attributed to the bombing war or the kind of fighting and atrocities characteristic of a brutal civil war. It is now clear that, while large numbers did flee, this included at least an equal proportion of Serbs and that many fled without forcible expulsion; and it is also clear that, while there were brutal killings, these fell far short of the ten thousand to fifty thousand claimed by NATO. It is also now on the record that NATO and the KLA were engaged in joint military actions during the bombing war and that expulsions were concentrated in areas of KLA strong support, pointing to a military logic to Serb actions.[10] The claim that the Serbs intended to do this anyway has never been supported by any evidence.

In Guatemala after 1947, the search was on for communists; in Kosovo, during and after the bombing war, the search was on for dead bodies (whereas there was no interest in or search for dead bodies in East Timor after the Indonesian massacres of 1999, in accord with the same propaganda service). The bodies found in Kosovo received great publicity, but the fact that this immense effort yielded only three thousand to four thousand bodies from all causes and on all sides, and the fact that it fell far short of the NATO-media propaganda claims during the bombing war, has received minimal attention. However, with Milosevic now transferred to The Hague, and a fresh demand arising for bodies whose deaths can be attributed to him, once again the media are coming through with fresh claims of bodies transferred from Kosovo under the villain's direction.

5. *War a Success, Refugees Returned to Kosovo*. But the refugees were produced by the NATO bombing policy itself, and they returned to a shattered country. Furthermore, after the NATO war, there was a REAL ethnic cleansing—in percentage terms the "largest in the Balkan wars" according to Transnational Foundation for Peace director Jan Oberg—with some 330,000 Serbs, Roma, Jews, Turks, and others driven out of Kosovo, while some 3,000 people were killed and disappeared. However, as this has taken place under NATO auspices, the mainstream media, insofar as they mention the real ethnic cleansing at all, have treated it as a semi-approved "vengeance." But

they have mainly dealt with the subject, as they did the post-Arbenz REAL terrorism, by eye aversion.

6. *Milosevic As the Source of the Balkan Conflict.* In virtually all mainstream accounts, it was "Milosevic's murderous decade" (Nordland and Gutman in *Newsweek*, July 9, 2001), Milosevic who "set Yugoslavia to unraveling" (Roger Cohen, *New York Times*, July 1, 2001), "the man who had terrorized the turbulent Balkans for a decade" (*Time*, April 9, 2001). The wars were a "catastrophe that Slobodan Milosevic unleashed" (Tim Judah, *Times* [London], June 29, 2001). This is comic book history that follows the standard demonization process and is refuted by every serious historian dealing with the area (Susan Woodward, Robert Hayden, David Chandler, Lenard Cohen, Raymond Kent, Steven L. Burg, and Paul S. Shoup).

Serious history takes into account, among other matters: (1) the fact that, long before 1990, Yugoslavia had persistent "deep regional and ethnic cleavages" with Croatia, Bosnia, and Kosovo, "all areas of high ethnic fragmentation whose suppression required a strong federal state";[11] (2) the effects of the Yugoslav economic crisis, dating back to 1982, and the IMF/World Bank imposition of deflationary policies on Yugoslavia in the late 1980s, and their consequences; (3) the post-Soviet collapse ending of Western support for the Yugoslav federal state, and German and Austrian collaboration in encouraging the Croatian and Slovenian secession from Yugoslavia without any democratic vote and without any settlement on the status of the large Serb minorities; (4) the West's and Western Badinter Commission's refusal to allow threatened ethnic minorities to withdraw from the new secession states; (5) the U.S. and Western encouragement of the Muslims in Bosnia-Herzegovina to hold out for unity under their control in the face of Serb and Croatian fears and opposition; and (6) the U.S. and NATO support of Croatia and its massive ethnic cleansing of Serbs in Krajina.

The media rarely mention these extremely important external, NATO-inspired causes of ethnic cleansing, or the fact that Milosevic supported many diplomatic initiatives such as the Owen-Vance and Owen-Stoltenberg plans, both unsuccessful because of U.S. encouragement of the Muslims to hold out for more. Heavy German and U.S. responsibility for the breakup of Yugoslavia; the NATO governments' help in the arming of Slovenia, Croatia, the Bosnian Muslims, and the KLA; and the U.S. sabotaging of efforts at negotiated settlements in the early 1990s are all well documented in Bogdanich's and Lettmayer's *The Avoidable War*. The film was shown on the History Channel on April 16, but has otherwise been ignored in Propaganda System Number One for good reason: it not only shows dominant NATO responsibility for the Balkan disaster, it makes the mainstream media's supportive propaganda role crystal clear.

7. *Milosevic's Nationalist Speeches of 1987 and 1989.* It is now rote "history" that in April 1987 Milosevic "endorsed a Serbian nationalist agenda" at Polje in Kosovo and did the same there on June 28, 1989—supposedly heralding his project of Greater Serbia and the coming wars to achieve it. People like Roger Cohen and Steven Erlanger who cite these as "inciting Serb passions" almost surely never bothered to read them (nor did Joe Knowles, who mentions Milosevic's "infamous" speech of June 28 in *In These Times* [Aug. 6, 2001]). In both speeches, Milosevic actually warns against the dangers of nationalism, and while he promises to protect Serbs, he is clearly speaking of the citizens of the Republic of Serbia, not ethnic Serbs; and he describes "Yugoslavia" as "a multinational community . . . [that] can survive only under the conditions of full equality for all nations that live in it" (June 28, 1989).

8. *Milosevic As Dictator.* The June 28, 2001, amended indictment of Milosevic notes that he was "elected" president of Serbia on May 8, 1989, was elected again "in multi-party elections" held in December 1990, was "re-elected" in December 1992, was "elected president of the Federal Republic of Yugoslavia" on July 15, 1997, and was defeated and ousted from power in an election in September 2000. But as Milosevic is on the U.S. hit list, he is referred to repeatedly in the media as a "dictator," a word they were extremely reluctant to apply to Suharto during his thirty-two years as a prized U.S. client. The designation of dictator created a problem for the media because they also found, and continue to find, the Serb populace guilty as "willing executioners" who were properly punished by bombing and who need to acknowledge their guilt. How a people suffering under a dictatorship and dictator-controlled media could be guilty of crimes committed elsewhere is unexplained, but in the U.S. mainstream media, the contradiction remains unchallenged.

9. *The Dictator As Responsible Killer.* In *Manufacturing Consent*, Chomsky and I showed how, in the case of the murder of Jerzy Popieluszko in communist Poland, the media repeatedly sought to prove that the leaders of Poland knew about and were responsible for the killing, whereas in cases where our own leaders or clients are involved, the media are not interested in high-level knowledge and responsibility. It was therefore a foregone conclusion that the media would jump on every claim that Milosevic was behind the deaths in the Balkan wars, and as the Tribunal has to confront the need for such proof to convict the demon, the media are working this terrain with vigor. Some of the alleged new evidence is clearly being leaked from the Tribunal itself (for example, Bob Graham and Tom Walker, "Milosevic Ordered Hiding of Bodies," *Sunday Times* [London], July 8, 2001), a form of propaganda once again revealing that it is not a judicial body but a political instrument. This evidence, which cites the very words used by the dictator in

Belgrade in March 1999 instructing his subordinates to commit crimes ("all civilians killed in Kosovo have to be moved to places where they will not be discovered," in Graham and Walker, "Milosevic Ordered Hiding of Bodies"), has the odor of NATO-bloc disinformation and should be treated with the utmost scepticism. And we may be sure the media will never ask why, with this instruction, "45 bodies" were left on the ground in Racak for the convenience of William Walker and other NATO propagandists.

## CONCLUSION

The U.S. propaganda system is at the peak of its powers in the early years of the twenty-first century, riding the wave of capitalism's triumph, U.S. global hegemony, and the confidence and effective service of the increasingly concentrated and commercialized mainstream media. It is a model propaganda system, its slippages and imperfections adding to its power, given its assured service in times of need. And as described above, in such times, its ability to ignore inconvenient facts, swallow disinformation, and work the public over with propaganda can easily compete with—even surpass—anything found in totalitarian systems.

## NOTES

1. See Edward Herman, "NAFTA, Mexican Meltdown, and the Propaganda System," chap. 14 in Edward Herman, *The Myth of the Liberal Media*, New York: Peter Long, 1999; Rachel Cohen, "For Press, Magenta Hair and Nose Rings Defined Protests," *EXTRA!* July/August 2000; "Action Alert: Police Violence in Genoa—Par for the Course? Media Complacency Helps Normalize Assaults on Demonstrators," *FAIR*, July 26, 2001.

2. On the history of this propaganda campaign, see Edward Herman, "Returning Guatemala to the Fold," in Gary Rawnsley, ed., *Cold-War Propaganda in the 1950s*, New York: Macmillan, 1999; more broadly, see Piero Gleijeses, *Shattered Hope*, Princeton, N.J.: Princeton University Press, 1991.

3. See Herman and Brodhead, *Rise and Fall of the Bulgarian Connection*, New York: Sheridan Square, 1986.

4. CNN Live At Daybreak, June 29, 2001.

5. See Christophe Chatelet, in *Le Monde*, Jan. 19, 1999; Professor Dusan Dunjic [a Serb medical participant in the autopsies], "The (Ab)use of Forensic Medicine," www.suc.org/politics/kosovo/documents/Dunjic0499html; J. Raino et al., "Independent Forensic Autopsies in an Armed Conflict: Investigation of the Victims from Racak, Kosovo," *Forensic Science International* 116 (2001), 171–85.

6. Peter Beaumont et al., "CIA's Bastard Army Ran Riot in Balkans," *Observer* (London), March 11, 2001.

7. "Important Internal Documents from Germany's Foreign Office," www.suc.org/kosovo-crisis/documents/ger-gov.html.

8. Christopher Hitchens, "Body Count in Kosovo," *Nation*, June 11, 2001; and Bugdan Denitch, "Citizen of a Lost Country," *In These Times*, May 14, 2001.

9. George Kenney, "Rolling Thunder: The Rerun," *Nation*, June 14, 1999.

10. Daniel Pearl and Robert Block, "War in Kosovo Was Cruel, Bitter, Savage; Genocide It Wasn't," *Wall Street Journal*, Dec. 31, 1999.

11. Lenard Cohen and Paul Warwick, *Political Cohesion in a Fragile Mosaic: The Yugoslav Experience*, Boulder, CO: Westview Press, 1983, pp. 152, 155.

# 10

## Biased Justice: "Humanrightsism" and the International Criminal Tribunal for the Former Yugoslavia

*Robert M. Hayden*

> Justice is the right to do whatever we think must be done, and therefore justice can be anything.
>
> —Meša Selimović, *Death and the Dervish*

Human Rights Watch (HRW) has hailed the new millenium as "the beginning of a new era for the human rights movement," based on "an evolution in public morality."[1] Its *World Report 2000* trumpets the trumping of state sovereignty by human rights,[2] because courts are willing to indict leaders and because organizations such as NATO are willing to intervene militarily against regimes that commit crimes against humanity. HRW cites the International Criminal Tribunals for the former Yugoslavia and for Rwanda, the incipient International Criminal Court, prosecutions of assorted Yugoslavs and Rwandans by Austrian, Belgian, French, German, and Swiss courts, and a Spanish judge's indictment of former Chilean dictator Pinochet. It then mentions the NATO military actions against Yugoslavia and the international intervention in East Timor. It concludes that all of this "foretells an era in which the defense of human rights can move from a paradigm of pressure based on international human rights law to one of law enforcement."[3]

The interlinking rhetorics of law, justice, and morality (along with their opposites of crime and injustice) underpin calls for "humanitarian [military] intervention," and the image of justice via international tribunals is dominant. HRW put "significant progress towards an international system of justice" to prosecute crimes against humanity at the head of its discussion of 1999 achievements[4] and is a strong proponent of the International Criminal Court. The link between tribunals and military intervention is explicit: "like the use of military intervention, the emergence of an international system of justice signals that sovereignty is no longer the barrier it once was to actions against crimes against humanity."[5]

The millennial shift includes a remarkable transformation of the capabilities of "human rights organizations," from persuasion to prosecution:

> Until now . . . human rights organizations could shame abusive governments. They could galvanize diplomatic and economic pressure. They could invoke international human rights standards. But rarely could they trigger prosecution of tyrants or count on governments to use their police powers to enforce human rights law. Slowly, this appears to be changing.[6]

HRW is not the only human rights organization that calls for governments to use their "police powers" to intervene in other states in the name of morality. Doctors without Borders, the organization that won the Nobel Peace Prize in 1999, is another. Bernard Kouchner, UN Governor of Kosovo after NATO's occupation of the place but otherwise one of the founders of Doctors without Borders, stated: "a new morality can be codified in the 'right to intervention' against abuses of national sovereignty. . . . In a world aflame after the Cold War, we need to establish a forward-looking right of the world community to actively interfere in the affairs of sovereign nations to prevent an explosion of human rights violations."[7] To Kouchner, this "right to intervene" is not "human rights imperialism" because

> Everywhere, human rights are human rights. Freedom is freedom. Suffering is suffering. Oppression is oppression. If a Muslim woman in the Sudan opposes painful clitoral excision, or if a Chinese woman opposes the binding of her feet, her rights are being violated. She needs protection. . . . When a patient is suffering and desires care, he or she has the right to receive it. This principle also holds for human rights.[8]

Chinese footbinding was last reported in the 1930s, and both the knowledge and the seriousness of a 1999 writer who calls for protection against it might thus seem doubtful. Yet Kouchner's personal elevation to administrative office as well as his organization's Nobel Peace Prize indicate that the NATO powers, at least, take him seriously. Certainly his sentiments echo those of Vaclav Havel, that "human beings are more important than the state. . . . the idol of state sovereignty must inevitably dissolve" and that NATO's war against Yugoslavia "places human rights above the rights of the state," thus demonstrating that "human rights are indivisible and that if injustice is done to one, it is done to all."[9]

Assertions of devotion to justice, however, are common in the world—probably every political actor makes public claims to be on the side of justice and to uphold morality. HRW and other human rights organizations that call for military intervention are thus acting as classic political figures, demanding the application of massive violence to those whom they define as immoral. As such, their own actions and the actions of those whom they support should be exposed to the same scrutiny that they claim to apply to others.

This article thus takes a close look at one of the most important elements of the new international legal order which human rights activists promote, the International Criminal Tribunal for the Former Yugoslavia (ICTY, or "the Tribunal"). It finds that the ICTY delivers a "justice" that is biased, with prosecutorial decisions based on the national characteristics of the accused rather than on what available evidence indicates that he[10] has done. Evidence of this bias is found in the failure to prosecute NATO personnel for acts that are comparable to those of Yugoslavs already indicted and in the failure to prosecute NATO personnel for prima facie war crimes. This pattern of politically driven prosecution is accompanied by the use of the Tribunal as a political tool for those Western countries that support it, and especially the United States: put bluntly, the Tribunal prosecutes only those whom the Americans want prosecuted, and the United States government threatens prosecution by the supposedly independent ICTY in order to obtain compliance from political actors in the Balkans. Further, judicial decisions by the ICTY render it extremely difficult, if not impossible, for an accused to obtain a fair trial, while the Tribunal has also shown a lack of interest in the investigation of potential prosecutorial misconduct.

An expose of the ICTY has its own intrinsic merits, but there is a wider point. The materials that are cited in this paper are almost all from readily accessible sources, and the *facts* discussed should be well known. Yet the arguments made here are not those commonly taken in regard to the ICTY by those who claim to be human rights advocates, which raises the question of why NATO actions that so clearly violate human rights, and Tribunal actions that so clearly violate fundamental fairness toward defendants, are not the subject of much concern by those who profess to support human rights. The answer is found in the transformation of human rights concepts, from protesting the application of state violence on nonviolent dissidents to demanding the application of massive violence on states deemed to be inferior. This transformation turns human rights into humanrightsism, with the new ism, like most isms, a repudiation in practice of the principles that it supposedly embodies. The ICTY is a particularly striking manifestation of humanrightsism because of the high principles that are routinely invoked to justify it, which are betrayed in practice.

## SELECTIVE PROSECUTION 1: CLUSTER BOMBS AND WAR CRIMES

In July 1995, Milan Martić, President of the Republika Srpska Krajina (the self-proclaimed Serb "Republic" in Croatia), was indicted before the ICTY for violations of the laws and customs of war, in that he had ordered a missile attack on the city of Zagreb in retaliation for the successful Croatian offensive of May 1995, which had driven Serbs from Slavonija.[11] What is interesting about this indictment is that what made the bombardment a war crime was that it was carried out by missiles that had been fitted with cluster-bomb warheads: "warheads containing 288 bomblets, all of which in turn have 400 small steel balls, which are scattered, along with bomblet fragments, on a lethal radius of ten metres. . . . It is used for soft targets, that is troops on the ground and vehicles, not for buildings or military installations."[12] Seven civilians were killed and many more wounded, and it was noted in the Rule 61 hearing that one rocket damaged a home for the aged and a children's hospital.[13]

The use of cluster bombs is key to the Martić indictment, and the nature of these bombs was described in detail in the Rule 61 hearing. As the indictment put it, the rocket in question could "be fitted with different warheads to accomplish different tasks: either to destroy military targets or to kill people. When the [missile] is fitted with 'cluster bomb' . . . it is an anti-personnel weapon designed only to kill people."[14] With this in mind, it is interesting to see the lack of response by the ICTY Prosecutor to NATO's May 7 attack on the city of Niš, when cluster bombs fell on the market, killing fifteen people, and the city's main hospital was also hit.[15] Over the course of the NATO bombings, nine hospitals were damaged or destroyed and over three hundred secondary and elementary schools and other educational institutions were damaged.[16] According to the *Philadelphia Inquirer*, the U.S. Defense Department says that "American planes dropped 1,100 cluster bomb canisters, with 220,000 bomblets, over Kosovo" while "British planes dropped about 500 bombs, each with 147 bomblets."[17] British authorities have acknowledged dropping large numbers of cluster bombs.

One can only wonder why the Prosecutor has not, thus far, seen NATO's use of cluster bombs against the city of Niš as being as serious as the Krajina Serbs' use of cluster-bomb warheads against the city of Zagreb. It will not do to say that NATO was only aiming at military targets and missed; Martić also said that he was aiming at military targets in Zagreb,[18] and, as we have seen, the Prosecutor has already taken the position that cluster bombs are not suitable for use against military targets but only to kill people. Further, it cannot be argued that the U.S. and British commanders did not know that they were risking civilian casualties. Martić's comment to a Western reporter that "I am very sorry if civilian targets were hit because our aim was to hit military targets"[19] may be compared to any of a large number of NATO statements about "collateral damage," including NATO's decision on about May 1 to stop even issuing such apologies.[20] While the Rule 61 hearing on Martić introduced evidence from interviews that showed that Martić targeted cities intentionally, this is also true of NATO generals, including, specifically, American ones, who have recently complained that French politicians did not permit them to attack even more sites in Yugoslav cities.[21]

The reason for the Tribunal's disinterest in NATO's actions is perhaps found in the views expressed by the official NATO spokesman, Dr. Jamie Shea, on May 16 and 17, 1999, when he was questioned during the daily NATO press conferences about the possibility of NATO liability for war crimes before the ICTY. Dr. Shea said on May 16 that "NATO is the friend of the Tribunal . . . NATO countries are those that have provided the finances to set up the Tribunal, we are among the majority financiers." He repeated the same message on May 17: NATO Countries "have established these tribunals . . . fund these tribunals and . . . support on a daily basis their activities." Therefore, he was "certain" that the Prosecutor would only indict "people of Yugoslav nationality."[22]

Any remaining doubts on this last point were put to rest in the last week of the second millennium, when several major newspapers reported that the ICTY Prosecutor was investigating the conduct of NATO pilots and their commanders during the Kosovo war,[23] including commissioning a preliminary study of NATO's use of cluster bombs by looking at the history of such weapons and how they have been used in previous wars.[24] While Milan Martić might well wonder why the Prosecutor had not found it necessary to make such a study before indicting him for using cluster warheads, NATO officials would seem to have little to fear. Within days of the first reports of prosecutorial interest in NATO, tribunal officials were reported as saying that the study was a preliminary, internal document that was highly unlikely to lead to indictments or even to be published.[25] While the Prosecutor had told the London *Observer* on December 26 that if the confidential report indicated that NATO broke the Geneva conventions she would indict those responsible, on December 30 she issued a press release saying that "NATO is not under investigation by the Office of the Prosecutor. . . . There is no formal inquiry into the actions of NATO during the conflict."[26] It is, of course, possible that this quick about-face was unrelated to U.S. government denunciations of the reported inquiry into NATO's actions.[27]

## SELECTIVE PROSECUTION 2: WANTON DESTRUCTION OF PROPERTY

In July 1995, the Prosecutor of the ICTY indicted Radovan Karadžić and Ratko Mladić. One of the sets of acts said to constitute a crime against humanity was "the systematic destruction of Bosnian Muslim and Bosnian

Croat homes and businesses. These homes and businesses were singled out and systematically destroyed in areas where hostilities had ceased or had not taken place."[28] They were also indicted for a "grave breach" of the Geneva Conventions because of "extensive destruction of property": that they had "individually and in concert with others planned, instigated, ordered or otherwise aided and abetted in the planning, preparation or execution of the extensive, wanton and unlawful destruction of Bosnian Muslim and Bosnian Croat property, not justified by military necessity, or knew or had reason to know that subordinates were about to destroy or permit others to destroy the property of Bosnian Muslim or Bosnian Croat civilians or had done so and failed to take necessary and reasonable measures to prevent this destruction or to punish the perpetrators thereof."[29]

With these indictments in mind, the enormous economic destruction of Serbia by NATO is relevant. According to the Group 17 economists (who form the core of the Savez za Promenu, the Serbian opposition coalition most favored by the United States, and thus who may be presumed to be fairly reliable observers), the economic damage caused by the NATO bombings to infrastructure, economic facilities, and noneconomic civil facilities was slightly over four billion dollars.[30] According to the BBC, "at least 30% of the adult population [of Serbia] is unemployed. The economic collapse was caused as NATO switched to infrastructure targets as the war continued"[31]—switched from military targets. In the first month of bombing alone, according to the European movement in Serbia, NATO targets included drug and pharmaceutical plants, tobacco plants and warehouses, printers, and shoe factories,[32] while the G17 economists listed as well wood, textile, and food industries, among others. There was clearly no "military necessity" for hitting these targets, unless "military necessity" is defined as meaning "anything the destruction of which might have a political impact." Neither can it be said that these were "collateral damage." NATO's generals and politicians made a very purposeful decision to attack nonmilitary infrastructure early in the war.[33] They planned the attacks very carefully and only one proposed target was ever rejected because of concerns about its relation to the military.[34] But the Yugoslav military was not the target. NATO generals told the *Philadelphia Inquirer* on May 21 that "Just focusing on fielded forces is not enough. . . . The people have to get to the point that their lights are turned off, their bridges are blocked so they can't get to work." Note that the purpose of destroying these bridges was not military; but this was clear when NATO destroyed the bridges in Novi Sad, five hundred kilometers from Kosovo, installations that clearly did not make the "effective contribution to military action" in Kosovo that would have rendered them legitimate targets under Art. 52 of Protocol I additional to the 1949 Geneva Conventions.

Aryeh Neier has noted that the UN commission that investigated war crimes in Bosnia concluded that "attacking the civilian population is a war crime."[35] There is no question but that, in attacking "infrastructure," NATO attacked civilians. Judging from the wording of the indictments of Karadžić and Mladić, we should expect indictments against those in NATO who planned and carried out these attacks, and against Bill Clinton and Tony Blair for having failed to take necessary and reasonable measures to prevent this destruction or to punish the perpetrators thereof. However, I would suspect that Jamie Shea's view, as quoted in the last section, is accurate, and that we should not expect to see the FOT (Friends of the Tribunal) indicted.

## SELECTIVE PROSECUTION 3: MURDER

On May 27, 1999, Slobodan Milošević, three other Yugoslav politicians, and a Yugoslav Army general were indicted by the Prosecutor of the ICTY for, among other charges, "murder, a violation of the laws and customs of war,"[36] for the deaths of Albanians who were killed by Serb/Yugoslav forces in Kosovo. It would seem, however, that NATO political and military leaders should also be liable for the charge of murder for, at the least, the bombing of the studios of Radio Television Serbia (RTS) on April 22, 1999. There is no question but that the RTS studios were civilian targets: NATO spokesman Jamie Shea had stated as much in an April 12, 1999, letter to the general secretary of the International Federation of Journalists, noting that "television and radio towers are only struck if they are integrated into military facilities."[37] No one has suggested that RTS studios played any military role. Indeed, NATO spokesman David Wilby had stated at NATO's news briefing on April 8, 1999, that RTS would not be bombed if it broadcast Western news broadcasts for six hours per day, which indicates clearly that there was no concern that the studios were integrated into the military. Bombing RTS was an intentional effort to widen the war to civilian targets,[38] which resulted in the deaths of at least sixteen civilians.

HRW agrees that the RTS studios did not constitute a legitimate military target and further states that "NATO failed to provide clear warning of the attacks," as required by the Geneva conventions.[39] Why the deaths of the sixteen journalists would not then be murders is not addressed by HRW.

At least, however, HRW recognizes the RTS dead to be journalists, more than can be said for the Committee to Protect Journalists (CPJ), which publishes a list annually of journalists killed on the job, worldwide.[40] CPJ's 1999 list intentionally excluded the RTS journalists on the grounds that what RTS broadcast was not journalism but propaganda.[41] Rather ironically, at the moment that the NATO bombs killed sixteen RTS people, the station was broadcasting an interview of Yugoslav President Slobodan Milosevic by an American scholar, who did the interview on behalf of a CBS affiliate in Texas. That interview had already been broadcast in the United States, so the CPJ presumably would regard CBS headquarters in New York as having been a legitimate NATO target.

In regard to charges of "propaganda," CBS would actually seem as vulnerable as RTS, but from the other side, if only it had had cruise missiles. In a speech to the National Press Club in Washington D.C., CBS anchorman Dan Rather referred to American attacks on Yugoslav water and power systems as "our" attacks, something that "we" did; and when questioned by a member of the audience on the propriety of a supposedly independent journalist associating himself with one side, Rather responded that

> I'm an American reporter. Yes I'm a reporter and I want to be accurate. I want to be fair. But I'm an American. I consider the U.S. government my government. So yes I do—when U.S. pilots in U.S. aircrafts turn off the lights, for me, it's "we." And about that I have no apology. . . . I'm an American, and I'm an American reporter. And yes, when there's combat involving Americans, [you] can criticize me if you must. Damn me if you must, but I'm always pulling for us to win. [applause from the audience][42]

Presumably, the CPJ would have protested had Rather been injured by Serbs in Belgrade (which he was not), and not only because of his status as a CPJ "Benefactor" who had given more than $25,000 to the organization (as did CBS News).[43] But can we say that he was not engaged in "propaganda" when he was "pulling for us to win"?

CPJ was founded in 1981 to "monitor abuses against the press and to promote press freedom around the world" and "accepts no government funding" in order to ensure its independence.[44] Yet this supposedly independent organization "pulled for us to win," adopting NATO's definition of legitimacy: NATO spokesman Wilby had justified attacking RTS by saying that it "is an instrument of propaganda. . . . It is therefore a legitimate target in this campaign,"[45] and the CPJ agreed. Thus the CPJ abandoned the principles it was founded to embody, in a striking manifestation of "humanrightsism."

## FAILURE TO PROSECUTE PRIMA FACIE WAR CRIMES: DEPRIVING A CIVILIAN POPULATION OF WATER

Art. 54 of the Protocol Additional to the Geneva Conventions of August 12, 1949, is about as unequivocal as humanitarian prohibitions of military targeting get. Entitled "Protection of objects indispensable to the survival of the civilian population," it states (Para. 2) that "it is prohibited to attack, destroy, remove or render useless objects indispensable for the survival of the civilian population, such as . . . drinking water installations and supplies . . . for the specific purpose of denying them for their sustenance value to the civilian population or to the adverse Party, whatever the motive."

On April 25, a "NATO official" who did not wish to be identified told the *Washington Times* that a new phase of the NATO campaign would aim to destroy electrical systems and water systems in Belgrade and in other major Serbian cities in order to take the war directly to civilians.[46] On May 23, "fifteen NATO bombs hit water pumps . . . in the northwestern town of Sremska Mitrovica for the second night in a row."[47] Attacks on May 24 "slashed water reserves by damaging pumps and cutting electricity to the few pumps that were still operative."[48] Only 30 percent of Belgrade's two million people had running water, and the city was down to 10 percent of its water reserves.[49] That these attacks were not aimed at military operations in Kosovo is clear from the remarks attributed by the *Washington Post* to a Pentagon official, who stated that the attacks had been limited to Serbia proper but that "NATO commanders are understood to be planning to extend the attacks to Kosovo."[50] A clearer example of NATO's targeting civilians in Serbia rather than soldiers in Kosovo would be hard to find.

To be sure, NATO responded to criticisms of these attacks by saying that it had not targeted water supplies but only the power system.[51] This was clearly not true in regard to Sremska Mitrovica, but in any event is irrelevant, because what is prohibited is also "rendering useless" a water system, and NATO acknowledged that it was aware that its bombing of electrical stations would do this: "We are aware this will have an impact on civilians," a NATO official told the *New York Times* on May 24.

Clearly, NATO committed a prima facie war crime, and the evidence that it did so knowingly is at least as strong as anything used in the speedy indictment of Milan Martić. However, as a spokesman for the International Relations Committee of the U.S. House of Representatives told the *National Post* (Ottawa), "You're more likely to see the UN building dismantled brick-by-brick and thrown into the Atlantic than to see NATO pilots go before a UN tribunal."[52]

## U.S. GOVERNMENT DIRECTION OF PROSECUTION 1: MILOŠEVIĆ BUT NOT TUDJMAN

The putative independence and impartiality of the ICTY was utterly compromised by the indictment on May 27 of Yugoslav President Milošević and four of his political associates. While there may be little question that Milošević is guilty of war crimes, "justice" that is not impartial cannot be seen as just. The failure of the Prosecutor to indict NATO or its clients would seem to confirm Jamie Shea's message that he who pays the prosecutor determines who is charged. It is particularly noteworthy that, while the Prosecutor has been reported unable to indict Croatian generals for the 1995 ethnic cleansing of the Krajina because the U.S. government has refused to provide requested information,[53] she made well-publicized visits to American and British officials to gather information with which to indict Milošević. When a Prosecutor who is a citizen of one NATO country seeks assistance from the governments of other NATO countries in order to indict the President of the country that NATO is attacking, not even the pretence of prosecutorial independence remains. The matter was well described by Nina Bang-Jensen of the Coalition for International Justice in testimony during the Kosovo war before the U.S. Congress's Commission on Security and Cooperation in Europe: the ICTY prosecutors "have to recognize . . . that even though they should make prosecutorial decisions independent of political considerations, and make their decisions in an unbiased legal and just way, they are wholly dependent on the cooperation of states in order to execute their orders. So they can be a little too pristine about their not wanting to acknowledge that they ultimately have to rely on political institutions."[54] In light of these comments, the independence of the ICTY seems compromised by the fact that the President of the Tribunal, Judge Gabrielle Kirk McDonald, had been the guest of honor of Ms. Bang-Jensen's organization a month before the testimony quoted and referred on that occasion to U.S. Secretary of State Albright as "the mother of the Tribunal."[55]

## U.S. GOVERNMENT DIRECTION OF PROSECUTION 2: THREATS AGAINST VUK DRAŠKOVIĆ

In July 1999, I was surprised when a close adviser to Vuk Drašković told me that the United States was threatening Drašković with indictment by the ICTY. If the Prosecutor's office were truly independent, such a threat could not be plausible. However, the *New York Times* has also reported that "Washington has threatened Mr. Draskovic with indictment by the international war crimes tribunal in the Hague for the activities of his short-lived Serbian Guard, a paramilitary group, in Croatia in 1991."[56] Since contacts in Washington inform me that a major task of the U.S. government's interdepartmental Balkans Task Force is now to support the Prosecutor's office, that Washington feels free to threaten indictments seems highly plausible.

## DENIAL OF A FAIR TRIAL 1: JUDICIAL DEFERENCE TO PROSECUTOR

Politicization of the ICTY Prosecutor's office is especially troubling in light of the extraordinary deference that the *judges* of the Tribunal afford the prosecutor. This deference was first shown in regard to a truly outstanding scandal in the first case tried before the ICTY, that of Bosnian Serb Duško Tadić.[57] In that case, no witness had testified to having seen Tadić personally commit an atrocity, such as murder or rape. However, the Prosecutor's final witness testified that not only had he seen Tadić rape and murder, but he had also been forced by Tadić to rape and murder as well. The witness was a Bosnian Serb who had been captured by the Muslims, convicted by them of genocide, and then presented to the ICTY Prosecutor as a witness against Tadić.

The witness testified under complete anonymity, his identity having been kept a secret even from the defense under a "protection order" meant to allay the fears of witnesses that they or members of their families would suffer retribution if they testified before the Tribunal. In permitting such protection orders, the ICTY adopted one of the less admired procedures of the Spanish Inquisition, which also concealed the identities of witnesses from the accused,[58] and so it is interesting that such American human rights advocates as the Jacob Blaustein Institute for the Advancement of Human Rights of the American Jewish Committee, the Center for Constitutional Rights, the Women's Human Rights Law Clinic of the City University of New York, and the Women Refugees Project of the Harvard Immigration and Refugee Law Program supported prosecution witness anonymity in a joint *Amicus* brief filed with the Tribunal.[59]

As it happened, the Defense was able to show that the witness, "Witness L," had lied.[60] The man had said that his father was dead and that he had no brothers, but a member of the defense team was able to discover that, in fact, he had a brother and that his father was not dead, and arranged to confront the witness with his father and brother by bringing them to The Hague. At that point, the witness not only confessed to lying about his family, but also claimed to have been forced by the Muslims, while he was in their custody, to agree to lie against Tadić, and was then trained by them in the testimony he was to give in the ICTY. Confronted with these lies, the Prosecutor in Tadić informed the court that it did not regard his testimony as reliable and invited the court to disregard it, and the identity of the witness, one Dragan Opaćić, was revealed.

At this point, the obvious questions would seem to have been why the witness lied and whether, in fact, he was trained to do so by the Bosnian government, which had made him available to the Tribunal. Indeed, the Trial Chamber did order the Prosecutor's office to investigate the matter in order to determine whether charges of perjury should be brought against the Witness. However, at this point, the Trial Chamber gave both the Prosecutor and the Bosnian government extraordinary deference.

On December 2, 1996, the Prosecutor sent a letter to Alija Izetbegović, President of the Presidency of Bosnia and Herzegovina, thanking him for his cooperation in investigating the Witness L matter and exonerating his government of wrongdoing.[61] Tadić's defense lawyers, who had gone to Sarajevo to investigate the matter themselves but who had been given the "cold shoulder" by the Izetbegović government,[62] first heard of this letter several weeks later, when I asked them for a copy of it.[63] The Trial Chamber accepted this action by the Prosector without questioning why the Prosecutor had never shown greater zeal in determining the truth of the witness's story before the defense challenged basic facts about it, an especially interesting question since the Prosecutor knew the identity of the witness and the defense, by virtue of the protection order, did not.[64] Since some parts of the witness's story seemed to indicate that the Prosecutor's office might also have been involved in training him to give false testimony, the Tribunal, in effect, asked the Prosecutor to investigate possible wrongdoing by her own office, while offering no support to the defense in its own efforts to investigate the matter.

To make matters even more odd, neither the judges nor the Prosecutor showed any interest in determining whether the witness had, in fact, been threatened by the Bosnian government or whether he would be mistreated were he to be sent back to that government. Opaćić, who said that he had been tortured into making a confession to genocide in Sarajevo, asked not to be returned to the Bosnian government, requesting asylum in Holland.[65] However, even though Opaćić had an attorney to represent him on these issues, he was returned to the Muslims, without prior notice being given to his attorney.[66] Opaćić's fears seemed not unreasonable—in at least one case similar to his, two supposed victims of a Serb who confessed to murdering them and was thereupon convicted of genocide were found alive, but the Bosnian government's courts refused a new trial.[67] Yet immediately after this false case received worldwide publicity, Opaćić was returned to the control of the Bosnian government, where he now is serving a ten-year sentence for "genocide" following a conviction based solely on his own confession, which he says was extracted from him by torture.[68]

When the Dutch *Argos* journalists asked the Tribunal for an explanation of this failure to investigate the Opaćić matter more thoroughly, or to consider his request for asylum, a Tribunal spokesperson said that

> Defense Counsel Vladimirof [sic] did not prove that all of Dragan Opacic's story was untrue. The only point that was established is that Opacic lied about his family members. His father wasn't at all dead, as he had claimed. And that

> is the basis upon which the prosecutor decided that Opacic was not a reliable witness. . . . Why Opaćić lied and whether the rest of his story was correct was not relevant to the Tadic case. He was no longer any use as a witness, and that is why we sent him back to Bosnia.[69]

Of course, Defense Counsel Wladimiroff had not proven more about Opaćić because his cross-examination of him was stopped as being in violation of the protection order,[70] and the Prosecutor had also objected even to the evidence about Opaćić's identity but was overruled.[71]

The questions of why Opaćić lied and especially of whether the Bosnian government and even the Prosecutor's office trained him to do so were basic to determining whether other witnesses might also have been trained to commit perjury. The *Tadic* defense did try to raise this question on appeal, in regard to the testimony of another witness who had been presented by the Bosnian government, but the Appeals Chamber did not accept this claim because the "circumstances" of the two witnesses were "different. Mr. Opacic was made known to the Prosecution while he was still in the custody of the Bosnian authorities, while [the other witness's] introduction was made through the Bosnian embassy in Brussels."[72] Why this particular difference might matter was not explained by the Appeals Chamber, which also failed to notice that, while Opaćić was in the custody of the Bosnian government because he was captured as a soldier in the Bosnian Serb Army, the second witness's name (Nihad Seferović) indicated that he was a Muslim and thus perhaps not as in need of persuasion to lie at the behest of the Muslim government as Opaćić had been.

In the Witness L matter, then, the judges of the ICTY afforded very great deference to the Prosecutor and an equally great indifference to the causes of the perjury of a prosecution witness who had been found by the Bosnian government, and to the implications of the possible causes of the perjury for defendant Tadić and for the witness himself (who claimed, apparently with justification, to have been the victim of mistreatment by the Bosnian government), and to future defendants who might be victimized by what may have been collusion by the Prosecutor and the Bosnian government.

## DENIAL OF A FAIR TRIAL 2: CHANGING THE TRIAL RULES AFTER THE TRIAL IS OVER

In its decision on a preliminary question before the start of the *Tadic* trial, the ICTY Appeals Chamber stated that charges under Art. 2 of the Statute of the Tribunal (covering "grave breaches" of the Geneva Conventions) apply only to persons or objects "to the extent that they are caught up in an international armed conflict."[73] The same interlocutory decision concluded "that the conflicts in the former Yugoslavia have both internal and international elements."[74] It argued that, had the Security Council considered the conflict international and bound the Tribunal to that position, an "absurd" conclusion would result:

> Since it cannot be contended that the Bosnian Serbs constitute a State, arguably the classification just referred to would be based on the implicit assumption that the Bosnian Serbs are acting not as a rebellious entity but as organs or agents of another State, the Federal republic of Yugoslavia (Serbia-Montenegro). As a consequence, serious infringements of international humanitarian law committed by the government army of Bosnia-Herzegovina against Bosnian Serb civilians in their power would not be regarded as "grave breaches", because such civilians, having the nationality of Bosnia-Herzegovina, would not be regarded as "protected persons" under Article 4, paragraph 1 of Geneva Convention IV. By contrast, atrocities committed by Bosnian Serbs against Bosnian civilians in their hands would be regarded as "grave breaches", because such civilians would be "protected persons" under the Convention, in that the Bosnian Serbs would be acting as organs or agents of another State, the Federal Republic of Yugoslavia (Serbia-Montenegro) of which the Bosnians would not possess the nationality. This would be, of course, an absurd outcome, in that it would place the Bosnian Serbs at a substantial legal disadvantage vis-a-vis the central authorities of Bosnia-Herzegovina. This absurdity bears out the fallacy of the argument advanced by the Prosecutor.[75]

In accordance with these decisions, the Prosecutor was required in the *Tadic* trial to prove that the conflict was, in fact, international. The Trial Chamber viewed the matter as controlled by the International Court of Justice's decision in the *Nicaragua* case,[76] that external support to a party in an internal conflict would only internationalize that conflict if the external party had "effective control" over the forces in question. The Trial Chamber, over the dissent of the presiding judge, found that the evidence showed only a coordination between the Bosnian Serb Army and the Yugoslav Army, not control of the latter by the former; and thus held that "on the evidence presented to it, after 19 May 1992, the armed forces of the *Republika Srpska* could not be considered as de facto organs or agents of the Government of the Federal republic of Yugoslavia (Serbia and Montenegro)."[77] Accordingly, the Trial Chamber found Tadic not guilty of charges under Article 2 of the Statute.[78]

The Prosecutor appealed that decision and won: the Appeals Chamber held that the Bosnian Serb forces were acting as "de facto organs" of the Federal Republic of Yugoslavia.[79] In doing so, the Appeals Chamber reached precisely the conclusion in the *Tadic* appeal that it had itself pronounced "absurd" in the interlocutory appeal in the same case. The fairness of a Tribunal that sets explicit rules before a trial and then changes them after it is over is certainly dubious, but that is what the ICTY has done.

Also dubious is the reasoning of the *Tadic* appeal. At trial, of course, the burden of proof rested with the Prosector to prove that the events in question took place in the context of an international conflict, and the Trial Chamber concluded that this had not been proved. The Appeals Chamber, however, noted that the Trial Chamber had not said what the nature of the conflict was after May 19, 1992. Since the burden was on the prosecutor to show that it was international, there was no burden on the defense to show that it was *not* international. Yet the Appeals Chamber phrases the question as whether the conflict "became . . . *exclusively* internal" after that date.[80] Since the *Tadic* interlocutory judgment had concluded that the conflict had *both* internal and international elements, this could not have been the question that the defense had been required to counter or, for that matter, that the Trial Chamber was required to determine.

Indeed, the Appeals Chamber itself recognized that the conflict was "*prima facie* internal," because it set up the legal question involved as determining "the legal criteria for establishing when, in an armed conflict which is *prima facie* internal, armed forces may be regarded as acting on behalf of a foreign power, thereby rendering the conflict international."[81] The Trial Chamber had undertaken a serious review of the facts in Bosnia in 1992 and had concluded that, while the Bosnian Serb forces were allied to those of the Federal Republic of Yugoslavia, "there is no evidence on which this Trial Chamber can conclude that the Federal Republic of Yugoslavia . . . and the [Yugoslav Army] ever directed . . . the actual military operations of the [Bosnian Serb Army], or to influence those operations beyond that which would have flowed naturally from the coordination of military objectives and activities" by the two armies.[82] The Trial Chamber based this conclusion in part on the fact that the Republika Srpska political leaders were popularly elected by the Bosnian Serb people and that these elected political leaders played a role in the activities of the Bosnian Serb Army.[83]

The Appeals Chamber, on the other hand, paid no attention to the activities of Bosnian Serbs as political or military actors in their own right. Instead, it concluded that, since the Bosnian Serb Army had received some financing and equipment from the Yugoslav Army, "participation in the planning and supervision of military activities" would constitute "overall control" by the Yugoslav Army, thus rendering the conflict "international." This reasoning, of course, negates the meaning of the term *control* by conflating it with *participation*. At this point, the Appeals Chamber's earlier acknowledgment that the conflict had both internal and international elements vanishes, and the *Tadic* appeal judgment reaches precisely the conclusion that the *Tadic* interlocutory judgment had rendered "absurd": that even though both the Bosnian Serbs and their victims were nationals of Bosnia and Herzegovina, the victims were "protected persons" because "they found themselves in the hands of armed forces of a State of which they were not nationals."[84]

The Appeals Chamber, perhaps aware that it was rejecting its own earlier conclusion even if unwilling to admit it, justified its new holding on the "object and purpose" of Article 4 of Geneva Convention IV, as "the protection of civilians to the maximum extent possible."[85] If this justification is valid, the distinction between "internal" and "international" conflicts that the Appeals Chamber affirmed in the *Tadic* interlocutory judgment is invalid—*but for* Tadic, *it is the interlocutory standard that must apply*. In any event, the *Tadic* appeals judgment then makes an extraordinary statement, that the applicability of the Geneva Conventions is not "dependent on formal bonds and purely legal relations."[86] The same judgment had already said, approvingly, that international law concerning State responsibility "is based on a realistic concept of accountability, *which disregards legal formalities*."[87] But legal formalities protect an *accused*—prosecutors, after all, need no protection, but the rest of us may benefit by the bounds put on prosecutorial zeal. The ICTY Appeals Chamber has thus clearly indicated that fairness of the proceedings for defendants is not high in its concerns.

In yet another striking lapse from both fundamental fairness and the principles of fair trials, the Appeals Chamber, apparently on its own initiative, introduced and discussed what it saw as evidence of FRY control over the Bosnian Serbs in 1995 as evidence that the FRY controlled the Bosnian Serb Army in 1992.[88] Since the same Appeals Chamber judges had refused to permit the *Tadic* defense to introduce additional evidence after the conclusion of the trial,[89] this seems grossly unfair. However, "legal formalities" in regard to evidence do not seem to have been among the stronger points of this Appeals chamber, which refers in the *Tadic* appeal to findings of the international character of the conflict in "three Rule 61 Decisions" in other ICTY cases.[90] Rule 61 proceedings are reviews of evidence in cases in which the defendant is not in custody, which "permit the charges in the indictment and the supporting material to be publicly and solemnly exposed."[91] Rule 61 proceedings are uncontested; in one, the Trial Chamber noted that powers of attorney had been lodged successfully by one defendant but refused the attorney access to the courtroom or any role in the proceedings.[92] Judicial presentation of the Prosecutor's uncontested allegations in cases other than the one at trial as being evidence on key issues in the latter seems grossly unfair.

For the Appeals Chamber, however, it would seem that justice is indeed the right to do whatever they think must be done, and therefore justice can be anything.

## PROBLEMS FOR AMERICA? STATE RESPONSIBILITY

The dissenting Trial Chamber judge in *Tadic* was an American, the greatest number of staff working in the Prosecutor's office were American, and it is likely that the U.S. government supported the Appeals Chamber's reversal of its own interlocutory decision in regard to the nature of the conflict. Yet if such a thing as international law ever does come into existence, in the sense of a legal order binding all international actors, the United States might regret elements of the appellate decision in *Tadic*. The view that because of the imposition on States of responsibility of "*de facto* agents" States should be allowed to disregard "legal formalities" would not only hold the United States responsible for the actions of the contras in Nicaragua but also for those of the Croatian Army in its 1995 offensives against Serbs in Croatia and Bosnia. It is no secret that the U.S. government arranged for the "private" firm Military Professional Resources, Inc. (MPRI) to train the Croatian Army, beginning in September 1994,[93] activity that is attributable to the U.S. government under the *Tadic* appeal judgment. That the American-trained and American-equipped Croatian forces were committing war crimes was known to the United States government; consider Richard Holbrooke's reference to the "harsh behavior of Federation troops during the [Sept. 1995] offensive," which would have produced "forced evictions and random murders" of Serbs had Banja Luka been taken—yet Holbrooke told the Croatian Defense Minister that "Nothing that we said today should be construed to mean that we want you to stop the rest of the offensive, other than Banja Luka. . . . We can't say so publicly, but please take Sanski Most, Prijedor and Bosanski Novi."[94] Indeed, Holbrooke himself admits telling Croatian President Tudjman that the actions of Croatian forces could be viewed "as a milder form of ethnic cleansing."[95] Yet he urged that the offensive continue. Of course, as one of Holbrooke's colleagues had put it when the offensive started, "We 'hired' these guys [the Croatian Army] to be our junkyard dogs because we were desperate. We need to try to 'control' them. But this is no time to get squeamish about things."[96] In addition to Holbrooke, then-U.S. Ambassador to Croatia Peter Galbraith has been reported to have "attended meetings when Croats planned war."[97]

In the unlikely event that the ICTY ever takes its mandate as a charge to render impartial justice, and follows the principles announced by its Appellate Chamber in the *Tadic* appeal, American political actors who trained, armed, and helped in the planning of Croatian offensives in which war crimes were committed should expect to be indicted, and the United Sates as a State should be charged with responsibility for the actions of its junkyard dogs and de facto agents, the Croatian Army. I do not expect this to happen, however. As Jamie Shea said, after all, the United States is the friend of the Tribunal, the United States is the major financier of the Tribunal.

What, then, does this politicization of the ICTY say about the chances of ever creating a regime of international law? We might ponder the view of a leading human rights advocate that the ICTY "was a significant advance over the tribunals at Nuremberg and Tokyo, because it had a mandate to prosecute and punish malefactors from all sides . . . and has carried out its charge. Accordingly, unlike its predecessors, it is not susceptible to accusations of victor's justice."[98] It is clear, however, that the ICTY is no more impartial than were these earlier tribunals. Instead of being victor's justice after the conflict, it is a tool meant to ensure victory during it.

## "HUMAN RIGHTS PECCADILLOES" AND HUMANITARIAN WAR CRIMES

To its credit, HRW has recognized that NATO's actions in its war against Yugoslavia signaled "a disturbing disregard for the principles of humanitarianism that should guide any such action"[99] and criticized, in particular, NATO's use of cluster bombs. Its report on "Civilian Deaths in the NATO Air Campaign" did say that civilian deaths resulted from nine "attacks on non-military targets that Human Rights Watch believes were illegitimate,"[100] and noted that "the use of cluster bombs was a decisive factor in civilian deaths in at least three incidents."[101] HRW also concluded that "NATO violated international humanitarian law," although it prefaced this conclusion with the interesting distinction that it had "found no evidence of war crimes."[102] However, HRW has not called for investigation of NATO actions with the goal of prosecuting those in NATO who have violated human rights. One must wonder why this is so. At the least, we should expect to see HRW issue a demand for an independent investigation that could facilitate prosecution of those in NATO who have committed the crimes that HRW says that NATO committed in Yugoslavia, comparable to HRW's December 1999 request that the UN Security Council appoint an independent commission of inquiry to investigate war crimes by Russian forces in Chechnya.[103] Instead, HRW demanded, in its report on civilian deaths, only that "*NATO and its individual member states*" "establish an independent and impartial commission . . . that would investigate violations of international humanitarian law and the extent of these violations, and would consider the need to alter targeting and bombing doctrine" and otherwise engage in "investigations."[104]

The HRW distinction between "war crimes" and (mere?) "violations of international humanitarian law" is specious (genocide, after all, is not a war crime), because the ICTY has jurisdiction over both kinds of delict.[105] Indeed, in convicting Croatian general Tihomir Blaskic, the presiding judge specified that the "extremely serious crimes" he committed included "acts of war carried out with disregards for international humanitarian law."[106] One might wonder whether the HRW call for an "independent and impartial commission" might be an acknowledgment of the truth of the Jamie Shea position that he who finances the Tribunal determines the prosecutions, and might thus imply that a really independent and impartial body should replace the ICTY, were HRW not explicitly calling for NATO to investigate, independently and impartially, itself.

The difference in standards applied to NATO and to Russia might be explained by a distinction in a 1998 *Washington Post* op-ed piece by HRW executive director Kenneth Roth.[107] Trying to assuage U.S. government concerns that new international judicial institutions could be used to accuse Americans of war crimes, Roth states that "clearly it is not U.S. policy" to commit genocide, war crimes, or crimes against humanity, and that "there is no prospect" of harassment of "democratic leaders who have at worst a few human rights peccadilloes to their record." Of course, Roth made this distinction before NATO committed what HRW identifies as violations of the Geneva conventions, but the distinction, perhaps, still holds: NATO, after all, is, by definition, democratic, so presumably its war crimes are peccadilloes not worthy of prosecution. The consequences of indictments of NATO personnel for war crimes for the new international judicial institutions that HRW wishes to promote were made clear by Senator Jesse Helms in his January 2000 speech to the UN Security Council:

> Any attempt to indict NATO commanders would be the death knell for the International Criminal Court. But the very fact that [the ICTY Prosecutor] explored this possibility at all brings to light all that is wrong with this brave new world of global justice, which proposes a system in which independent prosecutors and judges, answerable to no state or institution, have unfettered power to sit in judgment of the foreign policy decisions of Western democracies.[108]

Since HRW's executive director says that Western democracies commit human rights peccadilloes rather than war crimes, and the United States clearly controls the ICTY, Senator Helms's concerns are, clearly, baseless.

Another explanation might be said to lie in the extremity of the situation to which NATO responded in Kosovo: that "it took NATO's controversial bombing campaign before Belgrade would acquiesce in the deployment of international troops to stop widespread ethnic slaughter and forced displacement," and that the inspiration for "NATO's action was fundamentally humanitarian. . . . The desire to stop crimes against humanity was a major goal."[109] HRW's recounting of the events leading up to NATO's attacks closely tracks that of Bill Clinton, who asserted that NATO "had to act" when

Yugoslav forces "began an offensive" against the Albanians of Kosovo.[110] Assuming that he read the reports of his own State Department, the President must have known that his account was inaccurate: in a report issued two weeks before the President published his article in the *New York Times*, the State Department said that, until the NATO attacks were under way, Serb forces were engaged in "the selective targeting of towns and regions suspected of [Kosovo Liberation Army] activities," not a general offensive against the Albanian population.[111] This pattern of Serbian actions before NATO's offensive is confirmed by the OSCE in its massive report on events in Kosovo, which shows that Serbian forces, until NATO attacked, were fighting the KLA and not engaged in systematic ethnic cleansing.[112] HRW might have tacitly recognized this uncomfortable fact when it stated that "before using military force to stop crimes against humanity, planners at a minimum should be confident that intervention will not make matters worse by provoking a wider war or setting in motion a string of new atrocities."[113] Yet applying this criterion to NATO's actions would delegitimate them, which HRW clearly does not want to do.

The more fundamental problem in any event is HRW's assertion that war can be seen as humanitarian. Attacks against civilians are probably inevitable in any supposedly humanitarian intervention. Every nation has the right to defend itself, and at the level of practical politics, a nation that is attacked will try to resist the attacker. Winning the war thus requires defeating not only the army, but the nation: the civilian population. Thus the decision to attack a sovereign state is, logically, a decision to attack the civilian population of that state, not just the military. NATO's targeting of the civilian infrastructure of Serbia (and earlier, of Iraq) is thus logical, and the constant repetition that "NATO never targets civilians" was hypocritical, presumably meant to obscure the uncomfortable fact that humanitarian intervention requires the committing of humanitarian war crimes. At this point, the greatest triumph of the human rights movement, "humanitarian intervention," is revealed as its greatest defeat, because it transforms what had been a moral critique against violence into a moral crusade for massive violence. Of course, HRW could escape this trap by demanding the indictment of NATO leaders, but it would then precede the UN in being dismantled brick by brick and thrown into the Atlantic. While speaking truth to power is admirable, telling power what it wants to hear tends to bring more tangible rewards.

## HUMANRIGHTSISM

A month after NATO began its attacks on Yugoslavia, Vaclav Havel gave what seems to be a principled justification for the war:

> this is probably the first war that has not been waged in the name of "national interests," but rather in the name of principles and values. . . . This war places human rights above the rights of the state. The Federal Republic of Yugoslavia was attacked by the alliance without a direct mandate from the UN. This did not happen irresponsibly, as an act of aggression or out of disrespect for international law. It happened, on the contrary, out of respect for the law, for the law that ranks higher than the law which protects the sovereignty of states. The alliance has acted out of respect for human rights.[114]

Havel then states that human rights "are as powerful as they are because, under certain circumstances, people accept them without compulsion and are willing to die for them."[115]

Havel sounds great, but, in fact, even as he gave the speech quoted (April 29, 1999), he must have known that he lied. Few indeed were willing to die for human rights, particularly in the Czech Republic,[116] but rather NATO was engaged in killing for human rights. As Havel spoke, the alliance was targeting civilian "infrastructure" because attacking Yugoslav military targets would have exposed NATO pilots to danger. In the five days before his speech, NATO repeatedly bombed oil refineries in Novi Sad, causing massive pollution of the air and of the river Danube, bombed civilian targets in central Belgrade, and bombed a Serbian town on the Bulgarian border, destroying houses and killing civilians.[117] All but the last were intentional targeting, so damage to the environment and civilian deaths were not "collateral damage." Havel's speech is thus either politically cunning, as befits the elected president of a sovereign nation-state, or else evasive, avoiding the truth that Havel could not, as a long-term supporter of human rights, admit.

But the difference between Havel the advocate of human rights and Havel the War President embodies the difference between human rights as a principle for criticism of the actions of governments and humanrightsism as a justification for government actions that violate human rights. By humanrightsism, I mean what the *New York Times* has described as the "elevation" of human rights to a "military priority,"[118] since military priorities are, by definition, based on the threat and use of force. This "elevation" is actually a striking inversion of the principles that have guided the growth of human rights organizations. For example, Amnesty International long required that its "prisoners of conscience" not be advocates or practitioners of violence.[119] Humanrightsism, however, calls for violence.

I am aware, of course, of the revival of "just war" arguments by political philosophers[120] and politicians.[121] In regard to the latter, however, surely even Vaclav Havel realizes that all politicians justify wars by reference to "principles and values," and justification for attacks that are not based on self-defense are often less than reliable assessments. After all, were governments that apply force always candid in their reasons for doing so, HRW and other human rights organizations would not have been in business in the first place.

The question then, remains: why have human rights advocates ignored the actions by NATO and by the ICTY that they would condemn were they performed by, say, China or Russia or India?

This question is addressed directly in a brilliant and brave article by Dimitrina Petrovna, Executive Director of the European Roma Rights Center in Budapest.[122] Petrovna acknowledges that she herself was in favor of NATO intervention in Kosovo until she saw, soon after the bombing began, that it was escalating the human rights catastrophe for everyone in the Federal Republic of Yugoslavia, inside Kosovo and in Serbia, and that "from a campaign to defend the lives and rights of Kosovo Albanians, [the war] metamorphosed into something else: the monster of an escalated war."[123] While Petrovna herself then called for an immediate end to the bombing and a negotiated peace, few others in the human rights community did so. She notes that for east European human rights workers, their very status and funding could have been jeopardized by criticism of NATO and especially of the United States—NATO countries are, after all, the major financiers of more than just the ICTY. In the Western countries themselves, however, the reasons are more troubling. There, she notes, "human rights are becoming indistinguishable from official political ideology," producing "a gradual usurpation of the human-rights culture by the dominant powers, and the very argument for human rights is turning into an apologia for the global status quo, all in the interests of these very powers."[124]

From the evidence of NATO's actions in Kosovo and the ICTY's treatment of defendants, this transformation of human rights inverts the concept, from one premised on the protection of people from the violence of states to one justifying the application of violence by the world's most powerful states against weaker ones. With this transformation, human rights betrays its own premises and thus becomes its own travesty: humanrightsism.

## NOTES

1. Human Rights Watch, *World Report 2000: Introduction,* www.hrw.org/wr2k/Front.htm.
2. Human Rights Watch, "Human Rights Trump Sovereignty in 1999," press release, Dec. 9, 1999.
3. HRW, *World Report 2000.*
4. HRW, *World Report 2000,* at 1.
5. Ibid., at 6.
6. Ibid.
7. *Los Angeles Times*, Oct. 18, 1999.

8. Ibid.

9. V. Havel, "Kosovo and the End of the Nation-State," *New York Review,* 10 June 1999, 4, 6. The idea that "people" have rights superior to those of states is extended by John Rawls to mean that "liberal and decent Peoples," not states, should be the true actors in international society (Rawls, *The Law of Peoples* (Cambridge, MA: Harvard University Press, 1999), pp.23–29. Since each such "People" has a government (23) and a territory which it has the right to protect (29), it is very difficult to see how his distinction is meaningful—what, after all, is a State but a government united with a territory?

10. The gendered pronoun is intentional—no women have yet been charged by the ICTY.

11. *Prosecutor of the Tribunal v Milan Martic*, indictment, 25 July 1995 (hereafter, Martic indictment). Note: unless otherwise specified, references to ICTY documents are to versions on the Tribunal's web page, www.un.org/icty/.

12. *Prosecutor v Milan Martic*, ICTY case no. IT-96-11-R61; Rule 61 evidentiary review, 27th February 1996 (hereafter, *Martic* Rule 61 hearing), at 5. www.un.org/icty/transe11/960227IT.txt.

13. Ibid. at 18.

14. Martic indictment, para. 6.

15. BBC News Online, May 7, 1999.

16. *Times* (London), June 13, 1999.

17. *Philadelphia Inquirer*, Nov. 21, 1999, 1.

18. *Martic* Rule 61 hearing at 20.

19. *Martic* Rule 61 hearing at 20.

20. "At NATO, A Crash Course in Spin," MSNBC www service, May 1, 1999.

21. BBC News Online, Oct. 22, 1999.

22. 16 May comments, www.nato.int/kosovo/press/p990516b.htm; 17 May comments, www.nato.int/kosovo/press/p990517b.htm.

23. *Observer* (London), Dec. 26, 1999; *New York Times,* Dec. 29, 1999.

24. *New York Times*, Dec. 30, 1999, A5.

25. Ibid.

26. ICTY Press Release PR/ P.I.S./ 459-e, December 30, 1999.

27. *Washington Times*, Dec. 30, 1999; *New York Times* Jan. 3, 2000, A6.

28. *Prosecutor v Radovan Karadzic and Ratko Mladic*, indictment, July 25, 1995 (hereafter, Karadzic/ Mladic indictment), para. 29.

29. Ibid. at para. 41.

30. Grupa 17, *ZavršniRaćun: Ekonomske posledice NATO bomabardovanja* (Beograd: Stubovi Kulture, 1999), 9.

31. BBC News Online, Oct. 15, 1999.

32. www.msnbc.com/news, April 26, 1999.

33. See, e.g., *Wall Street Journal,* April 27, 1999, p. 1; BBC News Online October 15, 1999.

34. *Washington Post*, Sept. 20, 1999, A20.

35. Aryeh Neier, *War Crimes* (New York: Times Books, 1998), 169.

36. *The Prosecutor of the Tribunal against Slobodan Milosevic et al.*, indictment, May 27, 1999, jurist.law.pitt.edu/indict.htm.

37. Shea letter available at www.ifj.org/hrights/natoreply.html.

38. *Wall Street Journal*, April 27, 1999.

39. HRW, *Civilian Deaths in the NATO Air Campaign*, 14–15.

40. That the dead were simply employees of RTS—editors, technicians, mixers, makeup artists—is confirmed by Steven Erlanger, "An Ordinary Serb, Lost in Air Attack, Is Buried," *New York Times*, May 2, 1999, 13. I confess a personal connection: an old friend who worked at RTS as a night-shift translator had, fortunately, just left the building when it was hit. Had he not left he, too, would have been among the CPJ's propagandists even though, ironically enough, his past twenty years had been spent in the employ of the U.S. government, first in the Fulbright office, later in the embassy until it closed at the start of the war. Note that the RTS victims were not even "collateral damage," as NATO meant to hit them.

41. C. Glass, "When It's OK to Kill a Hack," *Spectator* (London), Feb. 5, 2000.

42. Transcript obtained from Sam Husseini of Accuracy in Media: sam@accuracy.org.

43. Benefactors and other major donors listed on www.cpj.org.

44. Ibid.

45. NATO news Briefing, April 8, 1999.

46. *Washington Times*, April 25, 1999, C9.

47. *Washington Post*, May 24, 1999 (World Wide Web Edition).

48. *Washington Post*, May 25, 1999, p. A1.

49. *New York Times*, May 25, 1999, p. A1.

50. *Washington Post*, May 25, 1999, p. A1.

51. BBC News Online, May 24, 1999.

52. *National Post*, May 22, 1999.

53. *New York Times*, March 21, 1999.

54. "Accountabiltiy for War Crimes: Progress and Prospects." Hearing before the Commission on Security and Cooperation in Europe, 106 Congress, 1st sess., May 11, 1999, 25.

55. "Remarks at the U.S. Supreme Court by Gabrielle Kirk McDonald on the Occasion of Receiving the ABA CEELI Award," April 5, 1999, as released by the ICTY: www.un.org/icty/pressreal/SPUSSC.htm.

56. *New York Times*, Oct. 15, 1999, A8.

57. Candor requires me to state that I was actually the very first *defense* witness to appear before the ICTY, in the *Tadic* case, on the question of the character of the conflict (national or international), a question discussed in the next section. My testimony was limited to constitutional and political issues in Yugoslavia and in Bosnia through 1992 (a précis of the testimony is found in my article in *The Fletcher Forum of World Affairs* 22, no. 1 [1998]: 45–64). Apart from one very brief meeting with Tadić in May 1996, at the request of his defense counsel, I had and have no personal acquaintance with Tadić or knowledge of the crimes for which he was accused.

58. H. Kamen, *The Spanish Inquisition* (New Haven, Conn.: Yale University Press 1997), 182, 194–195.

59. *Prosecutor v Dusko Tadic*, "Decision on the Prosecutor's Motion Requesting Protective Measures for Victims and Witnesses," August 10, 1995, at paras. 10–11.

60. The basic story of "Witness L" can be found in news accounts: e.g. *Internet Naša Borba* October 28, 1996, Reuters, Oct. 25, 1996, Associated Press, Oct. 25, 1996. Copies of an interrogation of "Witness L" by Tadić defense attorney Michail Wladimiroff and of an Oct. 25, 1995, statement by ICTY Prosecutor's investigator Robert Reid concerning Witness L's lies and accusations against the Bosnian government are in author's files. The most detailed account of the "Witness L" matter was broadcast on Dutch VPRO Radio's Argos program on Sept. 10, 1999, a transcript of which (in English) is available at www.domovina.net/opacice.html (hereafter, *Argos*).

61. Institute for War and Peace Reporting, *Tribunal Update no. 6* (Dec. 2–6, 1996).

62. Letter to author from Michail Wladimiroff, Nov. 11, 1996.

63. Fax letter from author to Michail Wladimiroff, Dec. 30, 1996; fax letter to author from Michail Wladimiroff, January 7, 1997.

64. It is in fact likely that the Defense was in violation of the protection order when it questioned people who, the defense thought, might have been related to the anonymous witness. Had they followed the rules, however, the defendant could not have had a fair trial.

65. *ICTY: Tadic Case: Update*, June 2, 1997.

66. *Argos.*

67. *New York Times*, March 1, 1997, 3; *Washington Post*, March 15, 1997, A15; *New York Times*, June 15, 1997, 10.

68. *Argos.*

69. Ibid.

70. Fax letter to author from Michail Wladimiroff, October 30, 1997.

71. Ibid.

72. *Prosecutor v Dusko Tadic, Judgment*, July 15, 1999 (hereafter, *Tadic* appeal judgment), para. 65.

73. *Prosecutor v Dusan Tadic, Decision on the Defense Motion for Interlocutory Appeal on Jurisdiction*, Oct. 2, 1995 (hereafter, "Tadic Interlocutory"), para. 81.

74. Ibid. at para 77.

75. Ibid. para 76.

76. *Case Concerning Military and Paramilitary Activities in and Against Nicaragua*, 1986 I.C.J Reports 14. Ironically, the defendant in Nicaragua was the United States, so the United States in *Tadic* was urging the abandonment of the position that had protected it in *Nicaragua*.

77. *Prosecutor v Dusko Tadic, Opinion and Judgment*, May 7, 1997 (hereafter, *Tadic* trial judgment), para. 607. The May 19, 1992, date was important because the Bosnian Serb Army was formally separated from the Yugoslav Peoples Army on or before that date, and the only evidence presented on the chain of command between the two armies after that date was that of a witness who said that "there was no real chain of command" between them and evidence that the Bosnian Serb Army used secure communications links that ran through Yugoslav Peoples Army headquarters in Belgrade for it own internal communications (Ibid. para. 598).

78. Ibid. para 608.

79. *Tadic* appeal judgment, para. 167.

80. Ibid. para. 86, emphasis added.

81. Ibid. §IV.B.3 (heading).

82. *Tadic* trial judgment, para. 605.

83. Ibid. para. 599.

84. *Tadic* appeals judgment, para 167.

85. Ibid. para. 168.

86. Ibid. para. 168.

87. Ibid. para. 121, emphasis added.

88. Ibid. paras. 157–160.

89. Ibid. para. 16.

90. Ibid. note 107.

91. *Prosecutor v Radovan Karadćić and Ratko Mladić*, Review of the Indictments Pursuant to Rule 61 of the Rules of Procedure and Evidence, July 11, 1996, (hereafter, *Karadćić and Mladić*, Rule 61 proceeding) para. 3.

92. Ibid. para. 4. Interestingly, the Trial Chamber described its actions in this uncontested Rule 61 proceeding as being in pursuit of the "mission" of "international criminal justice" of "revealing the truth about the acts perpetrated." Ibid. para. 3. Truth, apparently, can be found reliably in the uncontested allegations of the Prosecutor.

93. *Globus*, Oct. 20, 1995.

94. R. Holbrooke, *To End a War* (New York: Random House, 1998), p. 166.

95. Ibid. 160.

96. Ibid. 73.

97. *New York Times*, May 30, 1996, A7.

98. A. Neier, *War Crimes: Brutality, Genocide, Terror, and the Struggle for Justice* (New York: Time Books, 1998), p. 259.

99. HRW, *World Report 2000*, 5.

100. HRW, *Civilian Deaths in the NATO Air Campaign*, February 2000 (www.hrw.org/reports/2000/nato), "Summary."

101. Ibid.

102. Ibid. "International Human Rights Law and Accountability."

103. See www.hrw.org/campaigns/russia/chechnya.

104. HRW, *Civilian Deaths in the NATO Air Campaign*, "Summary," 7–8.

105. The Statute of the ICTY grants it jurisidiction over Grave Breaches of the Geneva Conventions of 1949 (Art. 2), Violations of the Laws and Customs of War (Art. 3), Genocide (Art. 4), and Crimes Against Humanity (Art. 5).

106. ICTY Press Release JL/P.I.S./474-E, March 3, 2000 (www.un.org/icty/pressreal/p474-e.htm).

107. *Washington Post*, Nov. 26, 1998, A31.

108. www.usis.it/wireless/wfa00120/A00120.htm.

109. HRW, *World Report 2000*, 1, 5.

110. *New York Times*, May 23, 1999, sect. 4 p. 17.

111. U.S. State Department, *Erasing History: Ethnic Cleansing in Kosovo*, May 1999.

112. OSCE, *Kosovo/ Kosova As Seen, As Told: The Human Rights Findings of the OSCE Verification Mission* (www.osce.org/kosovo/reports/hr/part1), part 1, chapter 3.

113. HRW, *World Report 2000*, 6.

114. V. Havel, "Kosovo and the End of the Nation-State," *New York Review,* June 10, 1999, 6.

115. Ibid. 6.

116. See M. Znoj, "Czech Attitudes toward the War," *East European Constitutional Review* 8, no. 3 (1999): 47.

117. U.N. Environment Programme and U.N. Centre for Human Settlements, *The Kosovo Conflict: Consequences for the Environment* (Switzerland: United Nations Environment Programme and the United Nations Centre for Human Settlements [Habitat], 1999), 17.

118. Editorial, *New York Times*, June 13, 1999.

119. See, for example, Amnesty International, *Yugoslavia: Prisoners of Conscience* (London: Amnesty International, 1985), 9–10: "the following violations of human rights in Yugoslavia are of concern to Amnesty International: the arrest and imprisonment of people for their non-violent exercise of internationally recognized human rights. . . . The vague formulation of certain legal provisions which enables them to be applied so as to penalize people for the non-violent exercise of their human rights."

120. For example, M. Walzer, *Just and Unjust Wars*, (New York: Basic Books, 1992), and J. Rawls, *The Law of Peoples,* Rawls' (81) assertion that "If the political conception of political liberalism is sound . . . then liberal and decent peoples have the right . . . not to tolerate outlaw states," seems, remarkably but as yet unremarked, a call for liberal *jihad.*

121. For example, W. Clinton, "A Just and Necessary War," *New York Times*, May 23, 1999, 4–17.

122. D. Petrovna, "The War and the Human Rights Community," *East European Constitutional Review* 8, no. 3 (1999): 97.

123. Ibid. 99.

124. Ibid. 101.

# 11

## Illegal Wars, Collateral Damage, and International Criminal Law

*Michael Mandel*

### INTERNATIONAL CRIMINAL LAW

My understanding of international criminal law is informed by my experience with the International Criminal Tribunal for the Former Yugoslavia (ICTY). In May 1999 I was part of a group of lawyers from North and South America who filed a war crimes complaint against sixty-eight individual leaders of the North Atlantic Treaty Organization (NATO) at The Hague. The leaders included all the prime ministers, presidents, foreign and defense ministers of the NATO countries, and various officials of NATO itself, that is to say Clinton, Albright, Cohen, Blair, Chrétien, etc., down through Javier Solana, Wesley Clark, and Jamie Shea. With a legal team from Canada, France, Great Britain, Greece, and Norway, we went to The Hague to make our case to Chief Prosecutor Louise Arbour and then to her replacement Carla Del Ponte. We filed volumes of legal briefs and evidence. Like literally thousands around the world, we demanded that Arbour and Del Ponte enforce the law against NATO. In March 2000 it became clear to us what we and others had long suspected, namely that the tribunal was a hoax, and we gave up on it. In June, Del Ponte announced that she had determined that NATO was not guilty of any crimes and that (rather illogically) she was not opening an investigation into whether they had committed any.[1] She released a report that was an amateur whitewash. Fortunately Amnesty International issued its own very careful and competent report at the same time—in fact, Del Ponte rushed to announce her results a week early to steal the thunder from Amnesty. Amnesty concluded NATO was guilty of war crimes.

I defy anyone to read the two reports and not conclude that the ICTY report is a fraud. Reflection on this experience with international criminal law has led me to the conclusion that the whole thing is in the tradition of the Trojan horse, a gift of which we must beware from the new Greeks of America who want to use it to hide their aggressive and violent imperial politics.

Another way of putting this is that I think Slobodan Milosevic had a very good point (English grammar apart) when he told the Hague judges on his first appearance before them that the Tribunal is "false tribunal, and indictments false indictments."[2] And when he said that the "trial's aim is to produce false justification for the war crimes of NATO committed in Yugoslavia,"[3] he was merely echoing the American State Department official who wrote the Statute for Madeleine Albright. Michael Scharf meant no criticism of the ICTY, only the governments, when he wrote in October 1999 that:

> [T]he tribunal was widely perceived within the government as little more than a public relations device and as a potentially useful policy tool. . . . Indictments also would serve to isolate offending leaders diplomatically, strengthen the hand of their domestic rivals and fortify the international political will to employ economic sanctions or use force.[4]

But treating the tribunal as one that perceived *itself* as merely a propaganda arm of NATO is the only way to make sense of its violation of the most basic principles of judicial impartiality. This is apparent, above all, in its failure to charge NATO leaders for the crimes they committed in the bombing campaign, something the Tribunal was legally required to do by its statute, not to mention morally required to do by the facts of the case. But it is also unmistakeable in the way it pursued the Serb authorities, clearly far more concerned with legitimating NATO's war on Yugoslavia than with doing justice. Here are some examples:

Racak, January 15, 1999. This was the event that the Americans used as a cause of war. It is still not clear whether this was a genuine massacre of forty-five defenseless Albanians by Serb soldiers or a monstrous hoax perpetrated by the KLA. But it didn't matter to the Americans whether it occurred or not. Up until then, the Security Council and independent observers judged the violence as provocation by KLA "terrorists" and retaliation by Serbs.[5] But the day after Racak, the head of the Organization for Security and Cooperation in Europe (OSCE) observer mission, William Walker, an American State Department official, decided to hold a press conference calling it a "massacre" and a "crime against humanity."[6] This was clearly an American political decision and not a moral one on Walker's part. Walker was an old hand at massacres. He was named in the indictment in the Iran-Contra affair and was a major player in other bloody, illegal Latin American adventures of the Reagan-Bush period. He was well known for turning the other way when

U.S.-backed paramilitaries killed priests in El Salvador in 1989. He must have been well known to Louise Arbour. Yet, within one day and with no further investigation, she was at the border of Kosovo with TV cameras declaring that she was "opening an investigation." Within four days, having consulted only with NATO officials, she declared it a war crime for which the perpetrators would be punished.[7]

Remember that despite a year's worth of powerful corroborated evidence accumulated and submitted by thousands to Arbour and Del Ponte on NATO crimes, they declared that they weren't even "opening an investigation." One day and one suspicious word were enough in Racak, when the Americans decided to change policy and go to war with Yugoslavia. Racak was the pretext for the war, and the ICTY legitimated the pretext.

Racak led directly to Rambouillet. The failure of the Serbs to agree to the United States' demands at Rambouillet was the justification for the bombing. Then, only days after the bombing had commenced, Arbour announced an indictment of the noted Serb paramilitary leader "Arkan" for alleged war crimes in Bosnia, an indictment that she had kept secret since 1997.[8] Why announce it then? She said it was to warn people against associating with him in further crimes in Kosovo.[9] As if all the players didn't know who Arkan was and that Arbour was after him. As if that could dissuade him from anything—given that he had far more serious things to worry about, like the assassins who would gun him down before the year was out. The only thing the announcement could do, and therefore what it was obviously meant to do, was demonize the Serbs and give credibility to the American justification for the bombing.

In early May, Arbour made successive television appearances with British Foreign Secretary Robin Cook and American Secretary of State Madeleine Albright. Cook made a great show of handing over war crimes dossiers that NATO had prepared against Yugoslav authorities, and Albright swore unswerving allegiance to the ICTY and promised it more money. But by the time Arbour appeared on TV with them, what Jamie Shea was calling "collateral damage"[10] (the death and maiming of civilian men, women, and children) was mounting, and well-founded, well- documented war crimes complaints against Cook and Albright had reached Arbour from thousands of citizens around the world (read Amnesty's report to see how well-founded they were). But did she care? She wasn't even embarrassed by a helpful hyperlink to the NATO website on the ICTY homepage throughout the "investigation" of NATO.[11]

The most egregious example of the tribunal's role as NATO's propaganda arm occurred when, midway through the war, on May 22 (as civilian casualties of NATO's bombing were sickening the world), Arbour announced the indictment of Yugoslav President Slobodan Milosevic for various crimes, including murder.[12] Apart from Racak, all of the charges concerned deaths that had occurred after the NATO bombing had commenced.[13] In other words, this indictment, based on undisclosed evidence supplied by NATO alone, came in the midst of a blistering bombing attack, for events which had occurred in some cases only *six weeks earlier* in the middle of the war zone. Though NATO tried to claim the indictment "embarrassed" them, the evidence all came from the Americans.[14] Any impartial prosecutor would have regarded this evidence as very suspicious, perhaps the basis for an investigation once the bombing had stopped, but for an indictment during a war? Of course, this has to be compared with the inability of the Tribunal to even "open an investigation" after one year of being provided with overwhelming evidence in the public domain of NATO leaders' crimes which, on the most conservative estimates, resulted in the deaths of far more civilians than those for which the Serb leadership was indicted.[15]

The purely propaganda nature of the Milosevic indictment became even clearer when Del Ponte took over from Arbour and said her first priority would be in gathering evidence against him,[16] in other words admitting that the indictment was preferred with most of the evidence still missing. When Milosevic first appeared in court, Del Ponte added hundreds of victims to the counts against him, but, apparently disappointed by the numbers, she announced—once again the announcement was made for effect, well in anticipation of the fact—that she would be bringing genocide charges against him for his part in the Bosnian civil war.[17] This in turn was aided by the Trial Division's judgment in *Krstic*[18] that "genocide" could consist of the murder of seven or eight thousand military-aged men (itself a very rough *maximum* estimate by the court) from one village in the middle of a military struggle over territory. A horrible crime, no doubt, but wouldn't it be enough to call it murder? Not if you wanted to Nazify the Serbs.

At the conclusion of the bombing, Arbour handed over the investigation of war crimes in Kosovo to the NATO countries' own police forces, notwithstanding their obvious motivation to falsify the evidence. When people started to question the paucity of the victims, compared to NATO claims (mass graves either did not exist or turned out to be individual graves), Arbour's replacement, Carla Del Ponte, made a well-publicized and improvised visit to the Security Council—I know it was improvised because she had to cancel a long-scheduled meeting with me to attend—to reassure the world that the victims could yet well amount to what NATO had, at least in its more modest moments, alleged. We've heard nothing from her since on this subject.[19]

So, whatever the guilt of the Serbs, this tribunal acted more like a NATO press office than a court; while this may not cast doubt on the guilt of the Serbs, it certainly casts a heap of it on the legitimacy of the ICTY.

But the real proof was in the failure to charge NATO, which is where I came in. Most of the world—according to reputable polls taken during the bombing—opposed this war.[20] Though supporters had some big names on their side (Wiesel, Sontag, Rushdie), we opponents did, too: Mikos Theodorakis, Claude Lantzmann—who called the war a "new Dreyfus Affair"—Alexander Solzhenytsin, Nelson Mandela, Roy Medvedev, Harold Pinter, Noam Chomsky, and Ramsey Clark.

Above all, we opponents did not believe the NATO countries, and particularly the United States, when they said they were acting out of necessity and for humanitarian reasons. There were a number of reasons for this. In the first place, in our experience, the United States had never before acted in its military interventions abroad out of humanitarian motives. It had a history of purely self-interested aggression in the world and zero respect for the lives of civilians: from the atomic bombs on Hiroshima and Nagasaki, through the napalming of Vietnam and the carpet bombing of Cambodia to the destruction of Iraq. This is a country that, for no legal or legitimate reason, keeps up a lethal sanctions regime, as well as a casual bombardment campaign (including the use of antihuman cluster bombs), that is reputably said to have killed thousands of Iraqi children every month for ten years.[21] The hypocrisy of the justification is, once again, almost beyond belief: "weapons of mass destruction" and the refusal to cooperate with international institutions. The first, when the United States is the master of nuclear weaponry and is the only country to have actually used it against humans, not to mention an admitted chemical warfare "research" program that caused the United States of America to refuse in 2001 to sign an international ban; the second when it is now widely accepted that the United States used arms inspection for spying on Iraqi defenses, the way they used the OSCE for bringing war to Yugoslavia.

This is the country that prevented the Security Council from intervening in Rwanda because it wasn't prepared to help and didn't want to look bad. This is a country that has underwritten repressive regimes from Somoza to Pinochet to Suharto to the Kuwaitis and the Saudis. Within the heart of NATO, Turkey has carried out a violent repression of the Kurds that has claimed thirty thousand lives, not two thousand like the one in Kosovo had before the intervention.[22]

Furthermore, the United States is a notorious violator of the human rights of its own citizens: a country of racial segregation, of poverty amidst prodigious wealth, of police brutality, bursting prisons, and the death penalty: the biggest prison population outside Russia;[23] and, unlike Russia (and Yugoslavia), which has banned the death penalty, during 1999 it executed two of its own citizens by lethal injection every week.[24] Not only that, and this is extremely important, in the Balkans itself, the United States, along with the rich countries of Europe, made a crucial contribution to the disintegration and descent into violence of the former Yugoslavia through aggressive economic policies motivated by pure greed as well as a desire to destroy Eastern European socialism.

The imposition of economic Shock Therapy (ST) on the Eastern European economies immediately plunged them into a deep depression. That's why they call it "shock" therapy. Yugoslavia lost two-thirds of its income in the early nineties.[25] The split-up of the country was also a function of ST: Yugoslavia couldn't afford the transfer payments necessary to keep the country together. But this wasn't the operation of immutable economic laws. It was imposed by the rich countries through their pseudo-independent financial institutions (the IMF and the World Bank) so that they could buy off East European productive resources at bargain basement prices and subject their economies to Western dominance in a "hub-and-spoke" arrangement that divided and conquered.[26] The European Union then recognized the Balkan republics on the basis of borders that were a recipe for civil war. What followed was the Bosnian civil war, whose bloody persistence was ensured by successive American administrations' relentless torpedoing of peace plans with a real chance of success, including the Lisbon plan of 1992 and the Vance-Owen plan of 1993. Remember that the "genocide" at Srebrenica didn't happen until 1995.

The NATO countries did precious little to stop the fighting. They cultivated the KLA, who were encouraged to engage in deadly provocations with the Serbs, inviting retaliation precisely to bring down NATO's bombs. NATO made noisy preparations for war for a year prior to the attack of March 24, 1999. Then there was the Racak affair, also a signal, and then the fake negotiations at Rambouillet. At Rambouillet, the NATO countries said they had ten nonnegotiable demands.[27] None of them included NATO presence or independence for Kosovo. The Serbs accepted every one of them, but not the Albanians. Then suddenly the terms changed, and the Serbs were presented with new terms that were impossible to accept and were meant to be so: a referendum on Kosovo's final status and total occupation of Kosovo by NATO, including a free hand in Yugoslavia itself.

The Americans withdrew the OSCE observers and commenced a bombing campaign ostensibly to enforce Rambouillet but really aimed at encouraging a refugee crisis that did not exist before the bombing but was an entirely foreseeably result of it (General Wesley Clark claimed only to be surprised at the size of it). This was then used to justify an intensification of the bombing, aimed mainly at breaking civilian morale, because NATO didn't want to risk their soldiers' lives. And they didn't lose one. Now *that's* "impunity."

And who could look honestly at the results of this war, unblinkered by the "official story" of the Western mass media, and conclude that this was a "humanitarian intervention"? A bombing campaign that, in dropping twenty thousand bombs on Yugoslavia, directly killed between five hundred[28] and eighteen hundred[29] civilian children, women, and men of all ethnicities and permanently injured as many others; a bombing campaign that caused sixty to one hundred billion U.S. dollars worth of damage to an already impoverished country;[30] a bombing campaign that directly and indirectly caused one million refugees to flee Kosovo in all directions;[31] a bombing campaign that indirectly caused the deaths of maybe thousands more, by provoking the violent retaliatory and defensive measures that were entirely predictable when you massively bomb one people on behalf of another and give a free hand to extremists on both sides to vent their hatred; a bombing campaign that led to the entirely predictable "ethnic cleansing" that has occurred in Kosovo since the entry of the triumphant KLA, fully backed by NATO's might, which has seen hundreds of thousands of Serbs and Roma (and the few Jews remaining) driven out of Kosovo and hundreds murdered, a murder rate about twice the American one, already one of the highest in the world.[32]

These results were to be expected, and NATO's military and political advisers must have contemplated them in their very careful planning of the war, which went back more than a year before the bombing commenced. So, in our view, the view of most of the world, it was the American government and business class, aided and abetted by their European counterparts, creating violent social conditions, destroying every chance to peacefully resolve them, and then imposing violent solutions. This was classic Americanism. Like poverty and murder in the midst of fabulous wealth, with the resulting tensions resolved by repression, including the death penalty. In other words, there were plenty of reasons to oppose this war.

Another reason I opposed it was the grotesque Holocaust analogy. Milosevic was a new Hitler. "Europe" had not seen this kind of thing since the Holocaust (of course, Africa had, and it continues to, South America had, Vietnam had). Maybe Benigni's film (*La vita è bella*), so lavished with Hollywood awards on the eve of the bombing, had made everyone think that trains and refugees were enough to make a Holocaust.

Trains and refugees do not make a Holocaust. The worst scenarios of Serb ethnic cleansing didn't even come close to the extermination program of the Nazis. You don't have to minimize the suffering of people killed in the thousands, terrorized, and expelled from their homes to distinguish between that and being hunted down one by one wherever we lived or wherever we ran in a methodical plan (that succeeded by about half) to wipe an entire people off the face of the earth. The Nazis, as Julie Birchill wrote, didn't put Jews on trains to Israel.[33] And what about the context? Did European Jewry have a separatist army like the KLA that was trying to take a piece of Germany away from the Nazis? If Srebrenica was "genocide," indeed "extermination" in the absurdly hyperbolic opinion of the ICTY judges in *Krstic*,[34] what was the Holocaust? And if only the West had merely "stood by"! Instead they locked their doors to Jewish immigration and sent people back to their deaths. "Outmoded notions of national sovereignty?" Had the world stood up for national sovereignty and international law when Hitler invaded Czechoslovakia, there would have been no Holocaust. And when the Allies were engaged in a fully legal war with Germany in Poland and they were begged by Jews to go five kilometers out of their way and bomb Auschwitz, which could have saved hundreds of thousands of Jewish lives, they couldn't be bothered because it didn't fit into their strategic plans. It seemed to me that if there were any analogy, it was that the West didn't give a damn about the Albanians any more than they did about the Jews.

A big part of the Holocaust analogy of course was the ICTY, the Nuremberg precedent and all that. This was something played up by the court itself, most notably in the ignorantly bloated rhetoric of Judge Gabrielle Kirk McDonald in speeches before the war, but also in small details such as the tasteless display of Prosecutor Louise Arbour's photo in the Anne Frank House in Amsterdam (which could be seen even as NATO's cluster bombs started to fall on Yugoslavia) with a quote arguing that she was continuing the work of punishing Anne Frank's murderers.

What were the real motives for the war if they were clearly not the humanitarian ones that NATO claimed? This was what made people of good will suspend their disbelief. It was hard to find the classic imperialist motives in this godforsaken part of the world. But there were, in fact, many war-making interests that converged here: the need to invent a new role for NATO after the Cold War; arms manufacturers' profits; a good place to test weapons; lucrative reconstruction contracts; a war *pour encourager les autres*, that is to say, a demonstration war for those who think they can oppose American will; a war against a weak enemy that could be fought without losing one American life in combat; security for the much-coveted Caspian Sea oil pipeline; even Monica Lewinsky—all these are far more plausible explanations than a sudden, isolated instance of humanitarianism on the part of the Americans.

One very important strategic interest seems to have been the United States' desperate desire, especially in the Clinton years, to free itself of the discipline of the United Nations (UN) system, including the Security Council's monopoly of the use of force, which, from Washington's point of view, puts far too much institutional power in the hands of rivals Russia and China. This is the powerful thesis of the Englishman Peter Gowan, that the Balkans was an excuse for the United States to redesign the world order in its own image.[35] Through the beggaring of the UN (including the firing of an independent secretary general Boutros Boutros-Ghali and his replacement with longtime NATO friend Kofi Annan) and through the expansion of NATO eastward, the United States has sought to establish NATO as the world's only legitimate active military interventionist force. Because, while the United States only has one vote at the UN and in the Security Council, by virtue of its military power, it *owns* NATO. Ninety percent of the military hardware used in the Kosovo war was American.[36] The other countries merely provided political cover.

There are always lots and lots of military and political reasons for going to war for a superpower, but the circumstances have to be right. The Balkans supplied about as good an excuse as could be hoped for, since humanitarianism could be a plausible justification (given the world's most powerful propaganda machine, the American news media) and the enemy was too weak to cause any losses. But the problem (or the *point* in Gowan's view) was that it was illegal, and over this there was no controversy.

This war was a conscious violation of international law and the Charter of the UN. The Charter authorizes the use of force in only two situations: self-defense or when authorized by the Security Council. The jurisprudence of the International Court of Justice is also very clear. For instance, it stated in its ruling against the United States' intervention in Nicaragua:

> In any event, while the United States might form its own appraisal of the situation as to respect for human rights in Nicaragua, the use of force could not be the appropriate method to monitor or ensure such respect. With regard to the steps actually taken, the protection of human rights, a strictly humanitarian objective, cannot be compatible with the mining of ports, the destruction of oil installations, or again with the training, arming and equipping of the contras.[37]

It should also be noted that the preliminary decision of the World Court in Yugoslavia's case against ten NATO countries does not in the slightest contradict this. This decision (to reject Yugoslavia's claim for preliminary measures against the attack) was taken on purely jurisdictional grounds, first, the United States' refusal to recognize the World Court's jurisdiction in general, and second, objections (by Canada and others) to jurisdiction in this specific case.[38]

So in the case of NATO's war on Yugoslavia, neither of the two exclusive bases for the use of force (Security Council authorization or self-defense) was even claimed by NATO. It should be pointed out that this is a very rare case of scholarly consensus (not seen in the case of Afghanistan, for instance): the war's illegality was not disputed by any legal scholar of repute, even those who had some sympathy for the war, for instance Professor Antonio Cassese, former President and Judge of the ICTY itself.[39]

Incidentally, as a violation of the UN Charter, the attack on Yugoslavia was also a violation of the NATO Treaty. The NATO Treaty (1949), so far as is relevant, reads as follows:

> [Preamble]: The Parties to this Treaty reaffirm their faith in the purposes and principles of the Charter of the United Nations and their desire to live in peace with all peoples and all governments.
>
> Article 1: The Parties undertake, as set forth in the Charter of the United Nations, to settle any international dispute in which they may be involved by peaceful means in such a manner that international peace and security and justice are not endangered, and to refrain in their international relations from the threat or use of force in any manner inconsistent with the purposes of the United Nations.
>
> Article 7: This treaty does not affect, and shall not be interpreted as affecting in any way the rights and obligations under the Charter of the Parties which are members of the United Nations, or the primary responsibility of the Security Council for the maintenance of international peace and security.

Another very important and uncontroversial legal element of all this was that the claimed humanitarian motives for the war, even if they were true, could not change its illegal character. In fact, the reason why there is such unanimity among scholars on the illegality of this war is that there is no "humanitarian exception" under international law or the UN Charter. Such an exception would have sounded distinctly Hitlerian to the drafters of the Charter, because that's how Hitler justified German aggression in World War II. This does not mean that there are no means for the international community to intervene to prevent or stop humanitarian disasters, even to use force where necessary. It just means that the use of force for humanitarian purposes has been totally absorbed in the UN Charter. A state must use only peaceful means or be able to demonstrate the humanity of its proposed intervention to the Security Council, including, of course, the five permanent members possessing a veto.

The apparent contradiction (that humanitarianism is a ground of intervention but only when authorized by the Security Council) is not so difficult to understand. It's as if the police arrested and imprisoned someone without trial, arguing that, since they had plenty of proof, why bother with the formalities?

It's well known that one of the justifications for the war was the supposed untrustworthiness of the Security Council. But imagine the police in the example just given claiming that the courts were so biased or inefficient that they couldn't be relied upon to convict the guilty. Now imagine the police making the same claim when they themselves were the ones sabotaging the courts. Because almost all the vetoing in the Security Council since the 1960s has been by the NATO countries: 86 percent of all vetoes between 1966 and 1997.[40] In the last ten years, the United States alone has accounted for 63 percent of the vetoes.[41] In March 2001, it vetoed the call for an international observer force to monitor the violence between Israel and the Palestinians.[42]

In fact, the Security Council was far from "paralyzed," as the NATO defenders like to put it. The Security Council had issued numerous resolutions authorizing action in this very conflict (Resolutions 1160, 1199, and 1203 of 1998, and Resolutions 1239 and 1244 of 1999, the last of which brought an end to the bombing). None of them authorized the use of force, of course, but not because the Security Council was incapable of doing so. The United States' war to expel Iraq from Kuwait in 1991 was explicitly authorized by Resolution 678 of November 29, 1990. Indeed, the NATO bombings during the Bosnian civil war were expressly authorized by Security Council Resolutions of 816 and 836 of 1993, "subject to close cooperation with the Secretary-General and UNPROFOR." This, of course, is not to defend either of these cases of the use of force, merely to show that the Security Council was far from incapable of authorizing it.

So the Gowan thesis is amply demonstrated by the facts: the United States had systematically undermined the UN system so that it could deliberately boycott it in this case and establish a new precedent. But to do this they had to appeal to a higher legality, not their own naked power, and that's where the ICTY came in. This UN organ would give the war the needed appearance of international legality, as a war fought essentially to prevent war crimes and to bring the criminals to justice.

Now it was only to be expected that, with most of the world opposed to the war, there would be quite a few lawyers who would feel the same way and who would harbor well-founded suspicions about the ICTY. With NATO bombing away and acting like a bull in a china shop with human life, they would be moved to call the ICTY's bluff by bringing charges against the NATO leaders for violations of the same Geneva Conventions that Arbour and company were charging the Serbs with. In fact, within a month of the commencement of the bombing, several more or less detailed legal complaints had been delivered to the ICTY, including one from the Faculty of Law of Belgrade University, one from Greece, on behalf of six thousand Greek citizens, one from England from a group called the Committee for the Advancement of International Criminal Law, one from a Committee of the Russian Duma, and our own complaint from Canada on behalf of law professors from York University in Toronto jointly with the American Association of Jurists, a group with members throughout the Western hemisphere. To this must be added the thousands of individuals from every corner of the globe who wrote to the ICTY endorsing our complaints or making their own.

In our case, we filed a complaint against sixty-eight named NATO leaders. The charges were: Grave breaches of the Geneva Conventions of August 12, 1949, (contrary to Article 2) namely, the following acts against persons or property protected under the provisions of the relevant Geneva Convention: (a) willful killing; (c) willfully causing great suffering or serious injury to body or health; (d) extensive destruction and appropriation of property, not justified by military necessity and carried out unlawfully and wantonly. Violations of the laws or customs of war (Article 3): (a) employment of poisonous weapons or other weapons to cause unnecessary suffering; (b) wanton destruction of cities, towns or villages, or devastation not justified by military necessity; (c) attack, or bombardment, by whatever means, of undefended towns, villages, dwellings, or buildings; (d) seizure of, destruction or wilful damage done to institutions dedicated to religion, charity and education, the arts and sciences, historic monuments and works of art and science. Crimes against humanity (Article 5): (a) murder; . . . (i) other inhumane acts.

Article 7 of the Tribunal Statute provides for "individual criminal responsibility" in this way:

> 1. A person who planned, instigated, ordered, committed or otherwise aided and abetted in the planning, preparation or execution of a crime referred to in articles 2 to 5 of the present Statute, shall be individually responsible for the crime.
>
> 2. The official position of any accused person, whether as Head of State or Government or as a responsible Government official, shall not relieve such person of criminal responsibility or mitigate punishment.
>
> 3. The fact that any of the acts referred to in articles 2 to 5 of the present Statute was committed by a subordinate does not relieve his superior of criminal responsibility if he knew or had reason to know that the subordinate was about to commit such acts or had done so and the superior failed to take the necessary and reasonable measures to prevent such acts or to punish the perpetrators thereof.

The legal case was based on two grounds. First, the illegality of the war. This was a classic war of aggression, which the Nuremberg Judgment had classified as the "supreme" crime: "To initiate a war of aggression . . . is the supreme international crime, differing only from other war crimes in that it contains within itself the accumulated evil of the whole."

Now this crime was not included in the ICTY statute as a specific crime. Evidently the United States didn't want it there, the way it desperately didn't want it in the International Criminal Court (ICC) Statute. Was it for "difficulty of definition" as is often said? As if war crimes and crimes against humanity were easy to define. Once again, Milosevic's explanation is the only one that makes sense: the ICTY was meant to legitimate aggression, so how could it make aggression a crime?

On the other hand the crime of aggression was not specifically excluded. And in the article on "crimes against humanity," there were the crimes of murder and other inhumane acts.[43] Murder is universally defined as causing death intentionally—which, in classic criminal law doctrine, always includes knowingly—and without lawful excuse.

Our case was simply that the NATO leaders planned and executed a bombing campaign that was contrary to the most fundamental tenets of international law and that they knew would cause the death and permanent injury of thousands of civilian children, women, and men. They admitted this over and over again, said they were sorry, but that's what happens in war, and went on bombing. On this ground alone, that is, the killing of hundreds or thousands of civilians knowingly and without lawful excuse, these leaders were guilty of *mass murder*. Milosevic and the other Serb leaders were indicted in The Hague for the murder of 385 victims.[44] The total victims of the 98 people executed for murder in the United States in 1999 was 129.[45] The NATO leaders murdered at least five hundred and perhaps as many as eighteen hundred.[46]

Here's what Chief Prosecutor Robert Jackson said on the subject at Nuremberg:

> Any resort to war—any kind of war—is a resort to means that are inherently criminal. War inevitably is a course of killings, assaults, deprivations of liberty, and destruction of property. An honestly defensive war is, of course, legal and saves those lawfully conducting it from criminality. *But inherently criminal acts cannot be defended by showing that those who committed them were engaged in a war, when war itself is illegal.* The very minimum legal consequence of the treaties making aggressive war illegal is to strip those who incite or wage them of every defense the law ever gave, and to leave the war-makers subject to judgment by the usually accepted principles of the law of crimes. (Emphasis added)[47]

And then there were the Geneva Conventions, which basically make it a crime, even in a legal war, to kill and injure civilians intentionally or carelessly, that is, not to take care to hit only military targets. But, according to admissions made in public throughout the war (for instance during daily NATO press briefings), according to eyewitness reports, and according to powerful circumstantial evidence displayed on the world's television screens throughout the bombing campaign—evidence good enough to convict in any criminal court in the world—these NATO leaders deliberately and illegally made targets of places and things with only tenuous or slight military value or no military value at all.[48] Places such as city bridges, factories, hospitals, marketplaces, downtown and residential neighbourhoods, and television studios. The same evidence shows that, in doing this, the NATO leaders aimed to demoralize and break the will of the people, not to defeat its army. Michael Dobbs, Madeleine Albright's authorized biographer, wrote in the *Washington Post* on July 26, 1999, that "it is obvious to anyone who visited Serbia during the war that undermining civilian morale formed an essential part of the alliance's war-winning strategy."

One reason civilian targets are illegal is that civilians are very likely to be killed or injured when such targets are hit. And all of the NATO leaders knew that. They were carefully told that by their military planners. And they still went ahead and did it. And they did it without any risk to themselves or to their soldiers and pilots. That's why this war was called a "coward's war." The cowardice lay in fighting the civilian population and not the military, in bombing from altitudes so high that the civilians, Serbs, Albanians, Roma, and anybody else on the ground, bore all the risks of the "inevitable collateral damage." Displacing all the risks onto the civilian population is contrary to the recognized laws of war. Indeed, there is persuasive evidence that, in some circumstances at least, NATO not only *knowingly* killed civilians, but *deliberately* set out to do so: for example on the Grdelica and Varvarin bridges (April 12 and May 30) and in the Nis marketplace (May 7).[49]

Starting in May 1999, along with many other lawyers and parliamentarians around the world, and thousands of individual citizens, we made our case to the Tribunal. We spent hours with Arbour and Del Ponte and their advisers. We filed written legal arguments and volumes of documentary evidence. In December of 1999, Del Ponte let it slip in an interview that she was studying our brief.[50] All hell broke loose. American military authorities said they would never cooperate.[51] Did Del Ponte call for sanctions? No, she unctuously apologized and backtracked.[52] By March of 2000, it was clear to us that she was a fraud, and we publicly denounced her as such.

Del Ponte announced her decision to the Security Council on June 2, 2000, but her report was only released on June 13.[53] Why did she anticipate the results? Only one explanation: she knew that Amnesty International was releasing its report on June 7 with a very different conclusion from the Prosecutor's, and she wanted to beat them to the punch. You should read these two reports in order to see whether Del Ponte's bleating about Milosevic can be given any credibility at all.

Amnesty's executive summary reads as follows:

> Amnesty International believes that in the course of Operation Allied Force, civilian deaths could have been significantly reduced if NATO forces had fully adhered to the laws of war. . . . NATO did not always meet its legal obligations

> in selecting targets and in choosing means and methods of attack. In one instance, the attack on the headquarters of Serbian state radio and television (RTS), NATO launched a direct attack on a civilian object, killing 16 civilians. *Such attack breached article 52 (I) of Protocol I and therefore constitutes a war crime*. . . . The International Criminal Tribunal for the former Yugoslavia should investigate all credible allegations of serious violations of international humanitarian law during Operation Allied Force with a view of bringing to trial anyone against whom there is sufficient admissible evidence. States should surrender to the Tribunal any suspect sought for prosecution by the Tribunal. (Emphasis added)[54]

Amnesty's report identifies three basic types of war crimes committed by NATO. First, attacks on civilian targets, such as the Belgrade RTS radio and television building, contrary to Article 52 (1) of Protocol I of the Geneva Convention (1977), made criminal by Article 2 of the Tribunal Statute. Secondly, for example, in the killing of civilians on bridges (Grdelica, Luzane, and Varvarin), the crime was the failure to suspend an attack after it became clear that would cause a loss of civilian life excessive in relation to the concrete military advantage to be anticipated, in contravention of Article 57 (2) (b). Thirdly, for example, in bombings that killed displaced civilians (e.g. Djakovica and Kori?a), insufficient precautions were taken to minimize civilian casualties, contrary to 57 (2)(a). Specifically on the "coward's war" question of bombing from 15,000 feet: "Also, aspects of the Rules of Engagement, specifically the requirement that NATO aircraft fly above 15,000 feet, made full adherence to international humanitarian law virtually impossible." Amnesty also found a lack of discrimination contrary to the Geneva Conventions in the use of cluster bombs: "The use of certain weapons, particularly cluster bombs, may have contributed to causing unlawful deaths."[55]

The Amnesty Report ends with nine illuminating case studies. They include the five selected by the Office of the Prosecutor's (OTP) Report and make for striking comparisons. The OTP report comes as something of a shock, not for its conclusion (which was expected, though admittedly not in the extreme form in which it came), but for the amateurishness and lack of shame with which it justifies that conclusion.

If it feels more like it was written by a lawyer for NATO than a judge, this shouldn't be surprising, because there is little doubt that the brief was in fact written by a NATO lawyer, if only an ex-NATO lawyer, one William J. Fenrick, Canadian Armed Forces Frigate Captain (ret.). Fenrick has been involved in the project from the beginning, leaving his position as Director of Law for Operations and Training in the Canadian Department of Defence to help set up the Tribunal in 1992. It's worth remembering that the tribunal was created at the insistence of the Americans, and that at the very moment of its creation, U.S. Secretary of State Lawrence Eagleburger publicly identified Serb leaders Milosevic, Karadzic, Mladic, and Arkan as war criminals. Fenrick became senior legal adviser of the Tribunal when it was officially launched in 1995. The OTP Report is unsigned, attributed to an anonymous "committee" charged with the case by Arbour in May 1999 (one week after we served our complaint), but amateur sleuths will notice that it quotes great swaths of an article authored by Fenrick in 1997—word for word and without quotation marks.[56]

On the other hand, the report often goes beyond even the lawyer's brief and comes as close as possible to being an actual NATO press release itself that might have been issued by Jamie Shea or James Rubin. These hard-nosed experts at the ICTY, with all their experience in investigating war crimes, declared that their operating investigative technique would be to read NATO's press releases and take them at face value:

> 90. The committee has conducted its review relying essentially upon public documents, including statements made by NATO and NATO countries at press conferences and public documents produced by the FRY. It has tended to assume that the NATO and NATO countries' press statements are generally reliable and that explanations have been honestly given.[57]

Can you imagine what kind of law enforcement a country would have if the police took alleged criminals' explanations at face value? Can you imagine how many indictments would have been issued against the Serb leadership if the OTP had stopped at the FRY press releases? It's not as if NATO had proved its veracity to the OTP by opening its books to them and making a full account. There was no investigation because NATO did not allow it:

> The committee must note, however, that when the OTP requested NATO to answer specific questions about specific incidents, the NATO reply was couched in general terms and failed to address the specific incidents.[58]

In fact, as far as the record goes (paragraph 12), the OTP sent one letter to NATO on February 8, 2000, and NATO replied ("in general terms," etc.) on May 10.[59]

So, having determined that NATO did not want to be investigated, the OTP had to absolve them without an investigation. Hence the "face value" principle. But even this would not do the trick entirely, because NATO made some pretty damning public admissions along the way. For instance, in bombing the Belgrade TV station, some NATO leaders claimed (most implausibly) that they did it to knock out FRY military communications, but others (e.g. Tony Blair) said they did it to strike a blow against Serb "propaganda" (i.e. they didn't like what the TV was saying)—an unmistakable war crime. That left only one thing to do: take the NATO version most favorable to NATO!

The report is so weak in its reasoning, so untroubled by inconsistency and double standards, that one can't help wondering whether the authors had spent too much time in The Hague's famous "coffee shops." For example, when they said that 500 deaths were too little for crimes against humanity, did they realize that Milosevic had been charged with 385? ("If one accepts the figures in this compilation of approximately 495 civilians killed and 820 civilians wounded in documented instances, there is simply no evidence of the necessary crime base for charges of genocide or crimes against humanity.") And what about paragraph fifty-six? Did they do the math on a napkin?

> 56. The committee agrees there is nothing inherently unlawful about flying above the height which can be reached by enemy air defenses. However, NATO air commanders have a duty to take practicable measures to distinguish military objectives from civilians or civilian objectives. The 15,000 feet minimum altitude adopted for part of the campaign may have meant the target could not be verified with the naked eye. However, it appears that with the use of modern technology, the obligation to distinguish was effectively carried out in the vast majority of cases during the bombing campaign.

*"Vast majority"!* What can this mean in a bombing campaign of thirty-eight thousand sorties? Seventy-five percent would mean 9500 sorties in which it did not comply with its legal obligations. Ninety percent? That would mean 3800. Ninety-nine percent? That would leave 380 sorties—more than enough to kill 500 people, if you're using the most powerful conventional weapons technology in the world. Even with all this, the OTP had major problems defending the decision not to even open an investigation, because the orthodox legal tests laid down by the Statute and deployed so handily to prosecute the Serbs became extremely inconvenient where absolving NATO was concerned. They had to undergo a major transformation.

The civilian principle of *l'obbligarietà d'azione penale* ("obligatory prosecution") written into the Statute in the clearest terms became a "discretion" to open an investigation. This discretion then became exercisable only when there was proof beyond any doubt that the accused were guilty. On this basis, of course, Milosevic never could have been charged. The clearest and most chilling example of this is the Grdelica bridge incident. On April 12, a NATO plane launched two separate laser-guided bombs that hit a passenger train crossing a bridge, killing at least ten people and injuring at least fifteen. NATO's explanation, offered by General Wesley Clark the next day at a news conference, was that the pilot was attacking the bridge and not the train and that the pilot did not see the train until the last second because it was going too fast.[60] According to the OTP, "It does not appear that the train was targeted deliberately."[61] Why? More work for the face value principle: *U.S. Deputy Defense Secretary John Hamre and General Wesley Clark, NATO's Supreme Allied Commander for Europe said so!* The OTP reproduced Clark's explanation in full:

> [T]his was a case where a pilot was assigned to strike a railroad bridge that is part of the integrated communications supply network in Serbia. He launched his missile from his aircraft that was many miles away, he was not able to put his eyes on the bridge, it was a remotely directed attack. And as he stared intently at the desired target point on the bridge, and I talked to the team at Aviano who was directly engaged in this operation, as the pilot stared intently at the desired aim point on the bridge and worked it, and worked it and worked it, and all of a sudden at the very last instant with less than a second to go he caught a flash of movement that came into the screen and it was the train coming in. Unfortunately he couldn't dump the bomb at that point, it was locked, it was going into the target and it was an unfortunate incident which he, and the crew, and all of us very much regret. We certainly don't want to do collateral damage.
>
> The mission was to take out the bridge. He realized when it had happened that he had not hit the bridge, but what he had hit was the train. He had another aim point on the bridge, it was a relatively long bridge and he believed he still had to accomplish his mission, the pilot circled back around. He put his aim point on the other end of the bridge from where the train had come, by the time the bomb got close to the bridge it was covered with smoke and clouds and at the last minute again in an uncanny accident, the train had slid forward from the original impact and parts of the train had moved across the bridge, and so that by striking the other end of the bridge he actually caused additional damage to the train.[62]

General Clark then showed the cockpit video of the plane that fired on the bridge:

> The pilot in the aircraft is looking at about a 5-inch screen, he is seeing about this much and in here you can see this is the railroad bridge which is a much better view than he actually had, you can see the tracks running this way. Look very intently at the aim point, concentrate right there and you can see how, if you were focused right on your job as a pilot, suddenly that train appeared. It was really unfortunate. Here, he came back around to try to strike a different point on the bridge because he was trying to do a job to take the bridge down. Look at this aim point—you can see smoke and other obscuration there—he couldn't tell what this was exactly. Focus intently right at the centre of the cross. He is bringing these two crosses together and suddenly he recognizes at the very last instant that the train that was struck here has moved on across the bridge and so the engine apparently was struck by the second bomb.[63]

Now the OTP's dismissal of this particular incident was rendered more complicated by the fact that a German computer wiz, Mr. Ekkehard Wenz, an opponent of the war acting entirely independently, analyzed the video and the technical information provided by NATO and discovered that the video shown by Clark had been speeded up to about five times its speed and that the plane was of a type in which there was both a pilot and a gunner. He concluded that the attack on the train must have been deliberate.[64] After a German newspaper report, NATO finally admitted in January 2000 that the video had been speeded up.[65] The OTP report does not dispute Wenz's points—nor naturally does the incident shake its faith in the trustworthiness of NATO's press releases—but says that this still does not prove his case:

> If the committee accepts Mr. Wenz's estimate of the reaction time available, the person controlling the bombs still had a very short period of time, less than 7 or 8 seconds in all probability to react. Although Mr. Wenz is of the view that the WSO intentionally targeted the train, the committee's review of the frames used in the report indicates another interpretation is equally available. The cross hairs remain fixed on the bridge throughout, and it is clear from this footage that the train can be seen moving toward the bridge only as the bomb is in flight: it is only in the course of the bomb's trajectory that the image of the train becomes visible. At a point where the bomb is within a few seconds of impact, a very slight change to the bomb aiming point can be observed, in that it drops a couple of feet. This sequence regarding the bombsights indicates that it is unlikely that the WSO was targeting the train, but instead suggests that the target was a point on the span of the bridge before the train appeared.[66]

Notice the standard: *another interpretation is equally available*. Only "equally available"—in other words, even though there was a fifty-fifty chance a dozen civilians had been murdered by NATO, which would put a different complexion on the whole bombing campaign, there would be no further *investigation*.

That aside, the OTP point is that if the train were deliberately targeted, the pilot would have followed it with his cross hairs. Unless, or course, he was trying to "fabricate an accident," which is Mr. Wenz's point, posted in a comment on July 12, 2000, for his group the Grdelica Organisation:

> As visible most clearly in the decelerated video, the target point during the *beginning* of the scene was the abutment of the bridge on the centre pier. Shortly after the train reached the bridge, the target point is *completely changed* from this point, which is the only reasonable point to take out truss bridges, towards a truss part, a loss that might damage the bridge but would not destroy the bridge at all (as happened). Since NATO maintained that missions were planned exactly, it is not very likely that truss bridges were intended to be dismantled brace by brace with 800,000 $ missiles. The reason to give up a "perfect" aiming point

> in favour of another unreasonable aiming point, in combination with the presentation of speeded video material, can only be that the previous aiming point wasn't the intended aiming point. In other words: this is the way to fabricate an "accident."[67]

Mr. Wenz also points out a number of other errors: that the bombs were not laser-guided but "TV-guided," that is, from a TV in the bomb which makes control much greater; that there was a third bomb that didn't hit the bridge at all, suggesting that the bridge was not the target; and that seven or eight seconds from the appearance of the train was plenty of time for a Weapons Systems Operator with only that duty to change the path of the target (in the whole video the target is changed six times in twenty-three seconds). In an e-mail to me, Wenz put it this way: "Sit back, close your eyes and count slowly from 21 to 28. Enough time?" Thus, Wenz's view is that the Weapons Systems Officer had plenty of time after he saw the train to put the bomb wherever he wanted.

So, the OTP analysis of the first bomb is completely unconvincing. But its analysis of the *second* bomb is nonexistent:

> 62. The train was on the bridge when the bridge was targeted a second time and the bridge length has been estimated at 50 meters (Wenz study para 6 g above at p.25). It is the opinion of the committee that the information in relation to the attack with the first bomb does not provide a sufficient basis to initiate an investigation. [*MM: Yeah, but what about the second one?*] The committee has divided views concerning the attack with the second bomb in relation to whether there was an element of recklessness in the conduct of the pilot or WSO. Despite this, the committee is in agreement that, based on the criteria for initiating an investigation (see para. 5 above), this incident should not be investigated. In relation to whether there is information warranting consideration of command responsibility, the committee is of the view that there is no information from which to conclude that an investigation is necessary into the criminal responsibility of persons higher in the chain of command. Based on the information available to it, it is the opinion of the committee that the attack on the train at Grdelica Gorge should not be investigated by the OTP.

This is nothing less than incoherent babbling. There is zero explanation of how firing a second bomb with knowledge that the train was on the bridge could not constitute recklessness (a consciousness that civilians might be endangered). Wenz has also pointed out that the bridge was subsequently repaired by Yugoslavia, not rebuilt, which means that NATO used some very expensive bombs to hit a bridge twice without destroying it.

We're talking here about *opening an investigation* in a case where the committee was divided in its views! Where there is no other plausible explanation. Milosevic had lots of explanations for Racak—quite credible in fact. Louise Arbour didn't wait to hear them before she "launched her investigation" the next day. On the other hand, listen to what Amnesty said about the Grdelica bridge incident:

> NATO's explanation of the bombing—particularly General Clark's account of the pilot's rationale for continuing the attack after he had hit the train—suggests that the pilot had understood the mission was to destroy the bridge regardless of the cost in terms of civilian casualties. This would violate the rules of distinction and proportionality.
>
> Yet, even if the pilot was, for some reason, unable to ascertain that no train was travelling towards the bridge at the time of the first attack, he was fully aware that the train was on the bridge when he dropped the second bomb, whether smoke obscured its exact whereabouts or not. This decision to proceed with the second attack appears to have violated Article 57 of Protocol I which requires an attack to "be cancelled or suspended if it becomes clear that the objective is a not a military one . . . or that the attack may be expected to cause incidental loss of civilian life . . . which would be excessive in relation to the concrete and direct military advantage anticipated." Unless NATO is justified in believing that destroying the bridge at that particular moment was of such military importance as to justify the number of civilian casualties likely to be caused by continuing the attack—an argument that NATO has not made—the attack should have been stopped.

The third incident discussed by the OTP was the deliberate attack by NATO on the RTS (Serbian TV and Radio Station) in Belgrade on April 23 in which sixteen people are believed to have been killed. The OTP concedes it would have been a crime if the station were taken out for propaganda purposes alone (as Blair's statement admits), but concludes that it may not have been (other statements) and thus does not open an investigation. The report also shifts the blame entirely to the FRY for allowing the civilians to stay at the station after they had been warned. As if a robber were to come to your house and tell you to leave and you didn't and he killed you, and any self-respecting judge would say he's not guilty of murder.

Here's what Amnesty said:

> Amnesty International recognizes that disrupting government propaganda may help to undermine the morale of the population and the armed forces, but believes that justifying an attack on a civilian facility on such grounds stretches the meaning of "effective contribution to military action" and "definite military advantage" beyond the acceptable bounds of interpretation. Under the requirements of Article 52(2) of Protocol I, the RTS headquarters cannot be considered a military objective. As such, the attack on the RTS headquarters violated the

> prohibition to attack civilian objects contained in Article 52(I) and therefore constitutes a war crime.
>
> The attack on the RTS headquarters may well have violated international humanitarian law even if the building could have been properly considered a military objective. Specifically, that attack would have violated the rule of proportionality under Article 51(5)(b) of Protocol I and may have also violated the obligations to provide effective warning under Article 57(2)(c) of the same Protocol.
>
> Article 51(5)(b) prohibits attacks "which may be expected to cause incidental loss of civilian life . . . which would be excessive in relation to the concrete and direct military advantage anticipated." . . . NATO must have clearly anticipated that civilians in the RTS building would have been killed. In addition, it appears that NATO realized that attacking the RTS building would only interrupt broadcasting for a brief period. SACEUR General Wesley Clark has stated: "We knew when we struck that there would be alternate means of getting the Serb Television. There's no single switch to turn off everything but we thought it was a good move to strike it and the political leadership agreed with us". In other words, NATO deliberately attacked a civilian object, killing 16 civilians, for the purpose of disrupting Serbian television broadcasts in the middle of the night for approximately three hours. It is hard to see how this can be consistent with the rule of proportionality.

One question which Amnesty did not deal with and on which the OTP took a firm stand concerned the effects of the illegality of the war. We had stressed to both prosecutors the importance of this. Our argument was that the illegality of the war and the lack of any real, as opposed to claimed, humanitarian justification made the killing of civilians murder and therefore a "crime against humanity." However, the OTP resolutely rejected this proposition:

> 30. Allegations have been made that, as NATO's resort to force was not authorized by the Security Council or in self-defense, that the resort to force was illegal and, consequently, all forceful measures taken by NATO were unlawful. . . . In particular, the legitimacy of the presumed basis for the NATO bombing campaign, humanitarian intervention without prior Security Council authorization, is hotly debated. That being said, as noted in paragraph 4 above, the crime related to an unlawful decision to use force is the crime against peace or aggression . . . the ICTY does not have jurisdiction over crimes against peace. . . . The ICTY has jurisdiction over serious violations of international humanitarian law as specified in Articles 2-5 of the Statute. These are *jus in belllum* offences.

The result is that the Tribunal gave NATO immunity for civilian deaths and injury that were merely part of the war, as if this were a legal war. This is a preposterous reading of the Statute and compares very unfavorably with Robert Jackson's statement at Nuremberg cited earlier. ("*But inherently crim-*

*inal acts cannot be defended by showing that those who committed them were engaged in a war, when war itself is illegal.")* Even if it were a correct reading, it would not save the ICTY's legitimacy that its Statute had been so crudely drawn to make American war crimes immune from punishment.

So my conclusion is that we are dealing in the ICTY with a corrupt tribunal. It can't even be trusted to give Milosevic a fair trial. But this is not the main point. Even if Milosevic were guilty, the failure to prosecute NATO crime renders this tribunal the opposite of what it claims to be. Not abstractly, but concretely. Imagine that one mafia boss makes war on another and then buys the police and the courts to prosecute only the other one. Who would feel safe? Naturally, only those who kiss the hand of the more powerful boss and pay him his *pizzo*. Then they would be free as birds to commit any crimes they wanted (so long as they didn't threaten Don Corleone's interests, of course). In other words, all you have to do is play ball with the Americans and you can do anything you want in Turkey, in Indonesia, in Colombia, in Saudi Arabia, and, I'm sad to say, in Israel.

## THE FUTURE OF INTERNATIONAL CRIMINAL LAW

What about the future? Maybe the ICTY was just a flawed prototype, like the Wright brothers' first airplane with its wobbly half-flight? On the other hand, if we take a look at what has happened with the International Criminal Court, it appears that corruption is the destiny of international criminal law.

The ICC statute, signed in Rome in 1998, is as full of holes as a plate of *bucatini alla matriciana.* Thanks to a big Western lobbying effort, it effectively leaves out the "supreme crime" of aggression and defines war crimes in a way congenial to the big powers (tending to exclude the kind they commit in their "humanitarian interventions" and "self-defense"). It also allows agreements between states to override the duty to arrest war criminals: Pinochet might not have even been subject to arrest in Britain under the ICC.

But the ICC has one good thing going for it: the judges and prosecutors are not subject to an American veto (like the judges and prosecutors of the ICTY via the Security Council). But that means the Americans will never ratify it. They've said so. They signed it on the last day possible for reasons of pure public relations (the way Israel did), with Clinton expressly saying that he recommended it not be ratified. Now nobody seriously thinks you can have an international criminal justice without the world's most powerful country to enforce it, as American critics of the ICC have not been shy in pointing out.[68]

The result is that the ICC operates as pure propaganda: it makes it seem that the punishment of America's enemies is part of a universal movement against impunity. In this way it operates like the detention of Pinochet who was held during the war in Yugoslavia and then released—"a great precedent" that will never be applied to him or anyone else the United States doesn't want tried. In fact, the war in Afghanistan has already provided another bit of proof for the unidimensional, war-legitimating function of international criminal law. The possibility of criminal proceedings against Osama bin Laden or other suspects in the September 11 attacks before an impartial international tribunal was repeatedly advocated by peace advocates and indeed the government of Afghanistan as a serious peace alternative, but rejected out of hand by the Americans because it didn't fit into their plans for war.

So international criminal justice seems destined to remain a hypocritical expression of power, as typically American as the death penalty and judicial review: repression as a solution to social problems and judges acting as an antidote to democracy[69]—as in the very election of President Bush II, where the U.S. Supreme Court, in a transparently biased decision, reversed its pro-federalist jurisprudence and ordered Florida not to count votes, evidently for fear that Bush might lose.

Finally, we should question the very vision of international criminal law.[70] Have we not learned the lessons of a century of criminology that violence has causes? International criminal law, like the "war on terrorism," seems designed to banish all talk of causes, beyond identifying this year's devil. But in a world of inequality gone berserk, we have more than enough causes to explain ethnic violence, and terrorism as well. Is it not obvious that we should try to foster the conditions that allow peace and human rights to flourish, instead of allowing them to be destroyed for reasons of greed, merely to come in afterward and punish the usual suspects?

## NOTES

The author wishes to thank Osgoode students Trung Nguyen and Melanie Banka for their research assistance in the preparation of this chapter. An earlier version of this chapter appeared as "Politics and Human Rights in International Criminal Law: Our Case Against NATO and Lessons to be Learned from It," *Fordham International Law Journal* 25 (2001): 95–128.

1. Prosecutor for International Tribunals Briefs Security Council, June 2, 2000 (Press Release SC/6870) at 222.

2. *Milosevic et al.* "*Kosovo*" (1998), Case No IT-98-37 (International Criminal Tribunal for the Former Yugoslavia, Trial Chamber), online: United Nations, www.un.org/icty/transe37/transe37.htm (date accessed: October 16, 2001).

3. *Ibid.*

4. M. Scharf, "Indicted for War Crimes, Then What?" *Washington Post*, October 3, 1999, B1.

5. See for example, Security Council Resolutions 1160 (March 13, 1998), 1199 (September 23, 1998); Report of the Secretary General Prepared Pursuant to Resolutions 1160 (1998), 1199 (1998) and 1203 (1998) of the Security Council (S/1998/1221—December 24, 1998); W. E. Ratcliff, "'Madeleine's War' and the Costs of Intervention. The Kosovo Precedent" *Harvard International Review* 22, no. 4 (Winter 2001): 71.

6. M. Ignatieff, *Virtual War: Kosovo and Beyond* (Toronto: Viking, 2000), Ambassador William Walker, U.S. Department of State, On-the-record briefing on the Kosovo Verification Mission, January 8, 1999 (Released by the Office of the Spokesman, Washington, DC, January 8, 1999) online: Department of State www.state.gov/www/policy_remarks/1999/990108_walker_kosovo.html (date accessed: August 16, 2001).

7. *Press Statement from the Prosecutor Regarding Kosovo Investigation*, 20 January 1999, CC/PIU/379-E online: United Nations, www.un.org/icty/pressreal/p379-e.htm (date accessed: October 20, 2001).

8. *Press Briefing—Statement by the Prosecutor*, March 31, 1999, CC/PIU/391-E, online: United Nations, www.un.org/icty/pressreal/p391e.htm (date accessed: August 20, 2001).

9. *Ibid.*

10. *NATO Press Conference*, March 30, 1999, online: NATO, www.nato.int/kosovo/press/p990330a.htm (date accessed: October 16, 2001).

11. Don't bother trying to find it anymore. It was removed sometime after the report was released and the presence of the link was ridiculed by at least one ICTY critic. I have a printout of the page from April 22, 2000, for anyone interested in seeing it.

12. International Criminal Tribunal for the Former Yugoslavia, Office of the Prosecutor, press release, "President Milosevic and four other senior FRY officials indicted for murder, persecution and deportation in Kosovo," *The Hague*, May 27, 1999 (JL/PIU/403-E) (www.un.org/icty—The Trial of Slobodan Milosevic, Archived Press Releases, date accessed: November 5, 2002).

13. *Ibid.*

14. Noam Chomsky, *The New Military Humanism* (Monroe, Maine: Common Courage Press, 1999), 98.

15. See "Civilian Deaths in the NATO Air Campaign," *Human Rights Watch* 12, no. 1 (D) (February 2000). Federal Republic of Yugoslavia, Federal Ministry for Foreign Affairs, *Economic Survey* (Belgrade, No. 2, November 10, 1999) where "more than 1800 [were] killed and 5,000 wounded . . . some 2,000 wounded persons will remain disabled for life."

16. *Statement by Carla Del Ponte Prosecutor of the International Criminal Tribunal for the Former Yugoslavia on the investigation and Prosecution of crimes committed in Kosovo*, September 29, 1999, PR/P.I.S./437-E, online: United Nations, www.un.org/icty/pressreal/p437-e.htm (date accessed: August 20, 2001).

17. *Ibid.*

18. *Prosecutor* v. *Radislav Krstic, ("Srebrenica")* (1998), Case No. IT-98-33 (International Criminal Court for the Former Yugoslavia, Trial Chamber) onlnie: United Nations, www.un.org/icty/krstic/TrialC1/judgement/index.htm (date accessed October 16, 2001).

19. After the arrest of Milosevic, Serb authorities announced they had found another eight hundred Albanian bodies that had been secretly transported to Serbia for burial during the war to cover up crimes in Kosovo. Without minimizing the terrible tragedy of each one of these deaths, it has to be said that even adding these would bring the "genocide" up to about three thousand victims.

20. An opinion poll taken in mid-April 1999 and published by the *Economist* showed enormous opposition to the war both outside and inside the NATO countries. The poll showed more than a third of the population opposed in my own country, Canada, and in Poland, Germany, France, and Finland, almost an even split in Hungary, an even split in Italy, and a majority opposed in the Czech Republic, Russia, and Taiwan ("Oh what a lovely war!" *Economist*, April 24, 1999). Historian Roy Medvedev wrote during the war that Russians were 95 percent opposed (Roy Medvedev, "La rabbia dei russi" ["The anger of the Russians"] *La Repubblica*, April 20, 1999, 1). Opposition in the world's two most populous states, China and India, was official and assumed to be widespread in the population (Chomsky 1999, 142; United Nations, Security Council Press Release, "Security Council rejects demand for cessation of use of force against Federal Republic of Yugoslavia" (SC/6659; March 26, 1999). A poll taken in Greece, a NATO country, between April 29 and May 5 showed 99.5 percent against the war with 85 percent believing NATO's motives to be strategic and not humanitarian. Interestingly enough, 69 percent of those polled were in favor of charging Bill Clinton with war crimes, 35.2 percent for charging Tony Blair, and only 14 percent for charging Slobodan Milosevic, not far from the 13 percent in favor of charging NATO General Wesley Clark and the 9.6 percent for charging NATO Secretary General Javier Solana ("Majority in Greece wants Clinton tried for war crimes," *Irish Times*, May 27, 1999). In the United States itself, despite the relentless pro-bombing reporting of CNN, public opinion was evenly divided, and toward the end of the campaign had fallen below 50 percent (Ignatieff 2000, 193).

21. See T. Ali, "Our Herods" *New Left Review, second series,* no. 5 (Sept./Oct. 2000): 3.

22. Chomsky 1999, *supra* note 15 at chapter 3.

23. Hiroyuki Shinkai and Ugljesa Zvekic, "Punishment," in Graeme Newman, ed., *Global Report on Crime and Justice* (New York: OUP, 1999), 92. *Sourcebook of criminal justice statistics Online*, figure 6.1, online: Bureau of Justice Statistics, www.albany.edu/sourcebook/1995/pdf/t6001.pdf (date accessed: October 16, 2001).

24. *U.S. Department of Justice—Capital Punishment 1999,* online: Bureau of Justice Statistics Bulletin, www.ojp.usdoj.gov/bjs/abstract/cp99.htm (date accessed: October 16, 2001).

25. *Trends in Europe and North America*, online: UN/ECE Statistical Yearbook, www.unece.org/stats/trend/yug.htm (date accessed: October 16, 2001); see also B. Allen, *Why Kosovo? The Anatomy of a Needless War* (Ottawa: Canadian Centre for Policy Alternatives, 1999), 12.

26. Peter Gowan, *The Global Gamble: Washington's Faustian Bid for World Dominance* (London: Verso, 1999).

27. "The Rambouillet process is based upon a group of non- negotiable principles and on a detailed general agreement concerning the provisional status of Kosovo for

a three-year period. These principles call for an immediate end to hostilities, broad autonomy for Kosovo, an executive legislative assembly headed by a president, a Kosovar judicial system, a democratic system, elections under the auspices of the OSCE within nine months of the signing of the agreement, respect of the rights of all persons and ethnic groups, and the territorial integrity of the Federal Republic of Yugoslavia, with Kosovo remaining within the country." Mr. Paul Heinbecker (Assistant Deputy Minister, Global and Security Policy, Department of Foreign Affairs and International Trade) testifying before The Standing Committee on National Defence And Veterans Affairs of the Canadian House of Commons (Tuesday, February 9, 1999; Canada, House of Commons, 36 Parliament, 1st Session, evidence, page 1536).

28. *Supra* note 16.

29. *Ibid.*

30. Economist Intelligence Unit, 1999; *Evening Standard* (London), August 24, 1999, 37.

31. The OSCE Kosovo Verification Mission (OSCE-KVM) Human Rights Division. "*Kosovo/Kosova As Seen, As Told,*" 1999, online: Organization for Security and Cooperation in Europe, www.osce.org/kosovo/documents/reports/hr/part1/ch14.htm#1 (date accessed: October 16, 2001).

32. *Ibid.* Online: www.osce.org/kosovo/documents/reports/hr/part1/ch19.htm (date accessed: October 16, 2001).

33. Julie Birchill, "40 reasons why the Serbs are not the new Nazis and the Kosovars are not the new Jews" *Guardian*, April 10, 1999, quoted in M. Hume, "Nazifying the Serbs, from Bosnia to Kosovo" in P. Hammond and E. Herman, eds., *Degraded Capability: The Media and the Kosovo Crisis* (London: Pluto Press, 2000), 75.

34. In the case of *Krstic* (*Prosecutor vs. Radislav Krstic*, ICTY IT-98-33, Trial Chamber, August 2, 2001) the ICTY decided that the 1995 Srebrenica massacre of a maximum eight thousand Bosnian Muslim men of military age was enough for the intent to destroy a national group "in part," namely, the part that lived in the small town of Srebrenica. But even there the killings were found to be part of a plan to displace the population permanently, which was arguable in the context of the jockeying for territory of the Bosnian civil war. Applying this to Kosovo would take the creative decision making of the ICTY to an entirely new level.

35. P. Gowan, "The Real Meaning Of The War Over Kosovo" in L. Panitch and C. Leys, eds., *The Socialist Register 2000: Necessary And Unnecessary Utopias* (London: Merlin Press, 1999).

36. Ignatieff 2000, *supra* note 6 at 206.

37. *Case Concerning the Military and Paramilitary Activities in and Against Nicaragua* (*Nicaragua* v. *United States of America*) *(MERITS)*, [1986] Judgment of June 27, 1986, I.C.J. Rep., 134–135, paragraphs 267 and 268.

38. *Case Concerning Legality of Use of Force (Yugoslavia* v. *Canada)* International Court of Justice, June 2, 1999.

39. A. Cassese, "Ex iniuria ius oritur: Are We Moving towards International Legitimation of Forcible Humanitarian Countermeasures in the World Community?" *European Journal of International Law* 10, no. 1 (1999): 23, 24.

40. S. Bailey and S. Daws, *The Procedure of the UN Security Council*, third edition (Oxford: Clarendon Press, 1998), 239.

41. *Ibid.*

42. *Security Council Press Release,* "Draft Resolution on Middle East Situation Rejected by Security Council" March 27, 2001, online: United Nations www0.un.org/News/Press/docs/2001/sc7040.doc.htm (date accessed: August 13, 2001).

43. *Statute of the International Criminal Tribunal for the Former Yugoslavia,* Art. 5.

44. *Milosevic, supra* note 15.

45. *Death Penalty Information Centre*, online: Essential Information, www.essential.org/dpic/dpicintl.html (date accessed: May 17, 2000).

46. *Supra* note 28.

47. *The Nürnberg Case, as presented by Robert H. Jackson, Chief of Counsel for the United States, together with other documents* (New York: Cooper Square Publishers Inc., 1971): 82–84.

48. See for example *Human Rights Watch, supra* note 27; *Amnesty International Report, infra* note 60, *NATO Crimes in Yugoslavia: Documentary Evidence, Volumes I and II* (Federal Republic of Yugoslavia, Ministry of Foreign Affairs, 1999).

49. Amnesty International. "NATO/Federal Republic of Yugoslavia 'Collateral Damage' or Unlawful Killings? Violations of the Laws of War by NATO during Operation Allied Force" *Amnesty International Report* (London: Amnesty International Publications, June 6, 2000) [hereinafter *Amnesty Report*].

50. Jerome Sokolovsky, "U.N. prosecutor investigating NATO's conduct in Yugoslavia bombing campaign" *Associated Press*, December 28, 1999.

51. Rowan Scarborough, "U.S. denounces U.N. probe of NATO bombing" *Washington Times*, December 30, 1999.

52. *Statement by Madame Carla Del Ponte, Prosecutor of the International Criminal Tribunal for the former Yugoslavia*, December 30, 1999, PR/P.I.S./459-E, online: United Nations, www.un.org/icty/pressreal/p459-e.htm (date accessed: October 16, 2001).

53. *Final Report to the Prosecutor by the Committee Established to Review the NATO Bombing Campaign Against the Federal Republic of Yugoslavia*, June 13, 2000, PR/P.I.S./510-E, online: United Nations, www.un.org/icty/pressreal/nato061300.htm (date accessed: October 16, 2001) [hereinafter *OTP Report*].

54. *Amnesty Report*, *supra* note 49.

55. *Ibid.*, 23.

56. Paragraphs 35–42 and 48–50 of the report are lifted verbatim from "Attacking the Enemy Civilian as a Punishable Offense" by William J. Fenrick, *Duke Journal of Comparative and International Law* 7 (1997): 539, 542–46, except for one bow to political correctness when the word "people" is substituted for "women." The sentence in the *Duke Journal* reads, "For example, bombing a refugee camp is obviously prohibited if its only military significance is that *the women* in the camp are knitting socks for soldiers." Whereas in the *OTP Report* it becomes: "For example, bombing a refugee camp is obviously prohibited if its only military significance is that *people* in the camp are knitting socks for soldiers." I myself only became aware of this be-

cause Fenrick himself proudly presented me with an offprint of his article when we argued our case in The Hague in November 1999.

57. *OTP Report, supra* note 53.

58. *Ibid.* 90.

59. *Ibid.*

60. *NATO Press Conference*, April 13, 1999, online: NATO, www.nato.int/kosovo/press/p990413a.htm (date accessed: October 16, 2001).

61. *OTP Report, supra* note 53, 59.

62. *Ibid.* 59.

63. *Ibid.*

64. *Comment on ICTY's Final Report to the Prosecutor by the Committee Established to Review the NATO Bombing Campaign Against the Federal Republic of Yugoslavia,* online: The Grdelica Organization www.balkanpeace.org/lan/lan10.shtml (date accessed: October 16, 2001) [hereinafter *Wenz*].

65. *Ibid.* 7.

66. *OTP Report, supra* note 53, 61.

67. *Wenz, supra* note 76, 12.

68. Ruth Wedgewood, "The International Criminal Court: An American View" *European Journal of International Law 10* (1999): 93; David J. Scheffer, "The United States and the International Criminal Court" *The American Journal of International Law* 93 (1999): 12.

69. Michael Mandel, "A Brief History of the New Constitutionalism, or 'How we changed everything so that everything would remain the same,'" *Israel Law Review* 32 (1998): 250.

70. Carrie Gustafson, "International Criminal Courts: Some Dissident Views on the Continuation of War by Penal Means" *Houston Journal of International Law* 21 (1998): 51.

# 12

## Intervention in Ethnic Civil Wars and Exit Strategies: Lessons from South Asia

*Maya Chadda*

Differences can sometimes mask commonalities. Superficially, there can be few geopolitical zones less comparable to South Asia than the Balkan peninsula—each defined by culture, evolution, and other features, which are discrete and apparently unique. Yet, while the thrust of history separates, there are specific experiences that contain transferable signs, signals, and warnings. India's 1971 military intervention in Pakistan's civil war, commonly known as the Bangladesh war, and in Sri Lanka, in 1987, took place at a different time and place from the post–Cold War NATO intervention in Kosovo. The Indian experience nevertheless foreshadows dangers that NATO will face in bringing the Kosovo intervention to a successful conclusion.

Among the two South Asian interventions, the one in Bangladesh is widely acclaimed as a "just" and successful intervention. The second, the induction of Indian peacekeeping forces in Sri Lanka, is regarded as a case of failure. The "success" in Bangladesh was limited to winning the war. It did not take into account the consequences that would flow from it. "Success" in Kosovo and Sri Lanka was defined as democratic outcome to intervention. At least that was the ostensible purpose for which it was undertaken. Each intervention illustrates, in a different way, the problems of effecting a "successful" exit from ethnic civil wars and the dangers of choosing between sovereignty and self-determination. The intervention in South Asia encountered some of the same dilemmas that the policy community has faced, and is likely to face, in Kosovo and elsewhere.

Why are exits from intervention in ethnic wars so difficult? Many have sought answers in bad timing and in confusion of objectives, motivations, and modalities of intervention. But most have looked at these from the "entry" point alone and concentrated on questions of the legal, political, and moral compulsions.[1] I wish to shift emphasis from the moral and normative questions to the dilemmas of fixing goals and bringing interventions to a successful conclusion. In short, to the question of an exit, when should a humanitarian intervention be brought to an end? And what problems does an intervening agency face when conditions for a successful withdrawal are defined as an extension of humanitarian relief, public order, and democracy? After all, none of the interventions discussed here are, or were, meant to be permanent military occupations. Exit considerations have to be, then, an important part of the original decision to intervene. Assessing the efficacy and desirability of an intervention requires envisioning it in its fullness—from the introduction of military forces to their withdrawal. And indeed, a clearer view of problems associated with achieving the local conditions in accordance with the declared objectives of the intervention will help fashion a more discriminating response to civil wars in deeply divided societies.

It is noteworthy that in the 1980s, under the leadership of General Colin Powell and Casper Weinberger, the United States had established guidelines that made exit an important precondition for intervention.[2] Under the pressure of proliferating humanitarian crises, the Clinton administration abandoned these guidelines and fell back on an ad hoc and case by case response, with one exception that endured from the earlier policies, that is, avoidance of combat casualties for the U.S. military. Faced with a fragmenting Yugoslavia, the west European states also overcame their reluctance and were persuaded to attempt political engineering in the Balkans. But neither Europe nor the United States gave much thought to preventing fragmentation, which we now know, led to the horror of ethnic cleansing and war. The ad hoc responses they made produced the next set of crises in disintegrating Yugoslavia. In 1999, these events converged in the war over Kosovo that began with the escalating violence between the Kosovo Liberation Army (KLA) and the Serbian troops. NATO mobilized its armed power to force Slobodan Milosevic to accept the Rambouillet accord. But the accord failed, and attention shifted to what NATO must do next. Although Serbia was defeated, in the events that followed, it gained important concessions from NATO for accepting the ceasefire. NATO's Kosovo war has been highly controversial. Scholarly opinion is divided on whether the intervention was a success or a case of "perfect failure."[3]

## COMPARING INTERVENTIONS

Most interventions fall into three broad categories. The first type of intervention is meant to bring relief from floods or famines or other large scale disasters without addressing its political causes (for example, the first Bush administration in Somalia); the second type is a humanitarian intervention that attempts to create a degree of political order, usually by putting in place a particular local or friendly political leader (for example, Haiti and Sierra Leone); the third type is an intervention that aims to remove the deeper causes of the humanitarian crisis by reconstructing the entire political system of the effected country, making it liberal, democratic, and even multicultural where necessary (Bosnia, Kosovo, East Timor, and the Clinton Administration in Somalia).

The first category of intervention is relatively easier to achieve in justification for both the entry and exit because its objectives are limited and time-bound. These objectives can fail, however, if a country is fragmented into warring factions that fight to deny rival factions humanitarian relief, as in the case of Somalia. At that point, the original objective has to be either expanded or abandoned. The second type of intervention is usually more conventional in its aims and "end game" strategy. Military force is used to replace a government or a leader believed to have caused the humanitarian catastrophe with a regime that is more friendly to the interests and preferences of the intervening agency. Once this is accomplished, military force is withdrawn. The 1994 interventions in Haiti and the 1971 Indian intervention in Bangladesh are cases in point. The 1999 NATO intervention in Kosovo and the 1987 Indian intervention in Sri Lanka fall into the third category, where the objective is to reconstruct political institutions and restructure political power to more evenly balance the demands of self-determination and national sovereignty.

Military interventions are then on a continuum, where one set of objectives can be replaced by the next stage of expanded objectives and resource mobilization. This was evident in the shifting objectives of intervening agencies in Sri Lanka and Kosovo. Indian leaders had assumed that the Indian Peacekeeping Force (IPKF) would have to stay for a brief period, just until the Liberation Tigers of Tamil Elam (LTTE) had handed over its arms and implemented the devolution package India and Sri Lanka had agreed to in the treaty. But once in Sri Lanka, India was forced to change the "end game" plan and expand its intervention objectives. Similarly, the NATO strategy kept shifting from no commitment to low commitment, from that to intensive bombing of Serbia and Kosovo, and finally, to the replacement of Milosevic with the more friendly Kostunica. Interventions can also be compared on the basis of motives and intent and the extent to which they represent a mix of humanitarian and strategic interests. Interventions that occurred before and after the end of the Cold War are comparable on the questions of intent. All three instances of interventions discussed here, two of which occurred during the Cold War and one after the collapse of the Cold War, show a mix of altruistic and strategic interest motives.

In fact, a closer look shows that the Indian interventions were not purely self-centered, and the NATO intervention in Kosovo not purely humanitarian in purpose. It is true that the Bangladesh war weakened Pakistan permanently and made India the dominant military power in the region. But Pakistan's attempt to crush the Bangladesh independence movement had produced a human tragedy of genocidal proportions. The only way to return the refugees was to end the civil war. That objective could not be achieved without military intervention and the establishment of a representative and tolerant leadership in Dacca. The atrocities committed by Pakistan in the 1971 civil war provided a justifiable basis for intervention: genocide and danger to regional peace.[4] The insertion of Indian peacekeeping forces in Sri Lanka was under an Indo-Lanka agreement freely contracted by the two countries. The Indian interventions were then on firm legal grounds. In contrast, the NATO intervention in Kosovo was of debatable legitimacy. Not only did NATO avoid going to the UN, it ignored the time-honored dictum that war should be an instrument of last resort.

Attribution of exclusively humanitarian motives to NATO's intervention ignores the realpolitik considerations that have shaped its policy in Yugoslavia. These considerations were evident in the hasty German recognition of Slovenia, Croatia, and Bosnia, which, in the view of many, triggered the nasty wars of Yugoslavia. Germany had not intended to trigger wars, but in acting from its domestic compulsions, Germany had ignored the regional consequences of its recognition.[5] Similar considerations were evident in the privileging of non-Serbian ethnic groups over Serbian nationalists, and in the refusal to grant the same rights to the Serbian nation, which were ostensibly the grounds for the creation of a separate Croatia and a multiethnic Bosnia.[6] Even more important, bypassing the UN, forestalled the Chinese and Russian veto over the bombing of Serbia, which made that decision far from universal. In fact, there was widespread opposition among the UN members to the bombing.[7]

The argument here is not that Serbia was innocent of crimes against humanity. Milosevic and Serb nationalists had committed horrendous acts of cruelty and butchery in Bosnia, but so had others, for example, the Croats and, later, the Kosovar Albanians against their Serbian minorities. Michael McGwire points out that "the U.S.-supported Croatian army, on the direct authority of Croatian President Franjo Tudjman, drove out nearly all the Serbs from Krajina and 'cleansed' the area of its 200,000 inhabitants. This was by far the largest expulsion up to that point and was achieved in four days." Yet NATO stood still.[8] NATO countries had failed to be evenhanded in applying the right of self-determination objectively to all the ethnic claimants to separate statehood in the Balkans. This lack of impartiality challenged the claims to purity of motives in Kosovo.

What were the realpolitik NATO objectives in Kosovo? They were not, in fact, too different from the Indian objectives in its own region of South Asia: to establish hegemonic influence enabling New Delhi (or NATO, in the case of the Balkan region) to structure interstate relations in the region and be able to punish and reward states that defy the contour of political/ ideological order advantageous to the hegemonic state. India has not succeeded in achieving this end, and Europe may fail to establish full control over every defiant nationalist in its backyard, but these failures do not negate the larger purpose that motivates the choices they might make and the reasons why they make them. The notion of "Greater Europe" as a fulcrum of Trans-Atlantic hegemony requires rearranging the defiant parts, including the recalcitrant fragments of the former Soviet empire, into one pliable whole.[9] The entire debate about whom to admit and not admit in the European Union underlines the desire to impose the United States's hegemony, in which NATO plays a lead role. The attempt to keep the Russians out of the diplomatic maneuvering at Rambouillet, and subsequently in peacekeeping, underlines such a motive.

There were more specific objectives as well. Germany's recognition of Croatia was opposed by France and England, but it fit German national interests. India's intervention in Bangladesh was meant to weaken its enemy, Pakistan. The Sri Lankan intervention was shaped by more complex motives. India was sincere in wanting to settle the Tamil-Sinhala conflict partly because it believed its preeminence in the region demanded it, and partly because it feared that a separate Tamil state on its southern tip might encourage separatist demands from its own fifty million Tamils inside India. NATO was not then acting from purely humanitarian motives, and the Indian responses were not devoid of high purpose. Nor can we argue that Indian interventions were less legitimate because they were not endorsed by the UN and involved military forces of a single country with obvious regional interests. On the other hand, legitimacy of the NATO intervention in Kosovo is widely disputed, although it was a collective enterprise.

This brings us to the third problem of comparability, that of scales. It is true that NATO can mobilize vast resources to back its objectives, but the asymmetry in scales and capabilities must be qualified by the reluctance to make long-term commitments to peacekeeping and the presence of deep and troubling differences over the conduct and modalities of intervention.[10] Besides, collective actions are prone to confusion of command and control, military and diplomatic objectives, and conflict over timing and pace of operations. Single-country interventions are less plagued by these problems. India was able to mobilize sufficient forces to secure its objectives in Bangladesh. This was not the case in Sri Lanka, but that is precisely why it provides a powerful message to those embarking on interventions in deeply divided societies in the grip of ethnic wars. Let me then turn to the two interventions in South Asia and sketch their course for the purposes of comparison.

## DESCENT INTO CIVIL WAR: BANGLADESH AND KOSOVO

The 1971 conflict between East and West Pakistan was rooted in the long history of ethnic tensions between the predominantly Bengali speaking Muslims of East Pakistan and the Urdu speaking Muslims of West Pakistan, specifically in the denial of political autonomy and sustained economic exploitation of the Bengali Pakistanis.[11] These tensions were aggravated during the ten years of military dictatorship (1958–1968) of General Ayub Khan, who largely represented the Pathan/Pushtun ruling classes in West Pakistan. Popular pressures ultimately brought the Ayub regime to an end. Pakistan's new military rulers promised elections and democracy. The elections of December 1970, however, held an unpleasant surprise for West Pakistan's ruling elite. It gave a majority to the Awami League, the main political party based in and representing the Bengali Muslims of East Pakistan. Zulfikar Ali Bhutto's Pakistan People's Party (PPP), based mainly in West Pakistan, was returned as the second largest party in Pakistan's National Assembly. The 1970 elections and Awami League's triumph produced an immediate political crisis in Pakistan. The West Pakistani elite could not tolerate granting of autonomy or power to its eastern wing, let alone permit ethnic Bengalis to rule all of Pakistan. Negotiations between Pakistan's military rulers, led by Yahya Khan, the PPP leader Zulfikar Bhutto, and Mujibur Rehman, the president of the Awami League, failed to produce a compromise. Yahya Khan declared the 1970 elections null and void, arrested Mujibur, and ordered the Pakistan army—which was already preparing for military operations—into East Pakistan.

Years of protest had forged a distinctive political identity among the ethnic Bengalis of East Pakistan.[12] They were convinced that, in refusing to share power, the Punjabi/Pathan leadership of West Pakistan was trying to crush the richer, more cosmopolitan cultural heritage of the Bengalis. Protest movements that had sprung up spontaneously over the years—around the issues of language, share of revenue, absence of investment and development in East Pakistan, discrimination in jobs and position of power—had produced a vibrant political society, in which the Awami League represented the apex organization speaking for the masses of Bengali Muslims.[13] Rejection of the election results opened the door to violence. The Bengali popular will hardened even more when the Pakistani army landed in East Pakistan to crush the rebellion. In the crackdown that followed, thousands were killed, Pakistani armed forces indulged in murder and rape, and millions fled across the border into India.[14]

In the previous months, India had begun training and providing arms to small, but well-organized, groups of militant Bengali nationalists. Indian involvement was, however, gradual. Rose and Sisson write that not until the "collapse of negotiations, arrest of Mujib, Yahya's declaring him to be a traitor and banning of the Awami League for all time to come" did India consider the possibility of intervention.[15] But even then, it remained circumspect and scrupulously avoided any overt challenge to Pakistan's sovereignty.[16]

There were two reasons for this caution. First, it was not clear until June 1971 that India would actually intervene. The support to Bengali nationalists was meant to provide them and India with a voice should Pakistan decide to settle the conflict without war. India needed the leverage to ensure that the refugees would be able to return. Besides, it was clear that the Bengali nationalists would not agree to the restoration of political status quo ante, even if they chose to remain within Pakistan. The Indian support for self-determination was not meant to then jeopardize the chances of a negotiated settlement. Second, Indian leaders thought it prudent to ascertain the strength and ideological orientations of the militant separatists and their relations with the moderate Bengali leaders. New Delhi wanted to prevent an extreme right- or left-wing leader from gaining a foothold in Bangladesh. It believed that ethnic peace could be established only under a moderate, democratic government. Most importantly, India was keenly aware of the dangers in privileging a secessionist movement in South Asia. Its own experience suggested that ethnic sentiments ebbed and flowed and were best constrained by the granting of federal autonomy within a democratic framework. India's gradual and cautious approach paid rich dividends in the 1971 war. In contrast, NATO was careless about respecting Yugoslavia's sovereignty and hasty in extending diplomatic recognition to its fragments, Croatia and Slovenia. NATO support of the KLA has endangered the prospects of a multiethnic democracy in the Balkans.

The Bangladesh military operation lasted about two weeks, and the Indian presence was withdrawn within three months from the time Indian forces intervened. After two weeks of rapid-paced intervention, which carefully avoided damage to civilians and local infrastructure, Indian forces triumphantly marched into Dacca. In contrast, the NATO bombing of Serbia and Kosovo inflicted great damage to their infrastructure. At the end of India's two-week military campaign, Pakistan had been defeated and ninety-thousand Pakistani soldiers had surrendered as prisoners of war. Having secured East Pakistan for a new government of Bangladesh, Indian armed forces withdrew in March 1972. India and the independent state of Bangladesh signed a Treaty of Friendship and Cooperation which promised that neither country would commit aggression against the other, neither would extend military support to a third country at conflict with one of the two, and in the event of military attack, each will undertake measures to eliminate the threat.[17] The Friendship and Cooperation Treaty had brought the Indian intervention to a conclusion and laid the basis for India's exit from Bangladesh. As we will see, the end of the military campaign in Kosovo leads to an entirely different set of outcomes.

The history of ethnic conflict between the Serbs and Albanian Kosovars can also be traced to complaints about social and cultural discrimination, oppression, and lack of political autonomy.[18] In early 1974, Yugoslavia had amended its constitution to make Kosovo an autonomous province of the Serbian republic. This had gone a long way in satisfying the Albanian desire for self-rule, but there were still those who pressed for independence and merger with neighboring Albania as a springboard for establishing a "greater Albania," which would include Kosovo and Macedonia.[19] Following Tito's death, there were widespread riots and a period of federally imposed martial law. In reaction, two hundred thousand Serbians began to protest discrimination by the Albanian majority in the province. In the early 1980s, there was a series of violent confrontations between the federal forces and Albanian Kosovar nationalists, which intensified tensions between Serbs and Kosovo Albanians. These confrontations also provided Milosevic, an ambitious and rising politician, with the justification to mobilize counter Serbian nationalism and seize power. Milosevic eliminated Kosovo's autonomy in 1990. In July 1990, 115 ethnic Albanians, members of the provincial parliament, declared Kosovo to be independent. These deputies had been elected in 1989 but had been prevented by Serbian authorities from discharging their duties.

The declaration of independence prompted a severe crackdown. In defiance, the Serbian alternate leadership held an extralegal referendum in September 1991, which overwhelmingly opted for independence. Serbian repression had produced a broad movement for independence, led by the Democratic League of Kosovo (LDK), which was headed by Ibrahim Rugova.[20] The LDK leadership embarked on building a network of social institutions independent of Serbian control. Educational institutions became the main bone of contention between the government school and the alternate Albanian schools that sprang up everywhere. In terms of political discrimination, Bangladesh and Kosovo had followed a parallel course, for example, the growth of protest-driven civil society led to further oppression, violence, and war, which brought intervention by external actors. But beyond the events that led to the ethnic polarization, the Kosovo conflict followed a distinctly different trajectory from that in Bangladesh.

From 1996 on, the story of Kosovo begins to resemble the turn of events in Sri Lanka. By 1996, the situation in Kosovo had reached an impasse. Militant Kosovars had begun to attack the police and personnel of the Serbian Interior Ministry (known by its Serbian acronym MUP). As attacks continued the next year, a new group, the Kosovo Liberation Army, emerged as the military arm of independent Kosovo.[21] The collapse of neighboring Albania in 1991 had already provided impetus to the Kosovar militancy. The KLA received a shot in the arm when rioting Albanians (in Albania) captured the state armory along with small arms and weapons and made them available to the KLA. The civic networks that had flourished in the early 1990s under Rugova and the LDK lost momentum as the KLA preempted the slogans and symbols of the Albanian nation in Kosovo.[22] This militarization of the Kosovar Albanians occurred against the backdrop of war and ethnic cleansing in Bosnia in which all sides were implicated, but the lion's share of blame belonged to the Bosnian Serbs and Milosevic. The Bosnian Serbs had indeed indulged in large-scale violence against civilians and "ethnic cleansing" of Serb-controlled areas. In Kosovo, the armed clashes between the MUP and the KLA had resulted in considerable civilian casualties. In April 1998, the "Contact Group" for the former Yugoslavia—the United States, the United Kingdom, France, Germany, and Italy—imposed sanctions on Serbia for human rights violations in Kosovo, and in October, NATO threatened air strikes.

Anxious to avoid a confrontation, Milosevic acceded to Western demands to allow two thousand unarmed international observers to monitor the cease-fire and to withdraw heavy weapons and equipment from Kosovo. The Serb forces in Kosovo were to revert to their level prior to February 1998, namely, twenty-two thousand (ten thousand police and twelve thousand army). As the Serbian army withdrew, the KLA moved forward, often occupying the Serb's former position. Instead of restraining the KLA, the United States invited the militants to talks in November and again in December. The KLA were anxious to draw the United States in on their side. That, they believed, was the way to gain independence from Serbia.[23] But the Serb reaction to the talks was understandably hostile. Civilian casualties mounted as the Serbian army responded with ruthlessness and force. In January 1999, forty-five civilians were massacred in Racak by the Serbian security forces.[24] NATO immediately threatened intervention. Afraid to take on NATO, Milosevic agreed to peace talks which were convened in Rambouillet, France, on February 6, 1999.

There are contradictory interpretations of what actually transpired at Rambouillet.[25] According to Christopher Hill, a member of the negotiating team at Rambouillet, Milosevic refused to budge and left NATO no option but to intervene. A growing number of expert observers, however, contend that Serbia had agreed to almost all the terms of the Rambouillet agreement and the war could have been averted had NATO not introduced a new set of military clauses in the appendix attached to the draft. Milosevic had accepted the political conditions demanded in the Rambouillet agreement. The military clause gave NATO ground forces unlimited authority and would have turned the FRY into an occupied country. This is not a proposal that any country could have willingly accepted, as a part of a negotiated settlement to conflict within its own borders. When the Serbs rejected the later version, NATO announced air strikes with the stated goal of preventing Serbian forces from attacking Kosovar civilians. The OSCE observers were pulled out of the area, and the bombing campaign began on the evening of March 24. Once the air strikes began, the Serbian security forces began a systematic drive to expel the Albanians from Kosovo. According to the statistics collected by the UN High Commission for Refugees, on March 23, the UNHCR was caring for 89,500 refugees outside Kosovo. A majority of these had fled from areas where the Serbian and KLA fighting was most intense. After the air strikes began, the numbers had swelled to seven hundred thousand.

There is also a great deal of controversy surrounding the civilian casualties before the NATO bombing in March. President Clinton and British Prime Minister Tony Blair talked about over one hundred thousand Albanians killed or missing in Kosovo. The UN forensic teams that eventually went to dig up the sites of mass graves came away with no more than 2,078 bodies. And according to the 13 May 2000 report in the *New York Times*, the forensic teams were unlikely to find too many more bodies. Although reprehensible and worthy of condemnation, this body count was nowhere near the figures cited by the NATO leaders when they decided to bomb Serbia. It is worth noting the commentary by Brian Mitchell in the *Investors Daily* on the question of genocide and killings by Serbian troops. He writes, "During the war, NATO officials issued rising estimates of Albanian victims, based on interviews with refugees. The estimates started at 3,200 in mid-April and rose to 6,000 the day the bombing ended, jumping to over 11,000 after NATO troops moved in. Officials also stressed that 100,000 and later 225,000 Albanian men were missing." On May 16, Defense Secretary Cohen said on CBS *Face the Nation* that he had seen reports of 4,600 Albanians killed, but he suspected the numbers to be higher than that. In Cohen's view, the number could reach close to 100,000 military-age men missing or murdered. By June 1, U.S. and NATO officials were claiming 225,000 men missing and 6,000 killed in summary executions. Within days, senior British officials had pushed the number of dead to 10,000. The 195 sites that yielded up to 2,108 bodies were supposed to have held 4,256 bodies. Many early reports of mass graves appear now to have been exaggerated. Mitchell observes, "The ICTY won't say how many mass graves it has found. Many mass graves have turned out like Ljubenic. At Ljubenic, Italian troops first claimed to have found a grave with 350 bodies."

This was "the largest suspected mass grave in Kosovo so far," according to the news service Agence France-Presse, says Brian Mitchell. The next day, the same news service reported that there were only five bodies found at the site. According to Mitchell, Emilio Perez Pujol, who headed a team of Spanish investigators in Kosovo, calculated that the final figure could be 2,500 at the most. This included lots of strange deaths that cannot be blamed on anyone in particular. Mitchell quotes Alice Mahon, who chairs a committee on the Balkans as a member of the British Parliament: "When you consider that 1,500 civilians or more were killed during the NATO bombing, you have to ask whether the intervention was justified."[26]

## BANGLADESH: IMPLICATIONS FOR KOSOVO

Although not identical in the course they took, what lessons does the Indian intervention in East Pakistan carry for Kosovo? First, India had acted on incontrovertible evidence of genocide. The evidence of genocide in Kosovo before the bombing was debatable and highly inflated, even by NATO accounts. It is not clear whether NATO countries actually knew this before the bombing or whether the experience in Bosnia had deeply colored their assessment of what might happen. Even if they feared what they did not know, NATO's insistence on the military appendix in the Paris peace talks, and in ignoring the culpability of the KLA, which was waging a war against the Serb forces, points to a bias against Serbia. The sequence of events at Rambouillet—the fact that Serbia had largely accepted the agreement and pulled back from the talks only when presented with the demand for allowing KFOR (Kosovo Forces) presence all over Yugoslavia—suggests that the last minute introduction of the military appendix was mischievous, and perhaps intended with the Serb reaction in mind. Sam Husseini, the communications director of the Institute for Public Accuracy baldly states that "Appendix B of the Rambouillet text allowed for the occupation of all of Yugoslavia, not just Kosovo. The State Department's insistence on that provision—which was dropped in the final agreement—indicates that top U.S. officials wanted war."[27] NATO did not use force as an instrument of last resort, as India had done in the case of Bangladesh. Instead, it served an ultimatum that it knew Milosevic could not accept.

Second, India's military intervention was carefully planned to avoid damage to the infrastructure and cause minimum amounts of civilian casualties. This was important to the stability and reconstruction of Bangladesh after the intervention. In this regard, the Indian operation was a remarkable success. The same cannot be said of the NATO operation. The bombing was said to have knocked off thirty-one bridges, half of Serbia's and Montenegro's airports, 70 percent of the power supply, two railway systems that link Serbia to Kosovo, most of its telecommunications system, and some of Serbia's factories, including the biggest car-producing factory.[28] The refugees became a flood only after the NATO planes rained death and destruction over Serbia.[29] In East Pakistan, India had not acted to prevent the human rights violations when they had initially occurred. This is because a separate Bangladesh was not a foregone conclusion until November 1971, and Pakistan was acting within its own sovereign borders. The post–Cold War interventions have been far less concerned about preserving national sovereignty. In discarding that cardinal principle of the international system, intervening agencies have been neither impartial nor caring about the consequences of their interventions.

The sequence of events suggests that, in Kosovo, NATO had a different "end game" plan than the one India had in East Pakistan. The Indian military intervention in Bangladesh was brief. Having created an independent state of Bangladesh and placed the reins of state power in the hands of moderate Bengali leadership, Indian armed forces were promptly withdrawn. The objective of intervention was to return the refugees to their homes, restore law and order, and stabilize the new nation with a friendly, preferably democratic government in power. All three goals were reflected in the Indo-Bangladesh treaty signed by Indira Gandhi and Mujibur Rehman on March 25, 1972. The treaty reaffirmed mutual friendship, a promise (on the part of each) to refrain from making strategic alliances with unfriendly countries (China and eventually Pakistan), and a promise of mutual defense in the event either was attacked by a third country. India was not committed to nation building or to remaining behind as a referee between Bangladesh's rival factions. It hoped that Bangladesh would follow the Indian example and build a multiethnic, multireligious, secular, democratic nation-state. India wished for this for both altruistic and compelling realpolitik reasons. Indian leaders argued that a democratic neighboring state was less likely to threaten the fragile ethnic equation in India's Northeast (areas adjacent to Bangladesh) or foment secessionist insurgency among its own contentious nationalities.

NATO's "end game" had at least three declared objectives. First, to stop the killing, second, to restore law and order, and third, to establish political institutions at local and provincial levels that would produce a democratic outcome, that is, make Kosovo into a self-sustaining, plural, democratic region. The bombing campaign and induction of peacekeepers backed by NATO's firepower stopped the killing and secured the return of the refugees, but the prospects for establishing durable institutions of democracy appear dim.

Why does NATO spend so much energy and firepower in Kosovo that it is reluctant to spend elsewhere in instances of human rights violations? The short answer is that NATO seeks to eliminate all vestigial influence Russia might have on its former allies and to ensure its hegemony over the extended Europe.[30] The motives behind India's intervention on behalf of Bangladeshis was not too different in intent. India certainly wanted to restore conditions that would allow the ten million refugees to return to their homes, but more importantly, it wanted unchallenged power to structure future interstate relations in the region. NATO is likely to be more successful than India has been in securing its hegemonic interests.

There were no significant shifts to be noted in India's exit policy in Bangladesh. India went in to install a friendly government in Bangladesh and withdrew when that was achieved. The same cannot be said of the NATO plans. Having imposed the new Rambouillet agreement on Serbia, which requires the latter to withdraw from Kosovo and hand over the administration of the province to the UN, the "end game" shifted to replacing Milosevic with pliable Serbian leaders in Pristina and Kosovo. In other words, from stopping the killing and securing promises of autonomy from Milosevic, the policy shifted to political engineering to the new distribution of political and institutional power in the entire region.

## SRI LANKAN CIVIL WAR AND INDIAN INTERVENTION: LESSONS FOR KOSOVO

The dangers of remaining behind as a mediator, enforcer, and referee are highlighted by India's failed intervention in Sri Lanka. Growing tensions had preceded the outbreak of violence between the Tamil minority and the Sinhala majority of Sri Lanka in the early 1980s. The Tamils constitute about 17 percent of Sri Lanka, and although the majority live in the Jaffna and Eastern Province, a large number had migrated to other parts in search of livelihood and incomes. Most scholars trace the current conflict to the rise of virulent Buddhist nationalism in the 1950s and its periodic resurgence thereafter. In these early decades, tensions between these two communities revolved around competition for jobs, access to higher education, and share of power in government and bureaucracy. Over the years, Sinhala chauvinism and Tamil nationalism had fed and reinforced each other, a situation that strongly echoes the history of ethnic conflict between the Serbs and Albanians in Kosovo.[31]

An added complication was the close political and cultural ties between Jaffna Tamils and Indian Tamils in the southern state of Tamil Nadu. Kosovo Albanians have drawn similar cultural and political support from fellow Albanians in adjacent countries. The Bengalis on both sides of the Pakistan-India border enjoyed a sense of shared identity which was mobilized when the civil war began. The Tamil Nadu politicians had similarly espoused the cause of Tamil nationalists—both of the moderate and the separatist variety—and provided them with money and political support. Despite pressures from its own Tamil nationality, the Indian government had resisted being drawn into Sri Lanka's ethnic conflict until the early 1980s. However, in July 1983, an ambush of thirteen soldiers by a militant Tamil group, the Liberation Tigers of

Tamil Elam (LTTE) plunged Sri Lanka into a civil war. More than 150,000 Tamils fled from the Sri Lankan army operation in search of safety to Tamil Nadu in India.[32]

The problem of shared ethnic nationalities across international boundaries can become an impediment in bringing humanitarian intervention to a successful conclusion. The Sri Lankan Tamils derive the cultural symbols of their nationalism from the notion of a greater Tamil nation, which includes Tamil Nadu and the Tamil minority in Malaysia, just as the Kosovar Albanians include in their notion of greater Albania the neighboring Albania and fellow ethnics in Macedonia.[33] The Albanian irredenta will have to be considered in any future negotiations to stabilize the region, as will the problem of acceptable boundaries. James Pardew, a senior U.S. adviser to the Bureau of European Affairs, warned in June 2001 that the insurgent National Liberation Army, supported and manned by the KLA in Macedonia, had escalated its attacks on the government and had begun the ethnic cleansing of the non-Albanian population in northern Macedonia.[34] Macedonia understandably fears the spillover effect of an independent Kosovo on its own Albanian population.

India, too, fears the spillover effect of the Sri Lankan Tamil independence movement on fifty million Tamils in the southern state of Tamil Nadu. It is partly to prevent a breakup of Sri Lanka and partly to support the Sri Lankan Tamil demand for autonomy (not secession) that India agreed to intervene. After all, the number of refugees from Sri Lanka was nowhere near the one created by Pakistani atrocities twelve years previously. However, as the civil war escalated in Sri Lanka, the scale and brutality of the violence also escalated. Both the LTTE and the Sri Lankan security forces had access to external sources of arms and money. The government of Colombo purchased arms from England, the United States, and Israel.[35] The militants received money and arms from fellow Tamils in Tamil Nadu and some from the intelligence agencies of the Indian government.[36]

Ethnic nationalities distributed across international borders become an impediment because intervening agencies frequently use them and then lose control over their activities. India's Sri Lankan involvement is a prime example of this conundrum. Militant organizations are also resourceful in developing independent ties with the fellow ethnics abroad or across the border. The LTTE developed strong ties with political parties in Tamil Nadu just as the KLA forged ties with political organizations in Albania and the Albanian minority in Macedonia. Until 1984, however, Indian support for the Tamil militants was limited. Mrs. Gandhi had kept the militants strictly under the supervision of the Indian intelligence agencies. For India, the militants were a leverage to prod Sri Lanka into making concessions (in deference to Indian interests) but were not to be trusted to act on their own. NATO regarded the KLA with similar ambivalence.

The Sri Lankan conflict shows that separatists can force intervening agencies into making far larger commitments than originally intended, oftentimes against their national interests. The limited Indian involvement in Sri Lanka's civil war went through a drastic change after the advent of the Rajiv Gandhi government in New Delhi in 1985.[37] Rajiv Gandhi sought a negotiated settlement of the conflict, but he made an important error in judgment. He extended recognition to militant groups as the legitimate representatives of the Sri Lanka Tamils. This was evident in the composition of delegates representing Tamil interests at the 1985 round of talks at Thimpu. The Rajiv shift in policy proved disastrous. It altered the balance between the moderate and militant element within the Tamil movement. It also freed the local Indian Tamil leaders to openly and without restraint provide political and financial support to the militants. As the moderate leaders became weak, the militants began to vie for control over the whole movement. Soon, rivalry turned to violence, and before long, the LTTE emerged as the sole representative of the Sri Lankan Tamils. The LTTE had physically eliminated the entire phalanx of moderate and rival militant leaders by 1988.[38] India expelled the LTTE from Tamil Nadu in late 1986 when it refused to cooperate with Colombo, but by early 1987, the LTTE had captured control over the northern province of Jaffna in Sri Lanka and did not need official sanctuary in Tamil Nadu. The LTTE's progression from a dependent client group to an independent actor able to impose its own agenda on the course of the civil war points to the dangers in nurturing militancy as a leverage and losing control over their activities.

Between December 1986 and July 1987, however, the militant attacks escalated. The Sri Lankan forces launched a counteroffensive and imposed an economic embargo on the province of Jaffna in the belief that economic hardships would drive a wedge between the LTTE and the Tamil population. Disturbed by the new offensive and fearing a large-scale massacre of the Tamils, who were already starving because of shortages of food, the Indian government decided to break the economic embargo. Despite warnings from Colombo that any Indian action would be a breach of Sri Lanka's sovereignty, the Indian air force dropped twenty-five tons of food and medical supplies over the Jaffna peninsula.[39] This set the stage for the signing of the Indo-Lanka Treaty of July 1987.

The prelude to the Indo-Lanka Treaty is similar in many ways to the one before the March bombing of Kosovo. The collapse of diplomatic initiatives at Rambouillet confronted NATO with two options, to continue negotiations or begin bombing. It chose the latter. In each situation, failure to comply was backed by force and involved making the warnings credible. The Indian "food bomb," as the parachuted supplies was commonly known, had violated Sri Lankan sovereignty and warned Colombo that New Delhi would not stand aside should it invade Jaffna. However, what followed in Sri Lanka could not be more different from the subsequent NATO dealings with Serbia and Milosevic.

It was President Jayewardene who requested Indian mediation in 1987. He also requested an Indian Peacekeeping Force (IPKF) to disarm the Tamil militants. The IPKF remained in Sri Lanka at Colombo's discretion, although mutual obligations dictated that India be consulted when Colombo wanted it to withdraw. No such provisions protect Serbia's autonomy or sovereignty. It is true that India's backing of Sri Lanka was conditional upon its agreement to devolve power and grant autonomy to the Tamils. But unlike at Rambouillet, the Indo-Lanka treaty was meant to protect Sri Lanka's sovereignty. India agreed to disarm the militants and deliver them to the negotiating table for a final settlement. The Indian devolution formula for Sri Lanka had evolved over the previous five years, during which New Delhi had made several attempts to settle the conflict.[40] It reflected, therefore, an acute sensitivity to the sentiments and issues that each side believed important. It is apparent that the United States and NATO did not really engage in the "give and take" that is usually the basis of any sincere negotiations; instead, they presented Serbia with an ultimatum that it was bound to reject.[41]

Two additional presumptions shaped NATO response: the belief that "ancient ethnic hatreds" had caused the Balkan tragedy and that Milosevic and Serbia were mainly to blame for the ethnic cleansing, atrocities, and butchery in the region. The first permitted NATO to justify the hasty recognition of Croatia and Slovenia and Bosnia, although the Croats had "cleansed" Krajina of nearly 250,000 Serbians. The second permitted NATO to justify its punishing actions against Milosevic and Serbia. The Indian policy in Sri Lanka did not rest on a one-sided assumption of guilt and blame.

In line with the intent of the 1987 Indo-Lanka treaty, India sought to retain the sovereignty of Sri Lanka's central courts and judicial system, parliament, and constitution. It did not attach provisions to create a parallel judicial system under the supervision and authority of external powers (in contrast to those envisaged under the supervision of the Implementation Mission of the OSCE) as the Rambouillet agreement requires.[42] Some comparisons of the key provisions in the two documents are instructive.

- **Military Dimensions:** The Indo-Lanka Treaty envisaged the redrawing of internal political boundaries, that is, recognition of Jaffna and the Eastern Province as the ethnic homeland of the Tamils, as Kosovo is to be for the Kosovo Albanians. The Rambouillet agreement also creates internal political and administrative divisions. The Serbian forces in Kosovo were restricted to the border zone and were to act only in self-defense, in response to a hostile act. But its response had to be in accordance with the

Rules of Engagement (ROE) established by the COMKFOR in consultation with the Chief of Implementation Mission (CIM). The latter was appointed by NATO. The Serbian Border Guard forces were confined to within five kilometers of the Border Zone and could not undertake any training or exercise activities without the prior express approval of COMKFOR. The Sri Lankan forces were not so restricted. When they chose to withdraw from the northern provinces, it was mainly to permit IPKF full freedom to fulfill its obligations under the 1987 treaty. Colombo retained both the veto power and full sovereignty over all parts of Sri Lanka.

- **Administrative Dimensions:** The Indo-Lanka Treaty required redrawing of administrative boundaries: merger of Jaffna and the Eastern Province, followed by the creation of an interim council in which all major players would have a voice. The Rambouillet agreement had set up a separate administration. Accordingly, the Organization for Security and Cooperation in Europe (OSCE), through its Implementation Mission (IM), was to "monitor and supervise implementation of law enforcement and related provisions of this Agreement. The Chief of the Implementation Mission (CIM) or his designee shall have the authority to issue binding directives to the Parties and subsidiary bodies on police and civil public security matters to obtain compliance by the Parties with the terms" of the agreement. In carrying out his responsibilities, "the CIM is required to consult KFOR as appropriate. The IM has the authority to: (a) Monitor, observe, and inspect law enforcement activities, personnel, and facilities, including border police and customs units, as well as associated judicial organizations, structures, and proceedings; (b) Advise law enforcement personnel and forces, including border police and customs units, and, when necessary to bring them into compliance with this Agreement." The Indo-Lanka treaty did not foresee an Indian role beyond disarming the militants and seeking peace while the Tamils and Sri Lankan government proceeded to establish the provincial Councils it had proposed.
- **Political Dimensions:** The Indo-Lanka Treaty proposed holding a referendum in three years or at the discretion of the government in Colombo to legitimize the merger of eastern and northern provinces. The Rambouillet accord envisaged elections under the IM authority and constitution of representative bodies for self-government in Kosovo. The Indo-Lanka treaty envisaged Sri Lanka to amend its constitution and federalize the country to permit autonomy to all its provinces (the Rambouillet agreement also requires the Serbian state to be a federal state). The new federal design envisaged a devolution package that empowered local bodies and local communities in Sri Lanka. Similar provisions are included

> in the Rambouillet agreement regarding taxation and policing power granted to communal bodies. The Indo-Lanka Treaty was designed to establish a multiethnic consociational government in Sri Lanka; the Rambouillet agreement is a design for Albanian ethnocracy in which one ethnic community dominates all others.

The subsequent story of India's exit from Sri Lanka is even more instructive in the kind of dangers NATO might encounter in Kosovo.[43] The LTTE refused to surrender the weapons, rejected the Indo-Lanka Agreement, and took up arms against the IPKF. Confronted with a defiant LTTE, the Indian government had to either abandon the treaty or fulfill its obligations. From being no more than a token presence, the IPKF was suddenly transformed into a peace enforcer and a constabulary force, precisely the role that the UN peacekeeping personnel in Kosovo will be required to play in Kosovo.

The main problem for India in Sri Lanka was curbing the LTTE's ambitions and securing its cooperation in the peace building and power sharing enterprise. That objective was lost in the battles between the IPKF and the LTTE. When the LTTE was losing, it sued for cease-fire and talks, when it gained an upper hand, the LTTE reneged on promises and went to war. It used the period of cease-fire to rebuild its arsenal and regroup its cadres for the next offensive. The IPKF did not press its advantage in the battlefield to finish off the LTTE. Its ambivalence had a purpose: to soften up the militants and secure their cooperation in implementing the Indo-Lanka Treaty. India reasoned that the LTTE represented Tamil nationalism and had to be a party to any future settlement. As pointed out earlier, NATO succumbed to similar temptation in using the KLA to weaken Milosevic.

Many have argued that the IPKF was unprepared for the kind of warfare it had to wage, was mistaken in its evaluation of the LTTE, and was overly constrained by diplomatic imperatives dictated by bureaucrats unfamiliar with the ground realities in northern Sri Lanka.[44] This was true and had undoubtedly contributed to the setbacks IPKF experienced initially. But these setbacks also tested the strength and determination of the LTTE and gave the IPKF a better handle on developing counterforce strategies. These had begun to pay off by 1989. The IPKF managed to negotiate a merger of Jaffna and the eastern province, and set up a rival Tamil army, the Tamil Volunteer Force, and an alternate leadership as a rallying point for the Sri Lankan Tamils. But none of these measures provided the IPKF with a successful exit strategy. The alternate leadership was unable to mobilize popular support. The IPKF mission—to devolve political authority and power to the Tamil local bodies through democratic process—seemed increasingly impossible. Prime Minister Premadasa, who has succeeded Jayawardene as the new president, opened secret communications in the hope of cutting a separate deal with the LTTE and bypassing India. Premadasa was inveigled into thinking that the LTTE would lay down arms and agree to a deal if he asked the IPKF to quit Sri Lanka. In the quagmire that Sri Lanka became during the years of 1988-1989, it was difficult to separate the enemies and allies. All pursued actions contrary to their public pronouncements.

Since the introduction of NATO and now the UN administrators in Kosovo, the level of violence has died down. There is no certainty, however, whether the UN will fulfill its mission of installing a stable democracy in Kosovo. Although the September 2000 elections replaced Milosevic with Kostunica and Ibrahim Rugova was elected to head the provincial council in Kosovo, the situation in the Balkans was far from stable. There are already reports of internecine warfare among factions of the KLA. The law and juridical bodies envisaged in the Rambouillet agreement are hardly self-sustaining. The return of the Albanian refugees has in fact led to "ethnic cleansing" in reverse.[45] Jeremy Scahill, an independent journalist working in Yugoslavia for *Pacifica Radio*, observed that "One year after the initiation of bombing of Yugoslavia, the country's Southmost province of Kosovo is as ethnically clean as it has ever been. Thanks in no small part to the tactics and actions of the U.S.-led KFOR forces, Serbs, Gypsies, and moderate Albanians have been forced to flee their homes by violent and extremist Albanian forces backed by the U.N. Currently, Albanian militias are invading areas of eastern Serbia (Beyond Kosovo) on a regular basis."[46] The KFOR needs to establish not only law and order but create a tolerant political culture based on respect for the rule of law. This is a tall order and beyond the abilities of an external actor.

There are uncanny parallels between the KLA and the LTTE. Both are proto-fascist organizations headed by a ruthless and brutal leadership. Each is dedicated to secession and seeks to create a territorial and national base for its exclusive rule. Each has eliminated rivals and undermined moderate political leaders. Both have been nurtured with arms, support, and money from the outside. And neither cares much for human rights or democracy. If the state of Tamil Elam comes into being, it is unlikely to be democratic. The same is true of the KLA and its vision for a separate Kosovo. The lesson of twenty years of civil war in Sri Lanka is that militant organizations have greater staying power than most are willing to concede and its leaders will torpedo political settlements that weaken their hold. NATO may have secured a cease-fire and withdrawal of all Yugoslav forces from Kosovo, but winning durable and self-sustaining peace may encounter some of the same dilemmas that India faced with the LTTE in Sri Lanka. By 1989, two years after the introduction of the IPKF and loss of over twelve hundred troops—this was not a remote control or virtual war—India was nowhere close to fulfilling its part of the agreement. The demand to "bring the boys home" grew in India. The Premadasa government wanted the IPKF out of Sri Lanka. India withdrew in March 1990.

The IPKF mission required it do what the OSCE and UN peacekeepers are required to achieve in Kosovo: to stop the killing, to rearrange the power relationship between conflicting parties, and to establish democratic process and institutions to make the new power arrangements permanent. India failed in these objectives. It failed mainly because the consensus that had produced the 1987 agreement broke down. India could not impose peace when both the LTTE and Colombo sought to improve its bargaining position by engaging in military offensives. The NATO mission in Kosovo will require it to bottle up both Serbia and the KLA in order to keep them from jeopardizing its nation-building effort and wholesale rearrangements implied in the implementation of the Rambouillet agreement.

It is true that KFOR and NATO are immeasurably stronger in resources and armed power as compared to the IPKF, but the latter's failures were not all because of size and inadequate technological and military strength. The main reason for failure was IPKF's inability to generate processes of popular participation and mechanisms of interethnic deliberation in the war-torn regions of Sri Lanka. And the LTTE was superbly positioned to play the role of the spoiler. It was able to do this with just a few acts of violence. While both interventions can be called reformist, the Rambouillet agreement went much further in its political engineering. The Indian experience in Sri Lanka suggests that restoring peace to an ethnically torn society requires sustained efforts of mediation at all levels of society and the creation of mechanisms to institutionalize the reconciliation process backed by funds and force.

## CONCLUSION

Although the Bangladesh war is hailed as a textbook case of a successful humanitarian intervention, its tactical success depended on the fact that the "imagined" nation of Bangladesh was already in place with a popular backing, a cultural base, a territorially compact ethnic homeland, and a representative political party and leadership. What remained was the removal of the Pakistani army and the establishment of an independent state. That midwifery role was performed by the Indian intervention. India's exit from Bangladesh was shaped by these same considerations. It exited when the nation-state of Bangladesh came into its own. Beyond that, it hoped that democracy and human rights would endure in Bangladesh. Had India continued to occupy Bangladesh on the argument of nurturing democracy, it would have had to stay indefinitely and commit forces and resources it could not afford. While Indian intervention had won the moderate nationalists a temporary victory, it had not resolved the dilemma between rival nationalism, nor the question of who should ultimately rule in Bangladesh. The deficiency of the 1971 intervention was in its failure to establish strong civilian constraints over the military elite. The balance between elected and unelected leaders tilted in favor of the latter in 1975, and Bangladesh's freedom, won with blood and tears, passed into the hands of military dictators.

There are, of course, successful examples of rooting democracy in former authoritarian nations. Postwar Germany and Japan became thriving democracies after defeat and destruction. Could Kosovo and Serbia follow the democratic path? Success depends on curbing all forms of extremist nationalism and channeling its destructive energies into the routine of democracy. Some have argued that Kosovo and Serbia do not possess the tradition of moderate liberalism and cosmopolitanism (as embodied in Konrad Adenauer) that the German political culture could draw upon. That, of course, leaves the question of Japan. Japanese history does not yield a tradition of liberal cosmopolitanism. Even if the "cultural" argument is therefore jettisoned, the European Union will have to commit to Kosovo and Serbia for several years and with hundreds of millions of dollars in aid. Experts are divided on the question of how willing Europe is to make such a commitment. Many have argued that there are no strong pro-intervention domestic constituencies in Europe, and a prolonged presence in neighboring states will increasingly become an onerous burden for the Europeans to carry.

The Kosovo situation falls between that of Bangladesh and Sri Lanka. Kosovo has already gained quasi-independence, not unlike East Pakistan between 1970 and March 1972. But, as in Sri Lanka, the official NATO objective was to retain Serbian sovereignty over Kosovo. Unlike India's policy in Sri Lanka and Bangladesh, NATO, however, is ambivalent about an independent Kosovo. It encouraged the pro-independence forces in Kosovo before the March bombing. After the bombing (and for the time being at least) it has retained the fiction of Serbia's sovereign authority over Kosovo. The democratization scheme embedded in the Rambouillet agreement will, however, reduce Serbian jurisdiction to a nominal level. This will leave a huge authority and legitimacy deficit in Kosovo and Serbia that must be filled with democratically elected leadership. But the need for democratic engineering is ever expanding. The adjacent state of Montenegro is similarly threatened with chaos and resurgent Serbian nationalism. Albanian nationalism threatens Macedonia. How will NATO contain the fallout of these resurgent nationalisms? Humanitarian interventions that seek to build a cosmopolitan, democratic order must engage in social engineering that depends for success not on the ability to coerce but to harness culture, history, quality of ethnic leadership, and the level of institutionalization to forge a democracy. In both Bangladesh and Sri Lanka, the champions of self-determination and autonomy—the LTTE and the military elements drawn from its early precursor, the Mukti Bahini—undermined multiethnic democracy and human rights. That lesson has great relevance for the questions that NATO and Washington will face in Kosovo.

Does this mean that the world community has no obligations to prevent and stop massive violations of human rights, as in East Timor, Rwanda, and Chechnya? There is, of course, no simple answer to this question, as evident from the intervention in the first instance and silence on the other two. Experience suggests that intervention is likely to be successful in stopping gross violations of human rights and killings. It is occasionally successful in achieving the second goal of reworking elite agreement over power sharing, but it is seldom successful in nation building or restructuring politics and society. The South Asian experience underlines these conclusions. They suggest that intervention should be the instrument of last resort; it should be firmly rooted in a broad international consensus and warranted by undisputed evidence of massive human rights violations; interveners may have to simultaneously pursue coercion and negotiations, but neither track should be allowed to overwhelm local elements of moderation and democracy. If moderate political leaders have been victims of ideological polarization and war, the intervening agencies have no alternative but to stay on in the role of a constable, referee, and mediator, and construct, piece by piece, the layered structures of popular participation and accountability. No one would disagree that the international order should uphold human rights and democracy, but that end demands that the means to achieve it meet the test of fairness, justice, and prudence, but above all, enduring political will. The European and U.S. response to the crisis in Yugoslavia does not meet this test.

## NOTES

1. Adam Roberts, "NATO's Humanitarian War over Kosovo," *Survival* 41 (Autumn 1999), 102–123; Noam Chomsky, *A New Generation Draws the Line: Kosovo, East Timor and the Standards of the West* (New York: Verso, 2001); Michael Ignatieff, *Virtual War: Kosovo and Beyond* (New York: Metropolitan Books, 2000); Ivo Daalder and Michael E. O'Hanlon, *Winning Ugly: NATO's War to Save Kosovo* (Washington, D. C.: Brookings Institutions Press, 2000); "The Meaning of Kosovo," *Ethics and International Affairs*, 14 (2000), 1–67.

2. Glenn Hastedt, "The Powell Doctrine," in *American Foreign Policy*, third edition, (New Jersey: Prentice Hall, 1997), 365.

3. Michael Mandelbaum, "A Perfect Failure," *Foreign Affairs* 78, no. 5, (September/October 1999), 7; Javier Solana, "NATO's Success in Kosovo," *Foreign Affairs* 78, no. 6 (November/December 1999), 114–121.

4. J. Bryan Hehir, "Intervention: From Theories to Cases," *Ethics and International Affairs* 9 (1995), 9.

5. There is no consensus among scholars on why Germany decided to recognize Croatia and Slovenia. Wolfgang Schloer argues that a "unique combination of situational factors, personal idiosyncrasies, inexperience and misperceived domestic pressures propelled the German decision." Beverly Crawford focuses on the elite perceptions as an explanation, others explain it in terms of geostrategic calculations. But it is noteworthy that both England and France had strongly opposed the German decision. For a superbly succinct discussion of this issue see Raju Thomas, "Self-Determination and International Recognition Policy," *World Affairs* (London) 160, no. 1 (Summer 1997), 18–20.

6. David Rieff, "In Bosnia, A Prelude to Partition," *New York Times*, 14 August 1996.

7. For discussion of UN endorsement, see Peter Rodman, "The Imperilled Alliance," *Foreign Affairs* 78, no. 4 (July/August 1999), 46–48.

8. Michael McGwire, "Why Did We Bomb Belgrade?" *International Affairs* 76, no. 1 (January 2000), 2 .

9. The Russians and Chinese opposed bombing of Serbia. Italy and Greece were reluctant and repeatedly called to halt the bombing. Even Germany wanted to pause within three weeks. A large number of countries in Asia, Africa, and the Middle East likewise condemned the illegal actions of NATO. The Russians were particularly upset and had sought to tighten their hold on recalcitrant minorities and regions within Russia in the event NATO should feel compelled to comment or interfere in their domestic conflicts. The stepping up of war in Chechnya and subsequent measures to weld Russia into seven administrative provinces supervised by appointees from the central state, and dismissals of provincial governors who had enjoyed a degree of autonomy from the central state, show the profound impact on Russia of intervention in Kosovo.

10. Although NATO showed solidarity during the campaign of bombing of Serbia, there were important dissenting voices within the NATO countries. The left-wing parties in Germany and Italy opposed the bombing. The Chirac and Jospin government was under serious attack from far-right Gaullists as well as anti-American leftists in France. Peter Rodman, "The Imperilled Alliance," 47.

11. Rajat Ganguly, *Kin State Intervention in Ethnic Conflicts: Lessons From South Asia* (New Delhi: Sage Publications, 1998), 101–108.

12. Mitra Das, *From Nation to Nation: A Case Study of Bengali Independence* (Columbia, MO: South Asia Books, 1981), chapters 4 and 5.

13. M. G. Kabir, "Religion and Nationalism in Bangladesh," *Journal of Contemporary Asia* 17, no. 4, (1987), 473–87. For the role of the Awami League, see M. Rashiduzzaman, "The Awami League in Political Development of Pakistan," *Asian Survey* 10, no. 7 (July 1970), 574–87.

14. Anthony Mascarenhas, *The Rape of Bangladesh* (New Delhi: Vikas Publications, 1972), provides a fascinating account of events leading to the Pakistan army's crackdown in East Pakistan.

15. Richard Sisson and Leo Rose, *War and Secession: Pakistan, India and the Creation of Bangladesh* (Berkeley: University of California Press, 1990), 141.

16. Rajat Ganguly, *Kin State*, 121.

17. S. S. Bindra, *Indo-Bangladesh Relations* (New Delhi: Deep and Deep Publications, 1982), 19.

18. Susan Woodward, "War: Building States From Nations," in Tariq Ali (ed.), *Masters of the Universe? NATO's Balkan Crusade* (London: Verso, 2000), 203–271.

19. Rod Nordland, "A Different Kind of War," *Newsweek* 137, no. 13, March 3, 2001, 41–42.

20. Barnett R. Rubin, *Toward Comprehensive Peace in Southeast Europe*, Council on Foreign Relations, New York, 1996, 57.

21. Ibid. 32.

22. Prem Shankar Jha has carefully reconstructed the rise of the KLA, the decline of Rugova and his LDK, and the nature of arms and assistance available to the KLA from Albania. See Prem Shankar Jha, "Tragedy in the Balkans: NATO's Monumental Blunder," *World Affairs* (Geneva) 3, no. 2 (April/June 1999), 103–105.

23. Ibid. 108.

24. In a private conversation, Ambassador Christopher Hill (then U.S. Ambassador to Macedonia and part of the team at the Rambouillet negotiations) said that the January incident in Racak was a turning point in NATO's decision to bomb Serbia. World Policy Institute, New York, May 4, 2000, conference on Southeastern Europe, "The federal Republic of Yugoslavia and the Future of the region." Mr. Hill was the Senior Director, Southeastern Europe, U.S. National Security Council in the Clinton administration.

25. Jason Vest, "The Real Rambouillet," Press Clips, *Village Voice*, May 12–18, 1999.

26. Brian Mitchel, "How Many Really Died in Kosovo?" *Investors Daily*, November 20, 1999. Also see John Laughland, "The Massacres That Never Were," *Spectator* (London), November 3, 1999.

27. "Bombing of Yugoslavia: One Year later," Institute for Public Accuracy, news releases, March 24, 2000. Also see "NATO's crimes," *Spectator* (London), March 11, 2000.

28. Prem Shankar Jha, "Tragedy in the Balkans," 98.

29. Robert Fisk, " The Trojan Horse That Started a 79 Day War," *Independent*, November 6, 1999.

30. Peter Gowan, "The Euro-Atlantic Origins of NATO's Attack on Yugoslavia," in Tariq Ali, *Masters of the Universe*, 3–46.

31. For accounts of Sri Lanka's descent into civil war and India's role in resolving the conflict, see Maya Chadda, *Ethnicity, Security and Separatism in India* (New York: Columbia University Press, 1997), chapter 6; Bruce Matthews, "The Situation In Jaffna—And How It Came About," *The Round Table* 290 (April 1984), 188–204; S. D Muni, "Sri Lanka's Ethnic Crisis," in Kalim Bahadur (ed.), *South Asia in Transition: Conflicts and Tensions* (New Delhi: Patriot Publishers, 1986). S. Ponnambalam, *Sri Lanka: The National Question and Tamil Liberation Struggle* (London: Zed Books, 1983); Sumantra Bose, *States, Nations, Sovereignty: Sri Lanka, India and the Tamil Eelam Movement* (New Delhi: Sage Publications, 1994).

32. S. D. Muni, "Indo-Sri Lanka Ethnic Factor," in K. M. de Silva and R. J. May (eds.), *Internationalization of Ethnic Conflict* (New York: St. Martin's Press, 1991), 117.

33. Barnett Rubin, *Toward Comprehensive Peace in Southeast Europe*, 30–31.

34. "Macedonian Peace Process," BBC News, November 21, 2001 (News.bbc.co.uk/1/hi/world/europe/1331772/stm).

35. J. N. Dixit, *Assignment Colombo* (New Delhi: Konarak Publishers, 1998), introduction, xii.

36. For a detailed discussion of the Indian Intelligence Agencies' roles in Sri Lanka's ethnic conflict, see Rohan Gunaratna, *Indian Intervention in Sri Lanka: The Role of India's Intelligence Agencies* (Colombo: South Asian Network on Conflict Research, 1993), 99–100.

37. For discussion of Rajiv Gandhi's Sri Lanka policy, *Indian Intervention*, see Rohan Gunaratna, 112–134.

38. J. N. Dixit, *Colombo*, 78.

39. Ibid. 104.

40. The Indian government's mediation efforts had produced several formulas for settling the Tamil Sinhala conflict. The notable among these were the Annexure C proposal in 1983–1984, the Thimpu talks in 1985, the proposal on December 19, 1986, and finally the devolution package detailed in the Indo-Lanka Treaty of 1987.

41. Ambassador Christopher Hill, in a conversation with this author (May 4, 2000, New York City), pointed out that Kosovo was not mentioned in the Dayton Accords because the Dayton talks concerned only Bosnia—therefore, there was no reason to mention Kosovo. This disingenuous explanation runs counter to the ground realities in the remaining Yugoslavia. Anyone even slightly familiar with the situation would have seen the importance of reaffirming Serbia's sovereign jurisdiction over Kosovo provided it respected human rights and refrained from using unnecessary force against Kosovar Albanians. That reaffirmation would have served as a warning to the KLA not to cross the line and provoke retaliation from the Serbian forces.

42. The text of the Indo-Lanka Treaty is available in J. N. Dixit, *Colombo*, 355–360. For the Rambouillet Agreement, see the website: monde-diplomatique.fr/dossiers/kosovo/rambouillet.html.

43. Rajat Ganguly, *Kin States*, 214–216. For a detailed account see J. N. Dixit, *Colombo*, 189–220.

44. Author's interview with General Amarsingh Kalkat, commander of the IPKF at the time of withdrawal. Interview took place at his residence in New Delhi, December 22, 1999.

45. David Rhode, "Kosovo Seething," *Foreign Affairs* 79, no. 3, (2002), 70.

46. Reported in the news releases, Institute for Public Accuracy, Washington D. C., March 24, 2000.

13

# Reflections on the Yugoslav Wars: A Peacekeeper's Perspective

*Satish Nambiar*

## THE SETTING

Any analysis of events in the former Yugoslavia must take note, at the very least, of what has transpired in the not too distant past. However, interpretations of history vary, especially that of the former Yugoslavia, both those recorded and espoused by the various religious and ethnic groups that live there, and those of external analysts and commentators. One's own interpretation of history, therefore, may color one's assessments and judgments of the politics of the region. My interpretation stems from my experience as the first commander of the United Nations Protection Force (UNPROFOR) deployed in the former Yugoslavia and, subsequently, from my reading and learning experience since my assignment there. My perspective is also conditioned, in part, by my experience as an Indian military officer with combat experience and as the Deputy Chief of Staff of the Indian Army with policy experience. In these positions, I have had to deal with war and insurgency on the Indian subcontinent, where there are some similarities and parallels with the former Yugoslavia in the nature of interethnic and religious conflicts and in the wars that stem from such struggles.

### Historical Context

For many centuries, the Balkan region was considered an object of spoils among the then imperial powers. (It is another matter that, at the end of the twentieth century and the beginning of the twenty-first century, it has received the rather dubious attention of today's "democratic" powers.) Among the many reasons for this was the fact that the Balkan people often clashed among themselves over religious and national differences. Though the Balkan peoples were mostly Slav in culture and, at that time, Christian in religion, jealousies and quarrels arose among them on account of the different nationalities. Insofar as Yugoslavia was concerned, most of its people were subjects of foreign empires, and many of their lands were the scenes of constant warfare. The Croats spent almost two centuries under the oppressive rule of the Ottoman Turks; then, from 1699 to 1918, much of current Croatia became part of the Austro-Hungarian Empire run from Budapest. The Croatian populated region of Herzegovina remained under Ottoman rule.

The various tribes of Orthodox Serbs were loosely united by the end of the thirteenth century, forming an empire, which was, however, beset by endemic dynastic conflict and territorial disruption, as the fortunes of war ebbed and flowed. The battle of Kosovo in 1389 snuffed out Serbian independence, and for the subsequent four centuries, the Serbs had, to endure Turkish rule. However, by 1830, Serbia had wrested autonomy from the Turks and, by 1878, independence. A series of wars, mostly successful, had, by 1914, enlarged the country to include Kosovo, the country's spiritual home, and much of Macedonia. In World War I, the Serbs, after some initial defensive victories, were overrun by the Central powers in 1915. Serbian military casualties were proportionately the highest of all combatant nations in that war; with 57 dead per thousand of population and 371 dead per thousand mobilized. The comparative figure for Britain was 16 and 125, respectively. It is, therefore, no great wonder that, when the Southern Slavs decided to unite against imperial domination, the others looked to the Serbs for leadership.

Bosnia-Herzegovina (BiH) was divided as early as the tenth century between the Catholic West and the Orthodox East. Most of the area was part of the unstable Serbian Empire until it, too, was occupied by the Turks. Turkish occupation changed the religious map of BiH through the conversion to Islam of many local Slav inhabitants. In 1878, the Province, along with the Sandjak region, was given to Austria-Hungary, robbing Serbia of what the Serbs regard as their homeland. The people of BiH, therefore, never really enjoyed an autonomous existence.

Settled by Slavic tribes since the seventh century, Macedonia became part of the Bulgarian Empire in the early thirteenth, then part of the Serbian Empire toward the end of that century. The area was seized by the Turks, even before Kosovo, and was dominated by them for five and a half centuries. Russia awarded Macedonia to Bulgaria in 1878, ostensibly on strong ethnic grounds, but the other powers forced its return to Turkey. The Balkan Wars of 1912–1913 led to its liberation but also to partition between Serbia, Greece, and Bulgaria. Macedonia, therefore, is another region without its own history and traditions, or even identity.

In 1918, a voluntary union, the United Kingdom of the Serbs, Croats, and Slovenes, was created. This comprised restored Montenegro and prewar Serbia (enlarged by the acquisition of Vojvodina from Hungary, and some bits of Macedonia from Bulgaria) and, from the ruins of the Austro-Hungarian Empire, Slovenia, Croatia, BiH, and the Sandjak. This came about because the Southern Slavs continued to be acutely apprehensive about their political survival. They feared their resubjugation by the major European imperial powers. In 1929, this united kingdom was renamed Yugoslavia, meaning "The land of the South Slavs."

In 1941, a German blitzkrieg overran the country, and Yugoslavia was partitioned. Germany and Italy annexed or occupied and administered large areas; Vojvodina reverted to Hungary, and most of Macedonia was awarded to Bulgaria, and the large puppet state of Croatia was created. There followed a war against the German, Italian, and Bulgarian occupiers, combined with a civil war between Croat Ustashe and Muslim supporters of the Axis on one side, Tito's communist-dominated partisans on another, and Serbian monarchist nationalists (Chetniks) in the middle. This was a struggle (centered in BiH) of viciousness hardly paralleled, in which about 1.8 million Yugoslavs (10.9 percent of the population) died. Over 50 percent of these deaths, including about half a million Serbs reportedly massacred by the Croatian Ustashe and their supporters during "ethnic cleansing" in Croatia, were the result of the civil war. The scars that existed, therefore, were not difficult to imagine. In fact, when the nationalist upsurge took hold in 1990, a number of those in positions of authority in government or political parties were, in one way or another, part of, or affected by, the events of the early forties.

Aided by the collapse of German power elsewhere, the partisans under Tito emerged victorious over the Axis, the Ustashe regime, and the monarchists. Tito then set about creating a Yugoslavia in which bourgeois nationalism would be eliminated in favor of socialist unity of the Yugoslav peoples, all of whom would be treated as equals. The country was divided into six federal republics—Serbia (including the provinces of Vojvodina and Kosovo), Croatia, Slovenia, Bosnia-Herzegovina, Montenegro, and Macedonia. These were purely administrative divisions and did not, indeed could never, reflect the boundaries of Yugoslavia's heterogeneous ethnic groups. Each republic, except Slovenia, contained substantial minorities.

The 1981 census showed that, in the Republic of Serbia, Serbia proper had 85 percent Serbs, the autonomous region of Vojvodina had 55 percent Serbs and 20 percent Hungarians, and the autonomous region of Kosovo had 75 percent ethnic Albanians and 12.5 percent Serbs. Croatia had 76 percent Croats and a substantial Serb minority of 11 percent. Montenegro had 20 percent Muslims, 10 percent Albanians, and 67 percent Montenegrins. Macedonia had

20 percent ethnic Albanians and 4.5 percent Turks, against a Macedonian population of 65 percent. The Republic of Bosnia-Herzegovina had a mix of about 39 percent Muslims, 32 percent Serbs, and 19.5 percent Croats.

## The Process of Disintegration

It should have been evident to political analysts that, if Communism brought what the West saw as oppression to the people of Central and Eastern Europe, it also brought stability to the group of countries that emerged with the collapse of the Russian, Ottoman, Austro-Hungarian, and German empires after World War I. Yugoslavia was formed as the Kingdom of Serbs, Croats, and Slovenes; Czechoslovakia was erected from the ashes of the Hapsburg Empire; Poland was reborn; Hungary was drastically diminished by the Triannon treaty; and Rumania was enlarged at Hungary's expense. But these new or extensively remodeled countries were promptly savaged by the Depression and then by World War II. They never had the time to develop democratic institutions or secure identities. From the start, this insecurity found expression in ethnic tensions and persecution of minorities.

In this sense, the outbreak of violence and bigotry on the volatile soil of Eastern Europe should not have come as a surprise. But the complacency among Western leaders, a "New World Order" fogginess, even a vague notion that history was ending, may have blurred thc fact that history was really beginning again, and at full throttle, with the disappearance of Communism. As a Western analyst is reported to have stated, "Communism was a freezer; it simply froze old hatreds. Unfortunately, the hatreds thawed before the European Union was strong enough to provide a concerted response in the absence of real American leadership in Europe."

When Tito came to power after the war, his main concern, in the overriding interest of Yugoslav unity, was to place a seal over Yugoslavia's civil strife and the atrocities committed. In some cases, this sealing of history was apparently quite literally so; concrete was poured over the pits in Herzegovina, where the bones of countless executed Serbs lay. In other cases, history was simply ignored in the hope that it would disappear. Tito apparently never visited the Jasenovac concentration campsite, the scene of the worst Ustashe crimes against the Serbs. The dangers inherent in Tito's policy of burying Yugoslavia's past started becoming clear toward the late eighties. The interethnic warfare of World War II, never acknowledged, never judged officially, lived on beneath the surface, ready to explode at the slightest provocation.

Instead of moving toward greater democracy after his break with Stalin in 1948, Tito began the elaborate balancing act that he was to maintain until the very end of his long life in 1980. This policy involved offering even greater autonomy to Yugoslav's constituent nations and placing himself at the fulcrum, rather than extending individual liberties, democratic institutions, and the scope for personal economic initiative that alone might have cemented Yugoslavia. The culmination of this policy, in the 1974 Constitution, was the raising of Bosnia's Muslims to the status of a constituent nation, a decision that gave Tito one more piece to manipulate in the balancing game.

With the collapse of the political and economic structure in Eastern Europe and the Soviet Union, it was inevitable that the Yugoslav model would come under serious threat. The collective leadership, with a rotatory presidency and a loose confederal arrangement wherein each republic had its own president, vice president, and foreign minister, among others, together with an autonomous economic regime, which had eight separate markets, contributed in no small measure to the process of disintegration. Nationalist parties in Slovenia, Croatia, Serbia, and BiH were easily able to exploit the resentments and frustrated ambitions, especially after the economic stagnation of the eighties.

## THE ROLE OF THE EUROPEAN POWERS

The West never had, and still does not have, a coherent policy or response to the conflict in the former Yugoslavia; indeed, the United States and Western Europe have at various times been divided by it, notwithstanding the facade of coordination in NATO's intervention in Kosovo. Economic progress and political opening were supposed to follow the demise of communism in Eastern Europe; that was to be the logical consequence of what the West saw as victory over totalitarianism. Instead, the Caucasus erupted, and Yugoslavia witnessed a reversion to intense nationalism. Against this madness, grand Wilsonian principles, like self-determination of peoples, and grand institutions, like the UN and NATO, proved no insurance. The obvious helplessness became evident not only because of the scale of fighting that took place but also because of the way NATO, the European Union, and the UN were revealed as cumbersome and divided before the ethnic conflicts of post-Communist Europe.

The fact that some understanding of the dimensions and seriousness of the emerging situation did exist is far outweighed by the apparent lack of understanding, or the unwillingness to do so, among many Western governments. Lord Carrington had apparently stated in a letter (on 2 December 1991) to Hans van den Broek, Minister of Foreign Affairs of the Netherlands (at that time President of the European Community Council of Ministers)—"There is a real danger, perhaps even a probability, that BiH would also ask for independence and recognition, which would be wholly unacceptable to the Serbs in that Republic in which there are something like one hundred thousand JNA troops, some of which have withdrawn from Croatia. Milosevic has hinted that military action would take place there if Croatia and Slovenia were recognised. That might well be the spark that sets BiH alight." Similarly, Perez de Cuellar wrote to Hans-Dietrich Genscher, Vice Chancellor and Minister of Foreign Affairs of the Federal Republic of Germany, on 14 December 1991—"I trust also that you will have learnt of the deep concern that has been expressed by the Presidents of BiH and Macedonia, as well as by many others, that early selective recognition could result in a widening of the present conflict to those sensitive areas. Such a development could have grave consequences for the Balkan region as a whole."

The incomprehension about the Yugoslav situation in much international, including transatlantic, debate at that time was staggering. Jacques Delors, then President of the European Commission, is reported to have remarked in the summer of 1991, when fighting broke out in Yugoslavia, "We do not interfere in American affairs. We hope they will have enough respect not to interfere in ours." U.S. Secretary of State James Baker's message, when he visited Belgrade in June 1991, was apparently that the United States was opposed to the breakup of Yugoslavia and opposed the use of force to hold it together; much too subtle for anyone, least of all the belligerents in the Balkans, to understand. Whatever veneer of unity and pretence of being able to come to grips with the problem, insofar as the Europeans were concerned, fell away altogether with Germany's extraordinary, unilateral recognition of Slovenia and Croatia. When the rest of the European Community and, ultimately, the United States decided there was no way back from that German decision, the die was cast. The world was officially committed to Tito's internal administrative borders as state boundaries, even though they were still being disputed on the ground by rival armies of the Serbs, Muslims, and Croats.

There does not appear to be much doubt that Germany, Austria, Hungary, and the Vatican encouraged nationalistic and secessionist forces in Slovenia and Croatia; the rest of the developments were an inevitable fallout. Equally inevitable was the Serb view that what they were being subjected to was a German plot to subjugate them once again. It could be debated whether even these countries anticipated the savagery of the conflict their actions brought about. If they did not anticipate it in context of events of unbelievable viciousness barely five decades ago, to which the generation now running the republics were witness, and whose scars had still not disappeared, it was indeed gross incompetence or utter callousness. If they did anticipate it and, even so, proceeded as they did, they have much to answer for. Either way, the European Community and the United States share much of the blame for the carnage that took place in the former Yugoslavia in the first half of the 1990s. It was not, therefore, surprising to those of us who were connected with the problem that this guilt complex led to the governments of these countries deflecting blame and responsibility onto the Serbs alone. The fact that the Serbs had a case, both in Croatia (as recognized in the Security Council resolution setting up UNPROFOR in February 1992) and in BiH (as evident even in the Dayton Agreement), was submerged in the symbolism and rhetoric indulged in by the West and by the Serbs' own heavy-handedness and stubbornness.

Insofar as BiH was concerned, the Western powers were even more culpable. It was evident, even to relative newcomers like us sent to the region to set up a UN force, that it was utterly ridiculous, in the aftermath of the ethnic divide created by the secession of Croatia and the conflict that followed, that these two communities could coexist in BiH, and that, too, under a majority Muslim government whom neither of them trusted and whose leadership had already decided to break away from Yugoslavia and from, what they termed, a Serb-dominated federation. It was never going to work. As Henry Kissinger wrote in the *Washington Post* in mid-May 1993:

> It is important to understand that BiH has never been a nation. There was no Bosnian ethnic group or a specifically Bosnian cultural identity. Located at the intersection of the Muslim, Greek Orthodox, and Catholic religions, and at the dividing line between the Ottoman and the Hapsburg empires, BiH has been the no-man's-land where nationalities displaced by endless wars were thrown together. Serbs, Croats, and Muslims who are descendants of Slavic Christians converted to Islam during Turkish rule, and are therefore considered turncoats by the other ethnic groups, have managed to co-exist only under foreign rule. The most irresponsible mistake of the current Bosnia tragedy was international recognition of a Bosnian state governed by Muslims. . . . But where Croatia and Slovenia had their own identity, Bosnia was a Yugoslavia in microcosm. It is a mystery why anyone could think that Croats and Serbs, unwilling to stay together in the larger Yugoslavia, could be induced to create a joint state in BiH, together with Muslims they had hated for centuries.

## European Conference on the Former Yugoslavia

When Slovenia and Croatia declared their independence, the Serbs, given the history of World War II, reacted vigorously. European Community intercession was sought by the then federal authorities of Yugoslavia, and in due course, Lord Carrington was appointed chairman of the Conference on Yugoslavia, with three elements to his mandate:

1. That the Conference would not start till a cease-fire was reached.
2. That there would be no changes in borders except by mutual agreement.
3. None of the six republics would be recognized as sovereign and independent, until a final comprehensive settlement was reached.

Of these three elements, two were violated even before the Conference got down to its work. The European Community itself contemplated recognition of Slovenia and Croatia and set up the Badinter Commission to examine if these and other republics met the conditions for recognition. Badinter's ruling that Slovenia satisfied the conditions led to its recognition; but even though the Commission ruled that Croatia did not wholly meet these conditions, the EC decided to go ahead and recognize it. Macedonia was considered as having satisfied all conditions, but its recognition was long held back because of Greek objections. On BiH, Badinter said that the conditions laid down by its own Constitution, which demanded consensus on the question of independence by all three communities, had not been satisfied. A referendum was called, in which the Serbs of BiH did not participate; yet the EC went ahead with recognition on the basis of the voting result.

These developments totally altered the terms of reference of the Peace Conference headed by Lord Carrington. The republics, having got what they wanted, were not interested in the Carrington endeavor anymore; it degenerated into a series of bilateral or trilateral interactions. The internal borders of Yugoslavia did not follow clear ethnic, economic, or strategic lines. Hence, serious problems arose when the international community, in according recognition to the existing republics, accepted the internal boundaries, however arbitrary or artificial, as the international frontiers of the new or reconstituted states. The immediate problem was that, once recognized, a state is entitled to insist on retaining all its territory, however strongly it is disputed; what was previously a civil war became a war between sovereign states.

Insofar as BiH was concerned, it was evident, even in March 1992, as the UN operation for Croatia was being set up, headquartered as it was in Sarajevo, that the Bosnian Serbs were against secession from Yugoslavia. It was therefore suggested to Lord Carrington and his Portuguese interlocutors (Portugal being president of the EC at that time) that they should meet in a constitutional conference, to which all agreed. On 28 March 1992, all parties apparently agreed on the principles of a new constitution taking account of the three national communities in a federal arrangement. Most unfortunately, at that crucial stage, the EC accorded recognition to BiH, and fighting erupted.

Notwithstanding this serious setback, Lord Carrington and Ambassador Cutilheiro continued their efforts at peacemaking in pursuance of an overall settlement. This was, however, a lost cause, and no one knew it better than Lord Carrington himself. But the gallant old man persevered. President Izetbegovic apparently told Lord Carrington that the principles agreed to earlier were no longer acceptable to him. On the other side, Dr. Karadzic, the leader of the Bosnian Serbs, told Lord Carrington that he no longer felt that the Bosnian Serbs could remain part of an independent BiH. The Bosnian Croat position was not articulated at that time, though efforts were already under way to strengthen their hold in areas of Herzegovina where they were in a majority.

Lord Carrington's assessment was that President Izetbegovic was not willing to resume negotiations because of the following:

(a) He was already head of an internationally recognized Republic.
(b) He expected large-scale international intervention in his favor. (Lord Carrington apparently tried to disabuse him of this, but unsuccessfully).
(c) He believed (erroneously) that the balance of advantage had changed; that the Muslim-Croat alliance increased his chances of success.

By the first week of May 1992, the efforts of the European Conference on Yugoslavia had foundered on the intransigence of the parties to the conflict, but sadly, more due to the duplicity and hypocrisy of its own components.

## THE UNITED NATIONS OPERATIONS

### Political Aspects

One of the major shortcomings of the United Nations operations in the former Yugoslavia was that it was launched much too hurriedly, without the degree of preparation essential for a venture so complex and demanding. Preliminary negotiations and discussions were conducted by the Secretary General's Special Envoy, Cyrus Vance, and by the senior staff of the United Nations Secretariat with the political and military leadership of the parties to the conflict prior to the submission of a report to the Security Council. It was evident, even at that time, that there were a number of contentious issues on which there were significant variations of interpretation. While these were apparently taken note of, they were glossed over in the hope they may get resolved or disappear as the operation got going. In actuality, these issues assumed serious proportions and continued to plague the operation.

It would be useful to recall what turned out to be prophetic remarks made by Secretary General Boutros Boutros Ghali in his report of 15 February 1992 to the Security Council,

> immediate UN deployment is the only remaining hope for avoiding an even more destructive civil war than that which prevailed during the second half of 1991. Many member states (obviously the West Europeans) also have urged me not to delay in recommending the deployment of a UN Force in accordance with the Plan (the Vance Plan evolved in December 1991). . . ; If it is only now that

> I am proposing such a force, it has been because of the complexities and dangers of the Yugoslav situation. . . . As will be evident from Section 1 of the present Report, there remain a number of unanswered questions about the extent to which the Force will, in practice, receive the necessary cooperation. *But after careful deliberation, I have come to the conclusion, that the danger that a UN peacekeeping operation will fail because of lack of cooperation from the parties, is less grievous than the danger that delay in its despatch will lead to a breakdown of the cease-fire, and to a new conflagration in Yugoslavia.*

In the intervening period between the approval of the Vance Plan by the Security Council in December 1991 and the Secretary General's report on the setting up of the Mission in February 1992, many developments had taken place that had substantially altered certain basic features on which the Plan was premised. However, the original plan was not modified to allow for the new ground realities. Thc Mission Headquarters did not have anyone on its staff who had been associated with the negotiating process and the positions taken by the belligerents. In the initial stages, therefore, the UNPROFOR hierarchy was unable to interpret and respond effectively to the positions taken by the parties to the conflict.

Serb ground positions had changed and were well beyond the boundaries of the *opstine* (municipalities) listed in the Vancc Plan. These areas became very contentious as UNPROFOR deployed and began to deal with the belligerents; at a certain stage, parts of these areas came to be designated as "Pink Zones" remaining under Serb control, much to the chagrin of the Croatian authorities. Croatia and Slovenia had since been recognized as independent nations by the European Community members and others; in due course, they were also recognized by the United Nations. Such recognition carried with it the aspect of sovereignty within existing borders; on this basis, the Croatian government took the view that the Krajina Serbs had no "locus standi" and therefore should not be dealt with by the United Nations force. While this position may have had some validity from their point of view, it was in conflict with the Vance Plan, which categorically set out that deployment in the areas designated as United Nations Protected Areas was to be an "interim arrangement" subject to a final political resolution, which was to be arrived at under the aegis of the European Conference on Yugoslavia.

In actuality, with the changed political situation, insofar as Croatia was concerned, and the civil war in Bosnia-Herzegovina having broken out, even before the allotted forces for the original mandate arrived in full, UNPROFOR was saddled with additional tasks—what came to be known as "mission creep." Between June and December 1992, the Security Council, in its immense wisdom, conferred nine extensions to the mandate of UNPROFOR—symbolic responses to assuage political pressures and that of the media in the

West. Well-drafted specimens of United Nations intentions, which remained on paper because the resources required to implement the resolutions either did not arrive at all or arrived well after the situation that they were meant to handle, had changed totally.

As UNPROFOR operations progressed, it soon became evident that shared responsibility between the United Nations and the European Community (with NATO preparing to make its presence felt in due course in Bosnia-Herzegovina) was an unsatisfactory arrangement, to put it very mildly. Regional organizations should either handle such operations on their own, under the umbrella of a Security Council resolution, or the operation must be completely under the United Nations. UNPROFOR experience was that, when situations emerged where positive results appeared likely, the European Community came on the scene in the hope of drawing credit; but the moment things went wrong, UNPROFOR was left to pick up the pieces—an art we gradually came to master, insofar as weathering the flak directed at us was concerned. In due course, with the rather dubious arrangements that were put in place for Bosnia-Herzegovina, it was inevitable that copies of reports, analyses, and recommendations emanating from UNPROFOR headquarters began finding their way to Brussels, some national capitals, and the office of the European Community negotiator. The annoying and unacceptable part of this development was that, using such information, attempts were made to arrive at arrangements with the belligerents without consulting UNPROFOR, in most cases, with disastrous results.

A vital requirement for any United Nations operation to be successful is that of continuous political support. Sacrificing this at the altar of political expediency is not only hypocritical but also a source of danger to the personnel in the mission area, who continued to work in a dedicated manner under most trying conditions. Regrettably, the operations in the former Yugoslavia have been characterized by a degree of symbolism, rhetoric, and hypocrisy, for which a heavy price has been paid in terms of human lives and suffering; posterity will no doubt judge the international community harshly for this.

## Military Aspects

Besides the great challenge of dealing with the complexity of the situation in the former Yugoslavia, another immediate challenge in setting up the Mission was that of molding a large, multinational force with military, civilian police, and international civilian staff from so many different regions, with different cultures and languages, different backgrounds and approaches to the problem, varying levels of training, varied types of equipment, and so on, into a single, cohesive force. That we were able to do so in a relatively short period of time is a tribute to the dedication, professionalism, understanding, and application displayed by all members of the Mission collectively, as contingents, as well as individually. This was, in many ways, the single most satisfying feature of one's experience with UNPROFOR.

A major problem faced by UNPROFOR was the inordinately long time it took for the various contingents to arrive in the mission area. It took almost four months for the complete military components of the mission to be deployed for the initial mandate, by which time, extensions to the mandate had already begun to be framed. Another serious problem was the time it took for the Mission Headquarters and the four sector headquarters to become effective, given the fact that the commanders and staff were gathered together at short notice from various corners of the globe; most of them had never even seen each other before. This type of arrangement may have worked in earlier years when the pressures and dangers in the mission areas were not so serious as they are today. In the case of UNPROFOR, when additional deployment for the execution of tasks in Bosnia-Herzegovina took place, the solution was to draw the core of the headquarters from NATO resources. Whereas this was no doubt effective from the operational point of view, it was an uncomfortable arrangement. The professional inclinations of the staff were to the tasks in hand, but they were often embarrassed by the demands placed on them by the parent organization, as well as by their national governments.

A vital aspect that surfaces from time to time is that of the command and control of a United Nations operation. In the case of UNPROFOR, notwithstanding the large number of contingents, and the fact that these included contributions from permanent members of the Security Council and many developed countries of the Western world, there were no major problems in this regard. This was as much due to the fact that no compromises on the subject were allowed as it was to the unqualified support the Mission received from the headquarters in New York. This is, however, an aspect that needs some emphasis. There can be only one option insofar as operational command of a mission is concerned; all forces deployed in the mission area must take their orders from the Head of Mission or the Force Commander and implement them in the right spirit. It is for the Head of Mission or the Force Commander to be careful and discreet in decisions that are sensitive. One needs to be realistic enough to recognize that, no matter what the efforts put in, the mutual interaction ensured, and understanding developed, national interests and national pride will always take precedence over any form of commitment to the United Nations flag. The experience of UNPROFOR was that, in itself, this is not a bad thing, provided such national interests and national pride of the contingents were harnessed toward the common purpose of the mission.

## Coordination with Aid Agencies

One of the major tasks that UNPROFOR had to undertake, particularly in Bosnia-Herzegovina, was to assist in the provision of humanitarian aid. In this context, the interaction between the United Nations forces and aid agencies, like the United Nations High Commissioner for Refugees (UNHCR), non-governmental organizations (NGOs), and the International Committee of the Red Cross (ICRC), merit some reference. It took some time for an institutionalized arrangement to be set up, primarily because of the magnitude of the problem and the fact that all organizations were struggling to cope with their own internal dynamics in the early stages, under fairly adverse conditions. In the process, some very serious reservations about one another developed, and it took a great deal of effort at various levels for it to dawn on all concerned that they were, in fact, working to a common purpose.

Insofar as aid agencies are concerned, it is essential that their efforts are coordinated, both in terms of aid effort as well as the assistance desired from the military; the best arrangement would be for the UNHCR to be the lead agency. The problem that remains is that most NGOs have an agenda of their own and are reluctant to subordinate themselves to any other organization, their argument being that they have to show results to those who fund their activities and whose aims and purposes may not totally coincide with those of the international community. At a seminar I attended at Oxford University in October 1995 on the subject of the role of the military in humanitarian emergencies, I was shocked to note the intense distrust of the military by most NGO personnel (and the other way, too). Sadly, at the end of the three-day seminar, my impression was that the gap between the military and the NGOs had not narrowed but may well have widened. This is a factor that senior commanders would have to apply themselves to in the field; and the United Nations Headquarters, as well as other international actors, may well consider applying themselves to this factor so as to correct the wrong perceptions that seem to persist on all sides.

## The Media and Public Information System

The importance of the media, both electronic and print, in whatever activity is undertaken, cannot be overstated. There is possibly no other single factor that has a greater influence on the evolution, preparation, and conduct of a peace operation than this. Some operations in the recent past were rushed into, without adequate preparation and thought, purely because of pressures generated by media reports; in other cases, conduct of operations in mission areas has been influenced by media coverage, even to the extent of being against the better judgment of commanders on the ground. It is therefore imperative that the international community recognize the impact of this vital aspect and, while using it to good effect to further the cause of international peace and security, have the strength to resist pressures for deployment of forces without all implications being taken into account and full preparations made.

A related aspect is the recognition of the equally vital importance of providing qualified staff and essential equipment for running an effective public information system as part of any peace operation, as it is being set up; wherever this has been done well, the mission's success has been largely assisted. And where it was conspicuous by its nonexistence for many months, as was the case in the former Yugoslavia, the mission was seriously handicapped, because, particularly in cases of ethnic, intrastate conflict, truth is invariably the first casualty. In fact, in such operations, this vital tool is required from the outset in order to deal with the propaganda put out by the parties to the conflict, as also by unprincipled media persons.

## THE ROLE ASSUMED BY THE WEST

To the extent possible, given the dependence on media reports, one continued to follow events in the Balkans with keen interest even on return to India. It was disturbing to note that many of the fears in regard to the command, control, and direction of the operations began to come true. It is unfortunate that the United Nations became a facade for the machinations of some members of the NATO grouping. Inevitably, the Mission appeared to have become a tool of this regional alliance. Even so, it was indeed tragic to note that the United Nations forces were given tasks that were not feasible without matching resources being made available; the most unfortunate was that of the security of what came to be called "safe havens" or "safe areas." The disastrous results of the callousness displayed by the Security Council hardly merit elucidation.

The much-acclaimed Dayton Accord is another reflection of the symbolism that has characterized most of the initiatives in the region. The Serbs of Bosnia-Herzegovina were given almost all they had asked for as early as the end of 1992—recognition as a separate entity and control of Serb majority areas, which was almost half the country, among other things. The Muslims and Croats of the Republic have been grouped into a federation, which, even to the casual observer of the scene, is a superficial arrangement that will last only as long as the NATO forces are present in some strength; the real fact is that the two communities are probably as antagonistic to each other as they are to the Serbs. Therefore, notwithstanding all the rhetoric, NATO will need to remain for a long period of deployment in Bosnia-Herzegovina. The saving grace may well be that, as economic activity picks up and the quality of life improves, the people of the region may feel less inclined to respond to the call of nationalism. But for that to happen, the West will need to infuse substantial financial inputs.

Even before the provisions of the Dayton Accord had begun to be properly implemented, Kosovo exploded. It is a matter of deep regret that the political leadership of the United States and the countries of Western Europe did not apply their efforts to a resolution of the Kosovo situation during the deliberations at Dayton in November 1995. It is inconceivable that anyone dealing with developments in the Balkans could have failed to recognize that Kosovo was a "tinderbox." The manner in which NATO has blatantly violated all norms of international behavior in dealing with the developments emerging from its own mishandling should be a matter of concern to the international community.

## The Kosovo Intervention

Notwithstanding my brief association with the region, I was surprised that, when the United States and the West bludgeoned the warring parties in the former Yugoslavia into signing the Dayton Accord in November 1995, the Kosovo issue was left unaddressed. In my view, this was unforgivable; as unforgivable as having delayed allowing the Bosnian Serbs recognition as a separate entity within BiH for three years, from the end of 1992 to 1995, with the resultant deaths, destruction and misery. It was inevitable that, after the developments in BiH, Albanian extremist elements (many of them possibly having fought in BiH) would displace the moderate elements in Kosovo, assert themselves, and provoke the Yugoslav authorities into a heavy-handed response.

Rambouillet was a farce enacted to justify NATO actions in due course. There could never have been any doubt that Yugoslavia would not agree to the secession of Kosovo and the stationing of NATO forces on its soil. The process at Rambouillet was in violation of the Vienna Convention on the Law of International Treaties. NATO intervention in the form of missile and air attacks on Kosovo and other areas of Yugoslavia was in violation of all international norms—the UN Charter and even NATO's own charter. Statements of Western leaders and the use of the Western electronic and print media to put out unabashed propaganda (and what is now beginning to be revealed as quite deliberate untruths) on alleged atrocities to demonize Milosevic and the Serbs were obviously to sustain the theory of intervention on humanitarian grounds.

The so-called humanitarian intervention was also a farce. More casualties resulted in Kosovo and other areas of Serbia because of NATO strikes than due to any actions of the Serb security forces. The Western media is itself now beginning to put out facts to indicate that allegations of genocide and mass killings had no basis. Recoveries of bodies from alleged mass graves not only refute the figures put out when the NATO bombings were being undertaken but indicate a gross overestimation that was no doubt deliberate. In fact, the irony is that there are many cases where the bodies recovered are those of Serbs.

There is hardly any doubt that the NATO decision to undertake missile and air strikes was a political one and not a military one. The expectation was that, within a couple of days of strikes, Milosevic would capitulate. (The BiH scenario may have played a part.) In actuality, it took seventy-nine days of relentless, one-sided (though the term *war* was used) missile and air strikes, near desperation by the NATO Alliance to find a face-saving way out, and some manipulation by Chernomyerdin to coax the Yugoslavs into the arrangement finally arrived at. Needless to say, many of the terms of the agreement were soon violated—the Serbs in Kosovo were killed or driven out without the NATO forces doing much about it, the Yugoslav authorities were not allowed back to man the borders with Albania, and so on.

As things stand, therefore, it would appear that, as long as the NATO forces remain, the KLA will remain in check somewhat. But if the former leave, inevitable moves for secession from Yugoslavia will be initiated, with the KLA now better equipped to deal with the Yugoslav forces. Moves for a Greater Albania may follow, with the impact already on Macedonia, and then Greece could follow. Equally, there will be moves for a Greater Serbia and a Greater Croatia. All in all, a most volatile scenario.

This will only be kept in check by the continued presence of NATO forces. As mentioned earlier, this is one means of keeping NATO going as an Alliance and of also ensuring continued American presence in Europe.

## THE CURRENT SITUATION

### Slovenia

Slovenia emerged relatively unscathed from the crisis primarily because of the homogeneous nature of its population, with over 90 percent being Slovene and no significant numbers being present in the other republics. She is actively attempting to secure membership of the EU and NATO and has the best chance among the former Yugoslav republics. There are indications that she is trying to mend relations with FRY in order to restore old economic ties.

### Croatia

Croatia has come off rather well from the whole crisis, despite having had to suffer some effects of the conflict and not having control over some of her territories for a period of time. The late President Tudjman, a committed and ruthless nationalist, can claim credit for having achieved all his nationalistic goals with single-mindedness of purpose and by exploiting the assistance afforded by Germany and Austria, in particular, and the patronage of the remaining Western powers, in general (even, to an extent, in Herzegovina). By sheer perseverance and initiative, he got back all the territories held by Serbs in Krajina and Eastern Slavonia—the former by force, and the latter by securing implementation of a UN mandate. In the process, he also got rid of a large number of Serbs from these areas. The percentage of Serbs left in Croatia is now much less than before the conflict started. The new political regime appears to be handling the emerging situation rather well and may be expected to usher in a benign atmosphere that would foster better relations with the other former Yugoslav republics and give the Serbs of Croatia a reasonable deal. Even so, economic recovery will be the key.

## Bosnia-Herzegovina

From a relatively tolerant and mixed society, the people of BiH have become an intensely nationalistic and polarized community. Extreme positions have emerged from the conflict that tore the country apart; there is much animosity between the communities, and the destruction wrought by the conflict is not only in physical terms but also in terms of values in society. Liberal Islamic values, conditioned by close association with Europe, have been replaced largely by more radical and fundamental attitudes. By the terms of the Dayton Accord, arrived at in November 1995, the Serbs got most of what they fought for, and, in fact, controlled before Dayton, except a slice of Sarajevo that they were keen to retain. The Croats continue to retain control of areas they claim as theirs. The Muslims were forced into a confederation with the Croats, an arrangement that neither is comfortable with and which is, in many ways, the most fragile part of the Accord; Mostar is proof of the intensity of distrust between these two communities. It is therefore not inconceivable that the Muslims are biding their time and, in the meantime, with the assistance of the West, led by the USA, and friendly Islamic countries, consolidating their position and building up their military capability. The Croats, who were forced into accepting the confederal arrangement because of the pressures put on Tudjman, may well be biding their time and could, at the first opportunity, try and link up with Croatia; the probabilities are relatively small now, given the present dispensation in Zagreb. It is therefore inevitable that, to prevent renewed outbreak of hostilities, NATO troops will need to remain in BiH in considerable strength and for a long time. This may be just as well for the Western Alliance, as it provides justification for its continued existence.

## Macedonia

Achievement of independence was relatively painless, though the events of the 1990s had a considerable adverse impact on the economic situation in the country. President Gligorov requested UN deployment at the end of 1992, while I was still in command of the UN forces, and I set up the mission in that country in early 1993, well before I left. It was evident to us that this request, though portrayed in the Western media as an insurance against the Serbs, had to do with worries about an upsurge of Albanian nationalism and the possible impact on Macedonia. In retrospect, one can see that the Macedonian leadership had anticipated that Kosovo would boil over soon after the events in neighboring BiH. That it took much longer was, in fact, the surprise. All reports indicated that the Macedonian people very strongly disapproved of NATO's bombing of Yugoslavia and the spill-over effects it had on Macedonia. The country's economy was badly affected. The political leadership and the majority community looked at the developments in Kosovo with considerable trepidation, with fears of a possible upsurge within the indigenous Albanian population in the context of moves toward a Greater Albania. Events in the recent past appear to indicate that the world may witness more destabilizing events in the Balkans.

## Montenegro

Throughout the events of the 1990s, Montenegro was solidly aligned with Serbia and also suffered much of the effects of the war in the region, both against Croatia and during the conflict in BiH. With the emergence in the Republic of a political leadership opposed to President Milosevic, many made moves to distance themselves from many of the decisions taken by him. However, the affiliation between the Montenegrins and the Serbs is fairly strong and may be expected to weather the impact of the efforts being made by the United States and Germany to wean the Republic away from Yugoslavia toward independence. There is a large Montenegrin population within Serbia, including Belgrade, and many of them are in positions of authority in Yugoslavia. Furthermore, the Republic's viability is closely linked with that of Serbia. Even so, it is a matter of some debate whether the link between the two republics will survive.

## Serbia

Just as the Iraqi people are paying a severe price for being governed by Saddam Hussein, Serbia paid the price for being led by Slobodan Milosevic. The sanctions imposed by the West took a heavy toll. Serbia also has to bear the equally heavy burden of hosting a large number of refugees displaced from Croatia, BiH, and, now, Kosovo. It has significant numbers of Hungarians in Vojvodina, small numbers of Croats and Muslims, substantial numbers of Montenegrins, and, apparently, a significant number of Albanians. (The bakeries and pastry shops in Belgrade were once run by this community.) Given the Serb history, and the community's pride within a persecution complex, it did appear unlikely at one stage that Serbia could be pressured into submission to the dictates of the United States and Western Europe. However, recent events reveal that economic compulsions will dictate the course of action. Milosevic has been handed over to the War Crimes Tribunal in The Hague in return for a substantial aid package.

## PROGNOSIS

There is, however, a ray of hope. One is given to understand that, despite all the damage and destruction caused by NATO actions against Yugoslavia and the sanctions imposed by the West, some reconstruction has been effected, electricity supplies restored, new houses built, hospitals repaired, and so on. Therefore, if the economies of the republics are given impetus, and there is an indication of attaining a better quality of life for the people of the region, some of the animosities may be set aside toward a more peaceful resolution of the problems.

# Index

# About the Contributors

**GORDON N. BARDOS** is Assistant Director of the Harriman Institute at Columbia University. He also serves as Executive Director of the Association for the Study of Nationalities (ASN), the world's largest scholarly organization devoted to the study of the problems of nationalism and ethnic conflict in the post-communist world. Since 1998, he has also worked as a Balkans consultant for Freedom House. A specialist on Southeastern Europe, he has written extensively on various aspects of the crisis in the former Yugoslavia. His recent articles are "Balkan Blowback? Osama Bin Laden and Southeastern Europe" in *Mediterranean Quarterly*, and "The Bosnian Cold War: Politics, Society and International Engagement after Dayton," in the *Harriman Review*. Primary research interests include problems of democracy in a multinational environment, comparative state- and nation-building processes, and the role of Islamic fundamentalist groups in Southeastern Europe. He is completing his Ph.D. at Columbia University.

**MILICA Z. BOOKMAN** is a professor of economics at St. Joseph's University in Philadelphia. She was educated at Brown University, London School of Economics, and Temple University. She is the author of eight books, including *Ethnic Groups in Motion* (Frank Cass, 2002); *After Involuntary Migration* (Lexington Books, 2002); *The Demogaphic Struggle for Power: The Political Economy of Demographic Engineering in the Modern World* (Frank Cass, 1997); *Economic Decline and Nationalism in the Balkans* (Palgrave-Macmillan, 1994); *The Economics of Secession* (Palgrave-Macmillan, 1992); and *The Political Economy of Discontinuous Development: Regional Disparities and Inter-Regional Conflict* (Praeger Publishers, 1991). Her articles have appeared in *Journal of Peace Research, Studies in Comparative International*

*Development, Soviet Studies, Communist Economies and Economic Transformation*, as well as in numerous edited volumes.

**MAYA CHADDA** is professor of political science at William Paterson University of New Jersey and is a research fellow at the Southern Asian Institute, Columbia University. She has taught at the Brooklyn College, New York University, and Cambridge University. Chadda holds an M.A. in Government from NYU and a Ph. D. from the Graduate Faculty, The New School of Social Research. Her publications include *Indo-Soviet Relations* (Vora & Co., 1968); *Paradox of Power: The United States Policy in Southwest Asia* (Clio Press, 1986); *Ethnicity Security and Separatism in South Asia* (Columbia University Press/Oxford University Press, 1997) and *Building Democracy in South Asia: India, Pakistan and Nepal* (Lynne Rienner Publishers, 1999). She frequently contributes to academic journals and newspapers. She is sought after for speaking engagements in public fora and frequently for expert opinion in mainstream television media. Maya Chadda has worked on the United Nations Development Program (UNDP) and on United Nations Family Planning Agency (UNFPA) as a consultant. In 1998 she was appointed the Director of Undergraduate Research for William Paterson University (responsible for setting up grant and scholarship programs) and served on the review board of the Woodrow Wilson Center and United States Institute of Peace, Washington D.C. and as a consultant to the John D. and Katherine T. MacArthur Foundation. Chadda is the U.S. editor of *Global Review of Ethnopolitics* (UK) and is a recipient of several grants, including the Rockefeller Residency Fellowship at Bellagio, Italy. In 1998 she was given the *Excelsior* award for excellence in academic achievement by the Association of Indians in America and the Network of Indian Professionals and is a member of the Council on Foreign Relations. Chadda currently serves on the Joint Task force of the CFR and Asia Society on South Asia.

**KELLY M. GREENHILL** is a 2002–2003 Olin National Security Fellow at Harvard University and a Ph.D. candidate in the Department of Political Science at the Massachusetts Institute of Technology, where she is completing a dissertation on the use of refugees as asymmetric weapons and bargaining tools. Ms. Greenhill has conducted research and analysis for a variety of organizations, including the U.S. Department of Defense, the United Nations High Commissioner for Refugees (UNHCR), and the Ford Foundation. Her work has appeared in journals such as *Security Studies, Breakthroughs*, and *Conflict, Security, and Development* (CSD). She holds a bachelor's degree in Political Economy and in Scandinavian Studies from the University of California, Berkeley, a master's degree in Political Science from MIT, and a C.S.S. in International Management from Harvard University.

**ROBERT M. HAYDEN** is Professor and Director of the Center for Russian and East European Studies at the University of Pittsburgh. He received his law degree (1978) and Ph.D. in anthropology (1981) from the State University of New York at Buffalo. He is an anthropologist of law and politics, concentrating on the invocation, manipulation, and change of normative systems of social ordering. He has done extensive work on the reconstruction of states and nations in the former Yugoslavia, following extensive fieldwork there. He has also done fieldwork in India and among the Senecas of New York state, and has also written on issues concerning the American legal system and its role in society. His most recent publication is *Blueprints for a House Divided: The Constitutional Logic of the Yugoslav Conflicts* (University of Michigan Press, 1999)

**EDWARD S. HERMAN** is a Professor Emeritus of Finance at the Wharton School, University of Pennsylvania, where he gave courses in micro- and macroeconomics and financial regulation for thirty years. He also taught courses on The Political Economy of the Mass Media and on The Analysis of Media Bias at the Annenberg School of Communication at Penn for a decade. He has a Ph.D. in Economics from the University of California, Berkeley, and has written extensively on economics, political economy, foreign policy, and media analysis. He has a regular "Fog Watch" column in the monthly *Z Magazine* and has published numerous articles on economics, finance, foreign policy, and media analysis in a wide array of professional and popular journals. Among his twenty-two published books are *The Political Economy of Human Rights* (2 vols., with Noam Chomsky, South End Press, 1979); *Corporate Control, Corporate Power* (Cambridge University Press, 1981); *Demonstration Elections: U.S.-Staged Elections in the Dominican Republic, Vietnam, and El Salvador* (with Frank Brodhead, South End Press, 1984); *Manufacturing Consent: The Political Economy of the Mass Media* (with Noam Chomsky, Pantheon, 1988); *The "Terrorism" Industry* (with Gerry O'Sullivan, Pantheon, 1990); *Beyond Hypocrisy: Decoding the News in an Age of Propaganda, With a Doublespeak Dictionary* (South End Press, 1992); *Triumph of the Market: Essays on Economics, Politics, and the Media* (South End Press, 1995); *The Myth of the Liberal Media: An Edward Herman Reader* (Peter Lang, 1999). Most recently he published *Degraded Capability: Media Coverage of the Kosovo War* (coedited with Philip Hammond, Pluto Press, 2000.)

**ALAN J. KUPERMAN** is Assistant Professor of International Relations at Johns Hopkins University's School of Advanced International Studies (SAIS) in Bologna, Italy. He is the author of one book, *The Limits of Humanitarian*

*Intervention: Genocide in Rwanda* (Brookings, 2001), a chapter in *The New American Interventionism: Successes and Failures* (Columbia University Press, 1999), and a Ph.D. dissertation, "Tragic Challenges and the Moral Hazard of Humanitarian Intervention: How and Why Ethnic Groups Provoke Genocidal Retaliation" (MIT, 2002). He also has published articles in *Foreign Affairs, Political Science Quarterly*, the *Washington Post*, the *Wall Street Journal*, and other journals and newspapers. He has received fellowships from the University of Southern California's Center for International Studies, Harvard University's Belfer Center for Science and International Affairs, the U.S. Institute of Peace, the Harvard-MIT MacArthur Transnational Security Program, the Brookings Institution, and the Institute for the Study of World Politics. Prior to his academic career, he worked as legislative director to Congressman Charles Schumer, legislative assistant to Speaker of the House Tom Foley, fellow at the U.S. Agency for International Development, and legislative director of the Nuclear Control Institute, a nonproliferation advocacy group. He holds a Ph.D. in Political Science from MIT, a Master's degree in International Relations and International Economics from SAIS, and a Bachelor's degree from Harvard University.

**P. H. LIOTTA** holds the Jerome E. Levy Chair of Economic Geography and National Security at the U.S. Naval War College. Previously he served as Fulbright scholar in Yugoslavia and as a military attache to the Hellenic Republic. He has traveled extensively throughout the former Soviet Union, Europe, and the Balkan peninsula. The author of ten books and over 250 articles in fields as diverse as poetry, criticism, education, international security, intervention ethics, and foreign policy analysis, his work has been translated into Arabic, Bosnian, Bulgarian, French, Greek, Italian, Japanese, Macedonian, Russian, Serbo-Croatian, and Spanish. Among his books are *Dismembering the State: The Death of Yugoslavia and Why It Matters* (Lexington Books, 2001) and the earlier *The Wreckage Reconsidered: Five Oxymorons from Balkan Deconstruction* (Lexington Books, 1999). He has received a Pulitzer Prize nomination and National Endowment for the Arts literature fellowship, as well as the first *International Quarterly* Crossing Boundaries Award and the Robert H. Winner Award from the Poetry Society of America. A member of the advisory board for the Research Institute for European and American Studies, he has also been a visiting lecturer at the University of Athens and Complutense University in Madrid and a visiting writer at SUNY Binghamton and the California Institute for the Arts.

**MICHAEL MANDEL** is Professor of Law at Osgoode Hall Law School of York University in Toronto, where he has taught since 1974. He received his

LL.B from Osgoode in 1972, his B.C.L. from Oxford University in 1973, and became Barrister and Solicitor of the Supreme Court of Ontario in 1976. Professor Mandel has held visiting professorships at law faculties in Israel (the Hebrew University of Jerusalem) and Italy (Torino and Bologna, where he runs a semiannual exchange program for Canadian students). He was a Jean Monnet Fellow at the European University Institute in Fiesole in 1991. Professor Mandel's primary scholarly interests are in international criminal law and comparative constitutional law. His book on the Canadian constitution, *The Charter of Rights and the Legalization of Politics in Canada*, is in its second edition and has been translated into French as *La Charte des Droits et Libertés e la judiciarisation du politique au Canada*. He has also published many articles in journals, in collections, and as occasional papers. He is a frequent contributor to the op-ed pages of Canada's newspapers and is often heard on radio and television. Michael Mandel has always been a peace activist. He has been a campaigner for nuclear disarmament and is a member of the Toronto Advisory Board of Canadian Friends of Peace Now. In May 1999, he led an international team of lawyers who brought formal complaints of war crimes against sixty-eight NATO leaders before the International Criminal Tribunal for the Former Yugoslavia. He is currently cochair of Lawyers Against the War, an international group of jurists formed in 2001 to oppose America's so-called War on Terror.

**MICHAEL MANDELBAUM** is the Christian A. Herter Professor and Director of American Foreign Policy at the Johns Hopkins School of Advanced International Studies in Washington, D.C. His essay in this volume is adapted from his editor's introduction and conclusion to *The New European Diasporas: National Minorities and Conflict in Eastern Europe* (The Council on Foreign Relations, 2000). He is the editor of eleven other books and the author or coauthor of eight, the most recent of which is *The Ideas That Conquered the World: Peace, Democracy and Free Markets in the Twenty-First Century* (PublicAffairs, 2002). He received his Ph.D. in political science from Harvard University.

**Lt. General SATISH NAMBIAR** (Retd.) is currently the Director of the United Services Institution of India, a defense and military think tank in New Delhi. Earlier, General Nambiar was the first UNPROFOR commander in the former Yugoslavia, from March 1992 to March 1993. He was former Director General of Military Operations and Deputy Chief of Army Staff, Indian Army. He has published articles on the events in the former Yugoslavia and contributed a chapter of his peacekeeping experience. He has been involved as a commentator and adviser in India dealing with the war in the Kargil sector of Kashmir and the violent secessionist movement in that Muslim majority province of India, which carry some parallels with the Kosovo and Chechnya situations.

**RAJU G. C. THOMAS** is the Allis Chalmers Professor of International Affairs at Marquette University in Milwaukee, Wisconsin. He was a Visiting Fellow at Harvard University (1980–1981 and 1988–1989), UCLA (1982–1983), the Massachusetts Institute of Technology (1988–1989), the International Institute for Strategic Studies in London (1991–1992), and the University of Wisconsin-Madison (1994). Between 1992 and 1997, he was the Co-director of the University of Wisconsin at Milwaukee and Marquette University's Joint Center for International Studies. Thomas's dozen books and edited/coedited books include *The Defence of India: A Budgetary Perspective* (Macmillan-India, 1978); *Indian Security Policy* (Princeton University Press, 1986); *South Asian Security in the 1990s* (IISS-London/Oxford University Press, 1993); *Democracy Security and Development in India* (St. Martin's Press/Macmillan, 1996); *The Great Power Triangle and Asian Security* (Lexington Books, 1982); *Energy and Security in the Industrializing World* (University Press of Kentucky, 1990); *Perspectives on Kashmir* (Westview Press, 1992); *The South Slav Conflict: Religion, Nationalism and War* (Garland/Taylor & Francis, 1996); *The Nuclear Non-Proliferation Regime* (Macmillan/St. Martin's Press, 1998); *India's Nuclear Security* (Lynne Rienner/Sage, 2000); and *Nuclear India in the 21st Century* (Palgrave-Macmillan, 2002). From 1997 to 2001, he wrote most of the sections on India for Jane's Sentinel/Jane's Information of Great Britain. Currently, he is working on two book manuscripts, *India's Search for Security* and *Markets and Politics in India*, and is coediting with Stanley Wolpert a four-volume *Encyclopedia of India* under contract with Macmillan-Gale. Thomas has published more than thirty-five book chapters and thirty articles in academic journals. He has delivered numerous overseas lectures in India, Pakistan, Sri Lanka, Britain, Canada, Australia, Japan, Malaysia, Singapore, South Korea, Sweden, France, and Germany. Between 1965 and 1969, he worked for British multinational corporations in India. Thomas has an M.A. degree in Industrial and Monetary Economics from Bombay University, a B.Sc.Econ. degree in Economics and International History from the London School of Economics, an M.A. in International Relations from the University of Southern California, and a Ph.D. in Political Science from UCLA.